Legalines

Editorial Advisors:
Gloria A. Aluise
Attorney at Law
Jonathan Neville
Attorney at Law
Robert A. Wyler
Attorney at Law

Authors:
Gloria A. Aluise
Attorney at Law
Daniel O. Bernstine
Attorney at Law
Roy L. Brooks
Professor of Law
Scott M. Burbank
C.P.A.
Charles N. Carnes
Professor of Law
Paul S. Dempsey
Professor of Law
Jerome A. Hoffman
Professor of Law
Mark R. Lee
Professor of Law
Jonathan Neville
Attorney at Law
Laurence C. Nolan
Professor of Law
Arpiar Saunders
Attorney at Law
Robert A. Wyler
Attorney at Law

CONSTITUTIONAL LAW

Adaptable to Tenth Edition*
of Choper Casebook

By Jonathan Neville
Attorney at Law

*If your casebook is a newer edition, go to www.gilbertlaw.com
to see if a supplement is available for this title.

THOMSON
™
WEST

REGIONAL OFFICES: Chicago, Dallas, Los Angeles, New York, Washington, D.C.

SERIES EDITOR
Linda C. Schneider, J.D.
Attorney at Law

PRODUCTION MANAGER
Elizabeth G. Duke

FIRST PRINTING—2007

Legalines®

**Features Detailed Briefs of Every Major Case,
Plus Summaries of the Black Letter Law**

Titles Available

Administrative Law	Keyed to Breyer	Criminal Law	Keyed to Kadish
Administrative Law	Keyed to Strauss	Criminal Law	Keyed to LaFave
Administrative Law	Keyed to Schwartz	Criminal Procedure	Keyed to Kamisar
Antitrust	Keyed to Areeda	Decedents' Estates & Trusts	Keyed to Dobris
Antitrust	Keyed to Pitofsky	Domestic Relations	Keyed to Wadlington
Business Associations	Keyed to Klein	Evidence	Keyed to Waltz
Civil Procedure	Keyed to Cound	Evidence	Keyed to Weinstein
Civil Procedure	Keyed to Field	Evidence	Keyed to Wellborn
Civil Procedure	Keyed to Hazard	Family Law	Keyed to Areen
Civil Procecure	Keyed to Rosenberg	Federal Courts	Keyed to Wright
Civil Procedure	Keyed to Yeazell	Income Tax	Keyed to Freeland
Conflict of Laws	Keyed to Currie	Income Tax	Keyed to Klein
Conflict of Laws	Keyed to Hay	Labor Law	Keyed to Cox
Constitutional Law	Keyed to Brest	Labor Law	Keyed to St. Antoine
Constitutional Law	Keyed to Choper	Property	Keyed to Casner
Constitutional Law	Keyed to Cohen	Property	Keyed to Cribbet
Constitutional Law	Keyed to Rotunda	Property	Keyed to Dukeminier
Constitutional Law	Keyed to Stone	Property	Keyed to Nelson
Constitutional Law	Keyed to Sullivan	Property	Keyed to Rabin
Contracts	Keyed to Calamari	Remedies	Keyed to Re
Contracts	Keyed to Dawson	Remedies	Keyed to Rendelman
Contracts	Keyed to Farnsworth	Sales & Secured Transactions	Keyed to Speidel
Contracts	Keyed to Fuller	Securities Regulation	Keyed to Coffee
Contracts	Keyed to Kessler	Torts	Keyed to Dobbs
Contracts	Keyed to Murphy	Torts	Keyed to Epstein
Corporations	Keyed to Choper	Torts	Keyed to Franklin
Corporations	Keyed to Eisenberg	Torts	Keyed to Henderson
Corporations	Keyed to Hamilton	Torts	Keyed to Keeton
Corporations	Keyed to Vagts	Torts	Keyed to Prosser
Criminal Law	Keyed to Johnson	Wills, Trusts & Estates	Keyed to Dukeminier

---

All Titles Available at Your Law School Bookstore

SHORT SUMMARY OF CONTENTS

Page

I.   **INTRODUCTION TO THE CONSTITUTION** 1

     A.   **Basic Document** 1
     B.   **Significant Amendments** 1
     C.   **The Process of Constitutional Interpretation** 2

II.   **NATURE AND SCOPE OF JUDICIAL REVIEW** 3

     A.   **Judicial Review of the Constitutionality of Legislation** 3
     B.   **Political Questions** 6
     C.   **Congressional Regulation of Judicial Power** 8
     D.   **Discretionary Review** 10
     E.   **Prerequisites to Federal Jurisdiction** 11

III.   **NATIONAL LEGISLATIVE POWER** 12

     A.   **Sources and Nature of National Legislative Power** 12
     B.   **The National Commerce Power** 15
     C.   **The National Taxing and Spending Powers** 27
     D.   **Foreign Affairs Power** 32
     E.   **Intergovernmental Immunities** 33

IV.   **SEPARATION OF POWERS** 40

     A.   **Presidential Action Affecting Congressional Powers** 40
     B.   **Congressional Action Affecting Presidential Powers** 48
     C.   **Privilege and Immunity** 56

V.   **STATE POWER TO REGULATE** 61

     A.   **Introduction** 61
     B.   **Absence of Federal Regulation** 61

VI.   **SUBSTANTIVE PROTECTION OF ECONOMIC INTERESTS** 89

     A.   **Development of Substantive Due Process** 89
     B.   **Judicial Control Over Legislative Policy** 94
     C.   **Decline of Substantive Due Process** 95
     D.   **"Taking" of Property Interests** 96
     E.   **The Contract Clause** 107

VII.   PROTECTION OF INDIVIDUAL RIGHTS: DUE PROCESS, THE BILL OF RIGHTS, AND NONTEXTUAL CONSTITUTIONAL RIGHTS 112

    A.   Fourteenth Amendment Due Process 112
    B.   The Right of Privacy 115
    C.   The Right to Travel 141
    D.   Cruel and Unusual Punishment 142
    E.   Procedural Due Process in Non-Criminal Cases 148

VIII.   FREEDOM OF EXPRESSION AND ASSOCIATION 152

    A.   Determining What Speech Should Be Protected 152
    B.   Unconventional Forms of Communication 179
    C.   Less Protected Speech 183
    D.   Prior Restraints 196
    E.   Administration of Justice 203
    F.   Government Property and the Public Forum 208
    G.   Government Support of Speech 214
    H.   Mass Media 222
    I.   The Right Not to Speak and Freedom of Association 232
    J.   Wealth and the Political Process 240

IX.   FREEDOM OF RELIGION 245

    A.   Introduction 245
    B.   Establishment Clause 245
    C.   Free Exercise Clause 262
    D.   Preference Among Religions 268
    E.   Conflict Between the Clauses 271

X.   EQUAL PROTECTION 274

    A.   Traditional Approach 274
    B.   Race and Ethnic Ancestry 278
    C.   Discriminations Based on Gender 306
    D.   Special Scrutiny for Other Classifications 314
    E.   Fundamental Rights 321

XI.   THE CONCEPT OF STATE ACTION 347

    A.   Introduction to the State Action Doctrine 347
    B.   Government Function 348
    C.   State Involvement or Encouragement 350
    D.   Later Developments 354

XII. CONGRESSIONAL ENFORCEMENT OF CIVIL RIGHTS **358**

    A. **Introduction** **358**
    B. **Regulation of Private Persons** **358**
    C. **Regulation of State Actors** **359**

XIII. LIMITATIONS ON JUDICIAL POWER AND REVIEW **366**

    A. **Case or Controversy** **366**
    B. **Standing** **367**
    C. **Timing of Adjudication** **374**

TABLE OF CASES **379**

TABLE OF CONTENTS AND SHORT REVIEW OUTLINE

Page

I. INTRODUCTION TO THE CONSTITUTION 1

A. BASIC DOCUMENT 1

B. SIGNIFICANT AMENDMENTS 1

1. The Bill of Rights 1
2. Civil War Amendments 1

C. THE PROCESS OF CONSTITUTIONAL INTERPRETATION 2

II. NATURE AND SCOPE OF JUDICIAL REVIEW 3

A. JUDICIAL REVIEW OF THE CONSTITUTIONALITY
OF LEGISLATION 3

1. Origins of Judicial Review 3
2. Judiciary Act of 1789 3
3. Review of Acts of Congress 3

a. Hamilton 3
b. Jefferson 3
c. The Judiciary Act 3

4. Assertion of Judicial Review Power 4
5. Review of State Legislation 5

B. POLITICAL QUESTIONS 6

1. Constitutional Decisionmaking by Other Branches 6

a. General guidelines 6
b. Type of government 7
c. Justiciability of challenges to impeachment actions ... 7

2. Legislative Districting 8

C. CONGRESSIONAL REGULATION OF JUDICIAL POWER 8

1. Introduction 8

a. Review of courts of appeals 9

       b.   Review of final judgments of the highest state courts   9

    2.   Withdrawal of Jurisdiction During Consideration of Case   9
    3.   Limits on Congress's Authority 10
    4.   Modern Attempts to Limit the Court's Jurisdiction 10
    5.   Limitation of Jurisdiction of Lower Federal Courts 10

D. DISCRETIONARY REVIEW **10**

    1.   Introduction 10
    2.   Rule of Four 10

        a.   Supervision of federal courts 10
        b.   Control over federal law 10
        c.   Important cases 11

    3.   Denial of Certiorari 11

E. PREREQUISITES TO FEDERAL JURISDICTION **11**

    1.   Introduction 11
    2.   Adequate State Ground 11

III. NATIONAL LEGISLATIVE POWER **12**

**A. SOURCES AND NATURE OF NATIONAL LEGISLATIVE
POWER** **12**

    1.   Exclusive Federal Powers 12
    2.   Exclusive State Powers 12
    3.   Concurrent Powers 12
    4.   Denied Powers 12
    5.   Necessary and Proper Powers 12
    6.   Scope of the Federal Legislative Power 13
    7.   The Bank of the United States 13

        a.   Scope of federal authority 13
        b.   Subsequent history of the bank 14
        c.   Modern approach to *McCulloch* 15

B. THE NATIONAL COMMERCE POWER **15**

    1.   Basic Commerce Clause Concepts 15

        a.   Overlapping nature of commercial regulation 15
        b.   Early approach to the Commerce Clause 15

    c.   Definition of commerce 16

    d.   Using the commerce power to regulate undesirable activity 17

    e.   Rate setting as commerce 18

  2.   Regulation of Economic Problems Through 1936 19

    a.   Introduction 19

    b.   Promotion of social values 19

    c.   Regulation of employment conditions 20

    d.   Further developments 21

  3.   Expansion of Commerce Power After 1936 21

    a.   The affectation doctrine 21

    b.   Manufacturing 21

    c.   Farming 22

  4.   Regulation of Police Problems 22

    a.   Exclusion from commerce 22

    b.   Regulation of local illegal activity 22

    c.   Regulation of local activity after interstate commerce ends 23

  5.   Protection of Other Interests Through the Commerce Clause 23

    a.   Introduction 23

    b.   Civil rights and private motels 23

    c.   Civil rights and private restaurants 24

    d.   Protection of environment through commerce power 24

  6.   Modern Limits on Congressional Power 25

C.   **THE NATIONAL TAXING AND SPENDING POWERS** **27**

  1.   Regulation Through Taxing 27

    a.   Introduction 27

    b.   Tax as a penalty 27

  2.   Regulation Through Spending 28

    a.   Introduction 28

    b.   Local vs. general welfare 29

    c.   Inducement of states permitted 30

    d.   Federal influence over state regulation through the spending power 30

D. **FOREIGN AFFAIRS POWER** 32

    1. Introduction 32
    2. Treaties 32
    3. Principal Case 32

E. **INTERGOVERNMENTAL IMMUNITIES** 33

    1. Origins of Immunities 33
    2. State Immunity from Federal Taxes 34

        a. General principles 34
        b. Taxation of state activities 34
        c. User fees 34

    3. State Immunity from Federal Regulation 35

        a. Introduction 35
        b. Recognition of state autonomy 35
        c. From *National League of Cities* to *Garcia* 35
        d. *National League of Cities* overruled 35
        e. Limit on congressional regulatory authority 37
        f. Limit on congressional power to use state officers directly 38

IV. **SEPARATION OF POWERS** 40

A. **PRESIDENTIAL ACTION AFFECTING CONGRESSIONAL POWERS** 40

    1. Introduction 40
    2. Emergency Lawmaking Power Denied to the President 40
    3. Authority to Enter Executive Agreements 41
    4. The War Powers 43

        a. Introduction 43
        b. Inherent powers 43
        c. War Powers Resolution 44
        d. Defining "war" 44

    5. Individual Rights and the War on Terrorism 45

        a. Joint resolution authorizing the use of military force 45
        b. Detention of United States citizens 45
        c. Detention of enemy combatants at Guantanamo Bay 47

B. **CONGRESSIONAL ACTION AFFECTNG PRESIDENTIAL POWERS** 48

1. Delegation of Rulemaking Power 48
2. Legislative Vetoes 48

    a. Introduction 48
    b. Rejection of legislative veto 48

3. Line Item Veto 50

    a. Introduction 50
    b. Constitutionality of line item veto 50

4. Appointments Power 52

    a. Introduction 52
    b. Limit on appointment power 52
    c. Delegation of spending power 52
    d. Creation of independent counsel 53

C. PRIVILEGE AND IMMUNITY **56**

1. Executive Privilege 56

    a. Introduction 56
    b. Military, diplomatic, or national security secrets 56
    c. Evidence in a criminal trial 56
    d. Screening of presidential documents 57

2. Executive Immunity 58

    a. Introduction 58
    b. Immunity for official acts 58
    c. No immunity for unofficial conduct 58
    d. Qualified immunity for presidential aides 60

3. Congressional Immunity Under the Speech or Debate Clause 60
4. Impeachment of the President 60

V. STATE POWER TO REGULATE **61**

A. INTRODUCTION **61**

B. ABSENCE OF FEDERAL REGULATION **61**

1. Development of Principles 61

    a. Early approach 61

  b. National vs. local issues 61
  c. Negative implications 62

   1) The Wilson Act 62
   2) Insurance business and the McCarran Act 63

2. Regulation of Incoming Trade 63

  a. Regulation of incoming commerce 63

   1) Protection of health and safety 63
   2) Preserving local price structure impermissible 64
   3) Less burdensome alternatives should be used 65
   4) Total exclusion of commerce 66
   5) Precision 66
   6) Protective tax schemes 67

3. Regulation of Outgoing Commerce 68

  a. Introduction 68
  b. Licensing requirements 68
  c. Local problems 69
  d. Relative interests 69
  e. Statutes fixing minimum prices 70
  f. Protection of reputation 70

4. Regulation to Protect the Environment and Preserve Natural Resources 70

  a. Introduction 70
  b. Importation of wastes 70
  c. Ban on polluting products 71
  d. Limits on local government control with interstate economic effects 71
  e. Conservation of wildlife 73

5. Neutral Corporate Anti-Takeover Statute 74
6. Traditional State Regulation of Transportation 75

  a. Basic principles 76

   1) Uniform national regulation not required 76
   2) No discrimination 76
   3) Balance of interests favors the state 76

  b. Promotion of a valid state interest 76
  c. Modern approach to transportation regulation 78
  d. Burden of proof 79

7. The State as a Market Participant 79

    a. Introduction 79
    b. Purchases 79
    c. Restricting exports of goods manufactured by the state 79
    d. Post-sale obligations imposed by the state selling its resources 80

8. Privileges and Immunities 81

    a. Introduction 81
    b. Hunting 82
    c. Justification 82
    d. Municipality's preference for its own residents on
       construction contracts 82

9. State Power to Tax 83

    a. Introduction 83

        1) Source of state power to tax interstate commerce 83
        2) Fourteenth Amendment considerations 83
        3) Commerce Clause considerations 83
        4) Import-Export Clause considerations 84
        5) Types of taxes 84

    b. Direct taxation of commerce 84

        1) Per se rule against direct taxation of commerce 84
        2) Elimination of per se rule 85
        3) Multiple tax burdens 85
        4) Severance tax paid mostly by out-of-state users 86

    c. Fair appointment 86

        1) Introduction 86
        2) Apportionment formulas applied to international corporations 87

VI. SUBSTANTIVE PROTECTION OF ECONOMIC INTERESTS 89

A. DEVELOPMENT OF SUBSTANTIVE DUE PROCESS 89

1. Philosophical Limits on Governmental Power 89

    a. Justice Chase 89
    b. Justice Iredell 89
    c. Comment 89

2. Bill of Rights Not Binding on States 89
3. State Constitutional Law 90
4. Fourteenth Amendment Considerations 90

    a. Substantive due process under the Fourteenth Amendment 90
    b. First look at the Civil War amendments 90
    c. Increased judicial intervention in economic regulation 92

        1) Development of substantive due process 92
        2) Concept of substantive due process 92
        3) Pivotal case 93

B. JUDICIAL CONTROL OVER LEGISLATIVE POLICY **94**

1. Introduction 94
2. Applications 94

    a. Maximum working hours 94
    b. "Yellow dog" contracts 94
    c. Minimum wages 94
    d. Business entry and economic regulations 94

C. DECLINE OF SUBSTANTIVE DUE PROCESS **95**

1. Introduction 95
2. Regulation of Prices and Wages 95
3. Regulation of Minimum Wage 95
4. Footnote 4 of *Carolene Products* 95
5. Regulation of "Closed Shop" Contracts 96
6. Regulation of Business Entry 96

D. "TAKING" OF PROPERTY INTERESTS **96**

1. Introduction 96

    a. Public use 96
    b. Taking 96

2. Public Purpose Requirement 96
3. Transfer to Private Party as Public Use 97
4. Regulation as a Taking 99

    a. Mining restrictions 99
    b. Extensive limitation on harmful activities 100
    c. Zone regulations 101
    d. Complete destruction of property value 102

		e.	Public access to property through private property	104
		f.	Nexus test	105
		g.	Challenge against regulation in place when property was purchased	106
		h.	Temporary restriction	106
	5.	Determining What Is Property		106
		a.	Economic legislation	106
		b.	Interest on client funds	107

E. THE CONTRACT CLAUSE **107**

	1.	Introduction	107
	2.	Development of Contract Clause Doctrine	108
	3.	Basic Requirements for a Valid Impairment	108
	4.	State Obligations	109
	5.	Private Obligations	110
	6.	Modern Trend	111

VII. PROTECTION OF INDIVIDUAL RIGHTS: DUE PROCESS, THE BILL OF RIGHTS, AND NONTEXTUAL CONSTITUTIONAL RIGHTS **112**

A. FOURTEENTH AMENDMENT DUE PROCESS **112**

	1.	Meaning of Due Process	112
	2.	Incorporation Doctrine	112
		a.	Right to trial by jury incorporated	112
	3.	Bodily Extractions and the Incorporation Doctrine	112
		a.	Introduction	112
		b.	Forced stomach pumping	113
		c.	Blood samples	113
	4.	Criminal Procedure and Retroactivity	114
		a.	Introduction	114
			1) Effect on truth-finding	114
			2) Reliance	114
			3) Effect	114
		b.	Applications	114

	1)	Exclusionary rule applied to the states	114
	2)	Right to counsel	114
	3)	Comment on defendant's failure to testify	115
	4)	*Miranda* warning	115
	5)	Right to pretrial counsel	115
	6)	Application to cases in progress	115

B.   **THE RIGHT OF PRIVACY**   **115**

1. Introduction   115

    a.   Family   115
    b.   Education   115
    c.   Procreation   116

2. Fundamental Privacy Rights   116

    a.   Marital privacy within the Bill of Rights   116
    b.   Further development of substantive due process   117

        1)   Contraceptives   117

3. The Abortion Issue   118

    a.   Introduction   118
    b.   Basic constitutional rule on abortion   118
    c.   Companion case to *Roe*   119
    d.   Government refusal to pay for abortions   120

        1)   1977 cases   120
        2)   Public funding of medically necessary abortions   121

    e.   Third-party consent   122
    f.   Ersosion of *Roe*   122
    g.   Parental notification   123
    h.   Regulation of abortion   124
    i.   Post-*Casey* anti-abortion measures   127

4. Family Arrangements and Parental and Marital Rights   130

    a.   Family living arrangements   130

        1)   Basic rule   130
        2)   Housing   130

    b.   The right to marry   131

c. Rights of parents to make decisions concerning the care,
    custody, and control of their children 132
d. Tradition and due process 132

5. Assisted Suicide 133

a. The right to die 134
b. Due process analysis 134
c. Equal protection analysis 136

6. Sexual Lifestyles 137

a. Introduction 137
b. Homosexuality 137
c. Liberty interest in homosexual conduct 139

C.   THE RIGHT TO TRAVEL **141**

1. Interstate Travel 141
2. International Travel 141
3. Modern Application to Passport Laws 141

D.   CRUEL AND UNUSUAL PUNISHMENT **142**

1. Introduction 142
2. The Death Penalty 142

a. Requirement of standards for the jury 142
b. Permissible standards 143

3. Mandatory Death Sentences 144
4. Other Challenges 144

a. Use of mitigating evidence 145
b. Racial discrimination 145
c. Juvenile offenders 146

E.   PROCEDURAL DUE PROCESS IN NON-CRIMINAL CASES **148**

1. Due Process and Entitlements 148

a. Introduction 148

1) Liberty 148
2) Property 148

b. Procedural due process requirements 148

	c.	Welfare benefits	149
	d.	Public employment	149
	e.	No property interest in enforcement of restraining order	149
	f.	Liberty	149
	g.	Use of rational basis standard	149
	h.	Pretermination process for public employees dischargeable only for cause	150

2. Determination of What Process Is Due 150

	a.	Introduction	150
	b.	Minimum procedural rights	150
	c.	Weighing test	151
	d.	Commitment of children to mental hospitals	151
	e.	Termination of parental rights	151

VIII. FREEDOM OF EXPRESSION AND ASSOCIATION **152**

A. DETERMINING WHAT SPEECH SHOULD BE PROTECTED **152**

1. Introduction 152

	a.	Constitutional provision	152
	b.	Balancing interests	152

		1)	Rationale	152
		2)	Presumption of validity	152
		3)	Special scrutiny	152

2. Advocacy of Illegal Action 152

	a.	Development of basic principles	152

		1)	Clear and present danger test	153
		2)	Public speech	153
		3)	Incitement	154
		4)	Intent	155

	b.	State sedition laws	155

		1)	Legislative facts	155
		2)	Rationale for free speech	156

	c.	Communism and illegal advocacy	156

		1)	Development of the clear and present danger approach	156

2)	The Smith Act	157
3)	Validity of Smith Act upheld	157
4)	Mere advocacy	158
5)	Advocacy and proof	158
d.	Modern distinction between advocacy and incitement	158
3.	Reputation and Privacy	159
a.	Group libel	159
b.	Public officials and seditious libel	160
1)	Introduction	160
2)	Public officials	161
c.	Private individuals and public figures	162
1)	General rule	162
2)	Private individual involved in public issue	162
3)	Determination of public figure status	164
d.	Privacy	164
1)	Introduction	164
2)	Matter of public interest	164
e.	Infliction of emotional distress	165
f.	Disclosure of private facts	166
g.	Disclosure of intercepted cell phone call	167
4.	Obscenity	168
a.	Introduction	168
1)	Difficulty of defining obscenity	168
2)	Approach to obscenity cases	169
b.	Rationale for regulating obscenity	169
1)	Possession and distribution of obscene materials	169
2)	State regulation of obscene films	169
c.	Inability to define obscenity	170
d.	Modern standard for defining obscene materials	171
5.	Offensive Speech	171

		a.	Fighting words	172
			1) Categorization approach	172
			2) Balancing approach	172
		b.	Hostile audiences	172
			1) Basic rule	172
			2) Protective suppression	172
		c.	Offensive words	173
	6.	Ownership of Speech		174
	7.	New Categories		175
		a.	Child pornography	175
		b.	"Virtual" child pornography	176
		c.	Sex discrimination and pornography	178
		d.	Racist speech	179

B. UNCONVENTIONAL FORMS OF COMMUNICATION **179**

	1.	Introduction	179
	2.	Draft Card Burning	179
	3.	Flag Burning	180
	4.	Sleeping in Public Parks	182
	5.	Building Closure	183

C. LESS PROTECTED SPEECH **183**

	1.	Near Obscene Speech		183
		a.	Zoning	183
		b.	Regulation of speech based on secondary effects	184
	2.	Prohibition of Public Nudity		185
	3.	Commercial Speech		187
		a.	Introduction	187
		b.	Scope of protection	187
		c.	Attorney advertising	188
		d.	Four-part analysis of commercial speech	189
		e.	Regulations on advertising and sale of tobacco products	189
	4.	Private Speech and *Gertz*		191
	5.	Content of "Fighting Speech"		192

6.   Statutory Inference of Intent from Conduct Not Allowed 194

D.   PRIOR RESTRAINTS **196**

1.   Early Cases 196

    a.   Licensing 196

        1)   Introduction 196
        2)   Permit to distribute circulars 196
        3)   Permit for door-to-door advocacy 197

    b.   Injunctions 198

2.   Obscenity and Commercial Speech 199

    a.   Injunctions after a determination of obscenity 199
    b.   Special rule for motion pictures 199
    c.   Informal sanctions 200
    d.   Restrictions on commercial speech 200

3.   Licensing "Professionals" 200
4.   National Security 201

    a.   Prevention of publication of sensitive government documents 201
    b.   Injunction permitted 202

E.   ADMINISTRATION OF JUSTICE **203**

1.   Trial Publicity 203

    a.   Reasonable protections 203
    b.   Restriction on pretrial reporting 203

2.   Newsgathering 204

    a.   Reporter's testimonial privilege 204
    b.   Privilege against searches 206
    c.   Right of access to courtroom proceedings 206

F.   GOVERNMENT PROPERTY AND THE PUBLIC FORUM **208**

1.   The Traditional Public Forum 208

    a.   Mandatory access to public forums 208

        1)   Distribution of literature 208

2) Permit to demonstrate 208

b. Equal access 208

1) Introduction 208
2) Ban on labor picketing 209

2. New Forums 209

a. Access to government charity drive 209
b. Utility poles 209
c. Airports 209

3. Privacy and the Public Forum 211

G. GOVERNMENT SUPPORT OF SPEECH **214**

1. Conditioning Federal Funds on Refraining from Speaking 214
2. Decency Standards for Federal Spending 215
3. Government as Educator and Editor 217

a. Armbands in public schools 217
b. Student newspapers 217
c. Control over library material 218
d. Requiring Internet filters in government-supported libraries 220

H. MASS MEDIA **222**

1. Access to the Mass Media 222

a. Access by statute 222

1) Access to newspapers 222
2) Access to the electronic media 223

b. Access by constitutional right 223
c. "Must carry" requirements for cable television 224

2. Content Regulation 225

a. Indecent speech 225
b. Publicly-funded broadcasting 226
c. Telephone messages 226
d. The Internet 226
e. Regulations of cable television 228
f. Regulation of time for cable programming 230
g. Restricting Internet speech to protect minors 232

  I.   **THE RIGHT NOT TO SPEAK AND FREEDOM OF ASSOCIATION** **232**

        1.   Right to Refrain from Speaking 232

               a.   State-mandated speech 232
               b.   State-permitted speech on private property 232
               c.   Access to a parade 233
               d.   Compelled support of government speech 234

        2.   Expressive Associations 235
        3.   Exclusive Membership Based on Sexual Orientation 236
        4.   Freedom of Association and Employment 237

               a.   Political patronage 237
               b.   Disclosures and disclaimers 238
               c.   Restriction of employee's speech 239

  J.   **WEALTH AND THE POLITICAL PROCESS** **240**

        1.   Campaign Expenditures 240

               a.   Introduction 240
               b.   Balancing approach to regulation of campaign financing 240

        2.   Campaign Finance Reform 242

IX. **FREEDOM OF RELIGION** **245**

  A.   **INTRODUCTION** **245**

  B.   **ESTABLISHMENT CLAUSE** **245**

        1.   Introduction 245
        2.   Aid to Religion 245

               a.   Basic test 245
               b.   Transportation 245
               c.   Tax exemptions 246
               d.   Public aid to parochial schools 247
               e.   Loans to private secular schools 247
               f.   Publicly financed school choice 249

        3.   Religion and Public Schools 251

               a.   Introduction 251
               b.   Statutory requirement of period of silence in public schools for
                      meditation or voluntary prayer 251

		c.	Released-time programs	253
		d.	Secular purpose analysis and restrictions on teaching particular subjects	253
			1) Posting of the Ten Commandments	254
			2) Prohibition on teaching evolution invalid	254
			3) Teaching of creation and evolution	254
		e.	Purpose	255
	4.		Official Acknowledgment of Religion	255
		a.	State-employed chaplains	255
		b.	Limitations on religious displays on government property	255
		c.	Prayer at graduation ceremonies	258
		d.	The Pledge of Allegiance	260
		e.	Prayer at school functions	260
		f.	Religious speech in public forums	262
C.	**FREE EXERCISE CLAUSE**			**262**
	1.		Conflict with State Regulation	262
		a.	Introduction	262
		b.	Development of belief-action distinction	262
		c.	Unemployment benefits	263
		d.	Other cases	263
			1) Exclusion of clergy from public office	263
			2) Social Security payments	264
			3) Conscientious objection	264
			4) Veterans preferences	264
			5) Tax-exempt status	264
		e.	Limitation on required accommodation	264
		f.	Excluding the study of religion from public scholarships	266
	2.		Unusual Religious Beliefs and Practices	267
		a.	Inquiry into truth of religious precepts forbidden	267
		b.	Belief in God	267
		c.	Draft-exemption definition	267
D.	**PREFERENCE AMONG RELIGIONS**			**268**
	1.		Introduction	268

2. Religious Gerrymandering 268
3. Litigation of Religious Disputes 269
4. Fundraising 270

E. **CONFLICT BETWEEN THE CLAUSES** **271**

1. Permissible Accommodation 271
2. Sales Tax Exemption 272
3. Day of Worship 272

X. **EQUAL PROTECTION** **274**

A. **TRADITIONAL APPROACH** **274**

1. Introduction 274
2. Standards of Review 274

   a. Development of equal protection doctrine 274

     1) Traditional approach 274
     2) The Warren Court's "new" equal protection 274
     3) The Burger and Rehnquist Courts 275

   b. Types of classifications 275

3. Practical Considerations 276
4. State Economic Regulation 276
5. Extent of Deference Accorded 277

B. **RACE AND ETHNIC ANCESTRY** **278**

1. Historical Background 278
2. Discrimination Against Racial and Ethnic Minorities 279

   a. Use of Fourteenth Amendment 279
   b. Separate but equal doctrine 280
   c. Proper distinction based on race 280
   d. School desegregation and repudiation of the separate
     but equal doctrine 281
   e. Application to secondary and primary schools 282
   f. Implementation of desegregation 282
   g. Blatant racial classifications 283

     1) Equal application to all races 283
     2) More than equal application required 283

	h.	Racial identification and classification	284
	i.	Judicial consideration of private bias in making child custody determinations	284
3.		De Jure and De Facto Discrimination	284
	a.	Introduction	284
	b.	Discriminatory administration of law	284
	c.	Relevance of discriminatory impact in finding a discriminatory purpose	285
		1) General rule	285
		2) Qualification test	285
	d.	Adverse effect alone not a violation	286
	e.	Disproportionate impact based on sex	287
	f.	Standard procedures resulting in disproportionate impact	288
4.		Remedying Segregation	288
	a.	Introduction	288
	b.	Early judicial remedies	289
		1) Public schools	289
		2) Acceleration of desegregation	289
	c.	Authority of district courts to order desegregation in southern metropolitan areas	289
	d.	Judicial remedies for northern schools	290
		1) All minorities	290
		2) Presumption	290
		3) Prima facie case	291
	e.	Type of proof needed	292
	f.	Limits on remedies	292
	g.	Incremental relinquishment of court control	293
5.		Repeals of Remedies and Structurings of the Political Process that Burden Minorities	293
	a.	Removal of authority from school district	293
	b.	Constitutional amendment	294
6.		Affirmative Action and Benign Discrimination	295
	a.	Introduction	295

b. Special state school admissions program for minorities 295
c. Post-*Bakke* university admissions policies 297
d. Race as a factor for law school admission 297
e. Race as a preferential factor for undergraduate admission 299

7. Affirmative Action in Employment and Government Contracts 300

a. Teacher layoffs 300
b. Public contracts 301
c. Rejection of state and local set-aside programs absent
   evidence of direct discrimination 301
d. Congressional authority to order remedial programs 304
e. Strict scrutiny of affirmative action 304

C. DISCRIMINATIONS BASED ON GENDER 306

1. Introduction 306
2. Development of the Intermediate Standard 306

a. Military benefits 306
b. Liquor regulation 307
c. Single-sex military school 308

3. Differences 310

a. Disability insurance 310
b. Statutory rape 310
c. Draft registration 311
d. Peremptory challenges 312

4. Remedial Discrimination 312

a. Widows' tax benefits 312
b. Military career regulations 312
c. Social Security survivors' benefits 312
d. Proof of dependency requirement 313
e. Social Security benefits 313
f. Women's college 313

D. SPECIAL SCRUTINY FOR OTHER CLASSIFICATIONS 314

1. Introduction 314
2. Illegitimacy 315

a. Introduction 315
b. Social Security benefits 315

	c.	Other benefits	316
3.		Sexual Orientation	316
	a.	Introduction	316
	b.	States cannot prohibit protection of homosexuality	316
4.		Alienage	318
	a.	Introduction	318
	b.	Control over employment of aliens	318
	c.	Federal restrictions on aliens	320
5.		Mental Retardation	320
6.		Other Challenged Bases for Discrimination	321
	a.	Age	321
	b.	Wealth	321

E. FUNDAMENTAL RIGHTS **321**

1.		The Right to Vote	332
	a.	Denial or qualification of the right to vote	321
		1) Impact of a poll tax	321
		2) Voter qualifications not based on wealth	322
		3) Additional restrictions on the franchise	323
	b.	Dilution through apportionment	324
		1) Federal versus state apportionment	324
		2) Justiciability of apportionment challenges	324
		3) Constitutional standards	324
		4) Super majorities	325
		5) Permissible deviation	325
	c.	Dilution through gerrymanders	326
		1) Political gerrymandering	326
		2) *Bandemer* called into doubt	327
	d.	Dilution and race	328
		1) At-large system	328
		2) Subective evidence of disriminatory intent	330

3) State redistricting plan designed only to separate voters on the basis of race 331

4) Race as a primary factor 332

e. Equality in counting votes 334

2. The Right to Travel 336

a. Introduction 336
b. State welfare 336
c. Durational residence requirements for voting 337
d. Duration of residency and distribution of state resources 337
e. Reconsideration of *Shapiro* 338

3. Access to the Courts 340

a. Administration of criminal justice 340

1) Right to a record on appeal 340
2) Right to counsel on appeal 340

b. Civil litigation 341

1) Divorce fee 341
2) Bankruptcy 341
3) Termination of parental rights 342

4. Welfare 342

a. Introduction 342
b. Family size and public assistance 343
c. Housing 343

5. Education 343

a. State spending for education 343
b. Education of children of illegal aliens 345

6. Medical Care: Abortions 346

XI. THE CONCEPT OF STATE ACTION 347

A. INTRODUCTION TO THE STATE ACTION DOCTRINE 347

1. Basic Issue 347
2. Approach of the Nineteenth Century 347

B. GOVERNMENT FUNCTION **348**

    1. Introduction 348
    2. The Conduct of Elections 348
    3. Private Company Towns 348
    4. Shopping Centers 349
    5. Public Parks 349
    6. Business Regulation 350

C. STATE INVOLVEMENT OR ENCOURAGEMENT **350**

    1. Introduction 350
    2. Enforcement of Private Contracts 351
    3. Additional Cases 351

        a. Civil damages 351
        b. Will provisions 351
        c. Trespass 352

    4. State Authorization of Discrimination 352
    5. State Licensing 353
    6. Private Use of Government Property 354

D. LATER DEVELOPMENTS **354**

    1. Publicly Funded Private School 354
    2. Warehouseman's Lien 355
    3. Government's Failure to Act 356

XII. CONGRESSIONAL ENFORCEMENT OF CIVIL RIGHTS **358**

A. INTRODUCTION **358**

    1. Statutes 358
    2. Case Law 358

B. REGULATION OF PRIVATE PERSONS **358**

    1. Private Conduct Under the Thirteenth Amendment 358

C. REGULATION OF STATE ACTORS **359**

    1. The Right to Vote 359
    2. Constitutionality of the Voting Rights Act of 1965 359
    3. Congressional Control over State Voting Requirements 360
    4. Limits on Congressional Enforcement Power 361

5. Further Restrictions 363

    a. State employees unable to recover for ADEA violations 363
    b. State employees unable to recover for ADA Title I violations 363
    c. State employees can recover under FMLA 364
    d. States not subect to federal court actions for patent infringement 364
    e. Recovery under ADA Title II 364
    f. No civil remedy under Violance Against Women Act 365

XIII. LIMITATIONS ON JUDICIAL POWER AND REVIEW **366**

A. CASE OR CONTROVERSY **366**

1. Advisory Opinions 366

    a. Introduction 366

        1) Cases and controversies 366
        2) Justiciability 366
        3) Common scenarios 366

2. Strict Necessity 366

B. STANDING **367**

1. Introduction 367
2. Lack of Direct Personal Injury 367
3. Congressional Power to Create Standing 368
4. Injury Must Result from Unconstitutionality 369
5. Requirement of Cause and Effect 369
6. Taxpayer Standing 369

    a. Historical approach 369
    b. Adequate nexus showing 370
    c. Citizens' standing 371
    d. Third-party standing 372

        1) Basic rule 372
        2) Exception 372

7. Public Interest Not Enough 372

C. TIMING OF ADJUDICATION **374**

1. Mootness 374

a. Capable of repetition 374
b. Criminal cases 375
c. Admission procedures 375

2. Ripeness 376

a. Possible threats are not sufficient 376
b. The importance of a constitutional determination 376

TABLE OF CASES **379**

I. INTRODUCTION TO THE CONSTITUTION

A. BASIC DOCUMENT

The Constitution of the United States currently consists of seven articles and 27 amendments. It was created in response to the inadequacies of the Articles of Confederation and was ratified by nine states, as was necessary in 1788. The Constitution separates the powers of the national government into three branches: executive, legislative, and judicial. Each branch was intended to remain independent yet subject to restraint by the other branches through a system of checks and balances. The Constitution also establishes the federal/state framework of government. The study of constitutional law is essentially an examination of the sources of governmental power and the limitations imposed on its exercise. Through the system of judicial review, the United States Supreme Court has the final say in interpreting the Constitution; hence the heavy reliance on studying decisions of the Supreme Court.

B. SIGNIFICANT AMENDMENTS

The articles of the Constitution contain important protections of individual liberty, including the writ of habeas corpus, prohibition of ex post facto laws, and the Privileges and Immunities Clause. Two groups of amendments, however, provide the majority of the civil liberties enjoyed in the United States today.

1. **The Bill of Rights.** Many of the states included a bill of rights in their constitutions, but none was included in the original federal Constitution. Adoption of the first 10 amendments, or Bill of Rights, was prompted largely by the concerns expressed during the state ratification conventions. These amendments did not affect state power; they were only limitations on the power of the federal government.

2. **Civil War Amendments.** The conquest over slavery in the Civil War presented serious social problems. The Thirteenth Amendment, which was ratified in 1865, provided legal backing for eradicating slavery, which had been recognized in the original Constitution. In 1866, Congress enacted the Civil Rights Act to prohibit racial discrimination practiced by the states. The President vetoed the Act on grounds that it was unconstitutional, and although Congress overrode the veto, the Fourteenth Amendment was proposed to overcome constitutional objections to the Civil Rights Act. It was ratified largely because Congress made ratification a condition for the rebel states to be represented in Congress. The Fifteenth Amendment prohibited the states from denying an individual the right to vote on racial grounds.

C. THE PROCESS OF CONSTITUTIONAL INTERPRETATION

Effective study of the Constitution requires more than just learning what "the law is." Many of the currently prevailing constitutional doctrines are relative new-comers, and some are even the exact opposite of the doctrines that prevailed in earlier times. To be effective, a lawyer must understand various approaches to an issue. Often there is no "correct" interpretation of the Constitution; the interpretation that persuades a majority of the Supreme Court Justices is the one that becomes the law.

II. NATURE AND SCOPE OF JUDICIAL REVIEW

A. JUDICIAL REVIEW OF THE CONSTITUTIONALITY OF LEGISLATION

1. **Origins of Judicial Review.** Although there was some debate at the Constitutional Convention about the role of the judiciary in reviewing legislative acts, nothing in the Constitution expressly gives the Supreme Court power to rule on the constitutionality of Acts of Congress or state statutes, nor power to review decisions of state courts. Article III merely creates the Supreme Court and extends the judicial power to "all Cases, in Law and Equity, arising under this Constitution, the Laws of the United States, and Treaties made . . . under their Authority." However, Section 2 spells out those cases in which the Supreme Court has original jurisdiction and specifies that in all other cases, the Court has appellate jurisdiction.

2. **Judiciary Act of 1789.** In the Judiciary Act of 1789, Congress created lower federal courts as permitted by the Constitution, but did not give them general jurisdiction in civil cases arising under federal law. The state courts were to exercise jurisdiction over such cases. The Supreme Court was authorized to hear three types of cases on appeal, all essentially involving state court rejection of claims made under federal law.

3. **Review of Acts of Congress.** The authority of the Supreme Court to review Acts of Congress is not set forth in the Constitution. In the early days of the Marshall Court there was a considerable dispute about whether the Supreme Court had such authority.

    a. **Hamilton.** The Federalist No. 78, written by Alexander Hamilton, argues that the judiciary is the least powerful of the branches of government in that it controls neither public funds nor the military. The independence of the judiciary allows it to guard the Constitution and the rights of individuals from improper actions of the other branches. Judicial decisions must be governed by the Constitution rather than by any contrary statute.

    b. **Jefferson.** Thomas Jefferson argued that each branch was responsible for determining the constitutionality of its own actions and that the judges should not be the ultimate arbiters of all constitutional questions, although he recognized that the courts would face constitutional questions more often than the other branches.

    c. **The Judiciary Act.** In the Judiciary Act of 1789, Congress also gave the Supreme Court power to issue writs of mandamus to United States officials. This grant of original jurisdiction arguably violated the specific provisions of Article III, Section 2 of the Constitution, setting the stage for the following case.

4. **Assertion of Judicial Review Power--**

Marbury v. Madison, 5 U.S. (1 Cranch) 137 (1803).

Facts. Marbury (P) and others were appointed justices of the peace for the District of Columbia by President Adams and confirmed by the Senate on Adams's last day in office. Their formal commissions were signed but not delivered. Madison (D), as Secretary of State, was directed by the new President, Thomas Jefferson, to withhold P's commissions. P brought a writ of mandamus directly to the Supreme Court under the Judiciary Act of 1789, which established United States courts and, in section 13, authorized the Supreme Court to issue writs of mandamus to public officers.

Issue. Is the Supreme Court empowered to review Acts of Congress and void those that it finds to be repugnant to the Constitution?

Held. Yes. P's action is discharged because the Court does not have original jurisdiction; section 13 of the Judiciary Act is unconstitutional.

♦   The facts demonstrate a plain case for mandamus action, and under the Judiciary Act this Court could so act.

♦   P claims that since the constitutional grant of jurisdiction is general and the clause assigning original jurisdiction to the Supreme Court (Article III, Section 2, Clause 2) contains no negative or restrictive words, the legislature may assign original jurisdiction to this Court in addition to that specified in the Constitution. But the clause specifies in what cases this Court is to have original jurisdiction, and that in all other cases its jurisdiction is appellate. P's contention would render the clause ineffectual, an impermissible construction. Therefore, the Judiciary Act's grant of original mandamus jurisdiction is unconstitutional and void.

♦   The grant of judicial power extends to all cases arising under the Constitution and laws of the United States. Since the Constitution is superior to any ordinary legislative act, it must govern a case to which both apply.

♦   The Supremacy Clause (Article VI, Section 2) declares that the Constitution and those acts of Congress made in pursuance thereof shall be the supreme law of the land. Thus, the Court must determine when such acts are actually made in pursuance of the Constitution. The power of judicial review is implicit in the Constitution.

Comments.

♦ In more recent times, the Court has asserted a broad judicial review power, claiming the responsibility of being the ultimate interpreter of the Constitution. Once a law is declared unconstitutional, the courts simply decline to enforce it. Both the states and the federal government are bound by the Supreme Court's decisions. [*See* Cooper v. Aaron, 358 U.S. 1 (1958)]

♦ *Bush v. Gore*, 531 U.S. 98 (2000), involved the 2000 Presidential election. The Florida Supreme Court ordered a manual recount of ballots cast in the 2000 Florida presidential election, but only in selected, heavily Democratic counties. The Florida Supreme Court later ordered a manual recount of the "undervotes" in all counties. These were ballots for which the machine did not record any selection for President. The Supreme Court held that the manual recount violated the Equal Protection Clause, and that because the deadline for counting ballots had elapsed, remanding the case to the Florida court for a constitutionally valid count would not be an appropriate remedy. The majority stated that the judicial system had been forced to confront the federal and constitutional issues. The dissent believed that the Court should not have taken the case and should not have ordered a stay of the Florida recount. According to the dissent, there was no fundamental constitutional principle at stake, and congressional statutes already addressed the issues.

---

5. **Review of State Legislation--**

Martin v. Hunter's Lessee, 14 U.S. (1 Wheat.) 304 (1816).

Facts. British subject Martin (D) was heir to the Virginia estates of Lord Fairfax, who died in England in 1781. Through state legislation confiscating the property of British loyalists, Virginia had conveyed title to Hunter. Hunter's lessee (P) brought an action of ejectment. D defended his title by virtue of two treaties between the United States and Britain that protected such British-owned property. The Virginia Court of Appeals sustained P's claim but was reversed by the United States Supreme Court. The Virginia court refused to comply with the reversal, and D again appealed.

Issue. Does the United States Supreme Court have appellate jurisdiction over the highest state courts on issues involving the federal Constitution, laws, and treaties?

Held. Yes. The Virginia court must obey the United States Supreme Court's rulings.

♦ The Judiciary Act of 1789, section 25, provides for review by the United States Supreme Court of final state court decisions rejecting claims under the federal Constitution and laws. The outcome of this case depends on the constitutionality of that section.

- Appellate jurisdiction is given by the Constitution to the Supreme Court in all cases where it does not have original jurisdiction, subject to congressional regulations.

- All cases involving the Constitution, laws, and treaties of the United States are included in the judicial power granted by the Constitution to the Supreme Court; hence, all such cases are properly subject to that Court's appellate jurisdiction, and section 25 of the Judiciary Act is valid.

- Such power is necessary for uniformity of decisions throughout the whole United States, upon all subjects within the purview of the Constitution.

Comments.

- In *Cohens v. Virginia*, 19 U.S. (6 Wheat.) 264 (1821), a case involving the illegal sale in Virginia of lottery tickets issued with congressional authority in the District of Columbia, the Court extended the *Martin* decision to permit review of state court criminal judgments.

- When the Supreme Court reverses a state court judgment, it normally remands for "proceedings not inconsistent with this opinion." This allows the state court to both review previously undecided issues and to reconsider its decision on matters of state law.

B. POLITICAL QUESTIONS

1. **Constitutional Decisionmaking by Other Branches.** The requirement of a justiciable Article III controversy is deemed to carry with it a limitation against the deciding of purely "political questions."

   a. **General guidelines.** The Court will leave the resolution of such political questions to the other departments of government. In determining whether there is a political question, the primary criteria are:

      1) A "textually demonstrable" constitutional commitment of the issue to the political branches for resolution;

      2) The appropriateness of attributing finality to the action of the political branches;

      3) The lack of adequate standards for judicial resolution of the issue; and

      4) The lack of adequate judicial remedies.

b.   **Type of government.** The fourth section of Article IV guarantees a republican form of government for each state. In *Pacific States Telephone & Telegraph Co. v. Oregon*, 223 U.S. 118 (1912), the company challenged a tax that had been adopted through a voters' initiative. The company claimed the initiative process was not republican but democratic. The Court held that the case involved a political question and was not cognizable by the courts. The issue could only be addressed by Congress. Congress had the duty to determine whether a state's government was republican, and when the state's senators and representatives are accepted into Congress, the state government's authority is thereby recognized as being constitutional. In effect, the company was challenging not the tax, but the state's status as a state.

c.   **Justiciability of challenges to impeachment actions--**

Nixon v. United States, 506 U.S. 224 (1993).

Facts. Nixon (P), a former federal district court judge, was convicted of making false statements before a federal grand jury. He was sentenced to prison, but refused to resign from his judicial office. The United States House of Representatives adopted articles of impeachment and presented them to the Senate. The Senate appointed a committee to hold evidentiary hearings. The committee made a report to the full Senate, which gave P three hours of oral argument to supplement the committee record. The Senate voted to convict P on the impeachment articles, and P was removed from his office. P then sued, claiming the Senate's failure to participate in the evidentiary hearings as a full body violated the Senate's constitutional authority to "try" impeachments. The lower courts held that P's claim was nonjusticiable. The Supreme Court granted certiorari.

Issue. May the courts review the procedures whereby the U.S. Senate tries impeachments?

Held. No. Judgment affirmed.

♦   A controversy is nonjusticiable when there is a "textually demonstrable constitutional commitment of the issue to a coordinate political department; or a lack of judicially discoverable and manageable standards for resolving it." [Baker v. Carr, *infra*]

♦   Applying this test requires the courts to determine whether and to what extent the issue is textually committed. In this case, Article I, Section 3, Clause 6 simply provides that the "Senate shall have the sole Power to try all Impeachments." This clearly gives the Senate exclusive authority to try impeachments.

♦   The use of the word "try" does not require a judicial trial; it is not an implied limitation on the Senate's method of trying impeachments. This is made clear by the inclusion of specific provisions such as the two-thirds vote requirement.

♦ Judicial review of the Senate's trying of impeachments would be inconsistent with the system of checks and balances. Impeachment is the only check on the judicial branch by the legislature, and it would be inconsistent to give the judicial branch final reviewing authority over the legislature's use of the impeachment process. The need for finality and the difficulty of fashioning relief also demonstrate why judicial review is inappropriate in this case.

Concurrence (White, Blackmun, JJ.). The Court should reach the merits of P's claim. But on the merits, the Senate fulfilled its constitutional obligation to "try" P. The Senate has wide discretion in specifying impeachment trial procedures, and the use of a factfinding committee is compatible with the constitutional requirement that the Senate "try" all impeachments. However, it is consistent with the Constitution that while the Senate serves as a means of controlling a largely unaccountable judiciary, judicial review insures that the Senate follow minimal procedural standards.

Concurrence (Souter, J.). Judicial review would be appropriate if the Senate were to act so as to seriously threaten the integrity of the results, such as by convicting based on a coin toss.

---

2. **Legislative Districting.** In early decisions, the Supreme Court consistently refused to review questions arising from a state's distribution of electoral strength among its political or geographical subdivisions. In *Baker v. Carr*, 369 U.S. 186 (1962), the Court decided that federal courts had jurisdiction over challenges to apportionment plans. The modern approach to *federal* elections requires that representation must reflect the total population as precisely as possible. More flexibility is permitted in apportionment of state legislatures, but grossly disproportionate districts are not allowed. State apportionment may not be used to further discrimination, but numerical deviations resulting from political considerations may be allowed.

C. CONGRESSIONAL REGULATION OF JUDICIAL POWER

1. **Introduction.** The Supreme Court's original jurisdiction, codified in 28 U.S.C. section 1251, mainly concerns controversies between two or more states. Congress cannot alter this jurisdiction. However, under Article III, Section 2, Clause 2, Congress has the power to regulate and limit the appellate jurisdiction of the Supreme Court. This power arguably applies at any time and at any stage of proceedings and may even allow Congress to withdraw particular classes of cases from the Court's appellate review. Congress has codified the Court's appellate jurisdiction in 28 U.S.C. sections 1254 and 1257.

a. **Review of courts of appeals.** Under section 1254, the Court may review cases in the courts of appeals by writ of certiorari, appeal of a party relying on a state statute held invalid under the Supremacy Clause (review restricted to the federal questions presented), and certification from a court of appeals.

b. **Review of final judgments of the highest state courts.** Under section 1257, the Court may review final judgments of the highest state courts by appeal, where the state court has found invalid a United States treaty or statute or where the state court has found valid a state statute challenged under the Supremacy Clause. The Court also may grant certiorari whenever the above issues arise, regardless of outcome, or where any title, right, privilege, or immunity is specially set up or claimed under the United States Constitution, laws, or treaties.

2. **Withdrawal of Jurisdiction During Consideration of Case--**

Ex parte **McCardle,** 74 U.S. (7 Wall.) 506 (1869).

Facts. After the Civil War, Congress imposed military government on many of the former Confederate states. McCardle (P), a newspaper editor in Mississippi, was held in military custody. P sought a writ of habeas corpus pursuant to an 1867 Act of Congress, but the federal court denied the petition. P appealed to the Supreme Court as provided by the 1867 Act. After a hearing but before the final decision, Congress repealed the portions of the Act that permitted the appeal.

Issue. Does congressional negation of previously granted jurisdiction preclude further consideration of matters brought to the Supreme Court based on that jurisdiction?

Held. Yes. Case dismissed.

♦ The Supreme Court's jurisdiction is conferred by the Constitution subject to such exceptions and under such regulations as Congress shall make. The first Congress established the federal courts and prescribed regulations for jurisdiction. Congressional affirmation of appellate jurisdiction implies the negation of all jurisdiction not so affirmed.

♦ Here, Congress has expressly removed jurisdiction previously granted. The Court may not inquire into the motives of Congress; without jurisdiction, the Court cannot proceed to consider the case.

♦ No judgment can be rendered in a suit after the repeal of the Act under which it was brought and prosecuted. Judicial duty requires rejection of ungranted jurisdiction as much as it requires exercise of valid jurisdiction.

Comment. This case represented the third major attempt to have the Court review the Reconstruction Acts, which had been passed over President Johnson's veto. The

McCardle decision has never been directly reexamined by the Court, although Justice Douglas doubted that its rationale would prevail today.

---

3. **Limits on Congress's Authority.** There are two basic theoretical limits on congressional authority over the Court's jurisdiction. First, Congress should not be able to interfere with the essential role of the Court in the constitutional scheme. This would include interference with the Court's independence, as by altering appellate jurisdiction in response to specific Court opinions. Second, Congress should not curtail jurisdiction in a manner that impairs the rights of litigants; *i.e.*, limits on jurisdiction should not violate litigants' due process and equal protection rights.

4. **Modern Attempts to Limit the Court's Jurisdiction.** In modern times, legislation to limit the Court's jurisdiction has been introduced in response to particularly controversial decisions, such as the *Miranda* decision, the busing decisions, the school prayer decisions, and the abortion decisions. To date, these proposals have not succeeded.

5. **Limitation of Jurisdiction of Lower Federal Courts.** Because Congress has the power to create lower federal courts, it can also limit their jurisdiction. Only in 1875 did the lower federal courts receive general jurisdiction to decide federal questions. At various times, Congress has removed certain types of cases from the jurisdiction of these courts.

D. DISCRETIONARY REVIEW

1. **Introduction.** The Supreme Court cannot handle all the cases brought before it. It is obligated to decide cases brought to it on appeal, but these are often disposed of summarily. Petitions for certiorari are granted on a discretionary basis. Most of the cases on the Court's docket are discretionary.

2. **Rule of Four.** The Supreme Court accepts cases brought to it on a writ of certiorari if at least four of the Justices want to grant the writ. (A vote of four Justices is also required to avoid a summary disposal of an appeal.) United States Supreme Court Rule 17 sets forth the type of cases the Court will likely hear by granting certiorari. These are:

    a. **Supervision of federal courts.** When a federal court of appeals renders a decision in conflict with another circuit or a state court of last resort, or has departed from the usual course of judicial proceedings, the Court will likely exercise its supervisory power.

    b. **Control over federal law.** When a state court of last resort decides a federal question in conflict with a federal circuit or another state court of last resort, the Court will likely review the decision.

c.   **Important cases.** Whenever a lower court decides an important question that the Supreme Court has not settled, or whenever the lower court decides a federal question in conflict with a Supreme Court decision, the Court will likely review the decision.

3.   **Denial of Certiorari.** In *Maryland v. Baltimore Radio Show, Inc.*, 338 U.S. 912 (1950), Maryland petitioned for a writ of certiorari to review a federal court of appeals opinion that the state believed misconstrued previous Supreme Court decisions. The Court denied certiorari. Justice Frankfurter wrote an opinion explaining that a denial of certiorari does not imply that the Court agrees with the opinion below. A denial means only that no four Justices agreed to grant certiorari. Justices have a variety of reasons for denying certiorari, and these reasons are not necessarily based on the merits. The Court cannot explain its reasons for denying certiorari, due to the variety of the Justices' reasons and the enormous burden that would be placed on their time to consider other cases.

E. PREREQUISITES TO FEDERAL JURISDICTION

1.   **Introduction.** The Supreme Court's only power over state judgments is to correct them where they incorrectly adjudge federal rights. The Court will not review severable state issues also decided in the case.

2.   **Adequate State Ground.** To avoid advisory opinions, review is denied where an adequate and independent state ground supports the judgment, since a reversal of the federal law interpretation would not change the outcome. Whether adequate and independent state grounds exist is a federal question, however. If a decision appears to rest primarily on federal law, the Court assumes that the state court felt bound by federal law unless it clearly states that its decision rests on an adequate and independent state ground. [*See* Michigan v. Long, 463 U.S. 1032 (1983)]

III. NATIONAL LEGISLATIVE POWER

A. SOURCES AND NATURE OF NATIONAL LEGISLATIVE POWER

Much of the Constitution deals with the allocation of governmental powers among the branches of government and between the federal and state governments. From an early date, the Supreme Court has had to determine the scope of these powers. It is useful to classify governmental powers as follows.

1. **Exclusive Federal Powers.** Certain federal powers specifically enumerated in the Constitution are exclusive by the terms of the granting provisions. Others are deemed exclusive because of the nature of the power itself, or because the power is denied to the states; *e.g.*, the powers to enter treaties, to coin money, and to collect duties on imports. Many of the early constitutional cases involved disputes over the scope of the enumerated powers, especially when Congress acted under the Necessary and Proper Clause of Article I, Section 8, Clause 18.

2. **Exclusive State Powers.** Under the Tenth Amendment, the federal government may not exercise power in a fashion that impairs the states' integrity or their ability to function effectively in the federal system. The states are sovereign within their sphere.

3. **Concurrent Powers.** Most of the enumerated federal powers do not specifically deny state power in the areas covered. Under the Supremacy Clause, however, federal law prevails over any conflicting or inconsistent state law. Hence, Congress may preempt an area when uniform national laws are deemed necessary. Many of the disputes among the states and the federal government arise from differing views as to the application of the Supremacy Clause.

4. **Denied Powers.** In addition to the specific limitations on state powers contained in Article I, Section 10, the Bill of Rights and other amendments deny powers to the federal and state governments; *e.g.*, Congress cannot establish a religion or abridge the freedom of speech.

5. **Necessary and Proper Powers.** The Necessary and Proper Clause of Article I, Section 8, gives Congress authority to make all laws necessary and proper to execute the enumerated powers and all other powers given by the Constitution to the federal government. The clause provoked controversy as the states met to ratify the Constitution. It allows Congress to take action not specifically authorized by the Constitution and has provided the basis for many decisions upholding federal laws. The Court has consistently held that

this clause does not grant a new and independent power, however; it simply makes effective the enumerated powers.

6. **Scope of the Federal Legislative Power.** Article I, Section 1, lodges all legislative power in Congress. This is the power to make laws and to do all things that are necessary to enact them, such as to conduct investigations and hold hearings. Article I enumerates many specific powers, but it also contains a broad provision in Section 8, Clause 18, which permits Congress to "make all Laws which shall be necessary and proper for carrying into Execution the foregoing Powers, and all other Powers vested by this Constitution in the Government of the United States, or in any Department or Officer thereof." The scope of the Necessary and Proper Clause has been a subject of intense debate.

7. **The Bank of the United States.** The meaning of federalism was initially clarified by the outcome of the controversy over the Bank of the United States. Nothing in the Constitution specifically granted Congress power to organize a Bank of the United States. However, Congress did create such a bank, as proposed by Secretary of the Treasury Alexander Hamilton, despite the objections of Thomas Jefferson and James Madison that Congress lacked power to do so. The original bank's charter expired after 20 years. Four years later, Congress established a second Bank of the United States. Many of the states objected to the bank and imposed stiff taxes on it. Maryland's tax on the bank became the basis for the first important Supreme Court opinion on federalism.

   a. **Scope of federal authority--**

McCulloch v. Maryland, 17 U.S. (4 Wheat.) 316 (1819).

Facts. The state of Maryland (P) imposed a tax requiring all banks chartered outside the state to print their bank notes on stamped paper if they established any branch or office within P's boundaries. The tax was similar to those passed in other states during a period of strong state sentiment against the Bank of the United States. The taxes were aimed at excluding the Bank of the United States from operating branches within those states. The bank fell within the statutory definition but issued notes on unstamped paper. Accordingly, P brought an action for debt collection against McCulloch (D), the cashier of the Baltimore branch of the Bank of the United States. The state courts imposed penalties on D, and D appeals.

Issue. Even though the Constitution does not expressly grant Congress the power to incorporate a bank, can it do so under a doctrine of implied powers?

Held. Yes. Judgment reversed.

♦ Under the Necessary and Proper Clause, any appropriate means that Congress uses to attain legitimate ends that are within the scope of the Constitution and not prohibited by it, but are consistent with the letter and spirit of the Constitution, are constitutional.

♦ The federal government is one of enumerated powers, which are found in the Constitution. However, the Constitution cannot contain an accurate detail of all the subdivisions of governmental powers and of all the means by which they may be carried into execution. Otherwise, the Constitution would become nothing more than a legal code. The government must have the ability to execute the powers entrusted to it through the best available means.

♦ Any means that directly executes a power enumerated in the Constitution may be considered incidental to the enumerated power. The word "necessary" in the Necessary and Proper Clause does not limit Congress to indispensable means; rather, the term enlarges the powers vested in the federal government. Congress has discretion in choosing the best means to perform its duties in the manner most beneficial to the people.

♦ The creation of a corporation is one of those powers that can be implied as incidental to other powers or used as a means of executing them. The incorporation of the Bank of the United States is a convenient, useful, and essential instrument in the performance of the fiscal operations of the federal government. The United States is a sovereign, and thus, has the power to create a corporation.

Comment. This case is one of the most important in the history of the Court because it established the doctrine of implied powers and emphatically articulated the supremacy of the federal government. The opinion went far beyond the needs of the specific case to promote a powerful federal government. Many commentators at the time objected that the idea of the nation as a union of sovereign states was being undermined. Instead of giving Congress only those additional powers that were needful or indispensable, the Necessary and Proper Clause was now a grant of discretionary power. However, exercise of this discretion must be based on powers granted by the Constitution.

━━━━━━━━━━━━━━━

b. **Subsequent history of the bank.** In 1832, Congress extended the charter of the bank, but President Andrew Jackson vetoed the legislation. Among other things, he objected to the windfall that the original private stockholders would have received upon extension of the charter. He also objected that many of these stockholders were foreigners. He found insufficient precedent to sustain the legislation, because Congress had been inconsistent over the years in its support and because the states were primarily against it. The Supreme Court's opinion was not determinative; President Jackson felt that each branch of the government had to determine for itself the constitutionality of a proposal, and he did not view the bank as necessary and proper.

c. **Modern approach to *McCulloch*.** In *U.S. Term Limits, Inc. v. Thornton*, 514 U.S. 779 (1995), the Court held that the states do not have power to add to the qualifications for members of Congress as provided in the Constitution. This means that states cannot impose restrictions on who appears on general election ballots, so they cannot impose term limits. The Court had previously ruled that Congress cannot change the qualifications specified by the Constitution. [Powell v. McCormack, 395 U.S. 486 (1969)] The majority in *U.S. Term Limits* held that the power to add qualification was not within the "original powers" of the states, so it could not be reserved to the states by the Tenth Amendment. This was the same principle followed in *McCulloch*, which rejected the argument that the Constitution's silence on the subject of state power to tax corporations chartered by Congress implied that the states had reserved power to tax them. Justice Kennedy, concurring, believed that *McCulloch* rejected the idea that the people can delegate power only through the states or through their capacities as citizens of the states, but instead the people have a federal right of citizenship. Justices Thomas, O'Connor, and Scalia, and Chief Justice Rehnquist dissented, concluding that all governmental power stems from the consent of the people of each individual state, not the consent of the undifferentiated people of the nation as a whole. Under this approach, the federal government has no authority beyond what the Constitution confers, and the states can exercise all powers not withheld from them by the Constitution.

B. THE NATIONAL COMMERCE POWER

1. **Basic Commerce Clause Concepts.** Among the most important powers of government are its powers to regulate commerce and to tax goods and instrumentalities in commerce.

   a. **Overlapping nature of commercial regulation.** The states granted power to Congress to regulate commerce with foreign nations, and among the several states, and with the Indian tribes; if they had not done so, they could have erected trade barriers among themselves which would have destroyed the political union. [*See* U.S. Const. art. I, §8, cl. 3] In effect, the United States was intended to be a "common market," made up of individual states. The federal power to regulate commerce among the several states overlaps with each state's power to regulate commerce within its boundaries.

   b. **Early approach to the Commerce Clause.** Most early cases dealing with the Commerce Clause involved challenges against state action that allegedly discriminated against or burdened interstate commerce. The Commerce Clause acted primarily as a restraint upon state regulation. It was not until 1887 and the enactment of the first Interstate Commerce Act that the Commerce Clause was relied on as the basis for the affirmative exercise of federal power. This occurred when Congress attempted to solve certain national economic problems. After the Interstate Commerce Act, Congress enacted several other regulatory statutes, including the Sherman Antitrust Act of 1890. The primary issue faced by the Court in deciding commerce cases was the definition of "interstate commerce." Recall that states have power over commerce within their boundaries. Thus, federal power is concurrent with state power to some extent.

c.   **Definition of commerce--**

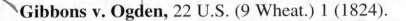

Gibbons v. Ogden, 22 U.S. (9 Wheat.) 1 (1824).

Facts. A New York statute granted the exclusive right to navigate by steamboat between New York City and Elizabethtown, New Jersey, to Livingston and Fulton, who in turn conveyed the right to Ogden (P). Gibbons (D) also operated boats along P's route. D's boats were licensed in the coasting trade under the federal Coasting Act. P sought and obtained a state court injunction prohibiting D's operation. D appeals, claiming that the power of Congress to regulate interstate commerce under the Commerce Clause is exclusive.

Issue. Is state regulation of commercial navigation that excludes federally licensed operators constitutional?

Held. No. Judgment reversed.

♦   P admits that Congress has the power to regulate commerce with foreign nations and among the several states, but would limit the meaning of commerce to traffic (buying and selling) or the interchange of commodities, and would exclude navigation. But one of the primary objects of the creation of the federal government was to grant the power over commerce, including navigation.

♦   The commerce power of Congress must be exercised within the territorial jurisdiction of the states, even though it cannot reach solely intrastate commerce. The power of Congress does not stop at the boundary lines of a state; it follows interstate commerce into the territory of a state.

♦   P attempts to analogize between the taxing power and the commerce power, claiming that since the taxing power is concurrent, the commerce power should be. But regulation of interstate commerce is an exclusive federal power. When a state regulates commerce with foreign nations or among the several states, it exercises the very power granted to Congress, and the analogy fails.

♦   State inspection laws are recognized in the Constitution, but do not derive from a power to regulate commerce. They act upon the subject before it becomes an article of foreign commerce.

- ◆ D has been granted, through a federal license, the privilege of employment in the coasting trade. P would restrict such trade to property transport, excluding passengers. Such a narrow interpretation would eventually "explain away the Constitution." Instead, safe and fundamental principles must be followed, and the coasting trade includes transport of both property and persons for hire.

- ◆ For these reasons, the federal license must be recognized, and state laws prohibiting exercise of such licenses are void.

Concurrence (Johnson, J.). Creation of a federal power over commerce was one of the main purposes of adopting the Constitution. This power must be exclusive.

Comment. The *Gibbons* case illustrates the difficulty in interpreting the language of the Constitution. The entire case revolved around the proper definition of the term "commerce." Some commentators look to the dictionary for definitions, others look to the context in which the term is used, and others attempt to determine the intent of the framers as expressed in letters and other writings. The most commonly used expression of the framers' intent is the Federalist Papers. In *Gibbons*, Chief Justice Marshall stated that the only limits on congressional power to regulate interstate commerce are political, not judicial. His broad definition included as commerce any commercial intercourse among the states.

---

d. Using the commerce power to regulate undesirable activity--

Champion v. Ames (The Lottery Case), 188 U.S. 321 (1903).

Facts. Champion (D) was arrested for shipping a box of lottery tickets by express from Texas to California in violation of the Federal Lottery Act, which prohibited importing, mailing, or causing interstate carriage of lottery tickets. Claiming that the Act was unconstitutional, D obtained a writ of habeas corpus. D appeals from a dismissal of the writ.

Issue. Does Congress have power under the Commerce Clause to regulate undesirable activity?

Held. Yes. Judgment affirmed.

- ◆ Lottery tickets are objects of commerce. They can be sold and transported. Hence, they can be regulated when trafficked from state to state. The power to regulate includes the power to prohibit.

- ◆ This statute does not interfere with traffic or commerce carried on exclusively within the limits of a state. A state could prohibit sales of lottery tickets within its boundaries; so may Congress, for the purpose of guarding the people of the

United States against the "wide-spread pestilence of lotteries," and to protect the commerce which concerns all the state, prohibit the carrying of lottery tickets from one state to another.

♦ Congress has the complete power to prohibit such commerce because it is the only governmental authority capable of protecting the public from the evils of interstate traffic of lottery tickets.

Dissent (Fuller, C.J., Brewer, Shiras, Peckham, JJ.). Congress does not have the power to suppress lotteries. Use of the police power has been reserved to the states by the Tenth Amendment. Furthermore, lottery tickets are not objects of commerce. This decision attempts to transform a noncommercial article into a commercial one simply because it is transported.

Comment. This is but one of several decisions that treat the commerce power almost as a federal police power. The rationale is simple—since Congress has plenary power over the channels or facilities of interstate commerce, it may prohibit their use for any activity that it deems adverse to public health and welfare. Congress may prohibit entry into interstate commerce of:

(i) Goods harmful to interstate commerce itself, such as diseased animals that might spread the disease;

(ii) Commercial items that are harmful, such as adulterated or misbranded articles; and

(iii) Noncommercial items that constitute an evil activity, such as stolen goods.

---

e. **Rate setting as commerce--**

Houston, East & West Texas Railway v. United States (The Shreveport Case), 234 U.S. 342 (1914).

Facts. The Houston, East & West Texas Railway (P) charged lower rates on its intrastate lines from Dallas and Houston to points eastward than on its interstate lines from Shreveport, Louisiana (near the Texas border), to points westward. All three cities competed for the same trade within Texas. The difference between the intrastate and interstate rates was so substantial that the ability of Shreveport merchants to compete in the east Texas markets was significantly impaired. The Interstate Commerce Commission ("ICC") found that the interstate rates charged out of Shreveport to points in Texas were unreasonable because conditions on both the interstate and the intrastate lines were similar. The ICC ordered P to desist from charging higher rates on its interstate lines. P unsuccessfully challenged the ICC order. P appeals.

Issue. Does Congress have the power under the Commerce Clause to control the intrastate charges of an interstate carrier in order to end injurious discrimination against interstate commerce?

Held. Yes. Judgment affirmed.

♦ The Commerce Clause gives Congress power to protect interstate commerce from impediments of local control that could destroy such commerce in violation of the policy behind the Constitution.

♦ Congressional power over interstate commerce necessarily extends to all other operations having a close and substantial relation to interstate traffic. In order to foster and protect interstate commerce, Congress may take all measures necessary or appropriate to that end including control of intrastate commercial activities that substantially affect interstate commerce.

♦ Here, the intrastate rates discriminated against interstate commerce. This constitutes sufficient grounds for federal intervention to protect interstate commerce by regulating rates.

Comment. One of the chief problems the Court struggled with during the rapid industrialization after the Civil War was the extent of congressional power under the Commerce Clause over intrastate commerce. The creation of a truly national market increased the tensions between local and interstate commerce as states tried to protect their industries against those of the sister states. *The Shreveport Case* set forth the substantial economic impact test, which guided many of the Court's decisions in this area.

---

2. **Regulation of Economic Problems Through 1936.**

   a. **Introduction.** Industrialization and the Depression presented many new social and economic problems for the nation to address. Congress and the President initiated new kinds of legislative programs to deal with these problems, often bringing government into the private sector through increased economic regulation. Although the Commerce Clause was raised as the constitutional basis for many of these laws, the Court narrowly construed the clause through 1936.

   b. **Promotion of social values--**

Hammer v. Dagenhart, 247 U.S. 251 (1918).

Facts. Dagenhart (P) sought to enjoin Hammer (D), the United States Attorney General, from enforcing the Child Labor Act, which prohibited the shipment in interstate commerce of any product that was produced or mined by child labor. P was the father of two children who were to be discharged in compliance with the law by the company for which they worked. The district court enjoined enforcement; D appeals.

Issue. May Congress prohibit the transportation in interstate commerce of goods manufactured by child labor?

Held. No. Judgment affirmed.

♦   Congress does not have general police power. Unlike *The Lottery Case*, *supra*, this case involves goods that are themselves harmless. Congress does not have power to prohibit movement of ordinary commodities.

♦   Manufacturing is purely a local activity, not subject to the congressional commerce power. The constitutional scheme must be respected; only the states may regulate purely local matters.

♦   Even though this result leaves those states without their own child labor laws with an advantage in interstate competition, Congress simply has no power to force states to exercise their police power or to equalize conditions among the states.

Dissent (Holmes, J.). The Child Labor Act does not meddle with state rights. When products are sent across state lines, the states are no longer within their rights. If there were no Constitution and no Congress, their power to cross the line would depend on their neighbors. Under the Constitution, control of such commerce belongs to Congress and not the states. Congress may carry out its views of public policy, whatever the indirect effect on the states. Instead of being encountered by a prohibitive tariff at her boundaries, the state encounters the public policy of the United States, which is for Congress to express.

Comment. This case illustrates the so-called "geographic view" of interstate commerce. This approach precluded congressional regulation over activity that begins and ends and at all times takes place within a single state. It was the first of many cases that frustrated attempts by Congress to deal with the social and economic problems created by the industrialization of America. The conflict between the legislature's and executive's broad view of congressional commerce power and the Court's narrow view of that power came to a peak during President Franklin D. Roosevelt's first term, when the Court struck down many of the programs of the New Deal.

---

    c.   **Regulation of employment conditions.** Just prior to 1936, the Court moved away from a geographic approach toward a direct/indirect analysis. Under this analysis, an activity that takes place entirely within a single state may be regulated by Congress if it has a direct effect on interstate commerce. This approach faded after 1936 as the Court broadened its view of the congressional commerce power. [*See* Carter v. Carter Coal Co., 298 U.S. 238 (1936)]

    d.   **Further developments.** The Court also held unconstitutional other aspects of the New Deal, including a federal retirement fund for interstate carriers [Railroad Retirement Board v. Alton Railroad, 295 U.S. 330 (1935)], and a fair labor code approved by the President [Schechter Poultry Corp. v. United States, 295 U.S. 495 (1935)]. The grounds for these decisions were mainly a restrictive interpretation of the federal commerce power.

F＆SA

3.   **Expansion of Commerce Power After 1936.**

    a.   **The affectation doctrine.** Beginning in 1937, the Court abandoned the "geographical" and "direct vs. indirect" approaches to federal regulation under the Commerce Clause. The Court's new position allowed Congress power to regulate any activity, whether interstate or intrastate in nature, as long as it has any appreciable effect on interstate commerce. This approach is called the "affectation doctrine." Under this approach, the term "affecting commerce" means burdening or obstructing commerce or the free flow of commerce, or having led or tending to lead to a labor dispute burdening or obstructing commerce or the free flow of commerce. [NLRB v. Jones & Laughlin Steel Corp., 301 U.S. 1 (1937)]

    b.   **Manufacturing--**

United States v. Darby, 312 U.S. 100 (1941).

Facts. The Fair Labor Standards Act of 1938 prescribed maximum and minimum wages for workers who manufactured goods for interstate commerce and prohibited interstate shipment of goods made by workers not employed in compliance with the Act. Darby (D), a lumber manufacturer, was charged with violating the Act. The district court quashed the indictment, finding the Act inapplicable to D's employees, who were involved in manufacturing, not interstate commerce. The United States (P) appeals.

Issue. May Congress establish and enforce wage and hour standards for the manufacture of goods for interstate commerce?

Held. Yes. Judgment reversed.

♦   The interstate shipment of manufactured goods is clearly subject to congressional regulation. Congress has in the past prohibited interstate shipment of various articles pursuant to public policy, and the Court has no control over legislative judgment of public policy. Prohibition of interstate shipment of goods covered by the Act is constitutional as long as the labor standards involved are properly within the scope of federal power.

♦ Congress has adopted the policy of excluding from interstate commerce all goods produced for that commerce that do not conform to the specified labor standards, and Congress may choose appropriate means of accomplishing that policy. Federal power extends to intrastate activities directly affecting interstate commerce. The means here adopted so affect interstate commerce as to be within Congress's power to regulate.

♦ The Act is directed at the suppression of "unfair" competition in interstate commerce—a valid purpose. Therefore, the Act is constitutional.

---

   c.   **Farming.** In *Wickard v. Filburn,* 317 U.S. 111 (1942), Wickard, the Secretary of Agriculture, imposed a marketing penalty upon the portion of Filburn's crop grown in excess of his allotment under the Agricultural Adjustment Act of 1938. Filburn sued to enjoin enforcement of the penalty, claiming that the application of the marketing quota to him was beyond Congress's commerce power, because he used the wheat on his own farm. The district court enjoined enforcement. The Supreme Court reversed, finding that the purpose of the Act was to restrict the supply of wheat to maintain a price, and that home consumption of the wheat did not detract from the economic effect of the excess crop, because it substituted for purchases on the open market. The fact that Filburn's effect was trivial was irrelevant because, taken together with many others similarly situated, it was far from trivial.

4.   **Regulation of Police Problems.**

   a.   **Exclusion from commerce.** As discussed in *The Lottery Case, supra,* Congress may exclude from interstate commerce products and transactions that harm the health, morals, safety, or welfare of the nation. Congress has used this approach in regulating crime as well, prohibiting interstate transportation of certain stolen property and other contraband.

   b.   **Regulation of local illegal activity.** In *Perez v. United States,* 402 U.S. 146 (1971), the Court upheld Congress's power to make "loan sharking" a crime and reaffirmed Congress's extensive power to regulate intrastate activities that affect more states than one. The Court reasoned that "extortionate credit transactions, though purely intrastate, may in the judgment of Congress affect interstate commerce," and as that class is within the reach of federal power, the courts have no authority to excise, as trivial, individual instances of the class.

c. **Regulation of local activity after interstate commerce ends.** Congress may regulate local business activity even after the interstate commerce ends, if the products traveled in interstate commerce. In *McDermott v. Wisconsin*, 228 U.S. 115 (1913), the Court held that Congress could require that labels meeting federal standards be attached to all "unsold" goods that travel interstate. This requirement facilitates inspection to enforce federal laws. In *United States v. Sullivan*, 332 U.S. 689 (1948), the Court reaffirmed *McDermott* and held that Congress could require a retailer to affix federal labels to the smaller containers into which he distributed the goods from a single large interstate container. The rationale for these decisions is that to enforce the Pure Food and Drug Act most effectively, Congress would have to authorize inspection and seizure when the goods are made available for final sale.

5. **Protection of Other Interests Through the Commerce Clause.**

a. **Introduction.** The Court now recognizes few, if any, federalism constraints on congressional power to regulate commerce. The federal commerce power embraces almost every phase of the economy, national or local, that taken separately or in the aggregate affects interstate commerce. The major function of the Supreme Court in this area has become one of statutory construction; *i.e.*, simply determining what Congress intends by its statutes that regulate commerce. Congress has elected to use this extensive power to protect civil rights within the sphere of commerce.

b. **Civil rights and private motels--**

Heart of Atlanta Motel, Inc. v. United States, 379 U.S. 241 (1964).

Facts. The owner of the Heart of Atlanta Motel, Inc. (P) refused to rent rooms to black persons. P sought a declaratory judgment that Title II of the Civil Rights Act of 1964 was unconstitutional. A three-judge federal court sustained the Act. P appeals.

Issue. May Congress prohibit racial discrimination by private motels that accept out-of-state business?

Held. Yes. Judgment affirmed.

♦ The legislative history of the Civil Rights Act contains numerous examples of how racial discrimination places burdens upon interstate commerce, which comprehends the movement of persons through more than one state.

♦ Even though the operation of the motel was local, if it is interstate commerce that feels the pinch, then it does not matter how local the operation is that applies the squeeze.

---

c. Civil rights and private restaurants--

Katzenbach v. McClung, 379 U.S. 294 (1964).

Facts. McClung (P), owner of a restaurant that excluded black persons from its dining accommodations, challenged Title II of the Civil Rights Act. The lower court granted an injunction against enforcement by Katzenbach (D), the Assistant Attorney General, finding that P would lose a substantial amount of business if required to serve black persons.

Issue. May Congress use its commerce power to forbid racial discrimination by a restaurant on the sole ground that slightly under one-half of the food it serves originates from outside the state in which it operates?

Held. Yes. Judgment reversed.

♦ Although the food originating out of state had "come to rest," the line of cases holding that interstate commerce ends when goods come to rest in the state of destination applies only with reference to state taxation or regulation, not to federal regulation of commerce.

♦ The fact that discrimination in restaurants resulted in sales of fewer interstate goods and that interstate travel was obstructed directly by it shows sufficient connection between the discrimination and the movement of interstate commerce to allow federal intervention.

♦ Once the court finds a rational basis for holding a chosen regulatory scheme necessary to the protection of interstate commerce, the only inquiry is whether the facts fit the scheme. Here, the lower court found that P serves food, a substantial portion of which has moved in interstate commerce. Hence, P is covered by the regulation.

Concurrence (Douglas, J.). This case is better decided under the Fourteenth Amendment, which gives Congress authority to act in this manner. The right of the people to be free of state action that discriminates against them because of race, like the right of persons to move freely from state to state, occupies a more protected position in our constitutional system than does the movement of cattle, fruit, steel, and coal across state lines. Deciding this case under the Fourteenth Amendment would put an end to strategies aimed at getting around the limitations inherent in using the Commerce Clause as a means of sustaining civil rights acts.

---

d. **Protection of environment through commerce power.** Congress has exercised its commerce power to protect the environment by establishing national surface mining and reclamation standards. The Court upheld the law in *Hodel v. Virginia Surface Mining & Reclamation Association*, 452 U.S. 264 (1981), based on congressional findings about the environmental and competitive effects of surface coal mining on interstate commerce. The plaintiff had argued that land as such is not subject to regulation under the Commerce Clause and that Congress could regulate land use only insofar as the Property Clause (Article IV, Section 3) grants it control over federal lands. The Court also upheld the restrictions on surface mining prime farmland, even though this portion of the statute applied to only 21,800 acres. [*Hodel v. Indiana*, 452 U.S. 314 (1981)]

6. Modern Limits on Congressional Power--

United States v. Morrison, 529 U.S. 598 (2000).

Facts. Morrison (D), a member of the varsity football team at Virginia Tech, assaulted and repeatedly raped Brzonkala, a female student, and made vulgar remarks about women. Brzonkala sued D under 42 U. S. C. section 13981, the Violence Against Women Act, which provided a damage remedy for a victim of gender-motivated violence. D claimed that section 13981's civil remedy was unconstitutional. The United States (P) intervened to defend the Act under the Commerce Clause or Section 5 of the Fourteenth Amendment. The lower courts held that Congress lacked constitutional authority to enact this civil remedy. The Supreme Court granted certiorari.

Issue. May Congress provide a federal civil remedy for a gender-motivated violent crime on the ground that the aggregate effect of such crimes substantially affected interstate commerce?

Held. No. Judgment affirmed.

♦ In *United States v. Lopez*, 514 U.S. 549 (1995), the Court held that Congress could not prohibit the possession of firearms within a school zone. The rationale was that possessing a firearm is a criminal act, not an economic one. Congress has authority to regulate interstate commerce, but it must show a substantial impact on interstate commerce of the actions it seeks to regulate or proscribe.

♦ In adopting the Violence Against Women Act, Congress made findings regarding the serious impact of gender-motivated violence on victims and their families, but used a but-for causal chain to show an impact on interstate commerce from these crimes. The Court has rejected this type of reasoning, since it would allow Congress to regulate any crime whose aggregated impact has substantial effects on any aspect of interstate commerce. This type of reasoning could as easily be applied to family law as well.

♦ The Constitution distinguishes between national and local issues, and the police power is one that was clearly left to the states and denied to the federal government. Congress has no authority to regulate noneconomic, violent criminal conduct based solely on the conduct's aggregate effect in interstate commerce.

♦ Section 5 of the Fourteenth Amendment does allow Congress to enforce the guarantee that no state shall deprive any person of life, liberty, or property without due process or deny any person equal protection of the laws. But this applies only to state action, not private conduct. Even if there had been gender-based disparate treatment by the state in this case, it would not have permitted Brzonkala's suit against D as a private party.

Concurrence (Thomas, J.). The very notion of a "substantial effects" test under the Commerce Clause is inconsistent with the Constitution. This test has led Congress to act as though there are virtually no limits to the Commerce Clause. The Court should adopt an approach more consistent with the original understanding.

Dissent (Souter, Stevens, Ginsburg, Breyer, JJ.). One difference between this case and *Lopez* is that here, Congress assembled considerable data showing the effects of violence against women on interstate commerce. This Act would have been constitutional at any time between *Wickard* and *Lopez*. The majority has revived a distinction between commercial and noncommercial conduct, which had been rejected in *Wickard*. The relative powers of the federal and state systems have changed substantially since the framing of the constitution. The Seventeenth Amendment was a major factor in this change, and the modern integrated national economy is a fact not reflected in the majority's notion of federalism.

Dissent (Breyer, Stevens, Souter, Ginsburg, JJ.). The distinction between economic and noneconomic is not easy to apply. Congress could have approached the same problem with legislation that focused on acts of violence perpetrated at public accommodations or by those who have moved in interstate commerce. The majority's approach could lead to complex rules creating fine distinctions that achieve random results.

Comments.

♦ In *Gonzales v. Raich*, 545 U.S. 1 (2005), the Court upheld federal laws that prohibited local cultivation and medical use and possession of marijuana, citing *Wickard, supra,* for the proposition that there was an interstate market for marijuana and that quantities intended for use under the California statute might be diverted into illegal uses. The Court distinguished *Lopez* and *Morrison* on the grounds that those cases fell outside Congress's commerce power in its entirety. Here, the Court deferred to congressional judgment that an exemption for a significant segment of the total marijuana market would undermine the orderly enforcement of the entire regulatory scheme. Justice Scalia concurred on the ground that Congress could prohibit intrastate controlled-substance activities to achieve the legitimate end of eradicating illegal substances from interstate commerce. Justice O'Connor, Justice Thomas, and Chief Justice Rehnquist dissented, claiming that under this approach, federal regulation of local activity is immune to a Commerce Clause challenge if Congress acts with a comprehensive, more intrusive statute, and that this case effectively gives Congress a general police power over the nation.

♦ The Court often relies on statutory interpretation to avoid constitutional issues. In *Jones v. United States*, 529 U.S. 848 (2000), the Court avoided a Commerce Clause issue by holding that a federal arson statute, which applied to buildings used in any activity affecting interstate or foreign commerce, did not apply to an owner-occupied residence not used for commercial purposes. In *Solid Waste Agency of Northern Cook County v. United States Army Corps of Engineers*, 531 U.S. 159 (2001), the Court held that the Clean Water Act does not cover nonnavigable, isolated intrastate waters used as habitat for migratory birds. The dissent in that case considered the economic aspects of birdwatching and hunting, as well as the migration of birds over state lines, to conclude that Congress's commerce power would extend to cover these waters.

C. THE NATIONAL TAXING AND SPENDING POWERS

1. Regulation Through Taxing.

    a. Introduction. Article I, Section 8 grants Congress power "to lay and collect Taxes, Duties, Imposts and Excises, to pay the Debts and provide for the common Defense and general Welfare of the United States." Congress may exercise its taxing power as a means of promoting any objective that is within an enumerated power. If Congress has the power to regulate the activity taxed, the tax is valid even though clearly enacted for a regulatory, rather than a revenue-raising, purpose. If Congress has no power to regulate the activity taxed, the validity of the tax depends on its validity as a revenue-raising measure, although incidental regulatory effects are permissible. Congress generally does not now rely on the taxing power to regulate because of its extensive regulatory powers under other provisions, but this is still an important federal power.

    b. Tax as a penalty--

Bailey v. Drexel Furniture Co. (The Child Labor Tax Case), 259 U.S. 20 (1922).

Facts. A few months after the *Hammer v. Dagenhart* decision, *supra*, as a means to circumvent that decision, Congress imposed an excise tax of 10% on the yearly net profits of any employer knowingly using child labor in his business without regard to whether goods produced were shipped in interstate commerce. Drexel Furniture Company (P) paid the tax and won a refund case in the lower courts. Bailey (D), the IRS Commissioner, appeals.

Issue. May Congress use its taxing power to accomplish objectives that it cannot reach under any of its other powers?

Held. No. Judgment affirmed.

♦ The major purpose of a tax should be to raise revenue. However, many legitimate taxes also have incidental regulatory effects. Such taxes when imposed by Congress are still valid if their principal purpose is to raise revenue.

♦ Taxes that have a principal purpose of regulating are not authorized by the Constitution. The tax here was imposed only on those who knowingly do not comply with the child labor standards. This is a clear element of scienter. Scienter is used in penalties, not taxes. The tax is clearly a penalty and designed for regulation rather than to raise revenue. It is therefore invalid.

♦ If this tax were validated, then all Congress would have to do to take control of any one of a great number of areas of regulation reserved to the states would be to enact a detailed measure of complete regulation of the subject and enforce it by a so-called tax.

Comment. In *The Child Labor Tax Case*, the Supreme Court indicated that the important thing is Congress's motive. This means that the Court looks at the taxing statute to see its purpose, its intended effect, and its effect in normal operation (*i.e.*, the Court examines the statute on its face). If the true purpose is to raise revenue, the tax is valid. In *United States v. Kahriger*, 345 U.S. 22 (1953), the Court upheld a tax on wagering, despite the tax's indirect effect of penalizing professional gamblers. The legislative history showed an intent to raise revenue, and the tax actually did raise funds, although the legislative history also showed an intent to suppress wagering. The penalty on wagering was considered as merely an indirect effect. Unless the penalty provisions are extraneous to the tax need, courts cannot limit the exercise of the taxing power. (As noted *supra*, after 1936 the Court expanded its view of the commerce power, and it became less necessary for Congress to use its taxing power to regulate.)

---

2. **Regulation Through Spending.**

   a. **Introduction.** The "general welfare" power of Article I, Section 8, is connected with the taxing and spending power. This clause can therefore be invoked only when there is an expenditure of money appropriated by Congress. Thus, Congress could not pass a law under the General Welfare Clause requiring seat belts in all cars. The rule is that Congress must tax for revenue and not merely regulatory purposes, and then it must spend for the general welfare. The spending must be for a national concern as opposed to a local one. However, the Supreme Court gives great deference to the determinations of Congress in deciding what is for the "common benefit." For example, the old age provisions of the Social Security Act were upheld, largely by ascribing wide latitude to congressional determination of the national interest. [*See* Helvering v. Davis, 301 U.S. 619 (1937)]

   b. Local vs. general welfare--

___

United States v. Butler, 297 U.S. 1 (1936).

___

Facts. The 1933 Agriculture Adjustment Act authorized the Secretary of Agriculture to extend benefit payments to farmers who agreed to reduce their planted acreage. Processors of the covered crops were to be taxed to provide a fund for the benefit payments. Butler (P) was receiver for a processor who had paid the tax. P brought suit to recover the tax paid on grounds that it was part of an unconstitutional program to control agricultural production. The court of appeals held the tax unconstitutional. The United States (D) appeals.

Issue. May Congress use its taxing and spending powers to operate a self-contained program regulating agricultural production?

Held. No. Judgment affirmed.

- ◆ The power of Congress to authorize expenditures of public monies for public purposes is not limited by the direct grants of legislative power found in the Constitution, but it does have limits. Appropriations cannot be made as a means to an unconstitutional end.

- ◆ Regulation of agricultural production is not a power granted to Congress; therefore, it is left to the states. Attainment of such a prohibited end may not be accomplished through the use of granted powers (here, the taxing powers).

- ◆ This scheme, purportedly voluntary, in reality involves purchasing, with federal funds, submission to federal regulation of a subject reserved to the states. Because the end is invalid, it may not be accomplished indirectly through the taxing and spending power.

Dissent (Stone, Brandeis, Cardozo, JJ.). Courts are concerned only with the power to enact statutes, not the wisdom of the legislature. The depressed state of agriculture is nationwide; therefore, the Act does provide for the "general welfare." There is no coercion involved, since threat of loss, not hope of gain, which is involved here, is the essence of economic coercion. Conditioning the receipt of federal funds on certain activity does not infringe state power.

Comment. This was one of the last of the series of cases striking down parts of the New Deal. Subsequent Commerce Clause cases indicate that the area involved in this case would not now be held to be one of purely local concern.

___

c. Inducement of states permitted--

Steward Machine Co. v. Davis, 301 U.S. 548 (1937).

Facts. The Social Security Act taxed employers of eight or more persons a certain percentage of the salaries of their employees; the funds were to go to the United States Treasury. If an employer contributed to a state plan, he got a 90% credit toward the contribution of his federal responsibility. All state plans had to be approved by the Secretary of the Treasury, however. Steward Machine Company (P) paid the tax and then sought a refund, claiming that the Act unconstitutionally sought to coerce the states to adopt state plans. P appeals lower court decisions upholding the Act.

Issue. May Congress reduce private employers' federal tax obligations by crediting payments made only to federally approved state plans?

Held. Yes. Judgment affirmed.

♦ In the economic crisis of a depression, the spending here was clearly for the general welfare.

♦ P claims the Act seeks to coerce the states. In reality, the Act merely provides for fairness by not permitting states with security plans to be penalized by the double taxation on their business that would result if there were no credit for payments to these state plans.

d. Federal influence over state regulation through the spending power--

South Dakota v. Dole, 483 U.S. 203 (1987).

Facts. South Dakota (P) permitted anyone 19 years old or older to purchase beer. Congress adopted a statute requiring the Secretary of Transportation, Dole (D), to withhold federal highway funds from any state that permits persons younger than 21 years old to purchase alcoholic beverages. P sought a declaratory judgment that the statute violated the Twenty-First Amendment and the limits on the congressional spending power. The district court found for D and the court of appeals affirmed. The Supreme Court granted certiorari.

Issue. May Congress refuse to provide federal highway funds to states that do not adopt federal age standards for the sale of alcoholic beverages?

Held. Yes. Judgment affirmed.

♦   It is not necessary to decide whether Congress could enact a national minimum drinking age, because the statute in this case relied on the spending power to encourage uniformity in state drinking ages without actually imposing a national drinking age.

♦   Congress clearly has authority to impose conditions on the receipt of federal funds, even to attain objectives it might not be able to attain directly. This authority is incident to the spending power.

♦   The spending power itself is limited in four ways: (i) it must be used in the pursuit of "the general welfare;" (ii) any conditions imposed must be unambiguous, so the states may make knowing choices; (iii) the conditions must be related to the federal interest in particular national programs; and (iv) the conditions must not be barred by other independent constitutional provisions.

♦   In this case, the statute is consistent with the first three limitations as it is intended to promote safe interstate travel. P claims the statute is impermissible because it violates the fourth limitation; *i.e.*, it is barred by the Tenth Amendment. However, the independent constitutional bar limitation does not mean Congress may not indirectly achieve objectives it could not achieve directly. The bar prevents Congress from inducing states to engage in otherwise unconstitutional behavior. Because a state may constitutionally raise its drinking age, Congress is not barred from imposing such a condition on the expenditure of federal funds.

Dissent (O'Connor, J.). This condition established by this statute is not reasonably related to the expenditure of federal funds for highway purposes. The minimum drinking age is at best tangentially related to highway safety. If Congress can impose a condition that is so minimally related to its spending objectives, then Congress can interfere in virtually all aspects of state government, merely by citing some effect on interstate travel.

Comment. *Sabri v. United States*, 541 U.S. 600 (2004), involved a federal statute that criminalized the bribing of a state or local official whose government agency received federal funds of over $10,000 in one year. After Sabri was indicted for attempting to bribe a local government official, he made a "facial challenge" to the statute, asserting that it was unconstitutional because it did not require proof that the bribe involved federal funds. The Court rejected Sabri's facial challenge, finding that Congress has authority under the Spending Clause to appropriate federal monies to promote the general welfare and, corresponding to that power, authority under the Necessary and Proper Clause to see that those monies are in fact spent for the general welfare, not frittered away in graft or on projects that are undermined when funds are siphoned off. The Court noted that it made little difference whether federal funds were involved or whether other funds, which would have freed up federal funds for other uses, were involved. Furthermore, the Court distinguished *Dole* because the bribery statute is a means to bring federal power to bear directly on individuals who convert public spending into unearned private gain, not a means for bringing federal economic might to bear on a state's own choices of public policy.

D. FOREIGN AFFAIRS POWER

1. **Introduction.** The powers of the federal government concerning foreign or external affairs are different in origin and nature from those involving domestic or internal affairs. In external affairs, federal power is exclusive; the states may not conduct foreign affairs. There is no allocation of this power between the states and the federal government.

2. **Treaties.** Article II, Section 2 grants the President the power to make treaties with foreign nations, provided that two-thirds of the Senators present concur. Such treaties become the supreme law of the land under the Supremacy Clause. The Tenth Amendment is not a limitation on the treaty power. Thus, pursuant to a treaty, Congress may legislate on matters over which it otherwise would have no power.

3. **Principal Case--**

Missouri v. Holland, 252 U.S. 416 (1920).

Facts. The Migratory Bird Treaty Act of 1918 implemented a treaty between the United States and Canada and prohibited killing or interference with migratory birds except as permitted by regulations made by the Secretary of Agriculture. Missouri (P) brought suit in equity to enjoin Holland (D), a United States game warden, from enforcing the Act. P claims the Act unconstitutionally interferes with state rights and that an earlier similar Act of Congress, not in pursuance to a treaty, was held invalid. The district court dismissed the action. P appeals.

Issue. May an Act of Congress implementing a United States treaty create regulations that would be unconstitutional if the Act stood alone?

Held. Yes. Judgment affirmed.

♦ The Tenth Amendment is irrelevant since the power to make treaties is delegated expressly. Furthermore, if the treaty is valid, the statute is equally so, being necessary and proper.

♦ The important national interest here can be protected only by national action in concert with that of another nation. Such a joint effort is possible only through a treaty. Since there is no specific constitutional restriction and the national interest requires it, the treaty and its implementing statute are valid.

◆   The state's interest, while sufficient to justify regulation in the absence of federal regulation, is too transitory to preempt specific national regulation, especially when the national action arises from exercise of the treaty power.

Comment. In *Holland*, the Court stated that "Acts of Congress are the supreme law of the land only when made in pursuance of the Constitution, while treaties are declared to be so when made under the authority of the United States." This raised the possibility that treaties could impinge on constitutional rights. However, in *Reid v. Covert*, 354 U.S. 1 (1957), the Court held that a treaty could not confer power upon Congress that is not provided for in the Constitution. Covert had been a civilian residing in England when a military court convicted her of murdering her serviceman husband there. Such a trial was permitted by a United States agreement with England, but the Court held that under the Constitution, a civilian could not be convicted by a military court.

E. INTERGOVERNMENTAL IMMUNITIES

1.   Origins of Immunities--

McCulloch v. Maryland, 17 U.S. (4 Wheat.) 316 (1819).

Facts. (*See supra.*)

Issue. Is the federal government supreme over the states so that a bank created by it pursuant to its constitutional powers is immune from taxation by the states?

Held. Yes. The federal government is supreme under the Constitution and its instrumentalities cannot be taxed by the states.

◆   The Constitution and the laws made in pursuance thereof are supreme. They control the constitutions and laws of the respective states and cannot be controlled by them. A state, which represents only a part of the people of the nation, cannot act to control the government of the whole country.

◆   The power to tax is the power to destroy. It is also the power to control. The tax that P imposed on the Bank of the United States is an attempt by that state to control an operation of the government of the whole. The tax, therefore, is unconstitutional.

Comments.

◆   This portion of the opinion gave a wide scope to the Supremacy Clause. A state law is void if it retards, impedes, burdens, or otherwise interferes with the accomplishment of the congressional purpose in enacting the federal law. Unless the United States government is supreme, it would be no better off than the weak government under the Articles of Confederation. Of course, the supremacy of the federal government still faced severe tests, including the Civil War, but this case fleshed out the constitutional framework for the relations among states and the federal government and provided a starting point for federal immunity from state regulation.

♦   In the early cases, immunity was reciprocal. Activities of the states were immune from federal taxation. In *Collector v. Day*, 78 U.S. (11 Wall.) 113 (1871), the Court held that a state judge's salary was immune from federal income tax. *Day* was reversed in *Graves v. New York ex rel. O'Keefe*, 306 U.S. 466 (1939).

----

2.   **State Immunity from Federal Taxes.** Although earlier cases exempted most state functions and activities from federal taxation based on reciprocity (since states could not tax the federal government), such immunity has been restricted in more recent cases.

    a.   **General principles.** A federal tax levied on all states would be valid as long as it does not discriminate against the states, does not unduly interfere with or substantially burden traditional state functions, and does not apply to revenue uniquely capable of being earned only by the state.

    b.   **Taxation of state activities.** As states began to undertake new functions resembling business enterprises more than sovereign activity (*e.g.*, hospitals), the courts began restricting state immunity.

        1)   Thus, state employees of a bistate corporation formed to build and manage tunnels and bridges were required to pay federal income taxes on their salaries. [*See* Helvering v. Gerhardt, 304 U.S. 405 (1938)]

        2)   State revenue may be taxed by the federal government if the revenue from the state activity is not uniquely capable of being earned by a state. In *New York v. United States*, 326 U.S. 572 (1946), the state of New York had been engaged in the sale of mineral waters, and the Court upheld a tax on this activity.

    c.   **User fees.** The federal government may impose a fee on states that benefit from a federal program, as long as the fee is (i) nondiscriminatory, (ii) based on a fair approximation of use, and (iii) not structured to produce revenue exceeding the total cost of the benefits conferred. In *Massachusetts v. United States*, 435 U.S. 444 (1978), the Court upheld an annual registration tax on all civil aircraft that fly in the navigable airspace of the United States, including aircraft owned by a state and used by it exclusively for police functions.

3. **State Immunity from Federal Regulation.**

   a. **Introduction.** The Court's interpretation of the Commerce Clause has made congressional choices the primary determinant of the scope of national regulation. The first decision in 40 years to hold a federal law unconstitutional for exceeding the commerce power was *National League of Cities v. Usery*, 426 U.S. 833 (1976), and it has since been overruled. [*See* Garcia v. San Antonio Metropolitan Transit Authority, *infra*] The vitality of the state autonomy limitation on the commerce power may well turn on the composition of the Court, as decisions in this area are usually five-to-four votes. For the present, however, it seems that the Court's only function in Commerce Clause cases is statutory interpretation.

   b. **Recognition of state autonomy.** In *National League of Cities v. Usery*, *supra*, the Court struck down amendments to the Fair Labor Standards Act that would have extended minimum wage and maximum hour protections to state employees. The Court held that Congress, in exercising its powers under the Commerce Clause, had impermissibly interfered with the integral government functions of the states because the amendments would have displaced state policies regarding the manner in which states chose to deliver the services their citizens required. This was seen as not comporting with the federal system. Four justices dissented. *National League of Cities* was overruled by *Garcia, infra*, a mere nine years later.

   c. **From *National League of Cities* to *Garcia*.** The Court summarized the test for governmental immunity in *Hodel v. Virginia Surface Mining & Reclamation Association*, *supra*. Under this test, four conditions must exist for a state activity to merit immunity from federal regulation under the Commerce Clause:

      1) The federal statute must regulate the states as states;

      2) The statute must address matters that are indisputably attributes of state sovereignty;

      3) The state's compliance with the federal regulation must directly impair its ability to structure integral operations in areas of traditional governmental functions; and

      4) The relation of state and federal interests must not be such that the nature of the federal interest justifies state submission.

   d. *National League of Cities* overruled--

Garcia v. San Antonio Metropolitan Transit Authority, 469 U.S. 528 (1985).

Facts. The San Antonio Metropolitan Transit Authority (D), a public mass transit authority, received substantial federal financial assistance. In 1974, Congress extended the minimum wage and overtime provisions of the Fair Labor Standards Act ("FLSA") to mass transit employees and virtually all state and local government employees. After *National League of Cities v. Usery*, *supra*, D told its employees that the FLSA no longer applied to them. In 1979, however, the United States Department of Labor determined that D's activity was not immune from FLSA. Garcia (P) sued D for overtime pay under FLSA. In a separate action, D sought a declaratory judgment that it was exempt from FLSA. The district court granted D's motion and denied P's cross-motion for partial summary judgment. P appeals.

Issue. May Congress enforce minimum wage and overtime requirements against a local government's mass transit authority?

Held. Yes. Judgment reversed.

◆　　If D is exempt from FLSA, it must be because of its status as a governmental agency, for if it were a private enterprise, Congress could clearly apply FLSA under the commerce power.

◆　　Under the four-part test of *Hodel*, *supra*, the third requirement—that the federal statute impair traditional governmental functions—is at issue here. This requirement has produced confusion and a variety of interpretations, with no clear constitutional distinctions between what is and what is not a "traditional governmental function."

◆　　The problem with these standards is that they ignore the principle of federalism, which allows states to experiment with ways to solve problems. Thus, there are no "traditional," "integral," or "necessary" governmental functions that should be more carefully protected than other governmental functions. Just as the "governmental/proprietary function" distinction used in cases involving state immunity from federal taxation eventually was discarded as unworkable, so the "traditional governmental function" analysis must be discarded.

◆　　The constitutional structure does impose limits on the commerce power. But the sovereignty of the states is limited by the Constitution itself, through the Supremacy Clause, the Fourteenth Amendment, and Article I, Section 10. The states have influence over Congress through equal representation in the Senate. State sovereign interests are more properly protected by procedural safeguards inherent in the structure of the federal system than by judicially created limitations on federal power. The limit on the commerce power is one of process, not result.

◆　　Nothing in the FLSA, as applied to D, destroys state sovereignty or violates any constitutional provision.

◆　　The states have been able to protect themselves. They receive significant federal aid. They are exempt from the operation of many federal statutes.

Dissent (Powell, J., Burger, C.J., Rehnquist, O'Connor, JJ.).

♦ The *National League of Cities* rationale has been followed in several cases. Departure from the doctrine of stare decisis requires special justification; the majority has undermined the stability of judicial decisions by so suddenly overruling *National League of Cities*.

♦ Under the majority's opinion, the Tenth Amendment is nothing more than meaningless rhetoric when Congress exercises its commerce power. The Court cites no authority for its view that the role of the states in the federal system depends on the grace of elected federal officials rather than on the Constitution as interpreted by this Court.

♦ *National League of Cities* adopted a familiar type of balancing test that requires weighing the respective interests of the states and federal government. Under the Tenth Amendment, the states' role is a matter of constitutional law, not of legislative grace. The Court holds that federal political officials invoking the Commerce Clause are the sole judges of the limits of their own power. Federal overreaching under the Commerce Clause undermines the constitutionally mandated balance of power among the states and the federal government.

♦ The Court's view ignores the understanding of federalism that has long been accepted. Congress is not free under the Commerce Clause to assume a state's traditional sovereign power, and to do so without judicial review. This relegates the states to precisely the trivial role feared by opponents of the Constitution.

Dissent (O'Connor, Powell, Rehnquist, JJ.). The proper resolution of this conflict is to weigh state autonomy as a factor in the balance when interpreting the means by which Congress can regulate the states as states.

Dissent (Rehnquist, J.). The judgment should be affirmed under Justice Powell's approach, Justice Blackmun's concurrence in *National League of Cities*, or Justice O'Connor's approach. I am confident that the principle will, in time, again command the support of a majority of the Court.

---

e. **Limit on congressional regulatory authority.** In *New York v. United States*, 505 U.S. 144 (1992), the Court declared unconstitutional a provision of the 1985 Low Level Radioactive Waste Amendment Act, which required that any state that did not regulate waste according to federal standards by 1996 must take title to the waste generated within its borders and become liable for all damages incurred by the state's failure to take title promptly. The Court held that while Congress may create incentives for states to adopt legislative programs consistent with federal interests (*e.g.*, by attaching conditions on the receipt of federal funds or by offering states the option of either regulating private activity in interstate commerce according to federal standards or having state law preempted by federal regulation), Congress may not "commandeer" states by compelling them to enact a federal regulatory program.

f.   Limit on congressional power to use state officers directly--

---

Printz v. United States, 521 U.S. 898 (1997).

Facts. The federal Brady Handgun Act required the United States Attorney General to create a national system to instantly check the background of prospective handgun purchasers. Pending establishment of the national system, the Act also required the chief law enforcement officer ("CLEO") of each local jurisdiction to conduct the background checks. Printz (P) and another sheriff challenged the statute under *New York v. United States, supra*. The lower courts upheld the statute. The Supreme Court granted certiorari.

Issue. May Congress compel state officers directly to enforce a federal regulatory program?

Held. No. Judgment reversed.

♦   There is no constitutional text that addresses the issue of congressional action compelling state officers to execute federal laws.

♦   Historical practice has required state judges to enforce federal prescriptions. But courts commonly apply the law of other sovereigns. The Full Faith and Credit Clause requires state courts to enforce obligations arising in other states. This practice does not mean that Congress can impress the state executive into its service. Other historical texts refer to the ability of the federal government to use state officers to execute federal laws, but none implies that this can be done without the consent of the states.

♦   The structure of the Constitution gives Congress the power to regulate individuals, but not states. The separation of the federal and state governments is one of the Constitution's structural protections of liberty. The power of the federal government would be augmented immeasurably if it could impress into its service the state police officers.

♦   Federal control of state officers would also affect the balance of powers among the three branches. The President is responsible for executing the laws, but the Brady Act transfers this responsibility to the CLEOs in the 50 states, without Presidential control.

♦   Under *New York, supra*, Congress cannot compel the states to enact or enforce a federal regulatory program. Congress cannot circumvent that prohibition by conscripting the states' officers directly. Such a practice would be fundamentally incompatible with the constitutional system of dual sovereignty.

Concurrence (O'Connor, J.). Nothing in this holding precludes Congress from imposing purely ministerial reporting requirements.

Dissent (Stevens, Souter, Ginsburg, Breyer, JJ.). The Commerce Clause itself supports the regulation of commerce in handguns by the Brady Act. Nothing in the Constitution would allow a local police officer to ignore a command contained in a federal statute enacted pursuant to an express delegation of power such as the Commerce Clause. The basic difference between the Articles of Confederation and the Constitution was the ability of the federal government to govern individuals directly. If the statute were directed at private individuals with relevant information instead of at public officials, it would present no structural problem. Allowing the Brady Act to impose this duty on state officers is less burdensome to state power than to require the government to create a vast national bureaucracy to implement the policy.

Dissent (Souter, J.). The Federalist Papers would support the United States's position in this case, although Congress should not be allowed to require administrative support without also paying fair value for it.

Dissent (Breyer, Stevens, JJ.). There is no need to set forth an absolute, inflexible rule in this case. Federal systems in Europe, for example, provide that constituent states implement many of the laws enacted by the central "federal" body.

Comment. In *Reno v. Condon*, 528 U.S. 141 (2000), the Court held that drivers' personal information gathered by state motor vehicle departments is a "thing in interstate commerce," because it is used by insurers, manufacturers, marketers, and others engaged in interstate commerce to contact drivers with customized solicitations. The Court unanimously held that Congress had authority to limit disclosure of this information by state authorities because the information is an article of interstate commerce under the Commerce Clause.

IV. SEPARATION OF POWERS

A. PRESIDENTIAL ACTION AFFECTING CONGRESSIONAL POWERS

1. **Introduction.** The Constitution provides for separation of powers, but there are gray areas in which responsibilities are shared to some extent. For example, the President may establish the national agenda and propose legislation, but only Congress can enact law. Yet the executive power also includes some legislative authority, such as the power to veto legislation under Article I, Section 7. Congress also may delegate essentially legislative power to administrative agencies operated under the executive branch.

2. **Emergency Lawmaking Power Denied to the President--**

Youngstown Sheet & Tube Co. v. Sawyer (The Steel Seizure Case), 343 U.S. 579 (1952).

Facts. The steelworkers, after prolonged negotiations, went on a nationwide strike during the Korean War. Citing the serious national interest in steel production, President Truman ordered Sawyer (D), Commerce Secretary, to seize the steel mills and keep them running. Youngstown Sheet & Tube Company (P) challenged the seizure as unconstitutional and unauthorized by Congress. Congress had earlier passed the Taft-Hartley Act, giving the President authority to seek an injunction against such strikes, but had rejected an amendment to permit government seizures to avoid serious shutdowns. The district court issued a preliminary injunction against D, which was stayed by the court of appeals. The Supreme Court granted certiorari.

Issue. May the President, acting under the aggregate of his constitutional powers, exercise a lawmaking power independent of Congress in order to protect serious national interests?

Held. No. Judgment affirmed.

♦ The President's power to issue the order must stem either from an Act of Congress or from the Constitution itself. Congress clearly gave no such power. In fact, it specifically rejected the means used by D.

♦ The President's authority as Commander in Chief does not warrant the seizure, as it is too far removed from the "theater of war." His general executive power is inapplicable since there is no relevant law to execute.

♦ The order does not direct that a congressional policy be executed in a manner prescribed by Congress but that a presidential policy be executed in a manner prescribed by the President. Such presidential usurpation of the lawmaking power is unauthorized and invalid.

Concurrence (Frankfurter, J.). Congress specifically expressed its will on the subject, which is that the President ought not have the powers he has here attempted to exercise.

 Concurrence (Douglas, J.). As a result of the condemnation provision of the Fifth Amendment, no condemnation would be lawful until Congress authorized or ratified it.

Concurrence (Jackson, J.). There are three categories of circumstances in which the President may act:

> First, he may act pursuant to the authorization of Congress. This situation gives him maximum authority because he acts under the powers granted to him by the Constitution plus all the authority delegated by Congress.
>
> Second, the President may act on the strength of his independent powers, absent any authorization by Congress.
>
> Third, he may act in ways contrary to the expressed will of Congress. In such a situation, his power is at its lowest ebb.

This case clearly falls under the third category, and the President's action can be sustained only if it was entirely within his constitutional domain and beyond the control of Congress. However, this action was not within his constitutional domain. The President cannot use his powers as Commander in Chief or his powers to control the nation's foreign policy to enlarge his mastery over the internal affairs of the nation.

Dissent (Vinson, C.J., Reed, Minton, JJ.). The President has a duty to execute the legislative programs of supporting the armed forces in Korea. The President's action was an effective means of performing his duty, and was clearly temporary and subject to congressional direction.

Comment. Two of the majority Justices were willing to agree with the dissent that the President did have inherent legislative powers to act in preserving the nation, but only when there was an absence of any provision passed by Congress purporting to deal with the situation. Here, these Justices pointed to the fact that Congress had passed the National Labor Relations Act, which set forth specific provisions to be followed by the President in case of strikes that threatened the national security.

-----

3. **Authority to Enter Executive Agreements--**

Dames & Moore v. Regan, 453 U.S. 654 (1981).

Facts. On November 4, 1979, American diplomatic personnel in Iran were captured and held hostage. On November 14, President Carter declared a national emergency and froze all Iranian assets in the United States. The next day, the Treasury Department issued regulations requiring licensing of any judicial process against Iranian interests and specifying that any such licenses could be revoked at any time. Dames & Moore (P) sued Iranian defendants for $3.5 million and attached Iranian assets pending the outcome of the litigation. On January 19, 1981, the United States, through Algeria, agreed to terminate all legal proceedings in United States courts against Iran, to nullify all attachments and judgments obtained therein, and to terminate such claims through binding arbitration. This agreement was implemented through an Executive Order. On January 27, P obtained a judgment against the Iranian defendants and attempted to execute the judgment on the attached property. The district court nullified the prejudgment attachments and stayed all further proceedings against the Iranian defendants in light of the Executive Order. P then sued Regan (D), the Treasury Secretary, for declaratory and injunctive relief against enforcement of the Executive Orders and regulations on grounds that they were unconstitutional and that the President had exceeded his authority in implementing the agreement with Iran. The district court denied P's claim. P appeals.

Issue. May the President, in response to a national emergency, suspend outstanding claims in American courts?

Held. Yes. Judgment affirmed.

♦ The questions presented by this case touch fundamentally upon the manner in which our republic is to be governed. Although little authority exists that is relevant to concrete problems of executive power, much relevant analysis is contained in *Youngstown Sheet & Tube Co. v. Sawyer, supra*. There the Court observed that exercise of executive power is closely related to congressional action; executive power is greatest when exercised pursuant to congressional authorization and weakest when exercised in contravention of the will of Congress.

♦ The International Emergency Economic Powers Act ("IEEPA"), by its terms, permits the President to "regulate [and] . . . nullify . . . any acquisition . . . of . . . any right . . . to . . . any property in which any foreign country or a national thereof has any interest." In essence, IEEPA was intended to permit freezing of assets to serve as "bargaining chips." P's attachment and judgment were obtained after the President had acted pursuant to this specific statutory authority. We conclude that IEEPA authorized the nullification of the attachments.

♦ IEEPA does not directly authorize the suspension of in personam lawsuits, which merely establish liability and fix damages and do not in themselves involve Iranian property. Neither does the Hostage Act of 1868 authorize such action. However, the general tenor of these enactments, combined with the International Claims Settlement Act of 1949, which created the International Claims Commission, indicates congressional approval of, or at least acquiescence in, executive agreements settling the claims of United States nationals against foreign countries.

♦ P can resort to the International Claims Commission as an alternative forum.

♦ This holding is limited to the narrow facts at hand where the settlement is a necessary element of a resolution of a major foreign policy dispute between our country and another and where Congress has acquiesced in the President's action.

---

4. **The War Powers.**

a. **Introduction.** Although the Constitution specifies that the President is commander in chief of the military, only Congress has the power to initiate or declare war. The interplay of these powers was not made clear in the Constitution. The Court has recognized the need to conduct foreign affairs and has largely deferred to the executive and legislative branches in this area. The Vietnam War called into question the entire matter of the relationship between Congress and the President in the conduct of war. Some commentators argued that the President had acquired more power in this area than was originally intended by the Constitution. Until President Theodore Roosevelt unilaterally sent troops into Panama in 1903, the Presidents did not initiate military action against foreign states without congressional approval. After World War II, troops were sent to several locations without congressional action, including Korea and Lebanon. The exact scope of executive and congressional powers in this area is not clearly defined by the Constitution. Consequently, each branch has been free to take initiatives to make national policy in this area. The basic issue is whether the President has the power to use armed forces against a foreign nation without the authorization of Congress.

b. **Inherent powers--**

United States v. Curtiss-Wright Export Corp., 299 U.S. 304 (1936).

Facts. Congress, by joint resolution, permitted the President to prohibit American arms sales to those countries involved in conflict in Chaco, if he found that such a prohibition would contribute to peace. Penalties for violation of such a prohibition were also specified. The President did order such a prohibition. Curtiss-Wright Export Corporation (D) was indicted for conspiracy to violate the prohibition. D challenged the indictment on the basis that the resolution was an invalid delegation of legislative power to the President. The lower court held the delegation unconstitutional. The United States (P) appeals.

Issue. May Congress delegate legislative-type power to the President to conduct foreign affairs?

Held. Yes. Judgment reversed.

♦ The power of the federal government in regard to external affairs is not delegated by the Constitution, but derives as a necessary concomitant of sovereignty. These powers are as broad as the powers held by any other nation.

♦ Furthermore, federal power is exclusive in this realm; the states have no concurrent power. Congress may delegate much broader powers to the President for conducting foreign affairs than it can for handling domestic affairs.

---

c. **War Powers Resolution.** In 1973, Congress adopted a joint resolution called the War Powers Resolution, 50 U.S.C. sections 1541-48, which spells out the President's authority to use the armed forces. If the President uses the armed forces in foreign nations under specified conditions without a congressional declaration of war, he must formally report to Congress. In the absence of any congressional action, the forces must (in most cases) be removed within 60 days. The constitutionality of the resolution has not been considered by the courts.

d. **Defining "war"--**

Campbell v. Clinton, 203 F.3d 19 (D.C. Cir. 2000).

Facts. On March 24, 1999, President Clinton (D) announced that NATO had begun attacks on Yugoslav targets. Two days later he submitted a report to Congress under the War Powers Resolution ("WPR") explaining the use of armed forces. On April 28, Congress voted down a declaration of war and an "authorization" of the air strikes. The WPR required the President to terminate any use of United States Armed Forces within 60 days unless Congress declared war or specifically authorized the action, but the conflict between NATO and Yugoslavia continued for 79 days. Campbell and other members of Congress (Ps) brought suit claiming the President had violated the WPR. The district court dismissed the suit for lack of standing. Ps appeal.

Issue. May members of Congress bring suit against the President for an alleged violation of the War Powers Resolution?

Held. No. Judgment affirmed.

Concurrence (Silberman, J.) No one can bring a suit like this because the claims of a violation of the WPR and the War Powers Clause of the Constitution are not justiciable. There is no constitutional test for what is war. Those cases in which a court has determined that the nation was at war did not deal with the issue of whether the President had "declared war" in violation of the Constitution. Under the *Prize Cases*, the President has independent authority to repel aggressive acts by third parties even without specific congressional authorization, and the courts may not review the level of force selected. If the President can respond to war initiated by another, a plaintiff who challenges the action would have to answer who started it, and the courts have no judicial standards to resolve such an issue. Judge Tatel's approach would require a President to obtain a declaration of war after the crisis is no longer acute, but this is a matter for the President's judgment, not that of the courts.

Concurrence (Tatel, J.). The courts may develop manageable standards for determining the existence of a war, just as they have developed standards regarding "an establishment of religion" or what constitutes an unreasonable search and seizure. In the *Prize Cases*, the Court determined that there was a state of war even though Congress had not declared war, defining war as that "state in which a nation prosecuted its right by force." In this case, the courts would need only to determine whether the President possessed legal authority to conduct the military operation, which involves legal, not political, issues.

---

5.   **Individual Rights and the War on Terrorism.**

    a.   **Joint resolution authorizing the use of military force.** In response to the attacks on September 11, 2001, Congress passed a joint resolution titled "Authorization for Use of Military Force" ("AUMF") that gave the President broad authority to use force against nations, organizations, or persons that the President determines aided the terrorist attacks. No particular enemy was defined. President Bush committed the United States military to combat in Afghanistan and Iraq and detained alleged enemy combatants inside the United States and at Guantanamo Bay, Cuba.

    b.   **Detention of United States citizens--**

Hamdi v. Rumsfeld, 542 U.S. 507 (2004).

Facts. Hamdi (P), a Lousiana-born Saudi-American, was captured in an active combat zone abroad, detained by the United States military as an "enemy combatant," and held in a naval brig in Virginia. P sought habeas corpus relief against Rumsfeld (D), Secretary of Defense, in federal court in Virginia, claiming that the Non-Detention Act of 1948 barred indefinite detention. The Fourth Circuit held that P was not entitled to habeas relief, despite being a United States citizen, because of military needs. The court held that the AUMF satisfied the requirement in the Non-Detention Act for an Act of Congress authorizing detention. P appeals.

Issue. Does the President have the authority to detain citizens who qualify as "enemy combatants" for an indefinite period of time with no opportunity for an impartial hearing?

Held. No. Judgment vacated and case remanded.

♦ D claims that the Executive has plenary authority to detain pursuant to Article II, but that question need not be addressed because Congress authorized detention through the AUMF. The detention of individuals falling into the limited category of combatants, for the duration of the particular conflict in which they were captured, is a fundamental incident to war and falls within the AUMF. There is no reason that the government cannot hold one of its own citizens as an enemy combatant.

♦ P claims that Congress did not authorize indefinite detention. He also claims that he faces the prospect of perpetual detention, because the "war on terror" is an unconventional war that does not fit within normal law-of-war principles. While indefinite detention is not authorized by Congress, there are active combat operations in Afghanistan against Taliban combatants, and the United States may lawfully detain Taliban combatants during these hostilities.

♦ Although the AUMF did authorize the detention of combatants such as P in the narrow circumstances of this case, the write of habeas corpus remains available to every person detained within the United States. The writ has not been suspended. P may properly seek a habeas determination on the issue of whether he falls within the category of hostile forces subject to detention. Due process demands that a citizen held in the United States as an enemy combatant be given a meaningful opportunity to contest the factual basis for that detention before a neutral decisionmaker.

♦ To satisfy the minimum requirements for such a hearing, the citizen-detainee must receive notice of the factual basis for his classification and a fair opportunity to rebut the government's factual assertions before a neutral decisionmaker. Evidentiary standards may be relaxed so that the government may use hearsay to support the classification. There may be a rebuttable presumption in favor of the government's evidence.

Concurrence and dissent (Souter, Ginsburg, JJ.). To the extent that the plurality rejects the government's proposed limit on the exercise of habeas jurisdiction, it is correct. However, the plurality goes too far when it agrees that P can be detained if his designation as an enemy combatant is correct. The AUMF does not refer to detention, so it cannot provide a basis for P's detention. The government has failed to justify holding P in the absence of an Act of Congress, criminal charges, a showing that P's detention conforms to the law of war, or a showing that section 4001(a) is unconstitutional. Without a showing of something more, P should be released. In a moment of genuine emergency, the President can detain a citizen if there is a reason to fear he is an imminent threat to the safety of the nation and its people, but such emergency power must be limited by the emergency. P has been held for over two years, so that exception does not apply here.

Dissent (Scalia, Stevens, JJ.). A citizen who wages war against the United States may be prosecuted for treason, but unless Congress suspends the usual protections under the Suspension Clause, a citizen cannot be detained without charge. The lower court decision should be reversed. The traditional treatment of enemy aliens that includes detention until the cessation of hostilities does not apply to American citizens. The criminal law process is the only means for punishing and incapacitating traitors. Unless the writ of habeas corpus is suspended, a citizen is entitled either to a criminal trial or a judicial decree requiring his release. The AUMF is not a suspension of the writ. The Court's opinion establishes a procedure that makes P's detention legal, but that is an incorrect application of the writ.

Dissent (Thomas, J.). The detention of P falls within the government's war powers, and the courts have no expertise or capacity to second-guess the decision to detain P. The President has constitutional authority to protect the national security and has broad discretion to exercise that authority. The courts should not interfere in these matters. Due process requires only a good-faith executive determination.

Comment. In *Rumsfeld v. Padilla*, 542 U.S. 426 (2004), Padilla, a United States citizen, was arrested in Chicago for participating in a plot to detonate a dirty bomb. He was held as a material witness under a warrant issued by a New York federal district court. Later he was declared an "enemy combatant" by the President and was turned over to the Department of Defense for detention. Padilla challenged his detention. The Second Circuit held that the President did not have authority to detain Padilla under section 4001(a). The Court reversed on jurisdictional grounds because Padilla should have filed his habeas petition in South Carolina against the commander of the brig where he was incarcerated rather than in New York where he had originally been detained. The four Justices in the minority opinion would have found Padilla's detention to be unauthorized under 4001(a). The dissent noted that Padilla was actually being detained for questioning, not for law enforcement or punishment.

---

c.   **Detention of enemy combatants at Guantanamo Bay.** The United States military captured several hundred foreign fighters in Afghanistan and held them as "enemy combatants" at Guantanamo Bay, a territory leased by the United States from Cuba since 1903. Under the lease, the territory remains under the "ultimate sovereignty" of Cuba. Some of the prisoners sought writs of habeas corpus in the federal district court for the District of Columbia. In *Rasul v. Bush*, 542 U.S. 466 (2004), the Court held that federal judges do have jurisdiction to consider such habeas petitions from Guantanamo detainees. The Court reasoned that although technically Cuba has sovereignty over the territory, under the lease, the United States exercises "complete jurisdiction and control" over the base and may continue to exercise such control permanently if it chooses. As such, Guantanamo Bay is in every practical respect a territory of the United States. Another consideration is the indefinite status of the detention and the lack of any legal procedure to determine the detainees' status. The dissenters argued that the decision extends the habeas statute to aliens beyond the sovereign territory of the United States to anywhere in the world and that Congress could have changed the habeas jurisdiction of federal judges if it wanted to.

B. CONGRESSIONAL ACTION AFFECTING PRESIDENTIAL POWERS

1. **Delegation of Rulemaking Power.** In principle, Congress cannot delegate its legislative powers to another branch of government. [Mistretta v. United States, 488 U.S. 361 (1989)] However, the Court has allowed Congress to delegate rulemaking power to executive agencies. For example, in *Yakus v. United States*, 321 U.S. 414 (1944), the Court upheld the delegation by Congress to an executive branch price administrator the authority to establish maximum prices and rents. Congress had stated the legislative objective, specified the means, and provided standards to guide the administrative determinations. Such delegations are upheld as long as Congress provides an "intelligible principle" that rulemakers must follow.

2. **Legislative Vetoes.**

   a. **Introduction.** Congress had occasionally included provisions in legislation that leave it some power to override executive action taken pursuant to the legislation. This device, called the legislative veto, had been praised for bringing greater efficiency to the government, but it raised potential conflicts with the principle of separation of powers among the branches of government.

   b. **Rejection of legislative veto--**

Immigration & Naturalization Service v. Chadha, 462 U.S. 919 (1983).

Facts. Chadha (P) was an East Indian who lawfully entered the United States on a nonimmigrant student visa. After his visa expired, the Immigration and Naturalization Service (D) held a deportation hearing. The immigration judge suspended P's deportation and sent a report to Congress as required by section 244(c)(1) of the Immigration and Naturalization Act. Section 244(c)(2) provided that either House of Congress could veto a suspension of deportation. The House of Representatives adopted a unilateral resolution opposing P's permanent residence, and P was ordered deported. P sought review in the Ninth Circuit, which held section 244(c)(2) unconstitutional. The Supreme Court granted certiorari.

Issue. May Congress employ the legislative veto device to oversee delegation of its constitutional authority to the executive branch?

Held. No. Judgment affirmed.

♦   Although this case has political ramifications, it is primarily a constitutional challenge that presents a bona fide controversy, properly subject to judicial action.

♦   Article I of the Constitution vests all legislative powers in both Houses of Congress. Every bill or resolution must be passed by both Houses and approved by the President (or his veto overridden) before it takes effect. These provisions are intended to secure liberty through separation of powers. The bicameral nature of Congress similarly insures careful consideration of all legislation.

♦   The action taken by the House in this case was essentially legislative in purpose and effect. The legislative veto replaced the constitutional procedure of enacting legislation requiring P's deportation (a private bill). Yet the Constitution enumerates only four instances in which either House may act alone—impeachment, trial after impeachment, ratification of treaties, and confirmation of presidential appointments. The legislative veto is not enumerated.

♦   Although the legislative veto may be efficient, efficiency is not the overriding value behind the Constitution. Separation of powers, as set up by the Constitution, may not be eroded for convenience. Therefore, the legislative veto is unconstitutional. Once Congress delegates authority, it must abide by that delegation until it legislatively alters or revokes it.

Concurrence (Powell, J.). There is no need to invalidate all legislative vetoes. This one is an unconstitutional exercise of the judicial function by the House because it decided the specific rights of P.

Dissent (White, J.). The legislative veto is a valid response to the dilemma of choosing between no delegation (and hence no lawmaking because of the vast amount of regulation necessary under our system) and abdication of the lawmaking function to the executive branch and administrative agencies. The legislative veto has been included in nearly 200 statutes, accepted by Presidents for 50 years, and allows resolution of major constitutional and policy differences between Congress and the President. Because the underlying legislation was properly enacted and because the Constitution does not prohibit it, the legislative veto is constitutional.

3. **Line Item Veto.**

   a. **Introduction.** Article I, Section 7 provides that "Every Bill which shall have passed the House of Representative and the Senate, shall, before it become a Law, be presented to the President of the United States; If he approves he shall sign it, but if not he shall return it, with his Objections to the House in which it shall have originated, who shall . . . proceed to reconsider it. If after such Reconsideration two thirds of that House shall agree to pass the Bill . . . and if approved by two thirds of [the other] House, it shall become a Law." This clause requires the President to approve or disapprove a complete law. For years, Presidents have requested a line item veto that would allow them to veto portions of statutes, leaving the balance intact. When Congress did enact a line item veto, the constitutionality of the statute was immediately challenged.

   b. **Constitutionality of line item veto--**

Clinton v. New York, 524 U.S. 417 (1998).

Facts. The Line Item Veto Act allowed the President, after making specific determinations, to cancel three types of provisions that have already been signed into law, including any item of new direct spending or any limited tax benefit. The cancellation becomes effective when Congress receives notice from the President, but Congress may render the cancellation void by passing a disapproval bill. President Clinton (D) applied the Act to cancel sections of two separate statutes, one that waived the federal government's right to recoupment of up to $2.6 billion in taxes from the state of New York and another that gave tax preferences to certain food refiners and processors. These provisions fell within the criteria set forth in the Act, and Congress did not pass a disapproval bill. The city of New York and others (Ps) sued, claiming the cancellations were unconstitutional. The district court consolidated the suits, found that Ps had standing, and held that the Act was unconstitutional. D appeals.

Issue. May Congress grant the President a line item veto that allows the President to cancel legislation after it is duly enacted and signed?

Held. No. Judgment affirmed.

♦ Article I, Section 7 allows the President to return a bill to Congress. This action takes place before a bill becomes law. By contrast, the cancellation provision in the Act occurs after the bill becomes law. A constitutional return applies to the entire bill, but a cancellation under the Act applies only to a part of a bill. These are constitutionally significant differences.

♦ The Constitution expressly permits the return of a bill, but it is silent regarding unilateral Presidential action that either repeals or amends parts of a duly enacted statute. Constitutional silence on a matter as important as Presidential action regarding statutes must be construed as an express prohibition on such actions. Presidents may either approve all parts of a bill or reject it completely.

♦ D claims that a cancellation is not actually an amendment or a repeal. In *Field v. Clark*, 143 U.S. 649 (1892), the Court allowed a Tariff Act that gave the President authority to suspend certain products' exemptions from import duties upon making certain findings. Such a suspension power differs from a cancellation power because exercise of the suspension power depended on conditions that did not exist when the Tariff Act was passed because the President had a duty to suspend under specified circumstances and because when the President did suspend the duties, he was executing congressional policy. A cancellation under the Act has none of these factors that justified upholding the suspension power. For example, the President can cancel a portion of a statute for his own policy reasons, independent of Congress. Congress cannot so alter the constitutional provisions without a constitutional amendment.

♦ The President has a traditional power to decline to spend appropriated funds. But never before this Act has Congress given the President the unilateral power to change the text of duly enacted statutes. The line item veto procedures are simply not allowed under Article I, Section 7.

Concurrence (Kennedy, J.). The Act threatens the liberties of individual citizens because liberty is always at stake when one or more branches of government seeks to transgress the separation of powers.

Dissent (Breyer, O'Connor, Scalia, JJ.). The Court appears to conclude that a cancellation is the equivalent of a repeal or amendment of a law, but it is not. A cancellation under the Act leaves the statutes as they were literally written, intact. In canceling a law under the Act, the President follows the law. He neither repeals nor amends anything. Congress has granted a contingent power to deny effect to certain statutory language in many other statutes. Finally, the Act does not violate the separation of powers because Congress retains the power both to disapprove a cancellation and to include in any bill a provision that says the act will not apply.

Concurrence and dissent (Scalia, O'Connor, Breyer, JJ.). The Court fails to observe that the Act applies only after the requirements of the Presentment Clause have been satisfied. This means that the Court's problem focuses on the President's power to prevent certain parts of duly enacted statutes to have full force and effect. Yet there is no difference between Congress allowing the President to cancel a spending item and allowing money to be spent on a particular item at the President's discretion. The latter approach has been allowed throughout history. If the Act had allowed the President to decline to spend any item of spending in the budget bills, it would have been constitutional. The Act uses a technically different approach, but it does not violate Article I, Section 7, and the doctrine of unconstitutional delegation is not a doctrine of technicalities.

4. **Appointments Power.**

    a. **Introduction.** Article II, Section 2 indicates that the President may appoint, with the consent of the Senate, ambassadors, consuls, Justices of the Supreme Court, and all other officers of the United States whose appointments are not otherwise provided for. In addition, Congress may vest the power to appoint "inferior officers" in the President alone, in the courts of law, or in the heads of departments, "as they think proper." With the increasing complexity of political problems, Congress has begun using the Appointments Clause to create unique offices having characteristics of more than one branch.

    b. **Limit on appointment power.** In *Buckley v. Valeo*, 424 U.S. 1 (1976), the Court relied upon this provision in holding that the composition of the Federal Election Commission established by the Federal Election Campaign Act was unconstitutional. Because of the enforcement powers of the commissioners, who were appointed by Congress, the Court held that they exercised executive powers, thus making them officers of the United States whose appointment was subject to the Appointments Clause.

    c. **Delegation of spending power--**

Bowsher v. Synar, 478 U.S. 714 (1986).

Facts. The Deficit Control Act of 1985 (Gramm-Rudman-Hollings Act) was enacted to reduce the federal budget deficit to zero over a period of years. Automatic reductions in federal spending were to take place in any fiscal year for which the deficit exceeded the statutory target. The reductions would take effect after the directors of the Office of Management and Budget and the Congressional Budget Office independently calculated the necessary budget reductions. These directors would then report their findings to the Comptroller General, who would make conclusions as to the necessary spending reductions. The President was then required to issue a "sequestration" order mandating the Comptroller General's conclusions. This order would become effective unless Congress reduced spending by legislation. An alternative procedure was also established in case the primary procedure was invalidated. The alternative procedure provided for an expedited congressional joint resolution that would become a sequestration order when the President signed it. Synar (P) and others challenged the statute. The district court held the reporting provisions unconstitutional. Bowsher (D) appeals.

Issue. May Congress assign to the Comptroller General the function of determining which accounts of the federal budget must be cut to meet deficit targets?

Held. No. Judgment affirmed.

- Standing in this case lies in one plaintiff, an employees' union whose members would not receive a scheduled increase in benefits if the Act is sustained.

- Although the Constitution gives Congress a role in appointment of executive officers, it does not give Congress an active role in supervising such officers. It has the power of removal only upon impeachment. Although Congress may limit the President's powers of removal, it cannot reserve for itself the removal power. Otherwise, Congress would have control over the execution of the laws in violation of separation of powers.

- Because Congress may not execute the laws, it cannot grant to an officer under its control the power to execute the laws. D argues that the Comptroller General performs his duties independently of Congress, but in fact Congress is the sole removal authority for the Comptroller General. Accordingly, the Comptroller General may not possess executive powers.

- Under the Act, the Comptroller General prepares a report by exercising his independent judgment. This is more than a mechanical function; it requires interpretation of the Act and application of judgment concerning a set of facts; this constitutes execution of the law. In fact, the President is required to comply with the report in ordering the reductions.

- Because the reporting procedures are unconstitutional, the fallback provisions are effective.

Dissent (White, J.). Whether Congress or the Comptroller General determines the level of funding available to the President to carry out its duties, the effect on the President is the same. The President has no authority to establish spending levels. Congress has not granted policymaking discretion; it has specified a detailed procedure based on specific criteria. The Act is an effective response to a serious national crisis, and presents no real threat to separation of powers.

---

d. **Creation of independent counsel--**

Morrison v. Olson, 487 U.S. 654 (1988).

Facts. The Ethics in Government Act of 1978, 28 U.S.C. sections 591 *et seq.*, provided for the appointment of an "independent counsel" to investigate and prosecute specified government officials for violations of federal criminal law. Under the Act, the Attorney General conducts a preliminary investigation of possible violations, and then reports to the Special Division, a court created by the Act. If the Attorney General determines that there are reasonable grounds to believe further investigation or a prosecution is warranted, she applies for appointment of independent counsel. The Special

Division then appoints such counsel and defines the counsel's prosecutorial jurisdiction. The independent prosecutor is required to comply with Department of Justice policies to the extent possible. The Attorney General may remove an independent prosecutor for cause; otherwise, the counsel's tenure expires upon completion of the specified investigations or prosecutions. The counsel notifies the Attorney General of the completion; alternatively, the Special Division may find the task completed. Certain congressional committees have oversight jurisdiction regarding the independent counsel's conduct. Pursuant to this Act, the Special Division appointed Morrison (D) to investigate allegations that Olson (P), an Assistant Attorney General, had lied in testimony to Congress. D obtained a grand jury subpoena against P. P moved to quash the subpoenas, claiming that D had no authority to proceed because the Act was unconstitutional. The trial court upheld the Act, but the court of appeals reversed. D appeals.

Issue. May Congress provide for the judicial appointment of independent counsel for purposes of investigating and prosecuting federal criminal offenses?

Held. Yes. Judgment reversed.

♦ Under the Appointments Clause, there are two classes of officers: (i) principal officers, who are selected by the President with the advice and consent of the Senate; and (ii) inferior officers, whom Congress may allow to be appointed by the President alone, by the heads of departments, or by the judiciary. Thus, if D is a principal officer, the Act violates the Constitution.

♦ The difference between principal and inferior officers is not always clear. It requires consideration of several factors:

> D may be removed by a higher executive branch official, despite having independent powers.

> D's authority is limited to performing specified, limited duties. D has no policymaking authority and must comply with Department of Justice policies.

> D's office is limited in jurisdiction to the terms of the appointment. It is also limited in tenure; it does not extend beyond the completion of the specific task given.

> Evaluation of these factors leads to the conclusion that an independent counsel is an inferior officer. However, P claims that Congress may not provide that an officer of one branch be appointed by officers of another branch.

♦ The clause itself does not forbid interbranch appointments, but instead gives Congress discretion to determine the propriety of vesting the appointment of executive officials in the courts. The limitation on this power is where it implicates the separation of powers or impairs the constitutional functions assigned to one of the branches. The very reason for the Act was to remove the appointment power from the executive branch, and the judicial branch is the most logical alternative. By making members of the Special Division ineligible to participate in any matters relating to an independent counsel they have appointed, Congress has protected the separation of powers.

♦ Article III limits the judicial power to cases and controversies. However, if the Appointments Clause gives Congress the power to authorize the courts to appoint officials such as an independent counsel, which it does, the appointment power is a source of authority independent of Article III. The additional powers granted to the Special Division, such as defining the counsel's authority and tenure of office, are incidental to the exercise of the appointment power itself.

♦ The Special Division also has power to terminate an independent counsel's office, which is an administrative power. This power must be narrowly construed to avoid constitutional problems. It is thus limited to removing an independent counsel who has served her purpose, but does not acknowledge that fact and remains on the payroll.

♦ P also asserts a separation of powers problem because the Attorney General can remove an independent counsel only by showing "good cause." In *Bowsher*, *supra*, for example, Congress could not involve itself in the removal of an executive officer. Under the Act in this case, however, Congress did not acquire a removal power over executive officials beyond its power of impeachment and conviction.

♦ The Attorney General retains the removal power, subject to the good cause requirement. But the Constitution does not give the President unbridled discretion to remove officials of independent agencies. Prior cases have distinguished purely executive officials from quasi-legislative and quasi-judicial officials, but this is an inappropriate distinction for analyzing removal powers. The proper question is whether the removal restrictions impede the President's ability to perform his constitutional duty. Because the independent counsel has a limited function, and because the Attorney General has removal authority for good cause, the good cause restriction does not unconstitutionally impede the President.

♦ The second separation of powers issue is based on interference with the role of the executive branch. However, the Act does not permit either congressional or judicial usurpation of executive functions. It also leaves the executive branch with the ability to supervise the counsel's prosecutorial powers.

Dissent (Scalia, J.). The power to conduct a criminal prosecution is a purely executive power, and the Act deprives the President of the exclusive control over the exercise of that power. It does not matter how much the Act reduces presidential control; the Act violates the separation of powers doctrine. In addition, P's appointment could only be constitutional if she is an "inferior" officer, but she is not inferior because she is not subordinate to another officer. The final infirmity of the Act is that it improperly imposes restrictions upon the removal of the independent counsel.

Comment. In *Mistretta v. United States*, 488 U.S. 361 (1989), the Court upheld the creation of the United States Sentencing Commission as an independent commission in the judicial branch, appointed by the President. The commission would have at least three federal judges. The Court concluded that because the judiciary has a traditional role in sentencing, judicial involvement on the commission was not incongruous.

C. PRIVILEGE AND IMMUNITY

1. Executive Privilege.

a. Introduction. Although not mentioned in the Constitution, a privilege has been recognized to protect against the disclosure of presidential communications made in the exercise of executive power. This privilege derives from both the doctrine of separation of powers and the inherent need to protect the confidentiality of high level communications.

b. Military, diplomatic, or national security secrets. Where the presidential communications relate to military, diplomatic, or sensitive national security secrets, the claim of privilege is given the utmost deference by the courts. However, other presidential communications are only presumptively privileged.

c. Evidence in a criminal trial--

United States v. Nixon, 418 U.S. 683 (1974).

Facts. The special prosecutor, acting for the United States (P) in the Watergate investigation, sought and received a subpoena ordering President Nixon (D) to produce various tapes and other records relating to presidential conversations and meetings, despite D's motion to quash and motions to expunge and for protective orders. The Supreme Court granted certiorari.

Issue. Does executive immunity give the President an absolute, unqualified general privilege of immunity from judicial process under all circumstances?

Held. No. Judgment affirmed.

♦   D contends that the case is merely an intra-branch dispute between officers of the executive branch and thus lacks the requisite justiciability. However, the special prosecutor has been given special authority to pursue the criminal prosecution and has standing to bring this action in the courts.

♦ The doctrine of separation of powers does not preclude judicial review of a President's claim of privilege, because it is the duty of the courts to say what the law is with respect to that claim of privilege, even if the judicial interpretation varies from the President's.

♦ The President's need for and the public interest in the confidentiality of communications is accorded great deference. But absent a need to protect military, diplomatic, or sensitive national security interests, in camera inspection of presidential communications will not significantly diminish the interest in confidentiality. Legitimate judicial needs may therefore outweigh a blanket presidential privilege.

♦ Applying a balancing test to the interests involved supports the district court's order. P sought the subpoena to assure fair and complete presentation of evidence in a criminal proceeding, pursuant to the fundamental demands of due process. The generalized assertion of privilege must yield to the demonstrated, specific need for evidence in a pending criminal trial.

---

d.   Screening of presidential documents--

Nixon v. Administrator of General Services, 433 U.S. 425 (1977).

Facts. Former President Nixon (P) challenged a law directing the Administrator of General Services (D) to take custody of P's papers and tapes and to (i) process and screen such records and to return to P those that are personal and private in nature and (ii) determine the scope of public access to those materials that are retained. The district court dismissed P's complaint. P appeals.

Issue. May the ex-President prevent Congress from regulating the disposition and use of presidential documents by claiming executive immunity?

Held. No. Judgment affirmed.

♦ The decision is limited to consideration of the facial validity of D's authority to take the materials into government custody subject to screening by government archivists.

♦ The Act does not violate the separation of powers doctrine because the control over the materials remains in the executive branch, of which D is an officer. Although Congress wrote the law, both succeeding Presidents support it. The proper inquiry focuses on the extent to which the law prevents the executive branch from accomplishing its constitutionally assigned functions. Here, there is no undue interference.

◆ Although executive privilege survives the individual President's tenure, the opinion of succeeding Presidents bears directly on the need to exercise the privilege. The screening process set up by D adequately assures protection of presidential confidentiality. The practice of establishing presidential libraries indicates that the expectation of confidentiality has always been limited and subject to erosion over time. The significant historical interest in such documents properly subjects them to congressional control.

Dissent (Burger, C.J.). Prior Presidents have been allowed to unilaterally provide for the disposition of their papers and there is no indication that Congress will be impaired without them.

---

2. **Executive Immunity.**

   a. **Introduction.** Executive officials are not given any express immunity in the Constitution. The case law seems to reject any implied immunity under the separation of powers doctrine.

   b. **Immunity for official acts.** In *Nixon v. Fitzgerald*, 457 U.S. 731 (1982), the Court held that absent explicit affirmative action by Congress, the President is absolutely, rather than qualifiedly, immune from civil liability for his official acts. In this action brought by a whistleblower who charged violation of his First Amendment and statutory rights when he lost his job with the Department of Defense, the Court stated that absolute presidential immunity is a functionally mandated incident of the President's office that is rooted in the doctrine of separation of powers. Just as with judges and prosecutors, who have absolute immunity, the President must make decisions on matters likely to arouse the most intense feelings. The public interest in his ability to deal fearlessly and impartially with these duties is a compelling one. The President's prominence would make him a target for numerous suits for civil damages. The President could not function if he were subject to inquiry about his motives and subject to trial on virtually every allegation of unlawful conduct. The proper protection against presidential misconduct is the constitutional remedy of impeachment. The dissenting Justices argued that this holding put the President above the law and that the better approach would make the scope of immunity depend on the function, not the office.

   c. **No immunity for unofficial conduct--**

Clinton v. Jones, 520 U.S. 681(1997).

Facts. In 1994, Jones (P) filed suit in federal court claiming that Clinton (D) had made sexual advances toward her in 1991, when P was an employee of the state of Arkansas and D was the Governor of Arkansas. P sought actual and punitive damages for D's alleged deprivation of her constitutional rights and for state claims. The allegations were unrelated to any of D's official duties as President and preceded his election. D filed a motion to dismiss on grounds of Presidential immunity. The trial court denied D's motion but ordered the trial stayed until the end of D's presidency on the ground that the public interest in avoiding litigation that might hamper the President outweighed any demonstrated need for an immediate trial. The court of appeals reversed the post-ponement of the trial, which it considered to be the functional equivalent of a grant of temporary immunity. The Supreme Court granted certiorari.

Issue. Must a claim by a private citizen against the President of the United States, based on actions allegedly taken before his term began, be deferred until the expiration of the President's term of office?

Held. No. Judgment affirmed.

♦   Certain public servants, including prosecutors, legislators, and judges, have immunity from suits for money damages arising out of their official acts, be-cause this serves the public interest in allowing such officials to perform their designated functions effectively, without fear of personal liability for a particu-lar decision. This rationale does not support immunity for unofficial conduct, however.

♦   There is no precedent to support D's position that he should have immunity for unofficial acts purely because of the identity of his office. The President is not above the laws, but is amenable to them in his private character as a citizen, and in his public character by impeachment.

♦   Despite the importance of the office of the President, whatever the outcome of this case, it will not curtail the scope of the official powers of the executive branch. The fact that a federal court's actions in this case may significantly burden the President's time and attention does not establish a constitutional violation. Courts have the authority to determine whether a President's official actions are within the law. Presidents are subject to judicial process in other areas, such as in complying with a subpoena. The separation of powers doc-trine does not require federal courts to stay all private actions against the Presi-dent until he leaves office.

♦   The district court did not grant immunity, but it did grant a stay until after D leaves office. This was an abuse of discretion because it did not take into ac-count P's interest in bringing the case to trial. Such a long delay would increase the risk of prejudice to P resulting from the loss of evidence, impaired memory, or perhaps even the death of a party. If greater protection of the President becomes necessary, Congress can provide appropriate legislation.

Concurrence (Breyer, J.). While there should be no automatic temporary immunity, the courts cannot unduly interfere with the President's performance of his duties.

Comment. The Court explained that the result might be different if the case were being heard in a state forum, where federalism might apply, and noted that it did not address the question of whether a court could compel the attendance of the President at any specific time or place.

---

  d. **Qualified immunity for presidential aides.** The Court held in *Harlow v. Fitzgerald*, 457 U.S. 800 (1982), that presidential aides are entitled to only qualified immunity. This is the normal type of immunity for executive officials, and it balances the interests of those citizens who suffer damages against the public need to protect officials who must exercise their discretion in an official capacity. Absolute immunity is available to such aides where the responsibilities of their office include such a sensitive function that such immunity is required and the liability claim is based on performance of that protected function.

3. **Congressional Immunity Under the Speech or Debate Clause.** Article I, Section 6 states that Senators and Representatives "shall not be questioned in any other place" for "any Speech or Debate in either House." This clause forbids criminal or civil proceedings against members of Congress for "legislative acts." In other words, neither acts that occur in the regular course of the legislative process nor the motivation for those acts may be used against a legislator in a judicial proceeding.

4. **Impeachment of the President.** Two Presidents (Andrew Johnson in 1868 and William Clinton in 1999) have been impeached and tried by the Senate. In both cases, the Senate voted to acquit. The Supreme Court has held that matters regarding congressional impeachments involve nonjusticiable political questions. Thus, whether the definition of impeachable offenses includes conduct besides statutory criminal offenses or whether it includes every criminal offense, is left to the judgment of Congress. The roles of the House and Senate, beyond the basic principle that the House may vote to impeach and the Senate holds a trial of the charges, are left to the discretion of the respective houses. Even the question of the appropriate sanction in the event of conviction is left to Congress.

V. STATE POWER TO REGULATE

A. INTRODUCTION

The modern approach to the Commerce Clause gives Congress absolute power over interstate commerce. Congress may permit a state to exercise this power or may prohibit a state from so doing. When Congress has in fact acted to prohibit state regulation, it has "preempted the field." Even when Congress has not acted, the very existence of the Commerce Clause forbids state regulation that places an unreasonable burden on interstate commerce. These areas have produced considerable litigation, partly because of the ambiguous nature of the standards involved and partly because of the large financial stakes affected. When Congress has not enacted legislation regarding the subject matter of commerce, the states may regulate local transactions even though they affect interstate commerce, subject to certain limitations. This principle applies to regulation of transportation as well.

B. ABSENCE OF FEDERAL REGULATION

1. **Development of Principles.**

    a. **Early approach.** In *Gibbons v. Ogden, supra*, Chief Justice Marshall discussed the relationship between federal and state regulation. Ogden had argued that the commerce power was like the taxing power; since the taxing power is concurrent, the commerce power should be. Marshall noted that regulation of interstate commerce is an exclusive federal power. When a state regulates commerce with foreign nations or among the federal states, it exercises the very power granted to Congress, and the analogy fails. The Constitution does recognize state power to inspect goods for health and safety, but such laws do not derive from a power to regulate commerce. Even though inspection laws may affect commerce, their existence does not imply that the states can directly regulate interstate commerce.

    b. **National vs. local issues--**

Cooley v. Board of Wardens, 53 U.S. (12 How.) 299 (1851).

Facts. Pennsylvania passed a statute requiring vessels entering or leaving the Port of Philadelphia to accept local pilots while in the Delaware River. The penalty for disobedience was one-half the pilotage fees. Cooley (D), consignee of two violating vessels, was sued by the Board of Wardens of the Port (P) for the penalty. P relied on a 1789 congressional statute that incorporated all then-existing state laws regulating pilots and that mandated conformity with subsequently enacted state regulation, such as the law in this case. D contended that Congress cannot delegate its powers in this manner. D appeals state court judgments for P.

Issue. May Congress permit the states to regulate aspects of commerce that are primarily local in nature?

Held. Yes. Judgment affirmed.

♦ Regulation of pilots is clearly a regulation of commerce. If Congress's power to regulate commerce is exclusive, the Act of 1789 could not confer upon the states the power to regulate pilots.

♦ The correct approach looks to the nature of the subjects of the power, rather than the nature of the power itself. Many subjects are national in nature, but some are local, like the one involved here. When a subject is national it is best governed by one uniform system and therefore requires exclusive legislation by Congress. But a local subject is best handled by the states, which can adapt regulation to the local peculiarities.

♦ The Act of 1789 manifests the understanding of Congress that the nature of this subject (pilotage of local ports) does not require its exclusive legislation. That understanding must be upheld, and the statute is constitutional.

Comment. This opinion was widely ignored at the time, although its approach was somewhat revived later on. After this case, the Court again applied the Marshall view that the states could not regulate interstate commerce. [*See, e.g.,* Paul v. Virginia, 75 U.S. (8 Wall.) 168 (1869)]

----

c.   **Negative implications.** Congress may validate state laws regulating commerce that, in the absence of such consent, would violate the Commerce Clause.

1)   **The Wilson Act.** In *Leisy v. Hardin*, 135 U.S. 100 (1890), the Court invalidated an Iowa law prohibiting the sale of liquors as applied to Illinois-brewed beer that was sold in the original package in Iowa. Later, however, after the passage of the federal Wilson Act, the Court held that a state may apply its prohibition laws to sales of intoxicating liquors in the original packages. In so ruling in *Wilkerson v. Rahrer*, 140 U.S. 545 (1891), the Court held that through the Wilson Act Congress had merely allowed certain designated subjects of interstate commerce to be divested of that character, so that the liquor, once imported, immediately fell within the local jurisdiction.

2) **Insurance business and the McCarran Act.** After passage of the McCarran Act of 1945, which deferred and limited the applicability of antitrust laws to the insurance business, the Court held that the Act validated state taxes that were discriminatory and invalid under Commerce Clause decisions. In *Prudential Insurance Co. v. Benjamin*, 328 U.S. 408 (1946), the plaintiff New Jersey company had objected to the continued collection of tax of 3% of the premiums received from business done in South Carolina, when South Carolina corporations were not similarly taxed.

2. **Regulation of Incoming Trade.** Where Congress has not acted, the states have power to regulate any phase of local business (*e.g.*, production, marketing, sales, etc.), even though such regulations may have some effect on interstate commerce, as long as they neither discriminate against, nor impose any unreasonable burden upon, interstate commerce.

   a. **Regulation of incoming commerce.** One way to develop a state's economy is to require businesses to operate within the state. The Commerce Clause prohibits such legislation if it burdens interstate commerce and is not necessary to promote a valid state purpose. Protecting local business against out-of-state competition is not a valid state purpose per se, but there may be valid reasons for excluding out-of-state products.

      1) **Protection of health and safety.**

         a) **Quarantine and inspection laws.** Quarantine and inspection laws enacted to protect public health are upheld as long as they do not discriminate against or unreasonably burden interstate commerce. [Hannibal & St. Joseph Railroad v. Husen, 95 U.S. 465 (1877)]

            (1) **Permissible regulation.** A local statute requiring that cattle or meat imported from other states be certified as free from disease by the state of origin has been upheld. The burden on interstate commerce caused by supplying such a certificate was outweighed by the public health objectives of the state law. [Mintz v. Baldwin, 289 U.S. 346 (1933)]

            (2) **Impermissible regulation.** Although having a valid "public health" purpose, a state law requiring local inspection of slaughterhouses prior to slaughter of livestock destined for local consumption has been held unconstitutional because it discriminates against out-of-state slaughterhouses (*i.e.*, it prevents importation of

sound meats from animals slaughtered in other states). [Minnesota v. Barber, 136 U.S. 313 (1890)]

    b)   **Protection of reputation.** State laws enacted to protect local, publicly owned natural resources are traditionally a proper exercise of the state's "police power," and will usually be upheld by the Court—*i.e.*, the Court tends to "balance the interests" in favor of such regulations. [Pike v. Bruce Church, Inc., *infra*]

    2)   **Preserving local price structure impermissible--**

Baldwin v. G.A.F. Seelig, Inc., 294 U.S. 511 (1935).

Facts. G.A.F. Seelig, Inc. (P), a New York milk dealer, purchased milk in Vermont at less than the minimum price set by New York law. New York denied P a license to deal in New York. The New York statute permitted price differentials based on transportation costs and applied special regulation to sales of imported milk. The purpose of the statute was said to be (i) to stabilize the supply of milk; (ii) to keep small farmers on the farms by not allowing cutthroat competition; and (iii) to keep the quality of milk up. P sued to enjoin enforcement of the statute, and the lower courts granted relief. Baldwin (D), a state official, appeals.

Issue. May a state protect intrastate producers against low-cost out-of-state competition to assure an adequate and safe supply of an essential commodity?

Held. No. Judgment affirmed.

♦   Distinctions between direct and indirect burdens on commerce are irrelevant when the purpose of a statute is to suppress competition between the states.

♦   The state may properly impose regulations to assure the health of its citizens, but not to assure their wealth. To uphold this statute as a valid exercise of police power with only incidental effects on commerce would "eat up the rule under the guise of an exception," and would lead to total emasculation of the law against state-levied import tariffs.

Comments.

♦   The statute in this case was an economic tool used to ultimately affect the health, safety, and welfare of the state's citizens. Did the Supreme Court rule against the use of economic tools to effect a safety measure indirectly? The Court did not seriously balance the interests here; it simply seemed to say that this type of regulation could not be used. The implication seems to be that direct regulation with a safety measure would be all right; *e.g.*, a requirement that everyone selling milk pasteurize it within five miles of the city. [*But see* Dean Milk Co. v. Madison, *infra*]

♦ The Court has upheld the imposition of a use tax by the consumer's state, even where a sales tax has previously been levied on the same transaction at the time of purchase outside the state, as long as a credit is given for the sales tax paid. [Henneford v. Silas Mason Co., 300 U.S. 577 (1937)]

3)   Less burdensome alternatives should be used--

Dean Milk Co. v. Madison, 340 U.S. 349 (1951).

Facts. An ordinance of the city of Madison, Wisconsin (D) prohibited (i) the sale of pasteurized milk unless processed at an approved plant within a five-mile radius of downtown Madison and (ii) the sale, importation, receipt, or storage of milk for sale in Madison unless originating at a farm inspected by Madison officials, who were not required to inspect any farms further than five miles from the city center. Dean Milk Company (P), an interstate milk processor and dealer, was denied a license to sell its products in Madison solely because P's plants were more than five miles away. The state courts upheld the ordinance, and P appeals.

Issue. May a local statute that has a valid purpose but discriminates against interstate commerce be upheld if there are nondiscriminatory yet effective alternatives?

Held. No. Judgment vacated and remanded.

♦ The ordinance has a valid purpose and is within the scope of local power. No federal regulation exists on the issue.

♦ However, the regulation has a discriminatory effect on interstate commerce. Local statutes cannot erect such barriers to interstate commerce even to further valid health and welfare objectives if reasonable nondiscriminatory alternatives are available to protect these local interests.

♦ The record discloses at least two such alternatives: United States Public Health Service inspections and out-of-town ratings and inspections. Permitting D to enforce a nonessential and discriminatory regulation would invite a multiplication of preferential trade areas contrary to the Commerce Clause.

Dissent (Black, Douglas, Minton, JJ.). There is no showing that P was unable to process its milk within the five-mile radius. Local determination of the best method of sanitary control should not be overruled by the Court. To do so elevates the right to traffic in commerce for profit above the power of the people to guard the purity of their daily diet of milk.

4) Total exclusion of commerce--

Breard v. Alexandria, 341 U.S. 622 (1951).

Facts. The city of Alexandria (P) prohibited door-to-door selling by vendors not having been requested or invited to come by the occupants of the home. Breard (D), a supervisor of a crew of house-to-house solicitors of subscriptions for national magazines, was convicted of violating P's statute. The magazines sold by D were mailed to subscribers by interstate mail. D appeals, claiming the statute discriminates against interstate commerce in favor of local merchants.

Issue. Is state regulation of door-to-door salesmen that prohibits sales of goods shipped in interstate mail constitutional as long as it prohibits sales of all goods by such means?

Held. Yes. Judgment affirmed.

♦ This statute was intended to protect the privacy and repose of the homes' occupants from the nuisance of repeated solicitations. Protection of the social, as opposed to the economic, welfare of the community is a valid objective.

♦ There is no less burdensome means of protecting against the harm in this case, unlike in *Dean Milk, supra*. D's knock on the door is the interstate commerce, and only by regulating that knock can the home be protected. D has no more right to sell in this manner than does any other seller, and the usual methods of seeking business are not denied to D.

Dissent (Vinson, C.J., Douglas, J.). Lack of discrimination on its face has not heretofore been regarded as sufficient to sustain an ordinance without inquiry into its practical effects upon interstate commerce. It is plain that this blanket prohibition against door-to-door solicitation discriminates against and unduly burdens interstate commerce in favor of local retail merchants with stores who would otherwise have to compete against D.

---

5) Precision--

Hunt v. Washington State Apple Advertising Commission, 432 U.S. 333 (1977).

Facts. A North Carolina statute required that all closed containers of apples sold, offered for sale, or shipped into the state bear "no grade other than the applicable United States grade or standard," and a related regulation required the USDA grade or none at all. The statute was intended to eliminate confusion resulting from a multiplicity of inconsistent state grades. The Washington State Apple Advertising Commission (P) brought an action against Hunt (D), a North Carolina official, challenging the statute as discriminating against interstate commerce. P had developed its own grades, widely recognized as superior to the USDA grades, and on which the reputation of its apples depended. The district court found for P. D appeals.

Issue. Must a local statute that has a valid, good-faith purpose but burdens interstate commerce actually achieve its stated purpose in order to be upheld against a Commerce Clause challenge?

Held. Yes. Judgment affirmed.

♦   When discrimination against interstate commerce is shown, the burden falls on the state to justify its regulation both in terms of the local benefits flowing from the statute and the unavailability of nondiscriminatory alternative ways to accomplish the same objectives.

♦   This statute is clearly discriminatory as it covers only closed containers of apples, the very means by which apples are transported in commerce. The record also discloses that feasible, effective, and less discriminatory alternatives are available.

♦   D recognizes that the statute burdens the interstate sale of Washington apples but claims that the burden is outweighed by the local benefits of protection of the public from fraud and deception. In reality, the statute does little to further D's goal, at least with respect to P's apples. It permits marketing under no grades at all; it directs its primary efforts at wholesalers and brokers, rather than the consuming public; and since P's grades are in all cases equal or superior to USDA grades, they could only "deceive" or "confuse" a consumer to his benefit. In light of the statute's ineffectiveness and the existence of reasonable regulatory alternatives, the statute is invalid.

---

6)   Protective tax schemes--

West Lynn Creamery, Inc. v. Healy, 512 U.S. 186 (1994).

Facts. The state of Massachusetts imposed a tax on any milk sales made by milk dealers to Massachusetts retailers. The tax applied whether the milk was processed in or out of Massachusetts. Once the tax was paid, the proceeds were distributed as a subsidy to Massachusetts milk dealers. West Lynn Creamery, Inc. (P), an out-of-state milk dealer licensed to sell milk in Massachusetts, sued Healy (D), the Massachusetts Department of Food and Agriculture Commissioner, to enjoin enforcement of the tax on the ground that it violated the Commerce Clause. The lower court denied relief and the

Massachusetts Supreme Court affirmed, stating that the tax and subsidy scheme was imposed evenhandedly on in- and out-of-state dealers, and only incidentally affected interstate commerce. The United States Supreme Court granted certiorari.

Issue. Does a state law that imposes a tax on in-state and out-of-state dealers alike, but then distributes the tax proceeds back to the in-state dealers only, violate the Commerce Clause?

Held. Yes. Judgment reversed.

♦ This Court has consistently declared unconstitutional state laws imposing protective tariffs that tax imported goods. Such a tax enables in-state dealers to better compete with out-of-state producers who offer a product at a lower cost.

♦ Although D's tax is imposed evenhandedly on dealers whether instate or out of state, the tax paid by the Massachusetts dealer under the scheme is entirely offset by the distribution of the tax proceeds. The result is the same as if D had imposed a protective tariff; milk produced out of state is more expensive, and the in-state dealer benefits.

Concurrence (Scalia, Thomas, JJ.). Nearly all subsidies, whether funded by taxes imposed on out-of-state products, in-state revenues, etc., "neutralize advantages possessed by out-of-state enterprises." Standing alone, this effect does not render a subsidy scheme unconstitutional. A state may subsidize its own industry provided that the subsidies are funded through nondiscriminatory taxes, the proceeds of which go into a general revenue fund rather than back to those in-state persons burdened by the tax.

Dissent (Rehnquist, C.J., Blackmun, J.). By imposing on the states commerce policies that have not been enacted by Congress, the Court erodes the principles of federalism.

---

3. **Regulation of Outgoing Commerce.**

   a. **Introduction.** *Dean Milk* involved a requirement that imported goods be partially processed within the state. States have also occasionally required that their products be processed within the state before being exported. Such requirements have not fared well despite assertions of valid state interests.

   b. **Licensing requirements--**

H.P. Hood & Sons, Inc. v. Du Mond, 336 U.S. 525 (1949).

Facts. A New York law required milk handlers to obtain a license prior to opening any new receiving depot. H.P. Hood & Sons, Inc. (P), a Massachusetts milk handler who already operated three milk-receiving depots in New York, was denied a license for a new depot. Du Mond (D), a New York official, found that the requested license would "tend to aid destructive competition in a market already adequately served," thus violating New York law, because it would deprive the local market of adequate milk supplies. The lower courts upheld the law. P appeals.

Issue. May a state suppress interstate shipment of local products as a means of protecting the health and safety of its people?

Held. No. Judgment reversed.

♦   Although a state may impose burdensome regulations in the interest of local health and safety, its attempt to advance its own purely commercial interests by curtailing the movement of goods in interstate commerce is impermissible. The police power does not extend to suppression of competition.

♦   The Commerce Clause was intended to encourage producers by assuring them free access to every market in the nation, with no customs duties or regulations to exclude them. It also protects consumers against exploitation by allowing freedom of choice among the products of every area in the country.

Dissent (Frankfurter, Rutledge, JJ.). The effect of this decision is that no matter how unimportant the interstate commerce affected, a state cannot prevent competition that has destructive effects on its economy. What is essentially a problem of striking a balance between competing interests should not be treated as an exercise in absolutes.

---

c.   **Local problems.** In *Milk Control Board v. Eisenberg Farm Products*, 306 U.S. 346 (1939), the Court upheld a Pennsylvania law requiring that a minimum amount be paid to local producers of milk. Eisenberg Farm Products had shipped its entire supply of milk to New York and objected to paying the Pennsylvania minimum price. The Court accepted the justification that the law attempted to regulate an essentially local problem, and only a small fraction of the milk bought in the state was shipped out of state (so that the main business affected by the regulation was not interstate commerce).

d.   **Relative interests.** The more compelling the state interest, the more regulation is tolerated. The Court may also consider the fact that the state regulation also furthers a national policy or interest, even though Congress has not specifically acted in this area. In *Parker v. Brown*, 317 U.S. 341 (1943), the Court upheld a state marketing program regulating the sale of the locally grown raisin crop (of which 95% entered interstate commerce), emphasizing that the state program coincided with congressional policies regulating agriculture during the war, and that raisin production involved essentially local problems.

e. **Statutes fixing minimum prices.** State laws imposing minimum prices on the sale of local natural resources have been upheld as proper "conservation" regulations. In *Cities Service Gas Co. v. Peerless Oil & Gas Co.*, 340 U.S. 179 (1950), the Court upheld a state law fixing minimum prices on all gas taken from local fields. The law was a proper measure for conservation of local natural resources, even though most of the gas was shipped in interstate commerce.

f. **Protection of reputation.** The Court, in *Pike v. Bruce Church, Inc.*, 397 U.S. 137 (1970), set forth the modern balancing test: If a state has a legitimate local purpose for regulating and the effects on interstate commerce are only incidental, the regulation will be upheld unless the burden is clearly excessive in relation to the local benefits. In *Pike*, the Court found that Arizona's interest in maintaining its reputation for fine produce did not justify a statute prohibiting shipment of produce to another state for packaging.

4. **Regulation to Protect the Environment and Preserve Natural Resources.**

a. **Introduction.** Environmental problems are often difficult to solve, particularly when the sources of pollution are out of state. States frequently impose environmental regulations, but the Court does not allow environmental concerns to override the Commerce Clause.

b. **Importation of wastes--**

Philadelphia v. New Jersey, 437 U.S. 617 (1978).

Facts. New Jersey (D) passed a law prohibiting importation into the state of solid or liquid wastes, in order to protect the public health, safety, and welfare from the consequences of excessive landfill developments. Philadelphia (P) and other cities, as well as New Jersey landfill operators, challenged the law under the Commerce Clause. The New Jersey Supreme Court upheld the law. P appeals.

Issue. May a state prohibit importation of environmentally destructive substances solely because of their source of origin?

Held. No. Judgment reversed.

♦ D's reason for passing the law may be legitimate, but the evils of protectionism can reside in the legislative means used as well as legislative ends sought. D's ultimate purpose may not be achieved by discriminating against out-of-state items solely because of their origin. D has failed to show any other valid reason for its discrimination.

♦ D's statute requires out-of-state commercial interests to carry the burden of conserving D's remaining landfill space in an attempt to isolate itself from a problem shared by all. Protection against such trade barriers serves the interest of all states, and may even work to the advantage of New Jersey in the future.

♦   D claims this statute resembles quarantine laws, which are exceptions to the general Commerce Clause rules. But quarantine laws merely prevent traffic in noxious articles, regardless of their origin. D claims no harm from the mere movement of waste into its borders and concedes that when the harm is felt (upon disposal) there is no basis to distinguish out-of-state waste from domestic waste.

Dissent (Rehnquist, J., Burger, C.J.). D's law essentially prohibits importation of items that could endanger its population, and should be upheld. The Court implies that the challenged laws must be invalidated because domestic waste may be used in the state's landfills. This fact ought not require D to exacerbate its problems by accepting out-of-state waste.

---

c.   **Ban on polluting products--**

Minnesota v. Clover Leaf Creamery Co., 449 U.S. 456 (1981).

Facts. Minnesota (D) banned the retail sale of milk only in plastic nonreturnable, non-refillable containers. Clover Leaf Creamery Company (P) successfully challenged D's law in the state courts under the Equal Protection and Commerce Clauses. D appeals.

Issue. May a state enact a statute that does not, on its face, discriminate against interstate commerce but that does cause a shift in an industry from a predominant out-of-state location to a predominant in-state location?

Held. Yes. Judgment reversed.

♦   Applying the familiar rational basis test, D's law is rationally related to its conservation interests and does not deny equal protection.

♦   D's ban applies to all plastic container manufacturers. While most of these are located out of state and production of the raw material for non-plastic containers is a major state industry, there is no discrimination against interstate commerce as such. There is an incidental burden on interstate commerce but it is not "clearly excessive" in light of D's legitimate purposes in imposing the ban.

---

d.   **Limits on local government control with interstate economic effects--**

C & A Carbone, Inc. v. Clarkstown, 511 U.S. 383 (1994).

Facts. To finance construction of a waste transfer station, Clarkstown (D) had to guarantee a minimum flow of waste to the station. D enacted a flow control ordinance, which required that all solid waste in the town be deposited at the station. C & A Carbone (P) was a private recycler with a sorting facility in D. D's ordinance increased P's costs, because P could obtain the necessary services out of state at a lower cost than D's station charged. P challenged D's ordinance. The lower courts upheld the ordinance. P appeals.

Issue. May a local government require that all solid waste within its boundaries be processed by a specific local processor?

Held. No. Judgment reversed.

♦ Although the ordinance has the effect of directing local waste to a local facility, the economic effects reach interstate commerce. P's facility receives waste from out of state. D's ordinance requires P to send the nonrecyclable portion of the waste to D's local facility, which increases P's costs and hence the costs to the out-of-state sources of solid waste. The ordinance also deprives out-of-state businesses access to D's local market.

♦ D claims that its ordinance does not discriminate against interstate commerce because it applies to all solid waste, regardless of origin, before it leaves the town. However, the ordinance does discriminate, because it allows only the favored processor to process waste within D's town limits. It is an example of local processing requirements that have been held invalid, such as the local milk pasteurizing requirement in *Dean Milk, supra*.

♦ In *Dean Milk*, the city of Madison had required that all milk sold in the city be pasteurized within five miles of the city limits. Although the ordinance had a valid purpose and was within the scope of local power, it had a discriminatory effect on interstate commerce, and reasonable nondiscriminatory alternatives were available to protect the local interests. In this case, D's ordinance is even more restrictive than the one in *Dean Milk*, because it leaves no room for outside investment.

♦ Discrimination against interstate commerce in favor of local business or investment is per se invalid, unless the municipality has no other means to advance a legitimate local interest. D has a variety of nondiscriminatory means to address its local waste disposal problems. The objective of fundraising is not adequate to justify discrimination against out-of-state businesses.

Concurrence (O'Connor, J.). D's ordinance is different from the ordinances the Court has previously held invalid, because it does not give more favorable treatment to local interests as a group as compared to out-of-state economic interests. Thus, it does not discriminate against interstate commerce. However, the ordinance does impose an excessive burden on interstate commerce when compared with the local benefits it confers.

Dissent (Souter, J., Rehnquist, C.J., Blackmun, J.). There is no evidence in this case that any out-of-state trash processor has been harmed. The ordinance treats all out-of-town investors and facilities to the same constraints as local ones, so there is no economic protectionism. The only right to compete that the Commerce Clause protects is the right to compete on terms independent of one's location. The ordinance merely imposes a burden on the local citizens who adopted it, and local burdens are not the focus of the Commerce Clause.

Comment. The Court has upheld express discrimination against interstate commerce where the statute serves a legitimate local purpose that cannot be served as well by an available nondiscriminatory means. For example, in *Maine v. Taylor*, 477 U.S. 131 (1986), the Court upheld a Maine statute prohibiting the importation of live baitfish because of the adverse biological consequences of non-native species and parasites.

---

e.   **Conservation of wildlife--**

Hughes v. Oklahoma, 441 U.S. 322 (1979).

Facts. Oklahoma (P) prohibited shipment of natural minnows for sale outside the state. Hughes (D), a licensed commercial minnow operator in Texas, transported a load of natural minnows from Oklahoma to Texas and was convicted of violating the statute. D challenged the statute as an unconstitutional burden on interstate commerce, but the state courts upheld the conviction on the authority of *Geer v. Connecticut*, 161 U.S. 519 (1896). D appeals.

Issue. May a state prohibit, as a conservation measure, transportation beyond its borders of natural wildlife captured within the state?

Held. No. Judgment reversed.

◆   *Geer* was an early case, virtually identical to this one, which upheld a similar state regulation on the theory that Connecticut, as representative for its citizens, "owned" game captured within its boundaries and could therefore retain it. *Geer* is now expressly overruled, and state regulation of wild animals must be considered pursuant to the same test that applies to regulation of other natural resources.

◆   The basic test requires consideration of (i) whether the regulation actually discriminates against interstate commerce, (ii) whether it serves a legitimate local purpose, and if so, (iii) whether alternative, less discriminatory means would be as effective.

♦ P's statute obviously discriminates against interstate commerce. Although conservation is a legitimate purpose, other more effective yet nondiscriminatory means are available. For example, P could limit the manner of natural minnow use within the state or could limit the permitted "catch" by both residents and nonresidents to assure conservation. Therefore, the statute is invalid.

Dissent (Rehnquist, J., Burger, C.J.). The statute is not discriminatory since no persons, residents or not, may export the natural minnows. The flow of interstate commerce is not affected, because there is no restriction on exports of hatchery minnows. The minimal burden resulting from requiring D to purchase hatchery rather than natural minnows is more than outweighed by P's interest in conservation.

---

5. Neutral Corporate Anti-Takeover Statute--

CTS Corp. v. Dynamics Corp., 481 U.S. 69 (1987).

Facts. Indiana adopted an anti-takeover statute that applied to all Indiana public corporations, defined as corporations with at least 100 shareholders; headquarters or substantial assets in Indiana; and 10,000 resident shareholders, 10% of its shares owned by residents, or 10% of its shareholders as residents. Under the statute, an entity that acquires control shares in a public corporation would not acquire voting rights unless the shareholders approved. Dynamics Corporation (P), which already owned almost 10% of the stock of CTS Corporation (D), announced a tender offer for another 7.5%. The same day, P filed a securities action against D. D then elected to be governed by the provisions of the anti-takeover statute. P amended its suit to claim that the anti-takeover statute violated the Commerce Clause. The district court held that the statute violated the Commerce Clause. The court of appeals affirmed. D appeals.

Issue. May a state adopt an anti-takeover statute that has the effect of making it more difficult for out-of-state entities to take control over a state's corporations?

Held. Yes. Judgment reversed.

♦ The principal focus of the Commerce Clause is to prevent state discrimination against interstate commerce. Indiana's statute does not discriminate against interstate commerce because it applies equally to domiciliaries of Indiana who make tender offers as well as to non-domiciliaries. It does not matter that, as P claims, most tender offers are made by out-of-state entities.

♦ The Commerce Clause is also concerned with statutes that subject interstate commerce to inconsistent activities, such as railroad regulations. However,

Indiana's statute does not present such a problem because it only applies to corporations the state has created, and no other state can regulate the voting rights of an Indiana corporation.

♦ The court of appeals held the statute unconstitutional because it could hinder tender offers. However, a corporation's very existence and attributes are a product of state law. Every state regulates the governance of corporations created by state law, and every such regulation has some effect on interstate commerce, particularly when shareholders live in other states. It is common for states to require supermajority votes to approve mergers, for example, and to provide for dissenting shareholders' rights.

♦ Indiana's statute does not prevent purchasers from acquiring control, but does impose regulatory procedures to protect shareholders of Indiana corporations by letting them decide whether a change in management would be desirable. This is a response to the threat of coercive tender offers, a threat Indiana could deem serious.

♦ D claims Indiana has no legitimate interest in protecting out-of-state shareholders, but it does have an interest in protecting shareholders of Indiana corporations, whether they are Indiana residents or not. Unlike the statute in *Edgar v. Mite Corp.,* 457 U.S. 624 (1982), this Act applies only to corporations that have a substantial number of shareholders in Indiana, persons whom Indiana has a legitimate interest in protecting.

Concurrence (Scalia, J.). The Court need only determine that the statute neither discriminates against interstate commerce nor creates inconsistent regulation. It is inappropriate for the courts to go further and determine whether the burden on commerce imposed by a state statute is excessive in relation to the local benefits.

Dissent (White, Blackmun, Stevens, JJ.). Indiana's statute substantially burdens the interstate market in corporate ownership and will have a greater impact as other states adopt similar statutes.

Comment. This case represents an apparent retreat from the balancing approach used in *Pike* and subsequent cases. Justice Scalia, concurring in *Bendix Autolite Corp. v. Midwesco Enterprises, Inc.,* 486 U.S. 888 (1988), expressly repudiated the balancing approach. Under his approach, a state statute would be invalid only if it accords discriminatory treatment to interstate commerce in a respect not required to achieve a lawful state purpose; it would be up to Congress, not the courts, to determine whether the purpose is not significant enough to justify the burden on commerce.

---

6. **Traditional State Regulation of Transportation.** Where the subject matter is traditionally subject to local regulation, the Court is more likely to

allow state regulation. Transportation has been one of the most highly regulated areas.

    a.   **Basic principles.** Over time, the Court has developed an approach to transportation problems that is fairly principled. To be constitutional, state regulation must not violate these principles:

        1)   **Uniform national regulation not required.** The subject matter must not inherently require uniform national regulation. [*See* Wabash, St. Louis & Pacific Railway Co. v. Illinois, 118 U.S. 557 (1886)]

        2)   **No discrimination.** The state regulation must not discriminate against interstate commerce so as to "substantially impede" the free flow of commerce across state lines. [*See* Seaboard Air Line Railroad Co. v. Blackwell, 244 U.S. 310 (1917)]

        3)   **Balance of interests favors the state.** The state interest underlying the regulation must not be outweighed by the burden on interstate commerce—*i.e.*, the "balance of interests" favors the state as opposed to the national interest.

            a)   **Public safety and welfare.** A state's interest in the public safety and welfare, where such is the predominant purpose of the state law, may justify obstruction of interstate commerce. For example, in *Bradley v. Public Utilities Commission*, 289 U.S. 92 (1933), the Court held that a state could restrict interstate truckers where the highway was already so badly congested by traffic that the proposed service would create excessive traffic hazards.

            b)   **Controlling competition.** While state interests in protecting public health and welfare are given considerable weight, a state's interest in controlling competition is not. For example, in *Buck v. Kuykendall*, 267 U.S. 307 (1925), the Court held that a state could not deny an interstate carrier a permit to use its highways simply because the state determined the territory was already adequately served.

    b.   **Promotion of a valid state interest--**

Southern Pacific Co. v. Arizona, 325 U.S. 761 (1945).

Facts. The Arizona Train Limit Law imposed restrictions on the number of cars permitted on any train operating within the state; it allowed 14 passenger cars or 70 freight cars. Arizona (P) sued Southern Pacific Company (D), an interstate carrier, for violation of the statute. D claimed that the statute unconstitutionally burdened interstate commerce. The trial court made extensive findings of fact and concluded that any possible safety benefits of the law were outweighed by increased hazards and that the law imposed unconstitutional burdens on interstate commerce. The Arizona Supreme Court accepted the legislature's findings and reversed, citing a lack of overriding federal legislation. D appeals.

Issue. In balancing the effect of a state regulation on interstate commerce against the state's safety and welfare interests, may a court consider the efficacy of the regulation in furthering the state's interest?

Held. Yes. Judgment reversed.

♦ Although Congress has refused to pass national legislation regulating train lengths, the state law may violate the Commerce Clause if it unreasonably burdens interstate commerce without an offsetting state safety benefit. Additionally, state regulation is precluded in those phases of national commerce that, because of the need for national uniformity, demand that their regulation, if any, be prescribed by a single authority.

♦ Constitutional doctrine mandates that the Court, and not the state legislature, is the final arbiter of competing state and national interests under the Commerce Clause.

♦ The serious impediment of state car limitations on interstate commerce indicates the need for uniform national legislation on the subject. By taking no action, Congress must have intended not to restrict the number of train cars permitted.

♦ Upon review of the record, it appears that the total effect of the law as a safety measure in reducing accidents and casualties is so slight or problematical as not to outweigh the national interest in keeping interstate commerce free from interference.

♦ *South Carolina Highway Department v. Barnwell Brothers*, 303 U.S. 177 (1938), is distinguishable because it dealt with state highways, which are of more local concern than railroads, and because there the record supported the state's safety findings.

Dissent (Black, J.). The Court in effect has found that the state legislature erroneously weighed the evidence before it as to train safety, and that regulation of train lengths would be unwise. The Court acts as a "super-legislature" instead of giving the traditional deference to legislative determinations.

Comment. A series of cases referred to as the *Full Crew Cases* upheld state laws dating from the early part of the century that required minimum crew sizes. The Court recognized that conditions had changed, but held that since there remained a possible safety benefit, the determination of state policy belonged to the legislature and not the courts.

---

c.   Modern approach to transportation regulation--

Kassel v. Consolidated Freightways Corp., 450 U.S. 662 (1981).

Facts. Consolidated Freightways Corporation (P) challenged an Iowa statute that, like Wisconsin's law in *Raymond Motor Transportation, Inc. v. Rice*, 434 U.S. 429 (1978), prohibited the use of 65-foot double trailers on Iowa highways, with certain exceptions. Kassel (D), an Iowa official, defended the law as a reasonable safety measure in light of the *Raymond* holding. The lower courts held the law unconstitutional as it seriously impeded interstate commerce while providing only slight, if any, safety. D appeals.

Issue. May the courts examine evidence to determine whether a state's purported interest in safety is real and substantial enough to justify applying its police power to burden interstate commerce?

Held. Yes. Judgment affirmed.

♦   A state cannot avoid a Commerce Clause attack merely by invoking public health or safety. The courts are required to balance the state's safety interest against the federal interest in free interstate commerce.

♦   Despite the "special deference" usually accorded to state highway safety regulations and D's serious effort to support the safety rationale, the record here is no more favorable to D than was Wisconsin's evidence in *Raymond*. P has demonstrated that D's law substantially burdens interstate commerce. Therefore, D's law is unconstitutional.

Concurrence (Brennan, Marshall, JJ.). D's law is unconstitutional under *Raymond* since it is protectionist. The plurality and the dissent insist on considering the legislative purposes advanced by D's lawyers. Separation of powers, however, requires that we defer to the elected lawmakers' judgment, not that we defer to the arguments of lawyers. D's statute exists because the governor of Iowa vetoed legislation that would have permitted 65-foot doubles, giving an essentially protectionist rationale for his action. This is an improper purpose. Safety became a purpose for the law only in retrospect, to defeat P's challenge.

Dissent (Rehnquist, J., Burger, C.J., Stewart, J.). Both the plurality and concurring opinions have intruded upon the fundamental right of the states to pass laws to secure the safety of their citizens. D's law is rationally related to its safety objectives. We are essentially reweighing the state legislature's policy choice, and are forcing D to lower its safety standards merely because its sister states' standards are lower.

Comment. In *Raymond, supra,* the Court also invalidated a prohibition against the use of double-trailer units on state highways because the state failed to show that the regulation contributed to highway safety, and because numerous exceptions to the regulation undercut the safety claims.

---

    d.   **Burden of proof.** When the challenged regulation significantly burdens interstate commerce, the state must meet a heavy burden of justification based on its interests. In *Bibb v. Navajo Freight Lines,* 359 U.S. 520 (1959), the Court held that a state may not impose even non-discriminatory safety regulations that conflict with the regulations of most other states where the asserted safety advantages are at best negligible. That case involved mudguards; 45 states permitted the conventional straight mudguards, but Illinois required the use of contour mudguards. The substantial burden on interstate commerce could not be justified by any compelling state safety consideration.

7.   **The State as a Market Participant.**

    a.   **Introduction.** The Court has recognized an exception to the normal Commerce Clause restrictions on state regulation when the state itself becomes a participant in the market. The proper scope of this exception has been the subject of much debate.

    b.   **Purchases.** In *Hughes v. Alexandria Scrap Corp.,* 426 U.S. 794 (1976), the Court permitted Maryland to impose more exacting documentation requirements on out-of-state junk-car processors than it imposed on in-state processors. The documentation was required to receive a "bounty" from the state of Maryland, which made the payments for each junk car, registered in Maryland, that was recycled. The purpose of the bounty was to improve the environment in the state. The Court reasoned that Maryland did not attempt to prohibit the flow of junk cars, but merely entered the market to bid up the value of Maryland junk cars. The state was a market participant, not a market regulator, so the Commerce Clause was not applicable.

    c.   **Restricting exports of goods manufactured by the state--**

Reeves, Inc. v. Stake, 447 U.S. 429 (1980).

Facts. In 1919, South Dakota began building a cement plant in response to regional cement shortages. By the 1970s, about 40% of the plant's output was sold to out-of-state buyers. Reeves, Inc. (P), a Wyoming cement distributor, bought 95% of its cement from the South Dakota plant. In 1978, however, the plant was unable to meet all orders, and the state Cement Commission, represented by Stake (D), "reaffirmed its policy of supplying all South Dakota customers first," with the remaining volume, if any, allocated on a first-come, first-served basis. P suffered losses and sued D, seeking injunctive relief. The district court enjoined D's practice, but the court of appeals reversed. P appeals.

Issue. May a state that itself produces cement limit sales only to its own residents in a time of shortage?

Held. Yes. Judgment affirmed.

♦ The basic distinction, articulated in *Hughes v. Alexandria Scrap Corp., supra,* between states as market participants and states as market regulators makes good sense and is sound law. The Constitution sets no limits on state power to operate freely in the free market. This is especially true where, as here, the state has acted as a sovereign in meeting the needs of its residents.

♦ The fact that South Dakota has made sales to P does not distinguish the case from one in which a state offered cement only to domestic buyers from the start.

♦ The preference for resident buyers is not protectionist but merely a means of serving its citizens. Nor is a natural resource at stake, so there is no danger of resource hoarding.

Dissent (Powell, Brennan, White, Stevens, JJ.). D's policy represents precisely the kind of economic protectionism that the Commerce Clause was intended to prevent. We agree that South Dakota could allocate cement to meet its public needs, but when it acts as a market participant to benefit private citizens, the effect is the same as if the state legislature had imposed the policy on private cement producers. Although a private business could properly exclude out-of-state customers, when a state adopts such a policy, it violates the Commerce Clause.

---

d. **Post-sale obligations imposed by the state selling its resources--**

South-Central Timber Development, Inc. v. Wunnicke, 467 U.S. 82 (1984).

Facts. The state of Alaska offered to sell its timber, but only with a contractual requirement that the timber be processed within the state before being exported. In return, the price for the timber was significantly reduced from what it otherwise would have been. South-Central Timber Development, Inc. (P) normally sold unprocessed logs to Japan. P sought an injunction in federal court, claiming the requirement violated the negative implications of the Commerce Clause. The district court granted the injunction, but the court of appeals reversed, concluding that a similar federal policy for timber taken from federal land in Alaska constituted implicit congressional authorization of the state plan. The Supreme Court granted certiorari.

Issue. When it sells its own natural resources, may a state impose post-sale obligations on the purchaser?

Held. No. Judgment reversed.

♦ The Commerce Clause limits the power of the states to impose substantial burdens on interstate commerce, although Congress may authorize state regulation of such commerce. Here, there was no indication that Congress intended to give such power to Alaska. The existence of a federal program similar to the state's is insufficient evidence to support an inference that the state's action was authorized by Congress.

♦ This case involves three elements not present in *Reeves, Inc. v. Stake, supra*: foreign commerce is restrained, the state is selling a natural resource, and the state imposes restrictions on resale. Commerce Clause scrutiny must be more rigorous because of these factors.

♦ The fact that the state acted through a contract is not enough. The market-participant doctrine must be limited to allowing a state to impose burdens on commerce within the market in which it participates. Here, Alaska has gone too far by imposing conditions that have a substantial regulatory effect outside of the market it has entered. This program does not fall within the market-participant exception.

♦ The protectionist nature of Alaska's program results in interference with interstate and foreign commerce. Thus, it violates the Commerce Clause.

Dissent (Rehnquist, O'Connor, JJ.). The plurality's decision seems to draw on antitrust law. But antitrust laws apply to a state only when it is acting as a market participant. The plurality thus concludes that Alaska is acting as a market regulator by relying on cases that are relevant only if Alaska is a market participant. The state is merely paying timber purchasers to hire Alaska residents to process the timber, a result it could accomplish in a variety of ways. It is unduly formalistic to hold that this method violates the Commerce Clause.

---

8. **Privileges and Immunities.**

   a. **Introduction.** Article IV, Section 2, Clause 1, the Privileges and Immunities Clause, states that the "Citizens of each State shall be entitled to all Privileges and Immunities of Citizens in the several States." This prohibits discrimination by a state against noncitizens (or nonresidents) of the state with respect to "essential activities" or "basic rights," unless justified by a substantial reason. To justify an exception, the state must show that the nonresidents are a peculiar source of the evil sought to be avoided, and that the discrimination bears a substantial relationship to the problem.

b. **Hunting.** In *Baldwin v. Montana Fish and Game Commission*, 436 U.S. 371 (1978), the Court held that a state may discriminate against nonresidents with respect to hunting permits by charging nonresidents $225 for a permit that would cost residents only $39. The reason is that sport hunting is not an activity that bears upon the vitality of the nation as a whole.

c. **Justification.** If the state's discriminatory scheme is overbroad, it will not withstand scrutiny under this clause. In *Hicklin v. Orbeck*, 437 U.S. 518 (1978), the Court determined that a state hiring preference for residents was an overbroad solution to the problem of unemployment because the preference extended to highly skilled state residents who did not have the problem of unemployment.

d. **Municipality's preference for its own residents on construction contracts--**

United Building & Construction Trades Council v. Mayor of Camden, 465 U.S. 208 (1984).

Facts. The city of Camden (D) adopted an ordinance requiring that at least 40% of the employees of contractors and subcontractors working on city construction projects be Camden residents. The United Building & Construction Trades Council of Camden (P) challenged the ordinance as violating the Privileges and Immunities Clause. After the state treasurer approved the ordinance in administrative proceedings, the state supreme court upheld it, holding that the clause does not apply to discrimination on the basis of municipal residency. P appeals.

Issue. Does the Privileges and Immunities Clause apply to municipalities that require contractors to hire the municipality's own residents to work on the municipality's construction projects?

Held. Yes. Judgment reversed and remanded for further fact findings.

♦   A municipality derives its authority from the state. If the state cannot discriminate in this manner, neither can a political subdivision of the state. Nor is the ordinance immune from attack because it discriminates against some in-state residents as well as out-of-state citizens. The former have the opportunity to directly change state law through the state legislature. The latter do not.

♦   P must first show that the ordinance burdens a privilege and immunity protected by the clause. The opportunity to seek employment is a fundamental privilege protected by the clause.

♦   The Privileges and Immunities Clause does not preclude discrimination against out-of-state residents if there is a substantial reason for the difference in treatment. Although D alleges several such reasons, including increasing unemployment in the city, declining population, and a depleted tax base, no trial has been held and no findings of fact have been made. The case must be remanded.

Dissent (Blackmun, J.). I don't believe that the Privileges and Immunities Clause applies to discrimination based on municipal residence.

---

9.   **State Power to Tax.**

   a.   **Introduction.**

   1)   **Source of state power to tax interstate commerce.** The Constitution does not expressly recognize or reject the states' power to tax interstate commerce, except to the extent that it vests the power to regulate or destroy in Congress. Therefore, the Supreme Court examines carefully state taxes on interstate commerce to determine their true nature and effect. While interstate commerce must pay its own way, the Court has to balance the state's right to secure revenue against the strong national interest in protecting the free flow of commerce from state to state and preventing state regulation (through taxation) of any area of commerce that requires uniform national regulation.

   2)   **Fourteenth Amendment considerations.** Fourteenth Amendment due process and equal protection problems with state taxation of interstate commerce revolve around jurisdiction. These familiar principles require that the benefits and protection afforded by the taxing state have a sufficient relationship to the subject matter taxed (certain "minimum contacts") so that the subject matter may be deemed to have a "tax situs" or "nexus" in the taxing state.

   3)   **Commerce Clause considerations.** The Commerce Clause requires that (i) the tax not discriminate against interstate commerce in favor of intrastate commerce, (ii) the tax not be an unreasonable burden upon interstate commerce, and (iii) the tax not result in multiple tax burdens (double taxation).

4) **Import-Export Clause considerations.** Article I, Section 10, Clause 2 provides that "[N]o State shall, without the Consent of the Congress, lay any Imposts or Duties on Imports or Exports, except what may be absolutely necessary for executing its inspection Laws." This is an absolute ban.

5) **Types of taxes.** States resort to a variety of taxing schemes. Each basic type of tax has its particular problems, but similar constitutional considerations apply to each.

   a) **Ad valorem property tax.** This tax is based upon the value of the property being taxed. It may be imposed on property used to transport goods interstate (instrumentalities of commerce), such as railroad cars, boats, or airplanes. It may also be imposed on goods either before interstate commerce begins or after it ends, but not while the goods are in transit.

   b) **"Doing business" tax.** The mere privilege of doing business may be taxable. States commonly impose income taxes on businesses, based on a percentage of the revenue earned in the taxing state. Other "doing business" taxes include privilege, occupation, license, and franchise taxes, which may be imposed as a flat fee or as a percentage of revenue.

   c) **Sales and use tax.** Sales taxes are imposed upon transactions taking place within the taxing state. Use taxes are imposed upon the use of goods purchased out of state and then imported. The use tax compensates for the loss of sales taxes and deters residents from buying goods outside the state merely to avoid the sales tax.

   d) **Severance tax.** States may impose a tax on the severance or extraction of minerals from the state because, once gone, such minerals cannot be replaced.

   e) **Highway and airport use tax.** States may tax the use of public commercial facilities that must be maintained by the state, as long as the tax is fair compensation for the use of the facility.

b. **Direct taxation of commerce.**

   1) **Per se rule against direct taxation of commerce.** The Court held in *Spector Motor Service v. O'Connor,* 340 U.S. 602 (1951), that a state could not apply its franchise tax to a transportation company that did not make deliveries in the state, even if the tax was imposed only on the company's net income attributable to business activities within the state. The privilege of doing interstate

business in a state could not be taxed, although the state could impose a tax for the use of its highways.

2) Elimination of per se rule--

Complete Auto Transit, Inc. v. Brady, 430 U.S. 274 (1977).

Facts. Complete Auto Transit, Inc. (P), a Michigan corporation that distributed General Motors cars from the railhead in Jackson, Mississippi, to dealers throughout that state, was assessed a state tax for "the privilege of doing business" within the state. P paid the tax, then instituted a refund action against Brady (D), a Mississippi state official. The state courts upheld the tax. P appeals.

Issue. Is a state tax levied on an interstate business for "the privilege of doing business" within the state per se unconstitutional?

Held. No. Judgment affirmed.

♦ Under *Spector Motor*, *supra*, any state tax specifically levied for "the privilege of doing business" within the state is per se unconstitutional. Upon examining this rule, we have concluded that it has no relationship to economic realities and stands only as a trap for the unwary draftsperson.

♦ The Court henceforth will consider the reality of the effect on commerce that any state tax has, and the formality-centered *Spector* case is overruled. P here has relied solely on the *Spector* rule, failing to allege insufficient nexus, discrimination, unfair apportionment, or lack of reciprocal state services. Since the *Spector* rule is hereby invalidated, P's challenge cannot stand.

♦ The relevant considerations for future cases are:

Is the activity sufficiently connected to the state to justify a tax?

Is the tax fairly related to benefits provided by the state to the taxpayer?

Does the tax discriminate against interstate commerce?

Is the tax fairly apportioned?

---

3) Multiple tax burdens. Although the *Complete Auto* test does not specifically mention multiple tax burdens, the Court continues to recognize that the practical effect of multiple taxation may be to impair interstate commerce. Cumulative tax burdens can be discriminatory. The concept of apportionment is considered *infra*.

4)   Severance tax paid mostly by out-of-state users--

Commonwealth Edison Co. v. Montana, 453 U.S. 609 (1981).

Facts. Montana (D) imposed a maximum 30% severance tax on all coal mined within its borders. Twenty-five percent of all known United States coal reserves and 50% of low-sulfur coal reserves are located in Montana. About three-fourths of this coal lies under federal land in the state. Most of this coal (about 90%) is exported to out-of-state utilities, so that the primary incidence of the tax falls on out-of-state energy consumers. Commonwealth Edison Co. (P), an out-of-state utility, challenged the tax as violating the Commerce and Supremacy Clauses. The Montana courts upheld the tax as a matter of law since it was levied on a purely intrastate activity. P appeals.

Issue. May a state provide for its own fiscal needs by imposing a high severance tax upon its unique state resources, the primary incidence of which falls on out-of-state consumers?

Held. Yes. Judgment affirmed.

◆   A severance tax is not immune from Commerce Clause scrutiny just because it affects goods prior to entry into the stream of interstate commerce. It must satisfy the four-part *Complete Auto* test. The first two prongs of that test are not at issue here, however.

◆   D's tax is imposed on all coal, regardless of its destination. There is no differential treatment such as that existing in other "discrimination" cases. The amount of tax paid depends on consumption of coal, not on any distinction between in-state and out-of-state use.

◆   The tax does not discriminate against interstate commerce merely because most of the coal moves across state borders. Under the Commerce Clause, the borders between the states are essentially irrelevant. Residents of one state do not have a right of access at "reasonable" prices to resources of another state, however richly endowed with natural resources.

Comment. Much of the opinion dealt with the fourth part of the *Complete Auto* test, *supra*.

c.   **Fair apportionment.**

   1)   **Introduction.** The fair apportionment rule has been attributed to both the Due Process and Commerce Clauses.

2) Apportionment formulas applied to international corporations--

Container Corp. v. Franchise Tax Board, 463 U.S. 159 (1983).

Facts. Container Corporation (P) manufactured paperboard packaging. It controlled 20 foreign subsidiaries in Latin America and Europe, most of which operated independently. However, P greatly assisted the subsidiaries in obtaining financing and equipment, and provided technical assistance and general supervision. P operated in California and filed state income taxes, but excluded its subsidiaries' income from the total unapportioned, taxable income of its unitary business. The Franchise Tax Board (D) assessed a greater tax liability by treating P's overseas subsidiaries as part of P's unitary business. This gave P a greater income, although it decreased the percentage of income apportionable to California. The final result was an increase in P's taxes, which P paid under protest. P then sued for a refund, but the California courts upheld the tax. P appeals.

Issue. May a state apply its unitary business and formula apportionment tax laws to the foreign subsidiaries of a corporation doing business within the state?

Held. Yes. Judgment affirmed.

◆ A state may not tax income earned outside its borders, but because of the imprecision of formal accounting, states are permitted to use formulas to apportion business income. The unitary business formula is used by most states and has been upheld as constitutional. There are two distinct aspects of this formula:

(i) The "unitary business" concept requires that the out-of-state activities be related in a concrete way to the in-state activities, as opposed to being a mere investment or a distinct business. Some part of the unitary business must be conducted within the taxing state.

(ii) The formula used to apportion income must be fair; it must be both internally consistent (meaning that if every jurisdiction used it, no more than all of the unitary business's income would be taxed) and externally consistent (meaning that the formula must reflect a reasonable sense of how income is generated). The formula may not discriminate against interstate or foreign commerce.

◆ The state courts held that, based on several enumerated factors, P's foreign subsidiaries were engaged in a unitary business with P. This conclusion is well within the realm of permissible judgment and should not be overturned.

◆ As to the question of fair apportionment, P has the burden to show that the income apportioned is out of all appropriate proportions to the business transacted within the state. At best, P has been able to show that the three-factor formula used by the state—based on payroll, property, and sales—has resulted in an increase of taxable income 14% greater than that which would have resulted from application of P's own accounting methodology. Such is within the margin of error of any method of attributing income among the components of a unitary business and P has not met its burden.

♦   Both the United States government and the foreign governments in which P's subsidiaries operate treat subsidiaries as separate corporations for tax purposes. While this would be irrelevant in an interstate case, greater scrutiny is necessary here because foreign commerce is involved. The tax imposed on P was not a property tax. It did not fall on foreign owners of an instrumentality of foreign commerce. And double taxation is not the inevitable result of D's taxing scheme. Thus, the tax is constitutional.

───────────────

VI. SUBSTANTIVE PROTECTION OF ECONOMIC INTERESTS

A. DEVELOPMENT OF SUBSTANTIVE DUE PROCESS

1. **Philosophical Limits on Governmental Power.** In *Calder v. Bull*, 3 U.S. (3 Dall.) 386 (1798), the Court refused to set aside state legislative action that overrode a judicial probate proceeding. The case is known best for the differing views of Justices Chase and Iredell on the nature and origin of legislative power.

    a. **Justice Chase.** Justice Chase expressed the view that legislative action is limited by the social compact that gave the legislature its power; *i.e.*, courts should be able to appeal to natural rights in making constitutional decisions.

    b. **Justice Iredell.** Justice Iredell, on the other hand, argued that constitutional limitations were the only restraint on legislative action. There is no reason why the courts should be able to define and apply natural law better than the legislature.

    c. **Comment.** The view expressed by Justice Chase is the approach generally taken today, partly by applying concepts of due process.

2. **Bill of Rights Not Binding on States--**

Barron v. Mayor & City Council of Baltimore, 32 U.S. (7 Pet.) 243 (1833).

Facts. Barron (P) sued the Mayor and City Council of Baltimore (Ds) for permitting street construction that had the effect of depositing silt in front of his wharf, making it inaccessible. P obtained a verdict for $45,000, which was reversed by the state court. P appeals on grounds that his property was not granted proper protection under the Fifth Amendment (*i.e.*, there was a "taking" without just compensation).

Issue. Does the Bill of Rights accord citizens of the United States protection from state government actions?

Held. No. Case dismissed.

♦   The limitations on government power expressed in the federal Constitution are applicable only to the government created by that instrument. Had the framers intended them to limit the powers of the state governments, they would have expressed that intention.

♦ Any limits on state powers can be found only in the respective state constitutions. For this reason the Court has no jurisdiction and must dismiss the case.

Comment. Although the Court readily presumed that the Bill of Rights did not apply to the states, it could have inferred otherwise from the fact that the language of all the rights is cast in general terms except the first, which specifically applies only to Congress.

---

3. **State Constitutional Law.** Most state constitutions contain a clause referring to "due process" or the "law of the land." Although these phrases originally were intended to establish a method of legal procedure, lawyers and state judges began to use them as a means of invalidating legislation. For example, in *Wynehamer v. People,* 13 N.Y. 378 (1856), the New York court held a state prohibition statute unconstitutional on due process grounds as applied to liquor already owned when the statute was enacted.

4. **Fourteenth Amendment Considerations.**

   a. **Substantive due process under the Fourteenth Amendment.** The concept of due process under the Fifth Amendment merely assured fair legal procedures, and applied only to the federal government. The Fourteenth Amendment Due Process Clause specifically prevents any state from depriving any person of life, liberty, or property without due process of law. Of course, the Fourteenth Amendment was adopted to prevent racial discrimination. However, the broad language used encouraged lawyers to try using it as a restriction on state regulation of business, not merely to attack the procedures used, but also to attack the substantive fairness of the regulations.

   b. **First look at the Civil War amendments--**

The Slaughter-House Cases, 83 U.S. (16 Wall.) 36 (1873).

Facts. The state of Louisiana granted a state corporation the exclusive right to operate facilities in New Orleans for the landing, keeping, and slaughter of livestock. The Butchers' Benevolent Association (Ps), a group of excluded butchers, sought an injunction against the monopoly on the grounds that they were prevented from practicing their trade unless they worked at the monopolist corporation and paid its fees. The state courts upheld the law. Ps appeal, based on four main grounds: (i) that the statute creates an involuntary servitude forbidden by the Thirteenth Amendment; (ii) that it abridges the privileges and immunities of citizens of the United States; (iii) that it denies Ps the equal protection of the laws; and (iv) that it deprives them of their property without due process of law, all under the Fourteenth Amendment.

Issue. Do the Civil War amendments grant United States citizens broad protection against the actions of state governments?

Held. No. Judgment affirmed.

♦ The proper interpretation of the Civil War amendments must reflect their historical setting. Thus, the meaning of "involuntary servitude" as used in the Thirteenth Amendment is restricted to personal servitude, not a servitude attached to property as Ps claim.

♦ The Fourteenth Amendment clearly distinguishes between citizenship of the states and citizenship of the United States. Only those privileges and immunities of United States citizens are protected by the Fourteenth Amendment. Privileges and immunities of state citizens upon which Ps rely here are unaffected, and rest for their security and protection in the power of the several states as recognized in Article IV. The Constitution does not control the power of the state governments over the rights of their own citizens except to require that a state grant equal rights to its own citizens and citizens of other states within its jurisdiction. Therefore, Ps, as citizens of the United States, have no privilege or immunity that has been infringed by the state law.

♦ The Equal Protection Clause of the Fourteenth Amendment is intended primarily to prevent state discrimination against blacks, although Congress may extend its scope to other areas. But Ps have not claimed a denial of equal justice in the state courts and therefore have no reason to have a remedy under the Equal Protection Clause.

♦ The restraint imposed by Louisiana upon the exercise of Ps' trade simply cannot be held to be a deprivation of property within the meaning of the Fourteenth Amendment. That clause should not be construed to cover such state restraint upon trade.

Dissent (Field, J., Chase, C.J., Swayne, Bradley, JJ.). These amendments were intended to protect the citizens of the United States against the deprivation of their common rights by state legislation. The majority holding as to the Privileges and Immunities Clause would add no more protection than existed prior to adoption of the amendment, making it meaningless. A distinguishing privilege of citizens of the United States is equality of right to the lawful pursuits of life throughout the whole country. To permit a state to interfere with such a basic privilege is to ignore the true purpose of the Fourteenth Amendment.

Dissent (Bradley, J.). A state infringes personal liberty when it grants a monopoly to individuals or corporations. A law that prohibits a large class of citizens from pursuing lawful employment deprives them of liberty as well as property without due process of law. Their occupation is their property, their choice their liberty. The law also deprives them of equal protection.

Comment. This case, the first requiring interpretation of these amendments, rendered the Privileges and Immunities Clause ineffective in protecting individual rights against invasion by state governments. Instead, the Court looked to the Due Process and Equal Protection Clauses. Ps in this case were not attacking the procedure used, but the actual fairness of the state-approved monopoly. Although the Court rejected the notion of substantive due process in this case, the scope of the clause was unclear for many years. Gradually, the Court began to examine the substantive reasonableness of state legislation.

---

c. **Increased judicial intervention in economic regulation.**

1) **Development of substantive due process.** As noted above, the state courts were the first to accept arguments in favor of some type of substantive due process. Then in *Munn v. Illinois*, 94 U.S. 113 (1876), the Court held that the Due Process Clause does protect private property, but a state may control such property if it is "affected with a public interest," so that a state could set maximum storage charges at central warehouses. Eventually, the Court began to scrutinize the substantive rights affected by legislation because there existed "fundamental rights" that were entitled to judicial protection. For example, in *Allgeyer v. Louisiana*, 165 U.S. 578 (1897), the Court invalidated a state law that prohibited the insuring of Louisiana property by any company not licensed to do business in Louisiana. Allgeyer had insured his property with a New York insurer in violation of the state law. The Court held that this statute deprived Allgeyer of his liberty to contract, without due process of law.

2) **Concept of substantive due process.** With the *Lochner* case that follows, the Court applied the following concepts of due process:

a) **Ends or purposes.** The Court examined the purposes of the legislation, asking whether the object was legitimate, appropriate, and/or necessary. Did the law promote in some way the health, safety, welfare, and/or morals of the people? These questions were answered from the language of the statute, the legislative record, and the history behind the passage of the statute. These were considered questions of law for the court.

b) **Means.** The Court also determined whether the means used to accomplish the legislation's purpose were reasonable and appropriate. That is, was there a real and substantial relationship between the means used and the legitimate end?

          c)   **Effect.** Finally, the Court inquired into the effect of the law on the liberty and property of the parties involved. If the effect was too drastic, then the law violated due process.

    3)   **Pivotal case--**

Lochner v. New York, 198 U.S. 45 (1905).

Facts. Lochner (D) was convicted of permitting an employee to work for him more than the statutory maximum of 60 hours per week. D appeals, claiming the law violated his freedom to contract under the Fourteenth Amendment Due Process Clause.

Issue. May a state generally prohibit private agreements to work more than a specified number of hours?

Held. No. Judgment reversed.

♦   The general right to contract in business is clearly part of the individual liberty protected by the Fourteenth Amendment. However, the right to hold both property and liberty are subject to such reasonable conditions as may be imposed by a government pursuant to its police powers.

♦   An earlier law restricting the work hours in certain dangerous occupations was upheld. The law here challenged, however, has no reference whatever to the health, safety, morals, or welfare of the public. The state claims an interest in the individual worker's health, but this goes too far; the individual's liberty must impose some restraint on the police power.

♦   This is not a substitution of the Court's judgment for the legislature's but merely a determination of whether the attempted regulation is within the state's police power.

Dissent (Harlan, White, Day, JJ.). There is room for debate about the validity of the state's interest in preventing more than 10 hours' work per day. Excessive work could impair the ability of workers to serve the state and provide for their dependents. The Court should not go farther than to determine that such reasons for the law exist.

Dissent (Holmes, J.). Many comparably restrictive uses of the police power have been upheld by the Court. The Constitution was not intended to embody a particular economic view but was framed to permit expression of dominant opinions, *i.e.*, that the laws freely reflect the people's choices. The law is not clearly unrelated to public health and ought to be upheld.

Comment. The Court applied principles of general constitutional law that formerly had been applied only in diversity cases. The Court began to define the limits of the police power where it excessively imposed upon individual freedoms, the scope of which the Court in turn was broadening. The Court began inquiring as to the propriety and reasonableness of the objectives sought through exercise of the police power.

B. JUDICIAL CONTROL OVER LEGISLATIVE POLICY

1. **Introduction.** After *Lochner*, the Court began substituting its judgment for legislative judgments in a variety of cases involving economic regulation. Most legislation held unconstitutional involved regulation of labor, prices, and entry into business.

2. **Applications.**

    a. **Maximum working hours.** The Court upheld a law fixing maximum work hours for women, distinguishing *Lochner* by the special state interest in healthy women. [Muller v. Oregon, 208 U.S. 412 (1908)] The Court later effectively overruled *Lochner* by upholding a general maximum work hour law in *Bunting v. Oregon*, 243 U.S. 426 (1917). In that case, the Court did not refer to *Lochner*, and substantive due process survived.

    b. **"Yellow dog" contracts.** In *Coppage v. Kansas*, 236 U.S. 1 (1915), the Court held that a state law that prohibited employers from requiring employees to agree not to join a labor union ("yellow dog" contracts) violated due process because it interfered with the right to make contracts. *Adair v. United States*, 208 U.S. 161 (1908), invalidated a similar federal law.

    c. **Minimum wages.** The Court invalidated a federal minimum wage law applicable only to the District of Columbia in *Adkins v. Children's Hospital*, 261 U.S. 525 (1923), again finding that interference with freedom to contract violated due process.

    d. **Business entry and economic regulations.** In a series of decisions that have been undermined by subsequent developments, the Court invalidated restraints on competition that curtailed entry into a particular type of business. [*See* New State Ice Co. v. Liebmann, 285 U.S. 262 (1932)—manufacture of ice requiring a certificate of convenience and necessity; Adams v. Tanner, 244 U.S. 590 (1917)—employment agency fees collected from workers] In *Weaver v. Palmer Brothers Co.*, 270 U.S. 402 (1926), although the Court recognized the validity of the state interest in curtailing business practices that might defraud or endanger consumers, the Court invalidated an absolute ban on the use of shoddy (cut up or torn) fabrics for bedding. The Court held that the ban was purely arbitrary since other secondhand materials could be used if sterilized and labeled.

C. DECLINE OF SUBSTANTIVE DUE PROCESS

1. **Introduction.** Some time after *Lochner*, the Court changed its earlier view and began to apply less strict scrutiny to economic regulation. Instead, it granted deference to legislative determinations of need and reasonableness.

2. **Regulation of Prices and Wages--**

Nebbia v. New York, 291 U.S. 502 (1934).

Facts. New York (P) passed a law establishing minimum and maximum retail prices for milk. The purpose was to aid the dairy industry, which was in a desperate situation because the prices received by farmers for milk were below the cost of production. Nebbia (D), a retail grocer, sold milk below the minimum price and was convicted of violating the statute. D challenges the statute as a violation of due process.

Issue. May a state strictly control retail prices, even where such control inhibits the use of private property and the making of contracts?

Held. Yes.

♦   As long as the Court finds the law to have a reasonable relationship to a proper legislative purpose, to be not arbitrary or discriminatory, and to have means chosen that are reasonably related to the ends sought, due process is not offended.

♦   No area is outside the province of state regulation for police power purposes, including the direct regulation of prices.

Dissent (McReynolds, Van Devanter, Sutherland, Butler, JJ.). This statute is not regulation but management. D is deprived of the fundamental right to conduct his business honestly and along customary lines, and consumers are deprived of their liberty to buy a necessity of life in an open market. The milk industry is not affected with a public interest.

3. **Regulation of Minimum Wage.** In *West Coast Hotel Co. v. Parrish,* 300 U.S. 379 (1937), the Court overruled several prior decisions and held that a state could, consistent with due process, impose a minimum wage on employer-employee contracts.

4. **Footnote 4 of *Carolene Products*.** In *United States v. Carolene Products Co.*, 304 U.S. 144 (1938), the Court held that Congress may prohibit the interstate shipment of food products that it deems injurious to the public health. Footnote 4 of the opinion sets forth principles regarding this varying

presumption of constitutionality. It noted that the scope of the presumption may be narrower when the legislation appears on its face to be within a specific prohibition of the Constitution, such as those of the Bill of Rights. Another area that may invoke a narrower presumption is when the legislation may restrict the political process that could lead to repeal of undesirable legislation. The third general area is legislation directed at particular religions or minorities.

5. **Regulation of "Closed Shop" Contracts.** In *Lincoln Federal Labor Union v. Northwestern Iron & Metal Co.*, 335 U.S. 525 (1949), the Court upheld a statute prohibiting employers from entering into "closed shop" contracts so as to exclude nonunion workers.

6. **Regulation of Business Entry.** The Court upheld a probably overly restrictive optician-optometrist regulation in *Williamson v. Lee Optical of Oklahoma*, 348 U.S. 483 (1955), a restrictive regulation of the business of debt adjusting in *Ferguson v. Skrupa*, 372 U.S. 726 (1963), and a local-ownership legislative scheme in *North Dakota State Board v. Snyders' Drug Stores Inc.*, 414 U.S. 156 (1973).

D. "TAKING" OF PROPERTY INTERESTS

1. **Introduction.** The Fifth Amendment provides in part that private property may not be "taken" for "public use" without just compensation. This clause is a restriction on both the federal and state power of eminent domain. Property rights may include tangible and intangible interests. The two most troublesome constitutional issues here are the meanings of the terms "public use" and "taking."

   a. **Public use.** Government may only exercise its power of eminent domain for a public use. This term is broadly defined by the Court. If the asserted use of the property is rationally related to a conceivable, articulated public purpose, the Court will defer to the legislative findings.

   b. **Taking.** Government action may affect property rights without constituting a "taking." Mere regulation that limits the use of the property, such as zoning laws, is not normally considered a taking under the Fifth Amendment. The Court merely determines whether justice and fairness require that the public compensate the private owner for the loss. As the following examples illustrate, the particular facts of each case are determinative.

2. **Public Purpose Requirement--**

Berman v. Parker, 348 U.S. 26 (1954).

Facts. Congress enacted the District of Columbia Redevelopment Act, which created a Redevelopment Agency to acquire and assemble real property for redevelopment of blighted areas. Berman (P) owned a well-maintained department store in a targeted area and objected to the appropriation of this property for the purposes of the project. The district court upheld the statute and its application to P. P appeals.

Issue. May the government, as part of a planned redevelopment, take private property that, by itself, neither imperils health or safety nor contributes to the existing blighted conditions?

Held. Yes. Judgment affirmed.

♦ Since Congress has power over the District equivalent to the power of a state over its own territory, we must consider whether this exercise of the police power exceeds specific constitutional limitations. The only review we can give is determining whether that power is being exercised for a public purpose and whether just compensation is given.

♦ The concept of the public welfare is broad and inclusive, and includes spiritual and aesthetic values. Thus, a legislature may deem it in the public interest to promote beautiful, balanced communities. Eminent domain is merely a means to that end. There are no prohibitions against action on an area rather than on a structure-by-structure basis.

♦ The fact that the property, once taken and consolidated, might be turned over to a private redevelopment company is not an improper means of attaining the ultimate objective. P's rights are satisfied by payment of just compensation.

Comment. The Court's modern view of "public" use demonstrates the extent of its deference to legislative findings. In *Hawaii Housing Authority v. Midkiff*, 467 U.S. 229 (1984), the Court permitted the Hawaii legislature to use eminent domain to allow tenants who owned their homes but not the land under them to purchase the real estate. In Hawaii, the state and federal governments owned 49% of the land and 72 private owners owned another 47%, leaving only 4% of the land for all other owners.

---

3.   **Transfer to Private Party as Public Use--**

Kelo v. New London, 545 U.S. 469 (2005).

Facts. State and local officials designated a portion of the city of New London (D) for economic revitalization. Kelo (P) and other property owners in the area refused to sell their property to D. D initiated condemnation proceedings, using its power of eminent domain. Ps' properties were not in poor condition, but D sought to condemn them because they were in the redevelopment area. Ps sued, claiming that the condemnation violated the Takings Clause. The Connecticut Supreme Court upheld the condemnation. The Supreme Court granted certiorari.

Issue. As part of a regional economic rejuvenation program, may a city take private property from one private party and give it to another private party?

Held. Yes. Judgment affirmed.

♦   The government cannot take the property of a private party for the sole purpose of transferring it to another private party, even with the payment of just compensation. However, the government may transfer property from one private party to another if future use by the public is the reason for the taking (*e.g.*, land for a railroad with common-carrier duties).

♦   Here, although D's taking is not to benefit specific individuals, D does not intend to open all of the condemned land to use by the general public. Also, unlike common carriers, the lessees will not be required to make their services available to all. However, to satisfy the "public use" requirement, condemned property need not be put to use for the general public, but it must serve a public purpose. Thus, the disposition of this case rests on a determination of whether D's plan serves a public purpose.

♦   D determined that the area was sufficiently distressed to justify an economic rejuvenation plan, and this determination is entitled to judicial deference. The plan clearly serves a public purpose, even if it does benefit individual private parties. Therefore, the condemnation does not violate the Takings Clause.

♦   Ps ask us to adopt a rule that economic development does not qualify as a public use. This position is not supported by precedent or logic. Promoting economic development is a long accepted governmental function.

♦   Nothing in our decision prevents the states from restricting the use of eminent domain powers.

Concurrence (Kennedy, J.). A taking that is intended to favor a particular private party, with only incidental and pretextual public benefit, would not be a valid taking. Although courts apply a rational basis review to this type of case, with a presumption that the government's actions are reasonable and intended to serve a public purpose, courts must treat plausible accusations of favoritism seriously.

Dissent (O'Connor, J., Rehnquist, C.J., Scalia, Thomas, JJ.). The majority concludes that the incidental public benefits resulting from the subsequent ordinary use of private property renders economic development takings "for public use." This effectively deletes the words "for public use" from the Takings Clause. But the fundamental limitation on takings prevents the government from taking property for the benefit of another private person. To let the government itself define what is public and what is private use eliminates the protection provided by the Fifth Amendment. Nearly any lawful use of real private property can be said to generate some incidental benefit to the public. Economic development takings should not be constitutional.

Dissent (Thomas, J.). The Court does not defer to legislative findings regarding, for example, what is a reasonable search of a home, and it should not diminish the protection provided by the Takings Clause by deferring to a legislative finding about "public purpose" either. The government can only take property if it actually uses or gives the public a legal right to use the property.

---

4.   **Regulation as a Taking.**

    a.   **Mining restrictions--**

Pennsylvania Coal Co. v. Mahon, 260 U.S. 393 (1922).

Facts. Mahon (P) sued to prevent the Pennsylvania Coal Co. (D) from mining coal under P's property. P's deed conveyed the surface but reserved the right to remove all the coal under the surface. P claimed that the Kohler Act, which prohibited the mining of coal in such a way as to cause the subsidence of any structure used as a human habitation, limits D's right to extract the coal. The trial court found that the statute destroyed D's previously existing rights and was therefore unconstitutional. The Pennsylvania Supreme Court held that the Act was a proper exercise of the state's police power. The Supreme Court granted certiorari.

Issue. May the state regulate mining so as to restrict a mineral rights owner's ability to extract coal?

Held. No. Judgment reversed.

♦   Government may enact laws that affect property values to some extent, without paying for the decrease in value. Some values are enjoyed under an implied limitation that yields to the police power, but the implied limitation must be limited or the Contract and Due Process Clauses are ineffective.

♦   Whether the effect on value constitutes a taking depends on the facts of each case. In this case, the Act goes too far because to make it commercially impracticable to mine coal is nearly the same as appropriating or destroying it. P assumed the risk of acquiring only surface rights, and the fact that that risk has become a danger does not justify giving P greater rights than P bought.

Dissent (Brandeis, J.). If D's activities released poisonous gases, the state's power to prevent the activity would be clear. It should be just as able to prevent mining so near to the surface as to present the danger of subsidence. There is no evidence that the value of the coal kept in place by the restriction is significant compared with the value of the whole property. The courts should not consider the reciprocity of advantage where the police power is exercised to protect the public from detriment and danger.

---

b. Extensive limitation on harmful activities--

Keystone Bituminous Coal Association v. DeBenedictis, 480 U.S. 470 (1987).

Facts. A Pennsylvania statute intended to prevent or minimize subsidence of surface land caused by coal mining required 50% of the coal under specified structures to remain in place for surface support. The Keystone Bituminous Coal Association (P) challenged the statute as an unconstitutional taking. P's members had acquired the mineral rights and support estates from landowners who retained only the surface estate. The statute would significantly reduce the amount of coal that could be mined. The district court found for DeBenedictis (D), and the court of appeals affirmed. The Supreme Court granted certiorari.

Issue. May a state prohibit, without compensation, the mining of coal that would have the effect of causing subsidence of surface land?

Held. Yes. Judgment affirmed.

◆ A land use regulation will be deemed a taking if it: (i) does not substantially advance legitimate state interests, or (ii) denies an owner economically viable use of his land. For example, *Pennsylvania Coal Co. v. Mahon, supra,* relied on the premise that the law protected only private interests and made it commercially impracticable to mine coal in the affected areas. The statute in this case does not suffer from these deficiencies.

◆ The statute has a clear public purpose—the protection of health, environment, and fiscal integrity to support the tax base. P's members' use of their coal rights is similar to a public nuisance, the control of which is supported by the notion of reciprocity of advantage. The public welfare and, in turn, each individual, is benefited greatly by the restriction placed on individual use of private property.

◆ P has not claimed or shown that the statute makes it commercially impracticable for its members to continue mining their coal, nor can P point to specific quantities of coal that it can no longer mine to prove a taking. Instead, the focus is on the nature of the interference with the rights in the property as a whole. When this is done, it is clear that less than 2% of P's members' coal is actually rendered unusable.

Dissent (Rehnquist, C.J., Powell, O'Connor, Scalia, JJ.). The differences between this statute and the one considered in *Pennsylvania Coal* are trivial. In this case, P's members' interests in specific coal deposits have been completely destroyed.

---

   c.   **Zoning regulations--**

Penn Central Transportation Co. v. New York City, 438 U.S. 104 (1978).

Facts. Penn Central Transportation Company (P) owned the Grand Central Terminal in New York City (D). The terminal was designated a "landmark" under the City Landmarks Preservation Law, which prohibited destruction of designated landmarks. P was denied permission to alter the terminal solely because of the Landmarks Law, which P then challenged as an unconstitutional taking. The trial court granted P relief, but the higher state courts all held for D. P appeals.

Issue. May a city restrict development of individual historic landmarks, beyond applicable zoning regulations, without a "taking" requiring payment of "just compensation"?

Held. Yes. Judgment affirmed.

♦   The question here revolves around two basic considerations: the nature and extent of the impact on P and the character of the governmental action.

♦   The "taking" may not be established by merely showing a government-imposed inability to further develop a property, nor is a diminution in property value determinative. Zoning laws have these effects yet are constitutional because they are part of a comprehensive plan for achieving a significant public purpose, as is D's law.

♦   P claims the law is discriminatory and arbitrary. Yet numerous other structures are likewise under the landmark regulations. Even if P does not receive benefits to completely offset its burdens, valid zoning laws may have a similar effect. If P finds application of the law to be arbitrary, it may obtain judicial review of any commission decision.

♦   The government has not taken P's airspace for its own purpose, but for the benefit of the entire public. It has done so pursuant to a legitimate interest in preserving special buildings.

♦   Finally, the impact on P is mitigated by the existence of Transferable Development Rights and by the fact that P has not been prohibited from making any improvements, but only the two drastic proposals that were rejected by D. Thus, P may be permitted the use of at least some portion of its airspace.

Dissent (Rehnquist, J., Burger, C.J., Stevens, J.). A literal interpretation of the Fifth Amendment would clearly favor P. Even the Court's more relaxed view should result in a decision for P. Clearly valuable property rights have been destroyed. A taking need not be a physical seizure. Destruction of rights is a taking, except in two instances: prohibition of nuisances and prohibitions covering broad areas that secure an average reciprocity of advantage, such as zoning laws. Neither exception applies here. The people generally, not P individually, ought to pay the cost of the recognized public benefit of having P's property preserved.

---

d. Complete destruction of property value--

Lucas v. South Carolina Coastal Council, 505 U.S. 1003 (1992).

Facts. Lucas (P) purchased two residential lots near the seashore, intending to build single-family homes. Two years later, South Carolina passed an anti-erosion law that barred making "occupiable improvements" that near the shore. This effectively barred P from building homes on his land. P sued, and the trial court found that he was entitled to compensation because his property was now valueless. The South Carolina Supreme Court reversed. The United States Supreme Court granted certiorari.

Issue. Must the government compensate a private landowner if the government's regulation prohibits all economically productive or beneficial uses of the land?

Held. Yes. Judgment reversed.

♦ In *Pennsylvania Coal Co. v. Mahon, supra*, the Court held that the Takings Clause extended beyond direct appropriations of property to regulations that go "too far." There are at least two categories of regulatory action that are compensable: (i) physical invasions, *e.g.,* requiring landlords to allow television cable companies to put cable in their apartment buildings [*see* Loretto v. Teleprompter Manhattan CATV Corp., 458 U.S. 419 (1982)]; and (ii) denial of all economically beneficial or productive use of land.

♦ The functional basis for allowing the government, without making compensation, to affect property values through regulation is the recognition that the government could not operate if it had to pay for every change in the law that affected property values, but this basis does not apply where the government deprives a landowner of all economically beneficial uses. Such regulation really presses the private property into a form of public service under the guise of mitigating serious public harm.

◆   P claims that the finding that his property has been rendered valueless requires compensation, regardless of the reason for the regulation. Prior opinions held that harmful or noxious uses of property may be proscribed by government regulation without compensation, but this really means that land-use regulation does not effect a taking if it "substantially advances legitimate state interests." But D cannot take land without compensation merely by reciting a noxious-use or benefit-conferring rationale. D could avoid paying compensation only if the nature of P's estate shows that the proscribed use interests were not part of his title to begin with; *i.e.*, that his bundle of rights did not include an expectation that the state would eliminate all economically valuable use.

◆   Confiscatory regulations cannot be newly legislated without compensation; they must inhere in the title itself, in the restrictions that background principles of the state's law of property and nuisance already place on land ownership. The fact that a particular use has long been engaged in by similarly situated owners, or that other landowners similarly situated are permitted to continue the use denied to P, demonstrates a lack of any common law prohibition on the use. In this case, it is unlikely that common law principles would have prevented P from building a house on the land, but this must be determined on remand.

Concurrence (Kennedy, J.). Where a regulation deprives the property of all value, whether it is a taking depends on whether the deprivation is contrary to reasonable, investment-backed expectations. The state supreme court erred in not evaluating P's reasonable expectations. And D did not act until after the property had been zoned for residential development and other parcels had been built on, so that the remaining lots have to bear the entire burden of the regulation.

Dissent (Blackmun, J.). The state may prevent any use of property it finds to be harmful to its citizens, and a state statute is entitled to a presumption of constitutionality. The record supports D's assessment that the building restriction is necessary to protect people and property, and the Court has departed from traditional rules by creating a new scheme for regulations that eliminate all economic value.

Dissent (Stevens, J.). The Court's new categorical rule is arbitrary since it distinguishes between a landowner whose property is diminished in value 95% and who recovers nothing, and a landowner whose property is diminished in value 100% and recovers its full value. The reliance on a common law exception prevents the states from developing the common law in response to new learning, such as the significance of endangered species and wetlands.

Comment. In *Loretto v. Teleprompter Manhattan CATV Corp.*, *supra*, the Court held that any permanent physical intrusion by the government is a taking requiring compensation. This rule applies regardless of the state's interest or the economic impact on the owner. The *Loretto* case involved a New York statute authorizing permanent cable TV installations for tenants of privately owned apartment houses. The tenant merely had to pay a one-time fee to the landlord of $1. The dissenting Justices noted that nonphysical government intrusions often diminish the value of property more than minor physical intrusions, and that therefore a per se rule for physical intrusion was inappropriate.

---

e. Public access to property through private property--

Nollan v. California Coastal Commission, 483 U.S. 825 (1987).

Facts. The Nollans (Ps) purchased a beachfront lot in southern California on the condition that they replace the existing structure with a new one. Ps applied to the California Coastal Commission (D) for permission to build a home like the others in the neighborhood, but D required Ps to grant a public easement across Ps' property to the ocean. Ps sued and won a judgment. D appealed, but meanwhile Ps built the house. The state court of appeals reversed, and Ps appeal.

Issue. If a state may not require an uncompensated conveyance of an easement over private property, may it require the conveyance as a condition to its approval of a land use permit for the property?

Held. No. Judgment reversed.

◆ It is clear that if D had simply required Ps to grant a public easement across their property, there would have been a taking. Such an easement constitutes a permanent physical occupation, and the right to exclude others is an essential stick in the bundle of rights that constitutes property.

◆ A land use regulation is permissible if it substantially advances legitimate state interests and does not deny an owner economically viable use of his land. If a condition is imposed short of an outright ban on construction, it must serve the same governmental purpose as the ban would. Otherwise, the condition is not a valid land use regulation but extortion. If the condition is unrelated to the purported purpose, the true purpose must be evaluated.

◆ In this case, D claims Ps' new house interferes with "visual access" to the beach, which in turn will cause a "psychological barrier" to the public's desire for access. These burdens on "access" would be alleviated by the easement over Ps' property. These arguments are nothing more than a play on words, however. The condition is not the exercise of the land use power for any of the state's purposes. It simply lacks any substantial advancing of a legitimate state interest.

◆ D's final justification is that the easement would serve the public interest, but a mere belief that the public interest would be served is insufficient. D must use its power of eminent domain to acquire the easement if it wants it.

Dissent (Brennan, Marshall, JJ.). The Court should defer to the state as long as the state rationally could have decided that the control used might achieve the state's objective. Instead, the majority has applied an inappropriately narrow concept of rationality. In fact, there is a reasonable relationship between the condition and the specific burden Ps' development imposes on public access. At any rate, the restriction is a minimal burden and the development increased the value of Ps' property much more than any diminution attributable to the easement.

Comment. Local governments have traditionally required developers to dedicate streets and utility easements within subdivisions, and frequently also require certain improvements that benefit the subdivision exclusively, such as paved streets or on-site utility facilities. However, some governments have required dedication of land for parks and schools, or a payment of money to develop parks and schools. Some courts disallow such requirements as not sufficiently attributable to the developer's activity to remove public responsibility for such improvements.

---

f.   Nexus test--

Dolan v. City of Tigard, 512 U.S. 374 (1994).

Facts. Dolan (P) petitioned the City Planning Commission of the city of Tigard (D) for approval to expand her store and pave her parking lot. D conditioned its approval on her agreeing to dedicate (i) a portion of her land on the floodplain for drainage system improvements and flood control and (ii) a portion of her land for a pathway for pedestrians and bicyclists. P sought an agency determination that the conditions were not related to the expansion of her store and thus were an unconstitutional taking under the Fifth Amendment. The agency ruled in favor of D, and the state lower courts affirmed. The Supreme Court granted certiorari.

Issue. Do the conditions imposed by D meet the required degree of connection to the projected impact of P's proposed expansion?

Held. No. Judgment reversed.

♦   The first determination that must be made is whether there is an "essential nexus" between the "legitimate state interest" involved and the conditions D seeks to impose. Here, such a nexus is present between both (i) preventing flooding and limiting development along the floodplain, and (ii) reducing traffic congestion and providing a path for alternative means of transportation.

♦   Having found that the nexus does exist, the next determination that must be made is whether the degree of the demands imposed by the conditions bears a "rough proportionality" to the projected impact of P's proposed expansion.

This issue was not reached in *Nollan, supra*. In meeting this standard, D must "make some sort of individualized determination that the required dedication is related both in nature and extent to the impact of the proposed development."

♦ D has failed to meet the required standard. Although preventing development along the floodplain would help deter flooding, D made no showing that dedicating the nondeveloped floodplain land to public use as opposed to leaving it to P's private use had any relation to flood control. Regarding the dedication for a pedestrian/bicyclist pathway, D has not made the required showing that the creation of a public pathway reasonably relates to the additional traffic that could result from P's expansion. Here, D has done no more than state that the pathway "could" offset some of the increase in traffic.

Dissent (Stevens, Blackmun, Ginsburg, JJ.). The correct inquiry should focus on whether the required nexus is present, and the condition's germaneness and nature should only be considered if the challenger makes a showing that the condition is grossly disproportionate to the possible adverse effect of the new development. The Court has incorrectly allocated the burdens of proof.

---

g. **Challenge against regulation in place when property was purchased.** The Supreme Court has held that a property owner can challenge a regulatory taking even when the restriction was in place when he purchased the property. [Palazzolo v. Rhode Island, 533 U.S. 606 (2001)]

h. **Temporary restriction.** *Tahoe-Sierra Preservation Council, Inc. v. Tahoe Regional Planning Agency*, 535 U.S. 302 (2002), involved a temporary moratorium on development. The Court held that the question of whether a temporary moratorium was a taking depended on the particular circumstances of the case. In some circumstances, it might be a per se taking under *Lucas*; in others, it would require case-by-case evaluation under *Penn Central Transportation Co. v. New York City*, 438 U.S. 104 (1978). The duration of the restriction is one of several factors for the courts to consider. The dissent noted that the moratoria in the case had lasted six years, a duration long enough to constitute a per se taking under *Lucas*.

5. **Determining What Is Property.**

a. **Economic legislation.** Under the Coal Act of 1992, Congress provided for retirement benefits by merging old benefit plans into a new fund, financed by annual premiums assessed against signatory coal operators. In *Eastern Enterprises v. Apfel*, 524 U.S. 498 (1998), the Court dealt with the impact of the Coal Act on a specific employer. Eastern

Enterprises ("Eastern") was a signatory to coal wage agreements executed between 1947 and 1964. This meant that Eastern was "in business" within the Coal Act's meaning, although it left the coal industry in 1965, after transferring its coal operations to a subsidiary. Under the Coal Act, Eastern was assigned the obligation for combined fund premiums respecting over 1,000 retired miners who had worked for the company before 1966. The Supreme Court held that it was a violation of the Takings Clause to force Eastern to bear the expense of lifetime health benefits for miners based on Eastern's activities decades before the benefits were even promised. While Congress has broad discretion to fashion economic legislation, a severe retroactive liability on a limited class of parties that could not have anticipated the liability is an unconstitutional taking, especially where the extent of the liability is substantially disproportionate. In this case, Eastern could be required to pay $50 to $100 million. The Act attached new legal consequences to the employment relationship that had terminated long before the Act was adopted. Justice Kennedy, casting the fifth and deciding vote, concurred in part, concluding that the Coal Act was contrary to due process regardless of the Takings Clause. The four dissenting Justices thought that the Takings Clause did not apply because the interest at stake was an ordinary liability to pay money to third parties, not a specific interest in physical or intellectual property. The dissent concluded that it was not unfair to require Eastern to pay the health care costs for its former employees.

    b.   **Interest on client funds.** When a client gives funds to an attorney, if the funds would not reasonably be expected to earn interest, all but one of the states provides that such funds be placed in a separate, interest-bearing account, the interest on which is paid to foundations that finance legal services for low-income persons. In *Phillips v. Washington Legal Foundation*, 524 U.S. 156 (1998), the Court held that such interest is the private property of the client for Takings Clause purposes on the basic legal concept that interest follows principal. The Court did not decide whether the funds were "taken" by the states, however.

E.   THE CONTRACT CLAUSE

    1.   **Introduction.** Article I, Section 10 provides that no state may pass any law that impairs the obligation of contracts. Note that the clause applies only to the states; there is no mention in the Constitution of a similar prohibition against the federal government. However, the Court has held that the Due Process Clause of the Fifth Amendment is broad enough to extend a similar prohibition to federal action. [Lynch v. United States, 292 U.S. 571 (1934)] The term "impairs" includes a substantial invalidation, release, or extinguishment of the obligation of a contract. "Obligation" includes the existing legal rules as well as the terms of the contract itself. This does not mean that the law can never change, but legitimate expectations of the parties cannot be impaired.

2. **Development of Contract Clause Doctrine.** The Contract Clause was a major restraint on state economic regulation in the 19th century. It applied to both private and public contracts. More recently, the Court has applied a balancing test approach. Not all substantial impairments of contracts are unconstitutional. Private parties may not claim immunity from state regulation through private contractual arrangements. Rights and duties may be modified by legislation necessary to an important and legitimate public interest as long as the impairment of the contract is reasonable.

3. **Basic Requirements for a Valid Impairment--**

Home Building & Loan Association v. Blaisdell, 290 U.S. 398 (1934).

Facts. Minnesota passed a law that permitted extensions of the period of redemption from a foreclosure and sale of real property under a mortgage. The Blaisdells (Ds) obtained such an extension. Home Building & Loan Association (P) challenged the extension as improper state interference in a private contract. The state defended the law as needed emergency legislation to deal with the Depression. The state courts upheld the law, and P appeals.

Issue. May a state alter existing contractual obligations in order to respond to emergency conditions?

Held. Yes. Judgment affirmed.

♦ An emergency does not create power, but it may justify the exercise of existing power. As maintenance of government is essential to having enforceable contracts, circumstances may arise when exercise of the police power to alter contracts is justified to maintain effective government.

♦ Legislation impairing contracts may be upheld when:

(i) The state legislature declares that an emergency exists;

(ii) The state law is enacted to protect a basic societal interest, not a favored group;

(iii) The relief is appropriately tailored to the declared emergency;

(iv) The imposed conditions are reasonable; and

(v)   The legislation is limited to the duration of the emergency.

♦   The statute at issue here meets all five of the requirements and is therefore constitutional.

---

4.   State Obligations--

United States Trust Co. v. New Jersey, 431 U.S. 1 (1977).

Facts. New York and New Jersey (Ds) formed the New York and New Jersey Port Authority by interstate compact. In 1962, both states passed statutes prohibiting financing of passenger railroad facilities with revenues pledged to pay the authority's bonds, unless the facility was self-supporting. In 1974, Ds retroactively repealed the 1962 statutes to permit greater subsidizing of mass transit. United States Trust Company (P), trustee and holder of Authority bonds, challenged the 1974 law on Contract Clause grounds. The state courts upheld the 1974 law, and P appeals.

Issue. May a state impair the obligation of its own contracts, based on its own determination of reasonableness and necessity?

Held. No. Judgment reversed.

♦   The Contract Clause does not require state adherence to a contract that surrenders an essential attribute of its sovereignty. This contract is purely financial and does not compromise the state's sovereignty. But impairment of Ds' duties is constitutional only if it is reasonable and necessary.

♦   Allowing a state to reduce its financial obligations whenever it wanted to spend the money for what it regarded as an important public purpose would negate all Contract Clause protection. For this reason, complete deference to legislative assessments of reasonableness and necessity is inappropriate. After independently examining the existence of less drastic alternatives, we hold that Ds' repealing acts are excessively harmful to P's contractual interests.

Dissent (Brennan, White, Marshall, JJ.). Elevation of the Contract Clause to the status of regulation of the municipal bond market, at the heavy price of frustration of sound legislative policymaking, is unwise and unnecessary. P's realistic economic interests are adequately protected by the political processes and the bond marketplace itself. The Court ought not restrict the legislature's responsiveness to changing public needs by preventing adoption of measures not plainly unreasonable and arbitrary. Ds' proper legislative decision ought to be upheld.

---

5. Private Obligations--

Allied Structural Steel Co. v. Spannaus, 438 U.S. 234 (1978).

Facts. Allied Structural Steel Company (P) established a pension plan, pursuant to IRS regulations, providing that qualifying employees would acquire pension rights but giving no assurance that any employee would not be dismissed at any time. P had an office in Minnesota that it began to close. A few months previously, Minnesota had passed a law that subjected employers to a "pension funding charge" upon termination of a pension plan or closing of a Minnesota office. The law had the effect of making several of P's otherwise unqualified employees pension obligees, resulting in a charge to P of $185,000. P sued Spannaus (D), a Minnesota official, for injunctive and declaratory relief. The federal district court held the Act valid. P appeals, claiming the law violates the Contract Clause.

Issue. Does the Contract Clause preclude state legislation that significantly expands duties created by private contract?

Held. Yes. Judgment reversed.

♦ The Contract Clause is not an absolute prohibition against any impairment of contracts. It does not operate to obliterate state police power, but it does limit a state's ability to abridge existing contractual relationships.

♦ The first issue is whether the state law has substantially impaired a contractual relationship. The challenged law nullifies express terms of P's contractual obligations and imposes a completely unexpected liability in potentially disabling amounts. Such severe impairment may be condoned only if justified by the need for the law.

♦ Unlike the law challenged in *Home Building & Loan Association v. Blaisdell*, *supra*, the law here is directed at a narrow class—those employers with voluntary private pension plans who either terminate the plan or close the Minnesota office. Nor was the law intended to deal with a broad and desperate economic emergency. It did not just temporarily change the contractual rights and duties, but imposed a permanent and immediate change.

Dissent (Brennan, White, Marshall, JJ.). The Contract Clause is simply an adjunct to the currency provisions of Article I, Section 10 and was intended only to prevent alteration of contracts that relieved one party of the duty to pay a debt. To "impair" a contract is not to add duties but to take away duties. Creating a previously nonexistent duty, as the Minnesota law does, is not an impairment of a contract but a valid exercise of the state's police power. The effect of the Court's adoption of these vague testing criteria, which are arguably satisfied by the statute in any case, is to invite judicial discretion to protect property interests that happen to appeal to them. The Contract Clause should simply not apply to laws that create new rights.

6. **Modern Trend.** Despite the apparent revival of the Contract Clause in *United States Trust Co.* and *Spannaus, supra,* the Court generally defers to state power. In *Energy Reserves Group v. Kansas Power & Light Co.,* 459 U.S. 400 (1983), the Court applied a three-part test. If the state substantially impairs a contractual relationship, it must have a significant and legitimate public purpose for so doing. If it does, and the contractual adjustment is reasonable and appropriate, the courts will defer to the state unless the state itself is a party to the contract. In *Exxon Corp. v. Eagerton,* 462 U.S. 176 (1983), the Court rejected a Contract Clause challenge to a law that prohibited oil and gas producers from passing through to purchasers an increase in the severance tax, thereby preventing producers from taking advantage of existing contract provisions for such a pass-through. The Court held that the alleged impairment of contractual obligations was incidental to a generally applicable rule of conduct and not a direct attack on the original contracts. The law applied to all producers, not just those with pass-through provisions in their contracts. The law was not constitutionally different from laws regulating rates, which override contractual prices.

VII. PROTECTION OF INDIVIDUAL RIGHTS: DUE PROCESS, THE BILL OF RIGHTS, AND NONTEXTUAL CONSTITUTIONAL RIGHTS

A. FOURTEENTH AMENDMENT DUE PROCESS

1. **Meaning of Due Process.** The Fourteenth Amendment Due Process Clause prevents any state from depriving any person of life, liberty, or property without "due process" of law. The effect of this clause on economic regulation has been discussed *supra*. Today, however, the clause is probably most meaningful as a protection of individual rights. The scope of the clause in this area has changed greatly over the years.

2. **Incorporation Doctrine.** Whether the Due Process Clause incorporated rights guaranteed at the federal level by the Bill of Rights is an important question. Some commentators and judges argued for total incorporation; *i.e.,* the Bill of Rights should apply fully to state action. Others argued that "due process" included only "fundamental" principles of liberty. The Supreme Court has consistently held that the Fourteenth Amendment only incorporates the Bill of Rights on a selective basis, although to date all provisions of the Bill of Rights have been incorporated except the Second, Third, and Seventh Amendments and the Grand Jury Clause of the Fifth Amendment. The concept of due process is not limited to the protections in the Bill of Rights, however.

   a. **Right to trial by jury incorporated.** In *Duncan v. Louisiana*, 391 U.S. 145 (1968), the Court stated that the right of trial by jury in serious criminal cases is fundamental to the American scheme of justice and qualifies for protection under the Due Process Clause of the Fourteenth Amendment against violation by the states. After discussing the increase in the selective incorporation of other guarantees of the Bill of Rights into the Due Process Clause, the Court held the Sixth Amendment guarantee of a right to jury trial applicable through the Fourteenth Amendment to state criminal cases which, if tried in a federal court, would be covered.

3. **Bodily Extractions and the Incorporation Doctrine.**

   a. **Introduction.** The relationship between the Due Process Clause and the specific protections of the Bill of Rights is best illustrated when an issue can be resolved through application of either provision. The Bill of Rights protects a person against "unreasonable searches and seizures" and against being forced to be "a witness against himself." These provisions are more specific than the Due Process Clause, but may not be enough by themselves to resolve issues arising, for example, from forced bodily extractions by police to obtain evidence.

b.   Forced stomach pumping--

Rochin v. California, 342 U.S. 165 (1952).

Facts. Police illegally entered Rochin's (D's) bedroom and saw two capsules on his nightstand. D took the capsules and swallowed them. The officers tried to retrieve the capsules. When they could not do so, they took D to the hospital and forcibly pumped D's stomach to obtain the capsules, which subsequent testing showed to contain narcotics. This evidence was used in a state court to convict D. D appeals.

Issue. May the police use forcible tactics to extract evidence by pumping the stomach of a suspect?

Held. No. Conviction reversed.

♦   If the methods of obtaining evidence "shock hardened sensibilities," as they did here, the evidence must be excluded under the Due Process Clause. Due process cannot be defined precisely, but it means that convictions cannot be brought about by methods that offend a sense of justice.

♦   Coerced confessions cannot be used as evidence, even if the statements are proven true by other evidence, because such coercion offends the community's sense of fair play and decency. To permit the brutal police conduct here would give brutality the cloak of law, thereby discrediting the law.

Concurrence (Black, J.). The Due Process Clause incorporates the Fifth Amendment's protection against compelled self-incrimination, and forced extraction of evidence such as occurred here is therefore unconstitutional. It is better to adhere to such specific guarantees in the Bill of Rights than to nebulous Fourteenth Amendment due process concepts.

Concurrence (Douglas, J.). The Fifth Amendment should apply to the states as well as the federal government. To rely on due process instead of the Fifth Amendment makes the law turn not on the Constitution but on the idiosyncrasies of the Justices on the Supreme Court.

---

c.   **Blood samples.** The Court permitted state police to take a blood sample from an unconscious person at an automobile accident scene. The person was convicted based on the blood test that showed intoxication. [Breithaupt v. Abram, 352 U.S. 432 (1957)] The majority deemed this a slight intrusion outweighed by the interests in scientific determination of intoxication, while the dissenters could not distinguish the case from *Rochin, supra*. Later, the Court upheld the taking of a blood sample from an injured person over his objection, again to prove intoxication. [Schmerber v. California, 384 U.S. 757 (1966)] By this time, the Court had held that the Fifth Amendment applied to the states, yet the situation in *Schmerber* satisfied the Fifth Amendment requirements.

4. **Criminal Procedure and Retroactivity.**

a. **Introduction.** The Court's decisions on matters of criminal procedure often drastically affect criminal prosecutions. Thus, it can be a determinative factor if a particular decision is applied retroactively, especially for those persons previously convicted. The Court bases its retroactivity decisions on the following factors:

1) **Effect on truth-finding.** If the new constitutional procedural requirement is intended to promote the truth-finding function of criminal procedure and raises questions about the accuracy of previous guilty verdicts, it will be given retroactive effect. Otherwise, the Court will consider two other factors.

2) **Reliance.** The degree to which police have relied on the existing procedural standards is one factor.

3) **Effect.** The practical effect a retroactive application would have upon the administration of justice is the other factor.

b. **Applications.**

1) **Exclusionary rule applied to the states.** In *Mapp v. Ohio*, 367 U.S. 643 (1961), the Court held that the Fourth Amendment's protection against unreasonable searches and seizures was incorporated by the Fourteenth Amendment so as to require state courts to exclude evidence obtained by unlawful searches and seizures. The ruling was not applied retroactively to final state convictions because the purpose of the exclusionary rule, deterrence of lawless police action, would not be promoted by a retroactive application, since any police violations would already have occurred. Also, the rule has no bearing on guilt.

2) **Right to counsel.** In *Gideon v. Wainwright*, 372 U.S. 335 (1963), the Court held that all defendants in felony prosecutions were entitled to counsel, and if they could not afford one themselves, the state must provide one. This holding was given complete retroactive effect because when a defendant had not been represented by counsel, it was impossible to tell whether his case was adequately presented and thus whether he was innocent.

3) **Comment on defendant's failure to testify.** The Court held that the Fifth Amendment's privilege against self-incrimination forbids adverse comment by a judge or prosecutor on a defendant's failure to testify, and that this applies to the states. [Griffin v. California, 380 U.S. 609 (1965)] However, the rule was not applied retroactively because the privilege against self-incrimination is not intended to protect the innocent from conviction, but to protect the individual's right to be let alone. The states had also relied on the existing rule in good faith for over 50 years.

4) *Miranda* **warning.** The *Miranda* rights case, *Miranda v. Arizona*, 384 U.S. 436 (1966), was applied only to those cases in which the trial began after the date of the *Miranda* decision. The Court reasoned that the voluntariness of confessions was already a basis for challenge, based on the totality of the circumstances of the interrogation. *Miranda* provided new safeguards, but existing challenges could be resolved through an involuntariness claim.

5) **Right to pretrial counsel.** In *United States v. Wade*, 388 U.S. 218 (1967), and *Gilbert v. California*, 388 U.S. 263 (1967), the Court granted the right to counsel at certain pretrial events such as line-ups. These holdings applied only to confrontations for identification purposes conducted after the date of the decisions, thus indicating the importance of police reliance on existing procedures.

6) **Application to cases in progress.** In *Shea v. Louisiana*, 470 U.S. 51 (1985), the Court held that changes in constitutional law, such as a suspect's right not to be interrogated once he has requested counsel, should apply to any defendants whose cases are still on direct review. The changed law would not apply to collateral review, however, in the interests of finality.

B. THE RIGHT OF PRIVACY

1. **Introduction.** Although substantive due process no longer imposes any serious restraints on economic regulations, the Court has revived the notion as a means of protecting certain fundamental personal rights not specifically enumerated in the Constitution, including the right of privacy. Early cases began to recognize privileges recognized at common law but not specifically mentioned in the Constitution.

   a. **Family.** In *Meyer v. Nebraska*, 262 U.S. 390 (1923), the Court recognized the rights to marry, rear children, and acquire useful knowledge as essential to the liberty protected by due process.

   b. **Education.** In *Pierce v. Society of Sisters*, 268 U.S. 510 (1925), the Court invalidated a state law requiring attendance at public school as violative of parents' liberty to direct the education of their children.

c. **Procreation.** In *Skinner v. Oklahoma*, 316 U.S. 535 (1942), the Court held that mandatory sterilization of certain felonious habitual criminals violated due process because it included relatively minor offenders and excluded major offenders, and because it involved a basic familial right.

2. **Fundamental Privacy Rights.** The right of privacy is nowhere mentioned in the Constitution. However, the Fourth and Fifth Amendments protect against invasion of privacy by search and seizure. The right of personal choice in matters of marriage and the bearing and rearing of children is so fundamental to society that it is afforded protection. Some consider this right to be protected by the Ninth Amendment, others by the "penumbra" of the Bill of Rights.

   a. **Marital privacy within the Bill of Rights--**

Griswold v. Connecticut, 381 U.S. 479 (1965).

Facts. Griswold (D), the Executive Director of Planned Parenthood in Connecticut and the organization's Medical Director for New Haven, gave information, instruction, and medical advice about contraception to married persons. D was convicted as an accessory to the crime of using contraceptives in violation of a Connecticut (P) statute prohibiting all such use. The conviction was upheld in all the state courts. D appeals.

Issue. Does a constitutional right of privacy exist that prohibits states from making use of contraceptives by a married couple a crime?

Held. Yes. Conviction reversed.

- The specific guarantees in the Bill of Rights have penumbras, or peripheral rights, that make the specific rights more secure. A right of educational choice has been noted in earlier cases, such as *Pierce* and *Meyer, supra,* even though it is not mentioned in the Constitution, because it is a peripheral right without which the specific First Amendment rights would be less secure.

- Various guarantees in the Bill of Rights create zones of privacy. The First Amendment protects the right of association with the related privacy. The Third Amendment protects the privacy of the home against quartering of soldiers. The Fourth and Fifth Amendments protect other facets of privacy, including the sanctity of the home. The Ninth Amendment protects rights retained by the people.

- This case involves a relationship lying within the zone of privacy created by several fundamental constitutional guarantees. The law at issue has a maximum destructive impact on that relationship. The privacy of marriage is older than the Bill of Rights. The association of marriage is for as noble a purpose as any involved in prior decisions protecting the right of association.

Concurrence (Goldberg, J., Warren, C.J., Brennan, J.). The Ninth Amendment expressly recognized fundamental personal rights not specifically mentioned in the United States Constitution. In determining which rights are fundamental, judges must look to the traditions and collective conscience of the people. Privacy in the marital relation is clearly one of these basic personal rights "retained by the people." The Court's holding does not interfere with a state's proper regulation of sexual promiscuity or misconduct, such as adultery and homosexuality.

Concurrence (Harlan, J.). The Fourteenth Amendment's Due Process Clause independently requires rejection of the Connecticut statute without reference to the Bill of Rights. The incorporation doctrine should not be used to restrict the reach of the Due Process Clause. (In his dissent in *Poe v. Ullman*, 367 U.S. 497 (1961), Justice Harlan argued that if the Due Process Clause were merely a procedural safeguard, it would be no protection against legislation that could destroy the enjoyment of life, liberty, and property, even through the fairest procedures. He argued that the meaning of due process is based on a balance between the demands of organized society and respect for individual liberty, guided by tradition, good judgment, and restraint.)

Concurrence (White, J.). Application of the law to married couples deprives them of "liberty" without due process of law.

Dissent (Black, Stewart, JJ.). While the law is offensive, it is not prohibited by any specific constitutional provision and therefore must be upheld. Constitutional amendments, not judge-made alterations, are the correct means of modernizing the Constitution.

Dissent (Stewart, Black, JJ.). The law is uncommonly silly since it is obviously unenforceable, but there is no general right of privacy found in the Constitution, so we cannot hold that it violates the Constitution.

Comment. More recently, the Court has simply held that the right of personal privacy is implicit in the concept of "liberty" within the protection of the Fourteenth Amendment Due Process Clause—*i.e.,* it is one of those basic human rights that are of "fundamental" importance in our society. [Roe v. Wade, *infra*]

---

    b.   **Further development of substantive due process.** Regardless of its source, the right of privacy is regarded as a fundamental right for due process purposes, which means that regulation in these areas can only be justified by a compelling state interest. The right of privacy protects the individual interest in avoiding disclosure of personal matters and the interest in independently making certain kinds of important decisions.

        1)   **Contraceptives.** In *Eisenstadt v. Baird*, 405 U.S. 438 (1972), the Court held that the decision whether to use contraceptives was

one of individual privacy; thus, the right belongs to single as well as married persons. In *Carey v. Population Services International*, 431 U.S. 678 (1977), the Court held that a state could not prohibit distribution of nonmedical contraceptives to adults except through licensed pharmacists, nor prohibit sales of such contraceptives to persons under age 16 who did not have approval of a licensed physician.

3. **The Abortion Issue.**

a. **Introduction.** It is currently held that a woman's decision to terminate her pregnancy is within her constitutionally protected right of privacy, and cannot be made conditional on parental or spousal consent. However, at some point during pregnancy, the state's interests in protecting the mother's life and in protecting prenatal life become sufficiently "compelling" to justify state regulation of abortion.

b. **Basic constitutional rule on abortion--**

Roe v. Wade, 410 U.S. 113 (1973).

Facts. Roe (P), unmarried and pregnant, sought declaratory and injunctive relief against Wade (D), a county district attorney, to prevent enforcement of Texas criminal abortion statutes. The district court invalidated the statutes.

Issue. May a state constitutionally make it a crime to procure an abortion except to save the mother's life?

Held. No. Judgment affirmed.

♦ P claims a constitutional right to terminate her pregnancy, based on the Fourteenth Amendment concept of personal "liberty," the Bill of Rights penumbras, and the Ninth Amendment. D claims a state interest in regulating medical procedures to insure patient safety and in protecting prenatal life.

♦ The right of privacy generally relates to marriage, procreation, and contraception, and includes the abortion decision, but is not without restraint based on the state's compelling interests. The state's interest in prenatal life cannot be based on the fetus's right to life, for a fetus cannot be considered a "person" in the constitutional sense. Unborn children have never been recognized in any area of the law as persons in the whole sense. However, the pregnant woman cannot be isolated in her privacy. The state may decide that at some point in time another interest, that of health of the mother or that of potential human life, becomes significantly involved. The woman's right of privacy must be measured accordingly.

♦ The state's interest in the health of the mother becomes "compelling" at approximately the end of the first trimester, prior to which mortality in abortion is less than mortality in normal childbirth. Only from this point forward may the state regulate the abortion procedure as needed to preserve and protect maternal health.

♦ The state's interest in potential life becomes "compelling" at viability. A state interested in protecting fetal life after viability may proscribe abortion except when necessary to preserve the life or health of the mother.

♦ The Texas statute challenged here is overbroad and cannot be upheld.

Concurrence (Stewart, J.). The Court has generally recognized freedom of personal choice in matters of marriage and family life as a liberty protected by the Fourteenth Amendment. The Texas statute directly infringes on that right and is correctly invalidated.

Concurrence (Douglas, J.). The present statute has struck the balance between the woman's and the state's interest wholly in favor of the latter. It is overbroad.

Dissent (White, Rehnquist, JJ.). There is nothing in the language or history of the Constitution to support the Court's judgment. The Court apparently values the convenience of the pregnant mother more than the continued existence and development of the life or potential life that she carries. This issue should be left with the people and to the political processes the people have devised to govern their affairs.

Dissent (Rehnquist, J.). An abortion is not "private" in the ordinary use of this word. The Court seems to define "privacy" as a claim of liberty from unwanted state regulation of consensual transactions, protected by the Fourteenth Amendment. But that liberty is not guaranteed absolutely against deprivation, only against deprivation without due process of law. The traditional test is whether the law has a rational relation to a valid state objective, but this test could not justify the Court's outcome. Instead, the Court adopts the "compelling state interest test," which is more appropriate to a legislative judgment than to a judicial one. The Court's conclusions are more like judicial legislation than determination of the intent of the drafters of the Fourteenth Amendment. Furthermore, the fact that most states have had restrictions on abortion for over a century indicates that the asserted right to an abortion is not so universally accepted as P claims.

c. **Companion case to *Roe*--**

Doe v. Bolton, 410 U.S. 179 (1973).

Facts. Doe (P) and other interested parties challenged the Georgia abortion statutes, which made abortion a criminal offense except when pregnancy would endanger the mother's life or health or resulted from rape, or when the fetus would very likely have severe defects at birth. Even in these circumstances, several conditions had to be met to legalize the abortion, of which the lower court found all but two to be valid. P appeals.

Issue. Must state regulation of abortion be closely related to achievement of valid state objectives in order to withstand a Fourteenth Amendment challenge?

Held. Yes. Judgment modified and affirmed. P challenged three procedural requirements and one residence requirement:

♦ The law required that all legal abortions be performed in accredited hospitals. However, the state made no showing that alternative facilities were incapable, and had no such requirement for nonabortion surgery. The requirement does not reasonably relate to valid state objectives. Additionally, it does not exclude the first trimester.

♦ All legal abortions were to be certified by a hospital abortion committee, yet any hospital or employee could refuse to participate in abortion. Also, medical judgment was necessary prior to committee approval. The condition is redundant and unnecessary.

♦ Separate confirmation by two doctors was required, but the judgment of a licensed attending physician should be adequate. The condition unduly infringes upon the physician's right to practice, without being rationally connected to the patient's need.

---

d. **Government refusal to pay for abortions.** Despite its strict scrutiny of regulation of abortion, the Court has held that the government may choose not to fund abortions.

1) **1977 cases.** *Maher v. Roe*, 432 U.S. 464 (1977), was the first major case in this area. The state had excluded nontherapeutic abortions from its Medicaid-funded program, although it did cover childbirth. The Court applied a rationality standard of review instead of strict scrutiny. The Court held that *Roe v. Wade* did not preclude the states from favoring childbirth over abortion, as long as they did not unduly interfere with the woman's freedom to choose an abortion. The dissent argued that the exclusion effectively forced indigent women to bear children instead of procuring a desired abortion. *Beal v. Doe*, 432 U.S. 438 (1977), and *Poelker v. Doe*, 432 U.S. 519 (1977), applied the same rationale to other programs.

2)   Public funding of medically necessary abortions--

Harris v. McRae, 448 U.S. 297 (1980).

Facts. The Medicaid Act, which mandates compliance with all its requirements by all states that elect to participate in its reimbursement program, was amended annually by various Hyde amendments, which denied public funding for certain medically necessary abortions. McRae (P), a Medicaid recipient in the first trimester of pregnancy who sought an abortion, sued for an injunction against enforcement of the restriction. The district court found all versions of the Hyde amendment unconstitutional. Harris (D), the Secretary of Health, Education, and Welfare, appeals.

Issue. May Congress, consistent with the Due Process Clause, deny public funding for certain medically necessary abortions while funding substantially all other medical costs, including costs of carrying pregnancy to term?

Held. Yes. Judgment reversed.

♦   A law is presumptively unconstitutional if it impinges on a recognized constitutional right. P asserts that *Roe v. Wade* recognized a constitutional right to the liberty to choose whether to terminate a pregnancy. However, a legitimate state interest in protecting potential human life was also recognized. That case placed limits on the state's ability to interfere with that choice.

♦   Here, P contests a completely different form of activity—state encouragement of an alternative activity consonant with legislative policy. *Roe v. Wade* recognized no constitutional entitlement to the financial resources needed to pursue the protected choice, and no such entitlement exists.

♦   P contends that the Hyde amendments tend to establish certain religious doctrines, in violation of the Establishment Clause. However, the fact that a statute coincides with a religious tenet does not, by itself, show an establishment of any religion.

♦   A classification is unconstitutional if based on "suspect" criteria, or if not rationally related to a legitimate government objective. Earlier cases such as *Maher v. Roe, supra*, have held that poverty, standing alone, is not a suspect classification. The amendments do clearly bear a rational relationship to the legitimate interest in protecting the potential life of the fetus. Therefore, there is no denial of equal protection.

Concurrence (White, J.). *Roe v. Wade* recognized the right to choose to undergo an abortion without coercive interference by the government. There is no such official interference here.

Dissent (Brennan, Marshall, Blackmun, JJ.). The amendments intrude upon the constitutionally protected decision of abortion by, in reality, coercing indigent pregnant women to bear children they would otherwise choose not to have.

Dissent (Marshall, J.). The amendments deny the constitutional right of choice to poor women at the cost of serious and long-lasting health damage.

Dissent (Stevens, J.). The government rules with partiality when it denies otherwise available medical benefits to a woman solely to further an interest in potential life, at the risk of that woman's health.

---

e. **Third-party consent.** In *Planned Parenthood v. Danforth*, 428 U.S. 52 (1976), the Court held that a state could not require a spouse's consent to an abortion, nor could it require parental consent. However, in *Planned Parenthood v. Ashcroft*, 462 U.S. 476 (1983), the Court held that a state could require authorization from a juvenile court as an alternative to parental consent.

f. **Erosion of *Roe*--**

Webster v. Reproductive Health Services, 492 U.S. 490 (1989).

Facts. Missouri adopted a statute that prohibits the use of public employees and facilities to perform or assist abortions not necessary to save the mother's life, prohibits the use of public resources to encourage or counsel a woman to have such an abortion, and requires a physician who has reason to believe a woman seeking an abortion is 20 or more weeks pregnant to perform tests to determine whether the fetus is viable. Reproductive Health Services (P) challenged the statute. The court of appeals held that these provisions were unconstitutional under *Roe v. Wade*. Webster (D) appeals.

Issue. May a state disregard the *Roe* trimester approach in regulating abortion?

Held. Yes. Judgment reversed.

◆ The statute includes a preamble stating that the "life of each human being begins at conception." While a state may not justify an otherwise invalid abortion regulation by adopting a specific view about when life begins, the language of the preamble here has not been used to restrict P's activities and need not be reviewed for constitutionality.

◆ The restriction on the use of public resources to perform an abortion is permissible. In *McRae*, the Court noted that Congress's refusal to fund abortions left an indigent woman with at least the same range of choices in deciding whether to obtain an abortion as she would have had if Congress had not subsidized any medical care. The same logic applies here—if a state is free to refuse to fund abortions, it is also free to deny the use of public facilities and employees to perform abortions.

◆ The viability-testing provision of the statute promotes the state's interest in potential human life; it creates a presumption of viability at 20 weeks that must be rebutted by the physician before performing an abortion. The only problem with this requirement is that it does not fit within the trimester approach adopted in *Roe*. The trimester approach has proven unworkable in practice, is not found in the Constitution, and has generated a series of legal rules that resemble a code of regulations, not a body of constitutional doctrine. Accordingly, the trimester approach of *Roe* is no longer binding.

◆ The testing requirement here is reasonably designed to ensure that abortions are not performed when the fetus is viable. Because this end is legitimate, the requirement is constitutional.

◆ Although this holding will permit governmental regulation of abortion that would have been prohibited under *Akron* and other cases, the goal of constitutional adjudication is to maintain a proper balance between that which the Constitution puts beyond the reach of the democratic process and that which it does not. The Court does not sit to remove politically divisive issues from the legislative process.

Concurrence (O'Connor, J.). The Missouri statute is not inconsistent with *Thornburgh*, which recognized that it is not constitutionally impermissible for a state to adopt regulations designed to protect its interest in potential life when viability is possible. This statute also differs from *Akron's* hospitalization requirement, which was an unnecessary and heavy burden. There is no reason to reevaluate *Roe*.

Concurrence (Scalia, J.). This opinion needlessly prolongs the Court's self-awarded sovereignty over a field it should not be in, because the answers to the questions posed are political and not judicial. *Roe* must be addressed because it is the only benchmark available. There are compelling reasons to go beyond this narrow ruling and address the entire *Roe* decision. If the issue is whether the Missouri statute contravenes *Roe*, we should examine *Roe*, not the contravention.

Dissent (Blackmun, Brennan, Marshall, JJ.). The plurality's judgment incites disregard for the law and our prior decisions. There was no need to reconsider the *Roe* framework in this case. The plurality threatens the hopes and visions of every woman in this country who had come to believe that the Constitution guaranteed her the right to exercise some control over her unique ability to bear children.

Concurrence and dissent (Stevens, J.). The preamble to this statute serves no identifiable secular purpose and therefore violates the Establishment Clause. It also implicates the privacy right to use contraceptives, in violation of *Griswold*.

———

g. **Parental notification.** In *Hodgson v. Minnesota*, 497 U.S. 417 (1990), four Justices held that a state may not preclude an abortion by an unemancipated minor unless both parents are notified 48 hours in advance. Four other Justices approved a "bypass" alternative that provided that if the basic requirement were judicially enjoined, the same requirement would be effective unless the pregnant woman received a court order permitting the abortion without notice because either (i) the minor was mature and could give informed consent, or (ii) the abortion without notification would be in her best interests. Justice O'Connor cast the deciding vote by joining each of the blocks, holding that the bare notification requirement was unduly burdensome because of the practical problems of notifying abusive, neglectful, or separated or divorced parents. She determined that the interference with the internal operation of the family is avoided by the judicial bypass alternative. Justice Scalia continued to "dissent from this enterprise of devising an Abortion Code."

> h.   **Regulation of abortion--**

Planned Parenthood of Southeastern Pennsylvania v. Casey, 505 U.S. 833 (1992).

Facts. Pennsylvania adopted an Abortion Control Act that required that a woman seeking an abortion must be given certain information at least 24 hours before the abortion; that the woman give informed consent prior to the abortion; that, if a minor, the woman obtain the informed consent of her parents unless a judicial bypass option is followed; that, if married, the woman certify she informed her husband; and that facilities providing abortion services must make certain reports about each abortion, including the woman's age, gestational age, type of abortion procedure, medical conditions and results, and weight of the aborted fetus. Compliance with the requirements is not required in certain medical emergencies. Planned Parenthood of Southeastern Pennsylvania (P) challenged the Act on its face by suing Casey (D), the governor. The district court held all the provisions unconstitutional, but the court of appeals upheld everything except the husband notification requirement. The Supreme Court granted certiorari.

Issue. May a state impose notification and consent requirements as prerequisites for obtaining an abortion?

Held. Yes. Judgment reversed in part.

♦   The three parts of the essential *Roe* holding are reaffirmed. These are: (i) the woman's right to have an abortion before viability without undue state interference; (ii) the state's power to restrict abortions after fetal viability, as long as there are exceptions to protect a woman's life or health; and (iii) the state's legitimate interest from the outset of the pregnancy in protecting the health of the woman and the life of the fetus that may become a child.

♦   Substantive due process claims require courts to exercise reasoned judgments, and the Court must define the liberty of all, not mandate a moral code. The

Constitution has been interpreted to protect personal decisions regarding marriage, procreation, and contraception. Defining one's own concept of existence, meaning, and the mystery of human life is at the heart of liberty. At the same time, abortion has consequences for persons other than the woman who is pregnant.

♦ *Roe* should be upheld under the principle of stare decisis because it has not proven unworkable, because people have relied on the availability of abortion, because under *Roe* women have been better able to participate equally in the economic and social life of the country, because no evolution of legal principle has left *Roe*'s doctrinal footings weaker than they were in 1973 when the decision was announced, and because there have been no changed circumstances or new factual understandings. Even if *Roe* is wrong, the error involves only the strength of the state interest in fetal protection, not the liberty of women. Overruling *Roe* simply because of a change in philosophical disposition would undermine the Court's legitimacy.

♦ Although *Roe* has been criticized for drawing lines, the Court must draw specific rules from the general standards in the Constitution. The trimester approach was not part of the essential holding in *Roe* and it both misconceived the nature of the pregnant woman's interest and undervalued the state's interest in potential life. It is therefore overruled and replaced with a line drawn only at viability. Under this approach, a law that serves a valid purpose not designed to strike at the right of abortion itself may be sustained even if it makes it more difficult or more expensive to obtain an abortion, unless the law imposes an undue burden on a woman's ability to make an abortion decision. Thus, the state may further its interest in potential life but cannot place a substantial obstacle in the path of a woman's choice.

♦ The state may adopt health regulations to promote the health or safety of a woman seeking an abortion. It may not prohibit any woman from making the ultimate decision to terminate her pregnancy before viability. After viability, the state may promote its interest in the potentiality of human life by regulating and even proscribing abortion except where it is necessary to preserve the life or health of the mother.

♦ With regard to the specific provisions of the Act, the definition of medical emergency does not impose an undue burden on a woman's abortion right. The informed consent requirement is also permissible because it furthers the legitimate purpose of reducing the risk that a woman may elect an abortion, only to discover later, with devastating psychological consequences, that her decision was not fully informed. The 24-hour waiting period does not impose substantial obstacles, and it is not unreasonable to conclude that the important decision will be more informed and deliberate if it follows some period of reflection. The exception for cases in which a physician reasonably believes that furnishing the information would have a severely adverse effect on the woman's physical or mental health accommodates the interest in allowing physicians to exercise their medical judgment.

♦ The spousal notification requirement does, however, impose an undue burden on a woman's choice to undergo an abortion and cannot be sustained. In well-functioning marriages, the spouses discuss important intimate decisions such as whether to bear a child, and the notification requirement adds nothing in such situations. However, millions of women are the victims of physical and psychological abuse from their husbands, and requiring spousal notification in these situations can be tantamount to preventing the woman from getting an abortion. The husband's interest in the life of the child his wife is carrying does not permit the state to empower him with a veto over the abortion decision. Men do not have the kind of dominion over their wives that parents have over their children.

♦ The parental consent provision has been sustained before, and provided that there is an adequate judicial bypass procedure, its constitutionality is reaffirmed. The recordkeeping and reporting requirements are also permissible, with the exception of whether the spouse was notified of the abortion.

Concurrence and dissent (Stevens, J.). The Court properly follows the principle that a developing organism that is not yet a "person" does not have a "right to life." The state's interest in protecting potential life is not grounded in the Constitution, but reflects humanitarian and pragmatic concerns, including the offense taken by a large segment of the population at the number of abortions performed in this country and third-trimester abortions specifically. But the woman's interest in liberty is constitutional; the Constitution would be violated as much by a requirement that all women undergo abortion as by an absolute ban on abortions. The 24-hour delay requirement should not be upheld because it presumes that the abortion decision is wrong and must be reconsidered. The state may properly require physicians to inform women of the nature and risks of the abortion procedure and the medical risks of carrying to term, but it should not be allowed to require that the woman be provided with materials designed to persuade her to choose not to undergo the abortion.

Concurrence and dissent (Blackmun, J.). The Court's decision preserves the liberty of women that is one vote away from being extinguished. The Court also leaves open the possibility that the regulations it now approves may in the future be shown to impose an unconstitutional burden.

Concurrence and dissent (Rehnquist, C.J., White, Scalia, Thomas, JJ.). *Roe* was wrongly decided, and it can and should be overruled consistently with the traditional approach to stare decisis in constitutional cases. Stare decisis is not a reason to retain *Roe*; the Court's legitimacy is enhanced by faithful interpretation of the Constitution. The Court's revised "undue burden" standard is an unjustified constitutional compromise that allows the Court to closely scrutinize all types of abortion regulations despite the lack of any constitutional authority to do so. The new "undue burden" approach is still an imposition on the states by the Court of a complex abortion code. Abortion involves the purposeful termination of potential life and is thus different in kind from the other areas of privacy recognized by the Court, including marriage, procreation, and contraception. Prohibitions on abortion have been part of the law of many of the states since before the Fourteenth Amendment was adopted; there is no deeply rooted tradition of unrestricted abortion in our history that justifies characterizing the right as "fundamental." A woman's interest in having an abortion is a form of liberty protected by the Due Process Clause, but states may regulate abortion procedures in ways rationally related to a legitimate state interest. The Act should be upheld in its entirety.

Concurrence and dissent (Scalia, J., Rehnquist, C.J., White, Thomas, JJ.). The states may permit abortion on demand, but the Constitution does not require them to do so. It is a legislative decision. The issue is not whether the right to an abortion is an absolute liberty or whether it is an important liberty to many women, but whether it is a liberty protected by the Constitution. It is not, because the Constitution says nothing about it and because long-standing traditions of American society have permitted it to be prohibited. Under the rational basis test, D's statute should be upheld. Instead, the Court perpetuates the premise of *Roe*, which is a value judgment, not a legal matter. The "undue burden" standard lacks meaningful content, and may be summed up by concluding that a state may regulate abortion only in such a way as to not reduce significantly its incidence. *Roe* nourished the deeply divisive issue of abortion by elevating it to the national level where it is much more difficult to resolve than it was at the state level. Political compromise is now impossible, and *Roe* has been a major factor in selecting Justices to the Court. The Court should not be concerned with predicting public perceptions but should do what is legally right by asking whether *Roe* was correctly decided and whether it has succeeded in producing a settled body of law. The answer to both questions is no, and *Roe* should therefore be overruled. The Court's reliance on value judgments instead of interpreting text has created political pressure directed to the Court, whereby various groups of people demonstrate to protest that the Court has not implemented the respective group's values.

———

i.   **Post-*Casey* anti-abortion measures--**

Stenberg v. Carhart, 530 U.S. 914 (2000).

Facts. Under *Roe v. Wade*, *supra*, and its progeny, the right to abortion varies with the viability of the fetus. Before fetal viability, a state law is unconstitutional if it imposes an "undue burden" on the woman's right to choose. Post-viability, the state's interest in promoting the potentiality of human life justifies greater regulation and even prohibition of abortion except where "necessary, in appropriate medical judgment, for the preservation of the [woman's] life or health." Nebraska adopted a statute that prohibited any "partial birth abortion" unless that procedure is necessary to save the woman's life. The statute defined "partial birth abortion" as a procedure in which the doctor "partially delivers vaginally a living unborn child before killing the unborn child," and defines the latter phrase to mean "intentionally delivering into the vagina a living unborn child, or a substantial portion thereof, for the purpose of performing a procedure that the person performing such procedure knows will kill the unborn child and does kill the unborn child." Violation of the law is a felony, and it provides for the automatic revocation of a convicted doctor's state license to practice medicine. Carhart (P), a Nebraska physician who performs abortions in a clinical setting, sought a declaration that the statute violates the Constitution. The district court held the statute unconstitutional. The eighth circuit affirmed. The Supreme Court granted certiorari.

Issue. May a state regulate abortion by banning a specified procedure if the statute has no exception for the health of the woman and would encompass an additional commonly performed procedure?

Held. No. Judgment affirmed.

♦   The differences between various abortion methods are critical in this case. During a pregnancy's second trimester (12 to 24 weeks), the most common abortion procedure is "dilation and evacuation" ("D&E"), which involves dilation of the cervix, removal of at least some fetal tissue using nonvacuum surgical instruments, and (after the 15th week) the potential need for instrumental dismemberment of the fetus or the collapse of fetal parts to facilitate evacuation from the uterus. When such dismemberment is necessary, it typically occurs as the doctor pulls a portion of the fetus through the cervix into the birth canal. The risks of mortality and complication that accompany D&E are significantly lower than those accompanying induced labor procedures (the next safest mid-second-trimester procedures).

♦   A variation of D&E, known as "intact D&E," is used after 16 weeks. It involves removing the fetus from the uterus through the cervix "intact," i.e., in one pass rather than several passes. The intact D&E proceeds in one of two ways, depending on whether the fetus presents head first or feet first. The feet-first method is known as "dilation and extraction" ("D&X"), more commonly called "partial birth abortion." The district court concluded that clear and convincing evidence established that the D&X procedure was superior to, and safer than, the D&E and other abortion procedures in some circumstances.

♦   The Nebraska statute lacks an exception for the preservation of the health of the woman. D claims that there is no need for a health exception because safe alternatives remain available and a ban on partial birth abortions would create no risk to women's health. However, the evidence showed that the D&X method could be safer than the D&E method in some cases. There are no definitive medical studies on this issue, so the state must provide a health exception to its regulation to avoid placing women at an unnecessary risk.

♦   D acknowledges that the statute would impose an "undue burden" if it applied to D&E procedures as well as to D&X. Because the statute refers to delivery into the vagina of a living fetus or "a substantial portion thereof," it encompasses a D&E procedure that involves a physician pulling an arm, leg, or other "substantial portion" of a still living fetus into the vagina before killing the fetus. Thus, the statute does not distinguish between D&E and D&X. Nebraska's Attorney General claims that his interpretation of the statute would mean that "a substantial portion" would mean "the child up to the head," but this interpretation is not controlling on the courts or law enforcement.

♦ Because all those who perform abortion procedures using the D&E method would fear prosecution, conviction, and imprisonment, the Nebraska law imposes an undue burden upon a woman's right to make an abortion decision.

Concurrence (Stevens, Ginsburg, JJ.). It is irrational for the state to conclude that either of these two equally gruesome procedures performed at a late stage of gestation is more akin to infanticide than the other.

Concurrence (Ginsburg, Stevens, JJ.). The statute imposes an undue burden because it prevents a woman from choosing the procedure her doctor reasonably believes will best protect her in the exercise of her constitutional liberty.

Dissent (Scalia, J.). Someday this decision will take its place alongside *Korematsu* and *Dred Scott*. This case represents a value judgment of the relative respect for the life of a partially delivered fetus and the freedom of the woman who gave it life to kill it. The majority value the former less or the latter more than the dissent. The decision about what limitations on abortion are "undue" should be left to the people of the various states.

Dissent (Kennedy, J., Rehnquist, CJ.). The majority's use of technical medical terms obscures for lay persons what this case is actually about. The D&E procedures P uses involve using instruments to grasp a portion of a developed and living fetus, such as a foot or hand, and then drag it out of the uterus into the vagina. He then tears this part away from the rest of the body, and the fetus often dies just as a human child would, by bleeding to death as it is torn limb from limb. In one case, removal of an arm did not result in death and the fetus was born as a living child with one arm. In the D&X procedure, the living fetus is delivered outside the uterus, where it may be moving on its own, with only the head remaining in utero. Then the abortionist tears open the skull with a pair of scissors and vacuums out the brain and other matter within the skull. In this case, the state has sought only to ban the D&X procedure. The majority in effect accepts P's argument that this ban does not further the state's legitimate interests because the D&E method can still be used and it is no less dehumanizing than the D&X method. The state should be allowed to find that the D&X procedure is not morally equivalent to the D&E procedure because it is more like infanticide. Substantial evidence supports the state's conclusion that its law denies no woman a safe abortion. And the state's own interpretation of its statute should be given deference.

Dissent (Thomas, J., Rehnquist, C.J., Scalia, J.). The *Casey* standard is not grounded in the Constitution, but is the product of its authors' own philosophical views about abortion. But given *Casey*, the majority now holds that states cannot constitutionally prohibit a method of abortion that millions of citizens find hard to distinguish from infanticide. Only in abortion cases does the majority disregard the basic principle that courts interpret statutes according to their plain meaning and do not strike down statutes susceptible of a narrowing construction. It is highly doubtful that this statute could be applied to ordinary D&E. And the state should not be required to include a health exception to this ban because there was no showing that any woman faced a significant health risk from the ban. In *Casey*, the majority stated that the states may express profound respect for fetal life, but the majority now prohibits 30 states from banning one rarely used form of abortion that they believe to border on infanticide.

---

4. **Family Arrangements and Parental and Marital Rights.**

   a. **Family living arrangements.**

      1) **Basic rule.** As discussed *supra*, the privacy of family life is a fundamental right. Numerous cases have raised questions about the scope of this aspect of privacy. The Court has continued to apply strict scrutiny to governmental interference with personal privacy in these areas.

      2) **Housing--**

Moore v. East Cleveland, 431 U.S. 494 (1977).

Facts. Moore (D) lived with her son and two grandsons, who were cousins. The city of East Cleveland (P) filed a criminal charge against D for her violation of a city ordinance restricting occupancy of a dwelling unit to members of a single family, defined by certain categories, none of which included D's arrangement. D moved to dismiss, but her motion was overruled, and she was convicted. The state courts upheld the conviction. D appeals.

Issue. May a local ordinance restrict occupation of dwelling units to certain specified categories of related individuals?

Held. No. Judgment reversed.

◆   The state courts based their decision on *Village of Belle Terre v. Boraas*, 416 U.S. 1 (1974). That case involved restrictions only on unrelated individuals.

◆   When the government intrudes on choices of family living arrangements, the legitimacy of the governmental interests and the effectiveness of the regulations must be carefully examined. This statute cannot stand such scrutiny since it only marginally, if at all, works to reduce overcrowding and traffic problems.

♦ P contends that a constitutional right to live together extends only to the nuclear family. Such legislative classifications are appropriate limits on substantive due process only if they reflect respect for and recognition of the basic values that underlie our society. The extended family has a strong tradition in our history, and the United States Constitution prohibits P from forcing all its people to live in certain narrowly defined family patterns.

Dissent (Stewart, Rehnquist, JJ.). The constitutionally protected freedom of association relates to promotion of speech, assembly, the press, or religion, not to an interest in the gratification, convenience, and economy of sharing the same residence. D's interest in sharing the dwelling cannot be equated with the fundamental decisions to marry and to bear and rear children, as the majority has done. P's line-drawing is no more onerous than other lines that have been upheld in earlier cases.

Dissent (White, J.). The Court ought not expand the substantive content of the Due Process Clause in order to strike down what it considers unfavorable legislation. The issue is whether there is actual deprivation of life, liberty, or property. The Due Process Clause should not be used to protect any right or privilege that the Court deems deeply rooted in the country's tradition from all but the most important state regulatory interests.

---

b. The right to marry--

Zablocki v. Redhail, 434 U.S. 374 (1978).

Facts. Redhail (P), a Wisconsin resident, was denied a marriage license for failure to comply with a Wisconsin statute requiring that an applicant who has a support obligation for a child not in his custody prove that the child is not a public charge and that he has complied with the support obligation. P challenged the statute and obtained declaratory and injunctive relief. Zablocki (D), the county clerk, appeals.

Issue. May a state protect the welfare of out-of-custody children by denying a marriage license to persons not fulfilling their support obligations to such children?

Held. No. Judgment affirmed.

♦ Marriage is a fundamental right, and significant interference with its exercise cannot be upheld unless closely tailored to effectuate sufficiently important state interests. Assuming the state's interests of protecting out-of-custody children and motivating applicants to fulfill prior support obligations are valid, the means used by the state unnecessarily impinge on the right to marry.

♦ The state's procedure relies on a collection device rationale that is inappropriate. The state has numerous other effective means for exacting compliance with support obligations that do not restrict the right to marry. In addition, the statute tends to impair an applicant's ability to improve his financial situation and thus improve his ability to meet prior support obligations.

Concurrence (Stewart, J.). The problem here is not discriminatory classifications but unwarranted encroachment on liberty protected by the Due Process Clause. The equal protection doctrine as applied here is no more than substantive due process by another name.

Concurrence (Powell, J.). The Court's rationale intrudes too broadly into the state's traditional power to regulate the marriage relation. This statute is improper only because it fails to provide for those without means to comply with child-support obligations.

---

c. **Rights of parents to make decisions concerning the care, custody, and control of their children.** *Troxel v. Granville*, 530 U.S. 57 (2000), involved a mother's challenge to a Washington statute that allowed anyone to petition for visitation rights at any time and authorized state superior courts to grant visitation when it would serve the best interest of the child. The Troxels had petitioned for the right to visit the two daughters of their deceased son. The girls' mother was not against all visitation, but she objected to the amount sought by the grandparents. After the superior court ordered more visitation than the mother thought was appropriate, the Washington Supreme Court struck down the statute, the court of appeals reversed, and the United States Supreme Court granted certiorari. The Court found that the Washington statute, as applied in this case, violated the mother's due process rights. The Court held that a judge may not override a fit parent's decision regarding third-party visitation merely because he feels that a "better" decision could be made or that visitation would be in the best interest of the child.

d. **Tradition and due process--**

Michael H. v. Gerald D., 491 U.S. 110 (1989).

Facts. California provided that a child born to a married woman living with her husband is presumed to be a child of the marriage. The presumption could be rebutted only in very limited circumstances, such as the impotence or sterility of the husband. Michael H. (P) claimed to be the father of Victoria, who was born to Carole D., who in turn was married to Gerald D. (D). P claimed that he had had an adulterous affair with Carole and that blood tests showed a 98.07% probability that he was the father. During the first three years of Victoria's life, she and Carole lived at times with P. P claimed that he had established a parental relationship with Victoria that was protected as a matter of substantive due process. The California courts rejected P's claim. P appeals.

Issue. May a state deny an adulterer's claim of paternity by applying a presumption that a child born to a married woman is the child of her husband?

Held. Yes. Judgment affirmed.

◆   P's argument is based on the premise that he has a constitutionally protected liberty interest in his relationship with Victoria. To be protected by the Due Process Clause, a liberty interest must not only be "fundamental" but also an interest traditionally protected by our society; *i.e.,* one so rooted in the traditions and conscience of our people as to be ranked as fundamental.

◆   There is no historical or precedential support for the power of a natural father to assert parental rights over a child born into a woman's existing marriage with another man. Thus, there is no basis for finding a fundamental right qualifying as a liberty interest.

Concurrence (O'Connor, Kennedy, JJ.). I agree with all of Justice Scalia's opinion except footnote 6.

Dissent (Brennan, Marshall, Blackmun, JJ.). In its attempt to limit the concept of liberty protected by the Due Process Clause, the Court seeks to tie the concept of liberty to "tradition." While tradition has been an important factor in due process cases, it is not the only factor. Several cases, including *Eisenstadt* and *Griswold*, recognized liberty interests that were not traditionally protected. The scope of the Due Process Clause is not limited to confirming the importance of interests already protected by a majority of the states.

Comment. The primary significance of this case is the dispute over footnote 6 of the Court's opinion, in which Justice Scalia stated that the Court should refer to the most specific level at which a relevant tradition protecting or denying protection to the asserted right can be identified. This would avoid the tendency toward arbitrary decisionmaking that results from permitting judges to base decisions on general traditions that provide imprecise guidance. Justices O'Connor and Kennedy, who concurred in the result but not with footnote 6, and Justices Brennan, Marshall and Blackmun, who dissented in the result and with footnote 6, would not confine due process analysis to the approach taken in footnote 6. Justice Scalia used the fact that O'Connor and Brennan reached opposite results by appealing to a broader tradition than he would have.

───────────────

5.   **Assisted Suicide.** In most states, patients may refuse even lifesaving medical treatment, or accept pain medication that can hasten death, but it is a crime to aid another to commit or attempt suicide. Many physicians assert that the assisted suicide ban prevents them from providing lethal medication for mentally competent, terminally ill patients who are suffering great pain and desire a doctor's help in taking their own lives, although it would be

consistent with the standards of their medical practices to provide this type of service.

a.   The right to die--

Cruzan v. Director, Missouri Department of Health, 497 U.S. 261 (1990).

Facts. Cruzan (P) was injured in an automobile accident and remained in a vegetative state, her body kept functioning by artificial nutrition and hydration procedures. P's parents asked that the medical procedures be terminated, which would cause P's death. When the hospital employees refused to do so without a court order, P's parents sued the Director, Missouri Department of Health (D) on P's behalf. At the trial, one of P's friends testified that P had said, prior to her accident, that she would not want to live if she became a "vegetable." Based on this evidence, the trial court granted P relief. The Missouri Supreme Court reversed on the ground that the evidence was insufficient to constitute clear and convincing proof of P's desire to have hydration and nutrition withdrawn. The Supreme Court granted certiorari.

Issue. May a state require proof by clear and convincing evidence of an incompetent patient's wishes as to the withdrawal of life-sustaining medical treatment?

Held. Yes. Judgment affirmed.

- ◆   The common law doctrine of informed consent to medical procedures, developed out of the law of battery, includes the right of a competent individual to refuse medical treatment. This right is a constitutionally protected liberty interest, and it may be assumed that a competent person has a constitutionally protected right to refuse lifesaving hydration and nutrition, but this right must be balanced against the relevant state interests.

- ◆   Missouri has determined that a surrogate may act on behalf of an incompetent patient such as P, but only if there is clear and convincing evidence of the incompetent's wishes as to the withdrawal of the treatment. Missouri has an important interest in the protection and preservation of human life. In this case, the choice between life and death is a deeply personal decision, and the state may safeguard the personal element by requiring a high standard of proof.

---

b.   Due process analysis--

Washington v. Glucksberg, 521 U.S. 702 (1997).

Facts. Washington (D) enacted a statute that prohibited assisting suicide. Glucksberg and other physicians (Ps) occasionally treated terminally ill, suffering patients and would assist these patients in ending their lives if not for D's ban on assisted suicide. Ps brought suit seeking a declaration that the statute violates the Fourteenth Amendment because Ps' patients have a liberty interest in a personal choice to commit physician-assisted suicide. The district court held the statute unconstitutional. The court of appeals initially reversed, but after an en banc hearing, affirmed the district court. The Supreme Court granted certiorari.

Issue. Is there a constitutional right to assistance in committing suicide?

Held. No. Judgment reversed.

♦ It is a crime to assist a suicide in almost every state, and almost every western democracy. This reflects the states' commitment to protect and preserve all human life. For over 700 years, the Anglo-American common law tradition has punished both suicide and assisting suicide.

♦ In modern times, the states' bans on assisted suicide have been reexamined and mostly reaffirmed. There have been modifications to reflect current medical technology, which can prolong life. For example, states permit "living wills," surrogate health care decisionmaking, and withdrawal or refusal of life-sustaining medical treatment. However, the states continue to prohibit assisted suicide. D's voters rejected a ballot initiative that would have permitted a form of physician-assisted suicide.

♦ The Court has previously applied the Due Process Clause so as to protect the right to marry, have children, educate one's children, enjoy marital privacy, use contraception, and have abortions. Under *Cruzan*, the Clause protects the traditional right to refuse unwanted lifesaving medical treatment. However, the extension of constitutional protection to an asserted right or liberty interest is only appropriate for those areas that are rooted in the nation's history and tradition, and even then only when there is a careful description of the asserted fundamental liberty interest.

♦ To recognize the right asserted by Ps, the Court would have to reverse centuries of legal doctrine and practice, including the policy choices of almost every state. In contrast, the right to refuse medication recognized in *Cruzan* reflected a long legal tradition. Forced medication was a battery at common law.

♦ Given that the right to assisted suicide is not a fundamental liberty interest, the Constitution still requires that D's ban be rationally related to legitimate government interests. That is satisfied here, where D has an interest in the preservation of human life, an interest in protecting the integrity and ethics of the medical profession, an interest in protecting vulnerable groups, and an interest in not opening the door to euthanasia, both voluntary and involuntary.

Concurrence (O'Connor, J.). There is no generalized right to "commit suicide." A terminal patient who suffers great pain may obtain medication to alleviate that suffering, even to the point of hastening death. Therefore, the state's interest in protecting those who are not truly competent or facing imminent death is sufficiently weighty to justify a prohibition against physician-assisted suicide. The democratic process will strike the proper balance in this area.

Concurrence (Stevens, J.). The value to others of a person's life is far too precious to allow the individual to claim a constitutional entitlement to complete autonomy in making a decision to end that life. But there may be situations where the individual's interest in choosing how to die might be paramount.

Concurrence (Souter, J.). The appropriate test would be to determine whether D's statute sets up an arbitrary imposition or a purposeless restraint contrary to the Due Process Clause. Substantive due process analysis requires a court to assess the relative weights of the contending interests. Statutes must give way when the legislation's justifying principle is so far from being commensurate with the individual interest as to be arbitrary or pointless. This case involves the right of a narrow class to help others in a narrow class under a set of limited circumstances. Ps note that D has largely repudiated the common law of suicide by decriminalizing suicide. A right to physician assistance in committing suicide is analogous to the right to physician assistance in abortion. D already allows doctors to administer pain relief medication that may hasten death. D could address its legitimate interests through a regulatory system.

Concurrence (Ginsburg, J.). I agree with Justice O'Connor.

Concurrence (Breyer, J.). Justice O'Connor's approach is persuasive. There may be a right to die with dignity, or a right to personal control over the manner of death, professional medical assistance, and the avoidance of unnecessary and severe physical suffering. Changes in medical technology may affect these types of cases in the future.

Comment. The Court noted that at one time, Oregon voters enacted a ballot initiative that legalized physician-assisted suicide. This prompted proposals in many other states. The Court specifically noted that its decision would allow the debate about physician-assisted suicide to continue.

---

c.   **Equal protection analysis--**

Vacco v. Quill, 521 U.S. 793 (1997).

Facts. New York made it a crime to assist suicide, but it was legal for a patient to refuse lifesaving medical care. Quill and other physicians and their patients (Ps) sued Vacco (D), the New York Attorney General, to challenge the ban on assisted suicide.

Ps claimed that the law violated equal protection because it gives different treatment to those competent, terminally ill patients who wish to hasten their deaths by self-administering prescribed drugs than it does to those who wish to hasten their deaths by directing the removal of life support systems. The district court upheld the law. The court of appeals reversed, finding a violation of equal protection because the unequal treatment was not rationally related to any legitimate state interests. The Supreme Court granted certiorari.

Issue. Does a ban on physician-assisted suicide violate the Equal Protection Clause?

Held. No. Judgment reversed.

♦ There is a clear distinction between assisting suicide and withdrawing life-sustaining treatment, and the distinction has been widely recognized in the medical and legal traditions. A patient who refuses life-sustaining medical treatment dies from the underlying disease or pathology, but a patient who ingests lethal medication dies from that medication. In the latter case, the doctor's intent is to end the patient's life, while in the former, it is merely to respect the patient's wishes. The law has long used a person's intent to distinguish between two acts that have the same result.

♦ The law does not treat people in the same class differently. Every competent person, regardless of physical condition, is entitled to refuse unwanted lifesaving medical treatment, and no one is permitted to assist suicide.

♦ The distinction between letting a patient die and making that patient die was reflected in *Cruzan*, which recognized not that patients have the right to hasten death but instead that patients have a right to bodily integrity and unwanted touching. The distinction between the two types of care is not arbitrary or irrational.

♦ D has the same reasons to recognize and act on this distinction as did Washington State in *Glucksberg*. These important public interests satisfy the constitutional requirement that the classification bear a rational relation to a legitimate end.

---

6.   **Sexual Lifestyles.**

   a.   **Introduction.** The Court has not expanded the right of privacy to every possible type of personal expression or association.

   b.   **Homosexuality--**

Bowers v. Hardwick, 478 U.S. 186 (1986).

Facts. Hardwick (P) was charged with committing sodomy with another adult male in P's bedroom in violation of a state law forbidding sodomy by any person. The district attorney decided not to pursue the case, but P sued, challenging the constitutionality of the statute as applied to consensual sodomy. The district court dismissed the suit, but the court of appeals reversed. The Supreme Court granted certiorari.

Issue. Does a person have a fundamental constitutional right to engage in consensual homosexual sodomy?

Held. No. Judgment reversed.

♦ Prior cases have recognized a right of privacy in matters of child rearing and education, family relationships, procreation, contraception, and abortion. None of those rights bears any resemblance to the right P claims to engage in homosexual sodomy. The precedent does not recognize a constitutional right to engage in any kind of private sexual conduct between consenting adults.

♦ Rights that qualify for heightened judicial protection are those fundamental liberties implicit in the concept of ordered liberty, such that neither liberty nor justice would exist without them, and those that are deeply rooted in the country's history and tradition. A right to homosexual sodomy falls within neither category. Sodomy is a common law offense that is still forbidden by 24 states. The Court must be prudent in expanding the substantive reach of the Due Process Clause.

♦ The fact that an offense takes place in the home does not make it immune from criminal sanction. Adultery, incest, and other sexual crimes may be punishable even when they are committed in a home. The *Stanley* case, *infra*, involved First Amendment freedoms and is distinguishable from this case.

Concurrence (Burger, C.J.). There is no such thing as a fundamental right to commit homosexual sodomy. The act has long been denounced as immoral. The states have legislative authority to forbid such conduct.

Concurrence (Powell, J.). P may have had an Eighth Amendment issue, since the statute permits a punishment of up to 20 years' imprisonment for a single act of private, consensual sodomy. However, that issue is not raised.

Dissent (Blackmun, Brennan, Marshall, Stevens, JJ.). P's claim that the statute impinges on his privacy and right of intimate association does not depend on his sexual orientation, because the statute does not apply only to homosexuals. The right of privacy extends to personal decisions such as how a person may define himself through sexual intimacy. There may be many "right" ways of conducting intimate sexual relationships and much of the richness of a relationship may come from the freedom an individual has to choose the form and nature of the intensely personal bond. Additionally, the right of an individual to conduct intimate relationships in the privacy of his own home is the heart of the Constitution's protection of privacy.

Dissent (Stevens, Brennan, Marshall, JJ.). The law applies as well to married persons, thereby affecting intimate decisions clearly protected by the Due Process Clause. Thus, the statute is overbroad at the least. The state cannot justify selectively applying the law to homosexuals.

---

c.   **Liberty interest in homosexual conduct--**

Lawrence v. Texas, 539 U.S. 558 (2003).

Facts. Police officers responding to a reported weapons disturbance entered an apartment where Lawrence resided. The officers found Lawrence and another man (Ds) engaging in a sexual act. Ds were arrested and convicted of "deviate sexual intercourse with a member of the same sex." Ds claimed that the applicable statute was unconstitutional under the Due Process Clause of the Fourteenth Amendment. The Texas state courts upheld the statute. The Supreme Court granted certiorari.

Issue. May a state criminalize private and consensual sexual activity between two men?

Held. No. Judgment reversed.

♦   In *Bowers v. Hardwick, supra,* the Court held that there was no fundamental right for homosexuals to engage in sodomy, so the Constitution did not prevent the states from making such activity illegal. This framing of the issue, however, limited the claim to the right to engage in certain sexual conduct. In reality, criminal statutes prohibiting certain sexual activity have more far-reaching consequences because they control a personal relationship that is within the liberty of persons to choose without being punished as criminals.

♦   The *Bowers* Court based its decision in part on proscriptions against homosexual conduct that have ancient roots. The historical premises relied on by the Court, however, have been reevaluated by scholars. The concept of the homosexual as being in a distinct category did not actually emerge until the late 19th century. Before that, sodomy laws were designed to prohibit non-procreative sexual activity, regardless of gender. Laws against same-sex couples were not enacted until the last third of the 20th century.

♦   The *Bowers* Court did note that societies have condemned homosexual conduct as immoral for many centuries. While many people may consider this a moral issue, the legal issue is whether the majority may use the power of the state to enforce these views on the whole society through the operation of the criminal law.

- In recent years, society has recognized that liberty gives substantial protection to adults in deciding how to conduct their private sex lives. The European Convention on Human Rights has been interpreted to preclude laws against consensual homosexual conduct in Europe, for example. Since the *Bowers* decision, 12 states have abandoned their laws against sodomy, and the remaining 13 states have a pattern of non-enforcement against consenting adults acting in private.

- *Romer v. Evans*, 517 U.S. 620 (1996), recognized that class-based legislation directed at homosexuals violates that Equal Protection Clause. This undermines the central holding of *Bowers* because the continued validity of *Bowers* demeans the lives of homosexual persons.

- The erosion of *Bowers* under *Romer*, the invalidity of many of the premises upon which *Bowers* was based, and the substantial criticism of *Bowers* by the states and the European Court of Human Rights suggest that *Bowers* should be overruled. It is time to recognize that *Bowers* was incorrectly decided, and it is hereby overruled.

Concurrence (O'Connor, J.). I do not join the Court in overruling *Bowers*, but I agree that the Texas statute here is unconstitutional under the Equal Protection Clause instead of the Due Process Clause. The Texas statute prohibits sodomy between homosexual partners, but not between opposite-sex partners. Texas has no legitimate state interest here, such as national security or preserving the institution of marriage.

Dissent (Scalia, J., Rehnquist, C.J., Thomas, J.). The Court has strongly rejected overruling *Roe v. Wade* out of *stare decisis* concerns, but the very conditions the Court finds applicable to *Bowers* also apply to *Roe*. The Court now allows us to overrule precedent if: (i) its foundations have been "eroded" by subsequent decisions; (ii) it has been subject to substantial and continuing criticism; and (iii) it has not induced individual or societal reliance that counsels against overturning. The Court's reasoning in this case calls into question laws against bigamy, prostitution, adultery, and related conduct. Until today, only fundamental rights qualify for heightened scrutiny protection, and all others may be abridged if the law is rationally related to a legitimate state interest. Homosexual sodomy is not such a fundamental right. The Court today effectively decrees the end of all morals legislation by holding that majoritarian sexual morality is not even a legitimate state interest.

Dissent (Thomas, J.). The Texas law is uncommonly silly and a waste of law enforcement resources, but there is no constitutional right of privacy that invalidates such laws.

Comment. The *Lawrence* opinion is the first Supreme Court majority opinion to cite an authority from European law as a factor in the decision. The Court took judicial notice of the laws in Europe, apparently concluding that it was useful to determine the extent of the governmental interest in proscribing such conduct.

C. THE RIGHT TO TRAVEL

1. **Interstate Travel.** The right to travel freely from state to state is constitutionally protected and is virtually unqualified, although the exact constitutional source for this protection is unclear.

2. **International Travel.** The right of international travel is not as absolute as interstate travel and may be regulated within the bounds of the traditional due process standard. Reasonable area restrictions for passports have been upheld because of substantial justifications of national security and foreign policy. [Zemel v. Rusk, 381 U.S. 1 (1965)] However, in *Aptheker v. Secretary of State*, 378 U.S. 500 (1964), the Court held unconstitutional a law forbidding issuing passports to members of organizations required to register as communist organizations. The law was overbroad since it applied to persons who may not be aware that they are members of an organization required to register. The law was also unrelated to the purposes or the areas of travel; it applied to all international travel.

3. **Modern Application to Passport Laws--**

Haig v. Agee, 453 U.S. 280 (1981).

Facts. Agee (P), a former CIA employee, began exposing undercover CIA agents in foreign countries. Haig (D), the Secretary of State, revoked P's United States passport, based on a regulation permitting revocation where the citizen's activities abroad "are causing or likely to cause serious damage to the national security or the foreign policy of the United States." D gave P a hearing and an opportunity for a prompt postrevocation hearing. P challenged the regulation as unauthorized by Congress and unconstitutional. The lower courts granted P relief. D appeals.

Issue. May the government revoke a passport based on national security and foreign policy considerations?

Held. Yes. Judgment reversed.

♦   Congress granted D broad authority to grant and issue passports. The challenged regulation is not inconsistent with anything Congress has done. Congressional silence is not to be equated with disapproval in foreign policy and national security matters.

♦   P is not penalized for his beliefs and speech but for his actions, which present a serious danger to American officials abroad and to the national security. Revocation of P's passport is an inhibition of action, not of speech.

♦   The right to hold a passport is subordinate to national security and foreign policy considerations and is subject to reasonable governmental regulation. D can take action to insure that P does not exploit the United States's sponsorship of his travel, and a postrevocation hearing satisfies due process.

Dissent (Brennan, Marshall, JJ.). Prior cases do not hold that a long-standing executive policy or construction is sufficient proof that Congress has implicitly authorized the secretary's action. An administrative practice must be demonstrated.

D. CRUEL AND UNUSUAL PUNISHMENT

1. **Introduction.** The Eighth Amendment prohibits infliction of cruel and unusual punishments. This protection has been held to be incorporated in the Fourteenth Amendment. [*See* Francis v. Reseweber, 329 U.S. 459 (1947)] The prohibition is primarily directed at the method or kind of punishment imposed for violation of criminal statutes, but the Court has left open the issue of whether it applies to certain noncriminal situations, such as involuntary confinement in mental or juvenile institutions.

2. **The Death Penalty.** A plurality of the Supreme Court has held that the death penalty is not per se cruel and unusual punishment. However, any arbitrary or capricious imposition of the penalty is unconstitutional.

    a. **Requirement of standards for the jury--**

Furman v. Georgia, 408 U.S. 238 (1972).

Facts. Furman and two others (Ds) had been convicted of murder and rape in Georgia and Texas and were sentenced to death after a jury trial. In each state, the judge or jury had unguided discretion to impose the death penalty. Thirty-seven other states had similar capital punishment statutes. Ds appeal their sentences.

Issue. Is the death penalty cruel and unusual punishment when it is administered in an arbitrary and random way?

Held. Yes. Judgments reversed.

Concurrence (Stewart, J.). The decision does not say that capital punishment is unconstitutional for all crimes and under all circumstances. The instinct for retribution must be recognized by the criminal law in order to preserve a stable society. But in these cases, the death sentences are cruel and unusual because of the randomness with which they are imposed.

Concurrence (White, J.). In the dictionary sense, the death penalty is cruel, but it is not in the constitutional sense as long as it is justified by the social ends it serves.

Because the penalty is so seldom imposed, it no longer serves the purpose of deterrence.

Concurrence (Douglas, J.). The death penalty is unconstitutional because it is demonstrably imposed more frequently against the poor and minorities. Such discrimination is cruel and unusual.

Concurrence (Brennan, J.). The death penalty is unconstitutional because it is unusually severe and degrading, it is probably inflicted arbitrarily, it has been rejected by the public because it is so infrequently imposed, and there is no reason to believe it fulfills any penal purpose better than imprisonment would.

Concurrence (Marshall, J.). The death penalty is excessive punishment serving no valid legislative purpose, and is abhorrent to moral values.

Dissent (Burger, C.J.). The legislatures, not this Court, should determine the validity of the death penalty because it depends on conflicting factual claims. The Eighth Amendment does not prohibit all punishments that the states cannot prove are necessary to deter crime.

Dissent (Blackmun, J.). Although I personally rejoice at the result, I cannot accept it as a matter of law.

Dissent (Powell, J.). The assessment of public opinion is a legislative, not a judicial, function. The Court should demonstrate more faith in the democratic process.

Dissent (Rehnquist, J.). The majority's holding is an act of will, not an act of judgment. It lacks humility and deference to the legislature.

---

b.   **Permissible standards--**

Gregg v. Georgia, 428 U.S. 153 (1976).

Facts. After *Furman, supra*, in which the Supreme Court held the Georgia capital punishment statute unconstitutional because it allowed imposition of the death penalty in a capricious and arbitrary manner, Georgia amended its law. A new bifurcated procedure was established, whereby the jury determined guilt at one stage and imposed a sentence at a second stage. In the sentencing stage, the jury may consider any aggravating or mitigating circumstances and must find at least one of 10 aggravating circumstances set forth by statute before it can impose the death penalty. Gregg (D) was found guilty of murder and sentenced to death under the new Georgia law. D appeals.

Issue. Is capital punishment constitutional under the Eighth and Fourteenth Amendments as long as the sentencing authority is provided proper guidelines in determining the sentence?

Held. Yes. Judgment affirmed.

♦ Although unappealing to many, capital punishment is essential to an ordered society that requires reliance on the legal process instead of self-help. On a number of occasions, we have both assumed and asserted the constitutionality of capital punishment.

♦ Because statistical attempts to evaluate the deterrent effect of the death penalty have been inconclusive, the resolution of this complex factual issue properly rests with state legislatures.

♦ Under Georgia's sentencing procedure, the jury's discretion is always circumscribed by legislative guidelines. The death penalty is available for only six categories of crime: murder, kidnapping for ransom or where the victim is harmed, armed robbery, rape, treason, and aircraft hijacking. After a verdict of guilty, a separate sentencing hearing is conducted, and the jury must find that one of 10 specified aggravating circumstances exists before imposing the death penalty. This satisfies the concerns of *Furman* as to those defendants who were being condemned to death capriciously and arbitrarily.

Concurrence (White, J., Burger, C.J., Rehnquist, J.). D's argument is essentially that the government is inevitably incompetent to administer the death penalty fairly and is actually an indictment of our entire system of justice. I cannot accept this as proposition of constitutional law.

Dissent (Brennan, J.). Our civilization and the law has progressed to the point that the punishment of death, for whatever crime and under all circumstances, is "cruel and unusual."

Dissent (Marshall, J.). The death penalty is unnecessary to promote the goal of deterrence or to further any legitimate notion of retribution, and is thus "cruel and unusual."

---

3. **Mandatory Death Sentences.** After *Furman*, 10 states changed their capital punishment statutes by providing for mandatory death penalties upon conviction for certain categories of murder. In *Woodson v. North Carolina*, 428 U.S. 280 (1976), and *Roberts (Stanislaus) v. Louisiana*, 428 U.S. 325 (1976), the Court held that a state may not empower a jury to impose a mandatory death penalty without consideration of all evidence relating to the crime and the background of the defendant as mitigating circumstances. In practice, the mandatory death sentence permitted the jury, without standards, to arbitrarily decide who should die and who should not.

4. **Other Challenges.**

a. Use of mitigating evidence.

1) In *Lockett v. Ohio*, 438 U.S. 586 (1978), Lockett was convicted of aggravated murder because she was sitting in the getaway car when her partner fatally shot a robbery victim. Lockett was sentenced to death because state law provided for a mandatory death sentence unless one of three mitigating circumstances existed. The Court reversed on the basis that a death penalty may not preclude consideration of any relevant mitigating factors.

2) In *Eddings v. Oklahoma*, 455 U.S. 104 (1982), the Court vacated a death sentence because the trial court refused as a matter of law to consider the defendant's emotional disturbance or the circumstances of his abused childhood. The state statute permitted consideration of any mitigating circumstances, but this was not enough where the judge in fact refused to consider some circumstances.

3) In *Walton v. Arizona*, 497 U.S. 639 (1990), the Court upheld a death sentence imposed by a judge under a statutory scheme that required imposition of a death sentence if one or more statutory aggravating circumstances were present and there were no mitigating circumstances sufficiently substantial to call for leniency. The state could properly impose on the defendant the burden to show sufficient mitigating circumstances, and the statute was not impermissibly mandatory because death was not an automatic sentence upon conviction. Justice Scalia concurred in the judgment, but noted that the Eighth Amendment jurisprudence would permit the Court to find (as four dissenting Justices did), that the sentencing court had unconstitutionally broad discretion to sentence to death instead of imprisonment and narrow discretion to sentence to imprisonment instead of death. This resulted from the *Furman* line of cases that channel the sentencer's discretion in imposing the death penalty and the *Woodson* line that forbids constraints on the sentencer's discretion to decline to impose the death penalty. In his view, *Woodson* and *Lockett* were rationally irreconcilable with *Furman* and should not be followed; instead, society should be enabled to specify which factors are relevant and which are not in the process of the individualized sentencing determination.

b. Racial discrimination--

McCleskey v. Kemp, 481 U.S. 279 (1987).

Facts. McCleskey (P), who was black, was sentenced to death for the murder of a white police officer during an armed robbery. In a federal habeas corpus action, he claimed the capital sentencing process administered by Georgia was done in a racially discriminatory manner based on a statistical study that showed that defendants charged with killing white victims were 4.3 times as likely to be sentenced to death as those charged with killing black victims, and that black defendants were more likely to be sentenced to death than non-black defendants. The lower courts denied relief. The Supreme Court granted certiorari.

Issue. Does statistical evidence that the death penalty is imposed more often when the victim is white than when the victim is black suffice to demonstrate unconstitutional discriminatory application of death sentencing procedures?

Held. No. Judgment affirmed.

♦ P cannot claim that the death sentence is disproportionate to the crime; instead, he claims his sentence is disproportionate to the sentences in other murder cases. But the sentencing procedures focus discretion on the particularized nature of the crime and the particularized characteristics of the individual defendant, so P's sentence was not "wantonly and freakishly" imposed and thus is not disproportionate.

♦ P claims that the system is arbitrary and capricious in application. There are always risks that prejudice may influence a jury's decision in a criminal case. But this risk does not become constitutionally unacceptable when statistics show a likelihood of racial prejudice, as long as there are adequate safeguards in place that are designed to minimize racial bias in the process. To use statistical studies such as this could undermine the entire criminal justice system, because the Eighth Amendment is not limited to capital punishment, and because there are several types of statistical disparities that could be shown.

Dissent (Brennan, Marshall, Blackmun, Stevens, JJ.). The statistical evidence demonstrates that there is a significant chance that race would play a prominent role in determining whether P would live or die. Although P cannot prove his sentence was arbitrary, he has demonstrated a risk that his sentence was imposed arbitrarily.

---

c. **Juvenile offenders--**

Roper v. Simmons, 543 U.S. 551 (2005).

Facts. Simmons (D) committed murder when he was 17 years old and was tried, convicted, and sentenced to death when he was 18. After his appeal and subsequent petitions for state and federal postconviction relief were rejected, the Court decided *Atkins v. Virginia*, 536 U.S. 304 (2002), and held that the cruel and unusual punishment clause prohibited the execution of a mentally retarded person. D filed a new petition for relief, claiming that under *Atkins* it was unconstitutional to execute a person who was under

18 when he committed the crime. The Missouri Supreme Court agreed. The Supreme Court granted certiorari.

Issue. Is it constitutional to execute a person who was under 18 when he committed the murder that led to his death sentence?

Held. No. Judgment affirmed.

♦ In *Stanford v. Kentucky*, 492 U.S. 361 (1989), the Court upheld the death penalty for juvenile offenders ages 16 and older. However, *Atkins* reflected an evolution in standards of decency. As in *Atkins*, the objective indicia of consensus in this case—the rejection of the juvenile death penalty in the majority of states, the infrequency of its use even where it remains on the books, and the consistency in the trend toward abolition of the practice—suggest that our society views juveniles as categorically less culpable than the average criminal.

♦ Juveniles have a lack of maturity and an underdeveloped sense of responsibility, which is why, in almost every state, persons under 18 cannot vote, serve on juries, or even marry without parental consent. Juveniles are also more susceptible to peer pressure. Furthermore, their character is not as well formed as an adult's is. For these reasons, it is morally misguided to equate the failings of a minor with those of an adult. But if the juvenile death penalty is not abolished, there is a danger that the brutality of a particular crime would overpower mitigating arguments based on youth.

♦ The determination that the death penalty is disproportionate punishment for juvenile offenders is confirmed by the fact that the United States is the only country in the world that continues to sanction the juvenile death penalty. The United Nations Convention on the Rights of the Child, which every country in the world has ratified except the United States and Somalia, expressly prohibits capital punishment for crimes committed by juveniles under 18.

Dissent (Scalia, J., Rehnquist, C.J., Thomas, J.). The Court's finding of a national consensus is based on the flimsiest of grounds. But even worse, the Court proclaims itself as the sole arbiter of our nation's moral standards by ignoring our people's laws. The meaning of the Constitution should not be determined by the subjective views of five members of the Court and like-minded foreigners. Fewer than half of death penalty states prohibit the death penalty for juvenile offenders, which cannot in any way constitute a national consensus for the Court's opinion. The Court's opinion is based on scientific studies that have not been tested in an adversarial proceeding and that, at best, conclude that, on average, juveniles are unable to take moral responsibility for their actions. The Court simply does not trust juries who consider the specifics of each case.

Comment. The dissent strongly objected to the citation of foreign sources to support constitutional interpretation. For example, the United States is one of only six countries that allow abortion on demand until the point of viability. *Roper* and *Lawrence*, both written by Justice Kennedy, cited foreign decisions and suggested a natural law approach.

————————

E. PROCEDURAL DUE PROCESS IN NON-CRIMINAL CASES

1. Due Process and Entitlements.

a. **Introduction.** Both the Fifth and Fourteenth Amendments protect against the deprivation of "life, liberty, or property" without due process of law. Although due process was traditionally used most often to provide procedural safeguards for criminal defendants, it also protects a range of liberty and property interests outside the criminal context. The liberty and property interests of which persons cannot be deprived without due process do not turn upon whether the interest involved is a "right" rather than a "privilege." Such a definitional approach has been rejected by the Court. The scope of liberty and property rights protected by due process, however, has not always been easy to describe.

1) **Liberty.** It is clear that "liberty" connotes more than freedom from the bodily restraints imposed by the criminal process. It includes at least the right to contract, to engage in gainful employment, and "generally to enjoy those privileges long recognized at common law as essential to the orderly pursuit of happiness by free men."

2) **Property.** Similarly, "property" includes more than just actual ownership of realty, chattels, or money. It includes "interests already acquired in specific benefits." However, there must be more than a mere abstract need or desire for, or unilateral expectation of, the benefit. The Constitution does not create property interests; there must be a legitimate claim to an existing interest already derived from state or federal law. Thus, there is a property interest in public education when school attendance is required [Goss v. Lopez, 419 U.S. 565 (1975)], in retention of a driver's license under prevailing statutory standards [Bell v. Burson, 402 U.S. 535 (1971)] (probably the high-water mark of "importance" to the individual as determinative), and in having continued utility service where state law permits a municipal utility company to terminate service only "for cause" [Memphis Light, Gas & Water Division v. Craft, 436 U.S. 1 (1978)].

b. **Procedural due process requirements.** Procedural safeguards against invasion of private liberty and property rights have gained increased attention in recent years. The Court applies a two-pronged test. The first question is whether the implicated right is a constitutionally protected interest in life, liberty, or property. If so, the courts must examine the procedural safeguards to determine their constitutional adequacy.

c. **Welfare benefits.** In *Goldberg v. Kelly*, 397 U.S. 254 (1970), the Court held that welfare benefits are an entitlement. By definition, a person entitled to receive welfare needs the assistance for essentials such as food, clothing, housing, and medical care. Termination of benefits despite a controversy over eligibility may deprive an eligible recipient of the necessities of life. The same governmental interests behind the welfare program also support its continuation to eligible recipients. These interests are not outweighed by the need to conserve governmental fiscal and administrative resources; the latter interests are not overriding in the welfare context. Thus, welfare benefits may not be terminated without due process.

d. **Public employment.** Whether there is a "property" interest in continued public employment is determined by state (or federal) law. There must be a legitimate claim to the benefit. [Board of Regents of State Colleges v. Roth, 408 U.S. 564 (1972)—termination of nontenured public employee does not affect a property right] A statute (or ordinance), the employment contract, or some clear practice or understanding must provide that the employee can be terminated only "for cause." [Arnett v. Kennedy, 416 U.S. 134 (1974)] There is no "property" interest if the position is held "at the will of" the public employer. [Bishop v. Wood, 426 U.S. 341 (1976)]

e. **No property interest in enforcement of restraining order.** In *Town of Castle Rock v. Gonzales*, 545 U.S. 748 (2005), a mother brought a section 1983 action against Castle Rock and the police officers who failed to enforce a domestic abuse restraining order against her estranged husband, who then killed their three children. The Supreme Court held that there was no liability under section 1983 because the officers had discretionary power as to when to enforce an order. The Court further held that the enforcement of the order was not something that the mother was entitled to, nor did she have a property interest in its enforcement.

f. **Liberty.** In *Paul v. Davis*, 424 U.S. 693 (1976), the Court held that the plaintiff suffered no deprivation of liberty as a result of his identification as an active shoplifter in a flyer produced by the local police and distributed to local merchants. Defamation resulting only in damage to one's reputation was held not to be a denial of protected "liberty." As a result, the definition of liberty was assumed to depend on state determinations. But in *Vitek v. Jones*, 445 U.S. 480 (1980), the Court held that a state law permitting involuntary transfer of a prisoner to a mental hospital implicated a liberty interest.

g. **Use of rational basis standard.** In an unusual set of concurring opinions, a majority of the Court held that a state scheme that permitted a hearing on an employment discrimination complaint only if processed within 120 days violated equal protection because the limitation was not rationally related to any legitimate governmental objective. [*See* Logan v. Zimmerman Brush Co., 455 U.S. 422 (1982)]

h. **Pretermination process for public employees dischargeable only for cause.** In *Cleveland Board of Education v. Loudermill*, 470 U.S. 532 (1985), a security guard employed by the board of education was discharged without a pretermination hearing for making false statements on his employment application. The state procedure did not provide for a pretermination hearing, although the guard was given one after discharge. The Supreme Court held that the guard possessed a property right in continued employment that could not be denied without due process, which in this case should have included, at a minimum, oral or written notice, an explanation of the evidence for the discharge, and an opportunity to present his side of the story. The Court rejected the notion that due process rights, which arise under the Constitution, could be limited by the state statute creating the property interest.

2. **Determination of What Process Is Due.**

   a. **Introduction.** In recent years the courts have given increased attention to the actual procedural safeguards against invasion of private liberty and property rights. Once the existence of a constitutionally protected interest in life, liberty, or property is established, the courts must examine the adequacy of the procedures afforded. The courts must weigh the following factors to determine the extent of the procedures required:

      1) The importance of the individual interest involved;

      2) The value of specific procedural safeguards to that interest; and

      3) The governmental interest in fiscal and administrative efficiency.

   b. **Minimum procedural rights.** Recall that *Goldberg v. Kelly, supra,* held that the government must provide an opportunity for an evidentiary hearing before it terminates public assistance to a recipient. However, a full judicial or quasi-judicial trial is not necessary to satisfy the requirements of due process. A fair hearing need only have the following attributes:

      1) Notice of the reasons for a proposed termination and a hearing at a meaningful time and in a meaningful manner;

      2) The right to confront and cross-examine adverse witnesses;

      3) The right to counsel, although the state need not furnish counsel in all cases;

4) A decision resting on the legal rules and evidence adduced at the hearing, shown by a statement of the reasons for the decision and the evidence relied on; and

5) An impartial decisionmaker.

c. **Weighing test.** Whether a prior hearing is required and the extent of procedural requirements are determined by weighing (i) the importance of the individual interest involved, (ii) the value of specific procedural safeguards to that interest, and (iii) the governmental interest in fiscal and administrative efficiency. [*See* Mathews v. Eldridge, 424 U.S. 319 (1976)—recipient of disability insurance benefits not entitled to an evidential hearing prior to the initial termination of benefits]

d. **Commitment of children to mental hospitals.** In *Parham v. J.R.*, 442 U.S. 584 (1979), the Court held that formal adversary hearings are not required when parents commit their children to state mental hospitals, because children's rights are circumscribed by parental interests and responsibilities.

e. **Termination of parental rights.** The Court has held that counsel need not be appointed when the state seeks to terminate an indigent's parental rights, except in particular circumstances. [*See* Lassiter v. Department of Social Services, 452 U.S. 18 (1981)]

VIII. FREEDOM OF EXPRESSION AND ASSOCIATION

A. DETERMINING WHAT SPEECH SHOULD BE PROTECTED

1. Introduction.

a. Constitutional provision. The First Amendment provides that "Congress shall make no law . . . abridging the freedom of speech, or of the press; or the right of the people peaceably to assemble, and to petition the Government for a redress of grievances."

b. Balancing interests. The right to freedom of expression is not an absolute right to say or do anything that one desires. Rather, the interests of the government in regulating such expression must be balanced against the very strong interests on which this right is based.

1) Rationale. The rationale behind freedom of speech is that such freedom will lead to the discovery of truth and better ideas through the competition of differing viewpoints. Such speech and action are necessary for a free society that is to be governed by democratic principles. They allow the people to bring about changes through nonviolent expression.

2) Presumption of validity. Legislation is normally presumed valid. This rule also applies for restrictions on expression, although freedom of speech is an important interest that cannot be restricted unless the government has a clearly overriding interest. A statute may be invalid on its face, which means that it is unconstitutional in all of its applications. More commonly, however, a statute is held unconstitutional only as applied to the particular fact situation presented by the case.

3) Special scrutiny. There is a general consensus that First Amendment rights are special. The issue in most cases involves the proper balance between the free speech interest and what countervailing government interest is being asserted. In some areas involving expression, the law is clear. In other areas, the law remains unsettled.

2. Advocacy of Illegal Action.

a. Development of basic principles. Certain types of expression may be punished as criminal acts. For example, a riot may constitute an expression of dissent, but damaging property is a criminal act. Speech that is likely to produce illegal activity may itself be illegal. World War I prompted a series of cases in which the Court dealt with advocacy of illegal action.

1) Clear and present danger test--

Schenck v. United States, 249 U.S. 47 (1919).

Facts. The Espionage Act of 1917 made it a crime to cause or attempt to cause insubordination in the military forces or to obstruct recruitment. Schenck (D) published a pamphlet that attacked the Conscription Act and encouraged disobedience to it. D distributed the pamphlet directly to draftees. D was convicted of attempting to cause insubordination. D appeals.

Issue. May Congress outlaw speech that presents a clear and present danger to an important governmental interest?

Held. Yes. Judgment affirmed.

♦ The right of free expression is not absolute but varies with the circumstances; *i.e.*, one is not free to falsely yell "fire" in a crowded theater.

♦ The first question is whether Congress is pursuing a proper end or purpose in the legislation. Here, it is. Congress has the right to prohibit the evils at which this statute is aimed, especially in time of war.

♦ The next question is to what extent Congress can go in seeking to effectuate its purposes; *i.e.,* how far can it go before it violates the First Amendment? Congress cannot make speech a crime unless there is a "clear and present danger" of action resulting from the accused's words that would lead to the legitimately proscribed evil.

♦ The evidence in this case supports the conviction.

Comment. The Court in *Schenck* also seemed to set up some sort of a scale concerning types of speech. At one end, receiving a low degree of judicial protection, is highly emotional speech, commands that do not appeal to reason or logic but that have the effect of force and advocacy of action ("Strike!"). At the other end, receiving a high degree of protection, is speech that has a high degree of ideological content (political ideas, debate, etc.).

---

2) Public speech--

Debs v. United States, 249 U.S. 211 (1919).

Facts. Debs (D) made two public speeches promoting socialism and denouncing capitalism and the War. He was convicted under the Espionage Act and appeals.

Issue. May a political speech denouncing public policy and advocating an alternative be made a criminal act?

Held. Yes. Judgment affirmed.

- D addressed potential draftees, encouraging them to resist the recruiting services as a way to oppose the War. His speech created a clear and present danger that his listeners would actually resist the draft, which is an illegal activity.

---

3)   Incitement--

Masses Publishing Co. v. Patten, 244 F. 535 (S.D.N.Y. 1917).

Facts. Patten (D), the New York postmaster, refused to accept for mailing a magazine published by Masses Publishing (P). D claimed the publication violates the Espionage Act. P seeks an injunction.

Issue. May the government refuse to permit use of the mails by private magazines that criticize public policy?

Held. No. Injunction granted.

- The Act prohibits false statements that interfere with the military or aid its enemies. P has not made such false rumors but has published political arguments.

- The Act forbids anyone from willfully causing disloyalty among the military. Although anyone who adopts P's views would be more prone to insubordination than one having faith in the existing policies, such an interpretation of causation would prohibit any expression of views counter to those currently prevailing, an impermissible restriction in a democratic society. Of course, one may not counsel or advise violation of the law as it now stands, but everyone is free to advocate changing the law.

- The Act also forbids willful obstruction of the enlistment service. But here only direct advocacy of resistance, or actual incitement, is prohibited. P has not done such an incitement.

Comment. The decision by Judge Learned Hand was reversed on appeal. The circuit court did not agree with the incitement test and deferred to the Postmaster General's discretion.

---

4)   **Intent.** In *Abrams v. United States*, 250 U.S. 616 (1919), the Court upheld the conviction of Abrams under amendments to the Espionage Act which broadened its coverage. Justice Holmes dissented, however. He felt that Congress could limit expression only where there was the present danger of immediate evil or an intent to bring it about. Both were lacking in this case. He also felt that the First Amendment did not leave the common law in force as to seditious libel, and implied that the majority did.

b.   **State sedition laws.** After World War I, several states enacted what became known as sedition laws.

1)   **Legislative facts--**

Gitlow v. New York, 268 U.S. 652 (1925).

Facts. Gitlow (D) was convicted and imprisoned for violating a New York law that prohibited language advocating, advising, or teaching the overthrow of organized government by unlawful means. There was no evidence of any effect resulting from D's actions. D appeals.

Issue. May states prohibit advocacy of criminal anarchy when there is no concrete result, or likelihood of such a result, flowing from such advocacy?

Held. Yes. Judgment affirmed.

♦   The state has penalized not doctrinal exposition or academic discussion, but language urging criminal action to overthrow the government. D's expressions clearly fit the statutory prohibition; his words were the language of direct incitement.

♦   The state has determined that such activity is so inimical to the general welfare that it must be controlled through use of the police power and suppressed in its incipiency. Because the statute is not arbitrary or unreasonable, it must be upheld.

♦   If the statute itself is constitutional and D's use of language falls within its reach, absence of actual results is irrelevant. The state's determination that these utterances involve sufficient likelihood of causing harm is not clearly erroneous.

Dissent (Holmes, Brandeis, JJ.). D's words did not constitute a present danger of an actual attempt to overthrow the government; they were too indefinite and ineffective. To say D's words were an incitement proves nothing, for every idea is an incitement, and may move the recipient to action depending on outside circumstances.

Whitney v. California, 274 U.S. 357 (1927).

Facts. Whitney (D) helped organize and became a member of the Communist Labor Party of California, an organization that advocated, taught, and aided criminal syndicalism as defined by the Criminal Syndication Act of California. She was convicted. D appeals, claiming that although she remained a member she did not intend that the party be an instrument of terrorism or violence.

Issue. May the state outlaw mere membership in a criminal organization even if the individual member intends no criminal acts?

Held. Yes. Judgment affirmed.

♦ The Act is not void for vagueness, and its purpose is clearly proper. The state may exercise its police power to outlaw organizations menacing the peace and welfare of the state.

♦ A person who abuses the right of association by joining such an organization is not protected by the Due Process Clause from punishment.

Concurrence (Brandeis, Holmes, JJ.). Freedom of expression is an end in itself. It is a safety valve for frustration, and it is a means for finding the truth through the competition of ideas. Suppression of free speech can be justified only if there exist reasonable grounds to fear that a serious evil would otherwise result, and reasonable grounds exist for believing that there is imminent danger that the serious evil will occur.

---

c.   **Communism and illegal advocacy.**

1)   **Development of the clear and present danger approach.** The clear and present danger test was kept alive by dissenting opinions until it was finally adopted, in modified form, by later opinions. In effect, it is a rule of evidence; *i.e.,* the government must show facts indicating a clear and present danger in order to be able to regulate expression. Evidence of the following is relevant:

a)   Any actual effect from the speech.

b)   The type of language used; *e.g.,* advocacy of action.

c)   The circumstances in which the words were spoken.

d)   The intent of the speaker.

2) **The Smith Act.** The Smith Act, 18 U.S.C. section 2385, makes it unlawful for any person to (i) knowingly or willfully advocate, abet, advise, or teach the duty, necessity, desirability, or propriety of overthrowing any government in the United States by force or violence; (ii) attempt to commit, or conspire to commit, any of such acts; or (iii) become a member of any organization advocating such acts, knowing its purpose.

3) **Validity of Smith Act upheld--**

Dennis v. United States, 341 U.S. 494 (1951).

Facts. Dennis (D) was convicted of participating in a conspiracy to organize the Communist Party in the United States. The party participated in activity prohibited by the Smith Act. D had been holding classes, giving speeches, and writing articles that advocated overthrow of the government. D appeals.

Issue. May Congress pass a law forbidding association with organizations advocating overthrow of the government?

Held. Yes. Judgment affirmed.

♦ Congress clearly has the power to protect the government from violent overthrow, and in exercising this power could properly limit any expression or utterance aimed at inciting such a result.

♦ The gravity of the evil (the possible overthrow of the government) is to be discounted by the improbability of its occurrence in order to determine whether a clear and present danger exists.

♦ In the trial court the jury is to decide whether D in fact violated the Act, and the judge is to decide the question of application of the Act to D's conduct in light of the clear and present danger test.

Concurrence (Frankfurter, J.). The First Amendment does not provide absolute immunity for all expression; some balancing of the competing interests is necessary. Congress has prime responsibility to adjust these interests; the Court merely decides whether the Constitution permits Congress to enact the Smith Act.

Concurrence (Jackson, J.). The "clear and present danger" test was designed as a rule of reason for isolated incidents. It is not a limitation on the power of Congress to deal with the threat of a conspiracy dedicated to overthrowing the government.

Dissent (Black, J.). "Reasonableness" is an inadequate standard for reviewing restrictions on First Amendment rights.

Dissent (Douglas, J.). Mere advocacy of communism should not be a crime. Free speech should not be eliminated unless there is a showing that the evils advocated are imminent. The clear and present danger test should be submitted to the jury.

Comment. After this case upheld the Smith Act, the government brought many actions against alleged communists. Although D here was a ringleader, it was thereafter thought that all that need be shown for a conviction of any person was that she was linked with an organization that advocated overthrow as fast as possible. In all cases, of course, there had to be some connection between the advocacy and the proscribed evil, although this could be supplied by judicial notice.

---

4)   **Mere advocacy.** The Smith Act does not prohibit "mere advocacy" or teaching of forcible overthrow as an abstract principle, apart from an effort to instigate action to that end. This is true even though such advocacy is engaged in with evil intent and uttered with the hope that it may ultimately lead to violent revolution. The urging of action for forcible overthrow is a necessary element of the proscribed advocacy.

5)   **Advocacy and proof.** By the time numerous cases against lower echelon communists prosecuted under the Smith Act reached the Supreme Court, Senator McCarthy had died and anti-communist fever had somewhat abated; the Court appeared to shift position. In *Yates v. United States*, 354 U.S. 298 (1957), the Court set aside convictions because jury instructions failed to give adequate guidance concerning the distinction between advocacy of abstract doctrine and advocacy of action. Mere advocacy is insufficient. The Court did uphold a conviction in *Scales v. United States*, 367 U.S. 203 (1961), but construed the Act to require specific intent to accomplish the organization's goals by resort to violence. Clear proof was required. Scales was the last defendant convicted under the Smith Act. In *Noto v. United States*, 367 U.S. 290 (1961), the Court reversed a membership clause conviction because of the insufficiency of evidence regarding illegal party advocacy. The Court specifically stated that convictions must be based upon particularized factual findings and not the supposed tenets of the party.

d.   **Modern distinction between advocacy and incitement--**

Brandenburg v. Ohio, 395 U.S. 444 (1969).

Facts. Brandenburg (D), a Ku Klux Klan leader, was convicted under an Ohio statute for advocating criminal terrorism and criminal syndicalism. His activities consisted of inviting television reporters to a secluded gathering where weapons were present and a speech was made. There was no threat of imminent lawless action. The state courts upheld the conviction. D appeals.

Issue. May a state law prohibit advocacy of civil disruption without distinguishing between mere advocacy and incitement to imminent lawless action?

Held. No. Judgment reversed.

♦   The constitutional guarantees of free speech and free press do not permit a state to forbid advocacy of the use of force or of lawlessness except where such advocacy (i) is directed to inciting or producing imminent lawless action and (ii) is likely to incite or produce such action.

♦   Ohio's law fails to make the required distinction, and cannot be upheld.

Concurrence (Black, J.). The Court cites the *Dennis* case, *supra*, but properly does not agree with the *Dennis* "clear and present danger" doctrine.

Concurrence (Douglas, J.). The line between permissible and impermissible acts is the line between ideas and overt acts. The "clear and present danger" test has no place under the Constitution.

Comment. Applying the *Brandenburg* incitement standard, the Court reversed a disorderly conduct conviction in *Hess v. Indiana*, 414 U.S. 105 (1973), a case involving a campus antiwar demonstration. The Court held that since the appellant's statement could be interpreted in various ways, there was no rational inference from the language that the words were intended to produce imminent disorder. The Court stated that words that only had a tendency to lead to violence could not be punished by the state.

━━━━━━━━━━

3.   **Reputation and Privacy.** Libelous speech is in somewhat the same category as obscenity—it receives little constitutional protection. However, the same difficult questions exist here also; *i.e.,* what constitutes libel and what tests should be used to distinguish protected from unprotected speech?

a.   **Group libel--**

Beauharnais v. Illinois, 343 U.S. 250 (1952).

Facts. Beauharnais (D) was convicted under a state statute that made it unlawful for any person to sell or publish any publication that portrayed a class of citizens of any race, color, or creed in a derogatory manner so as to expose them to derision or to be productive of a breach of the peace. D published a leaflet calling on Chicago officials to halt the encroachment of blacks on whites' property and neighborhoods, citing the black crime rate, possible "mongrelization," etc. D appeals the conviction.

Issue. May group libel be made per se illegal, even without a showing of a clear and present danger?

Held. Yes. Judgment affirmed.

♦   Every American jurisdiction punishes libels aimed at individuals. Libel is treated much as lewd and obscene speech; punishment of these types of expression does not violate the First Amendment. Such speech is not communication of information or opinion protected by the Constitution.

♦   Because the Fourteenth Amendment does not prevent the states from enforcing libel laws to protect individuals, it should not prevent laws against group libel unless they are unrelated to a legitimate government purpose. Illinois has a history of tense race relations. The legislature could certainly conclude that group libel tends to exacerbate these problems. It could also have found that group libel directly affects individuals in the group by impugning their reputations.

♦   There is no requirement for a showing of clear and present danger because libel is not within the protection of the Constitution.

Dissent (Black, Douglas, JJ.). Restrictions of First Amendment freedoms should not be judged by the rational basis standard. Criminal libel has always been intended to protect individuals, not large groups. Additionally, the words used by D were part of a petition to the government, and part of his argument on a question of wide public importance and interest.

Dissent (Reed, Douglas, JJ.). The statute is unconstitutionally vague. It forbids portrayal of a lack of "virtue" on the part of a class of citizens that leads to "derision." The meaning of these terms is too uncertain to describe a criminal offense.

Dissent (Douglas, J.). This type of speech can constitutionally be punished only with a showing that it provides a clear and present danger of causing disaster.

Dissent (Jackson, J.). The Fourteenth Amendment does not incorporate the First Amendment. Thus the states have more latitude than Congress.

————————————

b.   **Public officials and seditious libel.**

1)   **Introduction.** The First Amendment clearly protects disclosure and debate on matters of public interest. On the other hand, society must protect personal reputations against injurious falsehoods.

The conflict between these interests has produced some close decisions, but the Court has balanced the interests by creating a constitutional privilege for certain kinds of defamation. Thus, criticism of public officials relating to their official conduct cannot result in either criminal or civil liability for libel unless made with "actual malice." Society's interest in this type of expression is great, and public officials can normally refute false charges because they have access to the media.

2) Public officials--

New York Times Co. v. Sullivan, 376 U.S. 254 (1964).

Facts. Sullivan (P) was a commissioner of the city of Montgomery, Alabama, and supervised the police department. The New York Times Company (D) carried a full-page advertisement that included several false statements about repressive police conduct in Montgomery. Although P's name was not mentioned, the accusation of the ad could be read as referring to him. P sued for damages on grounds that D libeled him. The trial court awarded damages of $500,000, which were upheld in the state courts. The controlling state rule of law dealt with libel per se, established here by merely showing that D's statement reflected upon the agency that P supervised. Once libel per se is demonstrated, the only defense is the truth. D appeals.

Issue. May a state allow a public official to recover damages for a defamatory falsehood relating to his official conduct without proof of actual malice?

Held. No. Judgment reversed.

◆ The Constitution expresses a profound commitment to uninhibited debate on public issues. This protection does not turn on the truth of the ideas or beliefs expressed, nor does concern for official reputation remove defamatory statements from the constitutional shield.

◆ The deterrent effect of damage awards—without the need for any proof of actual pecuniary loss—is so great as to severely chill public criticism, which should be openly permitted under the First Amendment.

◆ Despite First Amendment considerations, a public official may recover damages for a defamatory falsehood relating to his official conduct if he proves the statement was made with actual malice (knowledge of falsity or reckless disregard of truth). P's proof falls short.

Concurrence (Black, Douglas, JJ.). D had an absolute, unconditional privilege to criticize official conduct despite the harm that may flow from excesses and abuses.

Comment. The Supreme Court has held that the same privilege to make statements about "public officials" exists for statements made about "public figures." In *Curtis*

Publishing Co. v. Butts, 388 U.S. 130 (1967), Wally Butts, the former director of athletics at the University of Georgia, was reported to have thrown a football game while at the University. In *Associated Press v. Walker* (decided with *Butts*), the Court held that General Walker, a retired Army general, was a public figure. The *New York Times* rule was extended to private plaintiffs involved in matters of public concern in *Rosenbloom v. Metromedia, Inc.*, 403 U.S. 29 (1971). Although *Gertz*, *infra*, rejected that distinction, it was resurrected to a certain extent in *Dun & Bradstreet, Inc. v. Greenmoss Builders, Inc.*, 472 U.S. 749 (1985). In that case (discussed further *infra*), a majority of the Court rejected the media-nonmedia distinction suggested by *Gertz*, and ruled that the *Gertz* requirements for private plaintiffs only apply to "matters of public concern."

---

c.   **Private individuals and public figures.**

1)   **General rule.** The *New York Times* rule applies to suits by public figures as well as by public officials. A person may become a public figure by achieving general fame or notoriety in a given community, either generally or as to particular issues. When the defamed person is neither a public figure nor a public official (or candidate for public office), "free speech" considerations are not as strong. Private individuals are more susceptible to injury because they do not usually have media access to counteract false statements published about them. Consequently, the states may impose whatever standard of defamation liability they choose, except that, for matters of public concern:

a)   The factual misstatement must be such as would warn a reasonably prudent editor or broadcaster of its defamatory potential;

b)   There must be a finding (by the trier of fact or the appellate court) that the publisher or broadcaster was at least negligent in publishing the misstatement (*i.e.,* liability without fault cannot be imposed); and

c)   Damages must be limited to "actual injury" (which includes any out-of-pocket loss plus impairment of reputation, personal humiliation, and mental anguish). An award of "presumed" or punitive damages is permissible only if the publication was made with knowledge of its falsity or in reckless disregard for the truth (*i.e.,* actual malice).

2)   **Private individual involved in public issue--**

Gertz v. Robert Welch, Inc., 418 U.S. 323 (1974).

Facts. Gertz (P), an attorney, represented the family of a victim killed by a police officer in the family's civil suit against the officer. Robert Welch, Inc. (D), publisher of *American Opinion*, printed an article, concededly untrue, that discredited P's reputation and motives. P sued D for libel. After a jury awarded damages to P, the trial court reconsidered and decided that D was protected by application of the *New York Times* rule, holding that discussion of any public issue is protected, regardless of the status of the person defamed. Because P was unable to prove that D acted with "actual malice," the court entered a judgment notwithstanding the verdict for D. The court of appeals affirmed. P appeals.

Issue. May a member of the press who published defamatory falsehoods about a person who is neither a public official nor a public figure, but who is involved in a public issue, claim a constitutional privilege against liability for injuries?

Held. No. Judgment reversed.

♦   The need to avoid self-censorship by the news media must be balanced against the legitimate interest in permitting compensation for harm resulting from defamatory falsehoods. Defamation plaintiffs are not all in the same class, however. Public officials and public figures have more access to the media to counteract falsehoods than do private individuals such as P. Private individuals are also more deserving of recovery because their public exposure is not voluntary. Therefore, the rationale behind the *New York Times* rule does not extend to private individuals.

♦   Involvement in a public issue, by itself, does not bring a private individual within the class covered by the *New York Times* rule. D was not a public official or public figure. To protect defamations whenever a "public issue" was involved would introduce new uncertainties and broadly expand the scope of the *New York Times* rule.

♦   States may define their own standards of liability for defamation by a publisher or broadcaster, but may not impose liability without fault. However, states may not permit recovery of presumed or punitive damages in the absence of proof of "actual malice" (knowledge of falsity or reckless disregard for the truth). The only permissible recovery for a private defamation plaintiff who establishes liability under any standard less demanding than the *New York Times* test is compensation for actual injury.

Dissent (Brennan, J.). The *New York Times* rule should apply to discussions of public issues.

Dissent (White, J.). The states should be free to impose strict liability in cases such as this.

3) **Determination of public figure status.** As discussed *supra*, a person may be a public figure for all purposes and in all contexts by gaining general fame or notoriety, or may become a public figure for special issues by becoming involved in the controversy. The critical element is the voluntariness of the public standing. A person is not a public figure simply because she is extremely wealthy and engaged in divorce proceedings of interest to the reading public. The fact that she files for divorce (and even holds press conferences during the proceedings) does not mean that she voluntarily chooses to publicize her married life, because going to court is the only way she can legally dissolve her marriage. [Time, Inc. v. Firestone, 424 U.S. 448 (1976)] Nor does a person become a public figure by being charged with a crime. [Wolston v. Reader's Digest Association, 443 U.S. 157 (1979)]

d. **Privacy.**

1) **Introduction.** The *New York Times* rule was also applied to suits for invasion of privacy, even if the plaintiff was not a public official or public figure, as long as the matter reported was of substantial public interest. The Court has not yet decided whether *Gertz* changes this rule for suits for invasion of privacy brought by private individuals.

2) **Matter of public interest--**

Time, Inc. v. Hill, 385 U.S. 374 (1967).

Facts. In 1952, Hill (P) and his family were held prisoners for several hours by escaped convicts. Thereafter, they moved and sought to avoid all publicity about their experience. *Life Magazine*, owned by Time, Inc. (D), published an article about a play that was loosely based on P's story, although it varied substantially from what really happened by adding violence. *Life* represented the play to be a reenactment of P's experiences. P sued for invasion of privacy and won. The judgment was based on a New York statute that gave no protection to fictitious publications about "newsworthy" persons. D appeals.

Issue. Does the constitutional protection for speech and press preclude recovery for false reporting of a matter of public interest in the absence of actual malice?

Held. Yes. Judgment reversed.

♦ Innocent or negligent erroneous statements upon public affairs must be protected if the freedoms of expression are to have the "breathing space" they need to survive. The play reported by *Life* is a matter of public interest.

♦ The indispensable service of a free press would be seriously impaired by a requirement that the press verify all facts printed about an individual. However, the constitutional guarantees are not impaired by sanctions against publication of known falsehoods or in reckless disregard of the truth (actual malice).

Concurrence and dissent (Harlan, J.). The proper test in a privacy case should be negligence. P has no reasonable prospect of being able to refute the false *Life* material. The state's interest in encouraging careful checking is much stronger here than it was in the *New York Times* case.

Comment. In *Zacchini v. Scripps-Howard Broadcasting Co.*, 433 U.S. 562 (1977), the Court held that a broadcaster cannot broadcast a performer's entire act on the news. Even though the broadcaster claimed the act was a newsworthy event, the Court held that the performer has a proprietary interest analogous to patent and copyright interests. The First Amendment does not immunize the media from an action for damages when a performer's entire act (for which compensation is usually paid) is published or broadcast without the performer's consent. This is the functional equivalent of broadcasting copyrighted material or a sporting event.

---

e. Infliction of emotional distress--

Hustler Magazine v. Falwell, 485 U.S. 46 (1988).

Facts. Hustler Magazine (D) published a parody of an advertisement in which Falwell (P), a nationally known minister, is depicted as describing a drunken incestuous rendezvous with his mother in an outhouse. The ad contained a disclaimer at the bottom. P sued for invasion of privacy, libel, and intentional infliction of emotional distress. After a directed verdict on the privacy claim, the jury found for D on the defamation claim on the ground that it contained no assertion of fact. The jury awarded P $200,000 on the emotional distress claim, however. The court of appeals affirmed. The Supreme Court granted certiorari.

Issue. May a public figure recover damages for emotional harm caused by the publication of an offensive parody intended to inflict emotional injury, but which could not reasonably have been interpreted as stating actual facts?

Held. No. Judgment reversed.

♦ Although the First Amendment promotes political debate by protecting even vigorous criticism of public officials, not all speech about a public figure is protected. A public figure may hold a speaker liable for damages to reputation caused by publication of a defamatory falsehood if the statement was made with knowledge that it was false or with reckless disregard of whether it was false or not.

♦ P claims a different rule should apply here where the state has sought to prevent emotional distress instead of damage to reputation. While an intent to cause emotional distress may be determinative in tort law, the First Amendment disregards the speaker's intent in the area of public debate about public figures. The alternative would deter political satirism.

♦ While D's parody may be more outrageous than normal political cartoons, there is no principled standard for distinguishing between more and less outrageous expression. Speech may not be suppressed for the sole reason that it offends society.

---

f.   Disclosure of private facts--

Florida Star v. B.J.F., 491 U.S. 524 (1989).

Facts. A Florida statute made it illegal to print, publish, or broadcast, in any instrument of mass communication, the name of the victim of a sexual offense. The Florida Star (D) obtained the name of B.J.F. (P), a rape victim, from a publicly released police report. D published P's name. P sued D and recovered $100,000 in damages. D appeals, claiming its publication was protected by the First Amendment.

Issue. May a state prohibit the press from publishing the name of a victim of a sexual offense if the name is released in a public police report?

Held. No. Judgment reversed.

♦ As a general rule, a newspaper that lawfully obtains truthful information about a matter of public significance may not be punished by state officials for publishing the information, absent a need to further a state interest of the highest order.

♦ In this case, the information published by D was truthful. D lawfully obtained P's name when the police released her name, even though the police were not required to disclose the information. The information about the violent crime is clearly a matter of public import.

♦ P claims that the statute furthers three important state interests: (i) the privacy of the victims; (ii) the physical safety of such victims; and (iii) the goal of encouraging victims to come forward. While these are highly significant interests, they are insufficient in this case because where the state itself disclosed the information, punishing the press is not a narrowly tailored means of safeguarding anonymity. In addition, the statute imposes a negligence per se standard so that liability follows automatically from publication; this means D would be liable even if P's name were otherwise known. Finally, the statute is underinclusive because it does not apply to dissemination of the victim's name through means other than an instrument of mass communication.

Concurrence (Scalia, J.). The third ground of underinclusiveness is sufficient to decide the case. The statute appears to prohibit the press from doing something that society in general is not prohibited from doing. Hence, the statute cannot be said to protect an interest "of the highest order."

Dissent (White, J., Rehnquist, C.J., O'Connor, J.). The reasons given by the Court do not support its result. D obtained the report that inadvertently included P's name in a room that contained signs that made it clear that the names of rape victims were not matters of public record and were not to be published. The government did not thus consider dissemination lawful. It is not too much to ask the press not to publish a victim's name. The negligence per se standard is inapposite here because the jury found that D acted with reckless indifference towards P, but on its face, the legislature could properly determine that disclosure of the fact that a person was raped is categorically a revelation that reasonable people find offensive. Finally, the law applies to all instruments of mass communication because the widespread distribution of rape victims' names is the objective at which the law is aimed.

Comment. The Court expressly declined to adopt a broad rule that truthful publication may never be punished, thereby preserving the need to assess the interaction between First Amendment and privacy rights on a case-by-case basis.

---

g.   **Disclosure of intercepted cell phone call.** During contentious union negotiations between a teachers' union and the school board, the union's chief negotiator used a cell phone to talk with the union's president. An unknown person intercepted and recorded their conversation. Vopper, a radio commentator, played a tape of the intercepted conversation on his radio show. In *Bartnicki v. Vopper*, 532 U.S. 514 (2001), the Court held that Vopper could not be held liable for damages under antiwiretap laws for broadcasting the phone call. The Court acknowledged that Vopper knew or should have known that the recording was illegal. However, the Court explained that although the government has a legitimate interest in protecting privacy, it cannot suppress speech by a law-abiding possessor of information in order to deter the conduct of a non-law-abiding third party. Furthermore, the tape involved a matter of public concern, and the Court decided that, in balancing the competing interests, privacy concerns must yield to the interest in publishing matters of public importance. Chief Justice Rehnquist, joined by Justices Scalia and Thomas, dissented, arguing that the decision diminished the purposes of the First Amendment by chilling the speech of millions of Americans who rely on electronic technology to communicate.

4. Obscenity.

    a. **Introduction.** Obscene publications are not protected by the constitutional guarantee of freedom of speech and press. Both federal and state governments may restrict such expression. The difficulty is in defining such speech. Freedom of expression is not an end in itself. To be protected, the speech must have some content of value to society. Obscene speech has no societal value, so it is unprotected, but speech that does not descend to the level of "obscene" remains protected.

        1) **Difficulty of defining obscenity--**

Roth v. United States; Alberts v. California, 354 U.S. 476 (1957).

Facts. Roth (D) was convicted of mailing obscene materials in violation of a federal obscenity statute. Alberts (D) was convicted of a similar state offense. Ds appeal their convictions.

Issue. Is obscenity presumptively without redeeming social value and therefore unprotected by the First Amendment?

Held. Yes. Judgment affirmed.

♦   The unconditional phrasing of the First Amendment was not intended to protect every utterance; *e.g.,* libel is unprotected. Obscenity is utterly without redeeming social importance. Therefore, obscenity cannot claim constitutional protection.

♦   Ds claim that their material does not create a clear and present danger to society, but merely incites impure sexual thoughts. It is true that mere portrayal of sex does not deny the material constitutional protection. But obscenity is not synonymous with sex. Obscenity deals with sex in a manner appealing to prurient interest. As such, it is unprotected.

♦   The test for obscenity, then, is whether to the average person, applying contemporary community standards, the dominant theme of the material taken as a whole appeals to the prurient interest.

Comment. After *Roth*, the Court was unable to make a majority statement on the proper standard for evaluating pornography until *Miller v. California, infra,* in 1973. In the meantime, however, the Court decided obscenity cases with plurality opinions. For example, in *Kingsley International Pictures Corp. v. Regents*, 360 U.S. 684 (1959), the Court invalidated a New York motion picture licensing law that banned films portraying acts of sexual immorality or presenting such acts as proper behavioral patterns. The Court held that the concept of sexual immorality differed from the concepts of obscenity or pornography, and that the state law prevented the advocacy of an idea protected by the basic guarantee of the First Amendment.

---

2) **Approach to obscenity cases.** In one opinion, Justice Stewart, writing about obscenity, stated "I cannot define it, but I know it when I see it." The Court seemed to follow this approach between 1967 and 1971 when it overturned obscenity findings in 31 cases. During this period, the Court never upheld obscenity findings when the material was textual, or when film or pictures showed only nudity. When film or pictures showed explicit sexual activity, however, the Court upheld obscenity findings.

b. **Rationale for regulating obscenity.**

1) **Possession and distribution of obscene materials.** The Court reversed a conviction for possession of obscene materials found in an appellant's home in *Stanley v. Georgia*, 394 U.S. 557 (1969). In so ruling, the Court held that the First Amendment grants the right to receive information and ideas and that there is a fundamental right to be free from unwanted governmental intrusion in one's home. However, in *United States v. Reidel*, 402 U.S. 351 (1971), the Court reversed the lower court's dismissal of an indictment under the federal law prohibiting the mailing of obscene materials. The Court rejected the lower court's contention, based upon the ruling in *Stanley*, that if a person has a right to possess obscene material, then a person also has a right to deliver it. The Court held that the indictment was not an infringement of the right to freedom of mind and thought or of the right to privacy in one's home.

2) **State regulation of obscene films--**

Paris Adult Theatre I v. Slaton, 413 U.S. 49 (1973).

Facts. Slaton (P), a state district attorney, filed civil complaints against Paris Adult Theatre I (D), seeking to enjoin exhibition of films claimed to be obscene. The films were available only to "consenting adults." The trial judge dismissed the complaint, but the Georgia Supreme Court reversed, holding that the films were without First Amendment protection. D appeals.

Issue. May a state prohibit commercial exhibition of "obscene" films to consenting adults?

Held. Yes. Judgment vacated and remanded.

♦ The state afforded D the best possible notice, as no restraint on exhibition was imposed until after a full judicial proceeding determined that the films were obscene and therefore subject to regulation.

♦ Obscene, pornographic films do not acquire constitutional immunity from state regulation merely because they are shown to consenting adults only. The states have power to make a morally neutral judgment that public exhibition of obscene material, or commerce in such material, has a tendency to injure the community as a whole, even if actual exposure is limited to a few consenting adults.

♦ While the right of privacy may preclude regulation of the use of obscene materials within the home, commercial ventures such as D's are not private for the purpose of civil rights litigation. Commerce in obscene material is unprotected by any constitutional doctrine of privacy.

♦ Incidental effects on human "utterances" or "thoughts" do not prevent state action to protect legitimate state interests where the communication is not protected by the First Amendment and where the right of privacy is not infringed. Such state action is permitted as long as it conforms to the standards of *Miller*.

Dissent (Brennan, Stewart, Marshall, JJ.). The Court's attempts to define obscenity have clearly failed. Governments cannot constitutionally bar the distribution even of unprotected material to consenting adults.

Dissent (Douglas, J.). The First Amendment makes it unconstitutional for me to act as a censor.

---

c. **Inability to define obscenity.** In *Memoirs v. Massachusetts*, 383 U.S. 413 (1966), the state had ruled that the book *Memoirs of a Woman of Pleasure* was obscene under Massachusetts law. The Court reversed in a plurality opinion. The Court stated that under *Roth*, material is protected unless it meets three criteria: (i) the dominant theme of the material taken as a whole appeals to a prurient interest in sex; (ii) the material is patently offensive because it affronts contemporary community standards relating to the description or representation of sexual matters; and (iii) the material is utterly without redeeming social value. The Court stated that a book could have redeeming social value even if the other two parts of the test are met. An indication of the social value of the material is the manner in which it is sold. If the seller's sole emphasis is on the sexually provocative aspects of the material, a court could accept his evaluation at its face value.

d.   Modern standard for defining obscene materials--

Miller v. California, 413 U.S. 15 (1973).

Facts. Miller (D) was convicted under a California statute of knowingly distributing obscene matter to unwilling recipients. The statute incorporated the *Memoirs* test of obscenity. D appeals the conviction.

Issue. Is the *Memoirs* test the appropriate measure of obscene expressions?

Held. No. Judgment vacated and remanded.

♦   Obscenity is not within the area of constitutionally protected speech or press. *Roth* presumed obscenity to be "utterly without redeeming social value," but the *Memoirs* case transformed that presumption into a necessary element of proof. *Memoirs* thus requires the prosecution to prove a negative, and that test cannot be upheld.

♦   Regulation of obscene material is restricted to works that depict or describe sexual conduct, and must specifically define that conduct. The basic guidelines for the trier of fact must be:

> Whether the average person, applying contemporary community standards, would find that the work, taken as a whole, appeals to the prurient interest;

> Whether the work depicts or describes, in a patently offensive way, sexual conduct specifically defined by the applicable state law; and

> Whether the work, taken as a whole, lacks serious literary, artistic, political, or scientific value.

♦   Under this test, material can be regulated without a showing that it is "utterly without redeeming social value."

Dissent (Brennan, Stewart, Marshall, JJ.). The difficulty in defining obscenity means that laws prohibiting it are necessarily vague. The Court has been able to resolve cases between parties but has not provided useful guidance to legislatures and other courts. Experience teaches that it is impossible to reconcile the First Amendment concerns in this area with the state's interest in regulating obscenity. The best solution is to permit government to regulate the manner of distribution of sexually-oriented material to protect juveniles and unconsenting adults, but not to wholly suppress such materials.

5. **Offensive Speech.**

   a. **Fighting words.**

      1) **Categorization approach.** In *Chaplinsky v. New Hampshire*, 315 U.S. 568 (1942), the Court held that a state may forbid the use in a public place of words that would be likely to cause an addressee to fight—so-called "fighting words." Chaplinsky had called the city marshall a "damned Fascist" and a "God damned racketeer." The Court held that fighting words are one of the "well-defined and narrowly limited classes of speech" not protected by the Constitution. Other classes included bribery, perjury, and criminal solicitation.

      2) **Balancing approach.** Because categorization presents such a high risk of being overinclusive, the Court has adopted a balancing approach to most content-based restrictions on speech. Balancing presents the danger of being susceptible to manipulation by those who apply the law.

   b. **Hostile audiences.**

      1) **Basic rule.** Free speech does not include the right to disrupt the community. Fighting words are not protected, but an unfavorable response by the audience is not necessarily enough to render the speech unprotected. In *Terminiello v. Chicago*, 337 U.S. 1 (1949), the Court held unconstitutional a breach of the peace statute that included a restriction on speech that stirs the public to anger, invites dispute, or causes unrest. One of the functions of free speech is the invitation to dispute; free speech is often provocative and challenging.

      2) **Protective suppression--**

Feiner v. New York, 340 U.S. 315 (1951).

Facts. Feiner (D) was addressing a street meeting and attracted a crowd, but there was no disorder. One man told the police officers that if they did not stop D, he would. The police asked D to stop speaking and arrested him when D refused to obey. He was convicted of disorderly conduct and appeals.

Issue. May police act to suppress speech that in their judgment is causing a breach of the peace?

Held. Yes. Judgment affirmed.

♦ D was accorded a full, fair trial, the result of which was a determination that D was arrested and convicted not for his speech but for the reaction it caused. The police were justified in acting to preserve peace and order.

Dissent (Black, J.). The police had a duty to protect D's right to talk, even to the extent of arresting the man who threatened to interfere.

Dissent (Douglas, Minton, JJ.). The police improperly sided with the person who sought to deny D's right to speak, and in effect became censors.

Comment. The problems of freedom of expression in public places really have two aspects—one is the idea of the content of the speech. For example, political dialogue or comment is clearly going to receive greater protection than is business advertising. The second element is clearly that of the conduct involved. As in *Feiner*, when there is a clear and present danger that the conduct involved will lead to harmful results, greater restrictions on the speech are permitted.

---

c.   **Offensive words--**

Cohen v. California, 403 U.S. 15 (1971).

Facts. Cohen (D) wore a jacket bearing the words "Fuck the Draft" in a Los Angeles courthouse corridor. He was convicted of violating a state statute that prohibited disturbing the peace by offensive conduct. He appeals after the state courts upheld his conviction.

Issue. May a state prohibit as "offensive conduct" public use of an offensive word?

Held. No. Judgment reversed.

♦   The government has the special power to regulate speech that is obscene, constitutes "fighting words," or intrudes on substantial privacy interests in an essentially intolerable manner.

♦   D's expression falls within none of these categories. D's jacket could not be considered erotic. Neither would D's jacket violently provoke the common citizen in the manner of fighting words. Persons present in the courthouse were not unwilling captives of the offensive expression; they could simply have averted their eyes. Thus, there was no intrusion on privacy interests.

♦   The state's regulatory attempt must fail because it would permit the state to outlaw whatever words officials might deem improper, thus running a substantial risk of suppressing ideas. Such power would permit official censorship as a means of banning the expression of unpopular views.

Dissent (Blackmun, Black, JJ., Burger, C.J.). D's antic was mainly conduct and involved little speech. As such, it could be regulated.

Comment. In *Gooding v. Wilson*, 405 U.S. 518 (1972), the Court reversed a conviction for using provocative words because the statute was overbroad. The Court apparently would uphold a statute applicable only to words that "have a direct tendency to cause acts of violence by the person to whom, individually, the remark is addressed."

---

6.   **Ownership of Speech--**

Harper & Row v. Nation Enterprises, 471 U.S. 539 (1985).

Facts. Harper & Row (P) contracted with former President Gerald Ford to publish his memoirs. P licensed a prepublication article to Time Magazine, which focused on Ford's pardon of former President Nixon. Before the Time article appeared, someone gave the editor of The Nation, which was published by Nation Enterprises (D), an unauthorized copy of the Ford manuscript. D published an article using copyrighted expression from the Ford manuscript. Time canceled its article, and P sued for damages. The district court found for P and awarded damages for the money that P lost when Time canceled. The court of appeals reversed, holding that the 300 to 400 words of copyrighted expression constituted "fair use." The Supreme Court granted certiorari.

Issue. Does the fair use provision of the Copyright Revision Act protect the use of verbatim excerpts in an unauthorized first publication of a work?

Held. No. Judgment reversed.

♦   Copyright law creates a monopoly that motivates and rewards the individual author for the benefit of the public. The copyright owner's rights are subject to certain statutory exceptions, including the "fair use" exception.

♦   The right of first publication is different from other rights under the Act because only one person can be the first publisher. It is the author's right to decide whether and in what form to release his work. The author's right to control the first public appearance of his undisseminated expression normally outweighs a claim of fair use.

♦   The fair use provision is intended to strike a balance between the First Amendment and the Copyright Act by permitting free communication of facts while still protecting an author's expression. D claims that not only the facts, but also the precise manner in which Ford expressed himself, were newsworthy and therefore a proper subject of fair use. However, there is no public figure exception to copyright protection.

♦ Freedom of speech includes a freedom not to speak publicly. D's use of the copyrighted material was intended to supplant P's valuable right of first publication for commercial purposes and was based on a stolen manuscript. D acted in bad faith. The equities in this case weigh against D.

Dissent (Brennan, White, Marshall, JJ.). Aside from when it quoted Ford, The Nation conveyed the historical information in its article in a way that did not so closely track Ford's language as to constitute an appropriation of literary form. The Court seems to be compensating P for the appropriation of information from the stolen manuscript. However, Copyright does not protect information and ideas, which are of most value in works of history. A court must not reject the fair use defense due to a concern that an author of history has been deprived of the full value of his labor.

---

7. **New Categories.**

a. **Child pornography--**

New York v. Ferber, 458 U.S. 747 (1982).

Facts. New York (P) enacted a statute that outlawed production and promotion (including distribution) of child pornography, regardless of whether the material was legally obscene. "Child pornography" consisted of any performance that includes sexual conduct by a child under 16 years old. Ferber (D) was convicted of selling two films of young boys masturbating. The New York Court of Appeals reversed the conviction, holding that the statute violated the First Amendment. The Supreme Court granted certiorari.

Issue. May a state prohibit distribution of all child pornography, even without requiring that it be legally obscene?

Held. Yes. Judgment reversed.

♦ Obscenity is not protected by the Constitution. States have even greater leeway in dealing with child pornography than with obscenity because of the compelling state interest in safeguarding their children's physical and psychological well-being.

♦ Distribution of child pornography is intrinsically related to sexual abuse of children because the distribution aggravates the harm to the child and because, without a market, the pornography would not be produced. Prohibiting distribution of obscene materials would not adequately promote the state's interest because the harm of abuse is unrelated to any possible literary, artistic, political, or social value of the material.

- Production of child pornography, of which distribution is an integral part, is illegal; the First Amendment does not protect against commission of a crime. There is no cognizable value in permitting production of child pornography.

- The definition used in the statute is sufficiently clear and precise. The statute is not overbroad. Even if it could conceivably extend to medical or educational material, such applications of the statute would be a tiny fraction of the materials prohibited. The cure in such instances is a case-by-case analysis of the circumstances.

Comment. *Massachusetts v. Oakes*, 491 U.S. 576 (1989), involved an overbreadth challenge to a statute that prohibited posing or exhibiting nude children for photographs or pictures, with educational or cultural purposes excepted. After the state supreme court held the statute overbroad and the Supreme Court had granted certiorari, the state legislature amended the statute by eliminating the exemptions and adding a "lascivious intent" requirement. The Court remanded for determination of the statute as applied, holding that the former law could not chill protected speech because it had been repealed. The dissenting Justices objected that this procedure minimized the legislature's incentive to stay within constitutional bounds because they could fix an overbroad statute prior to final appeal and not lose a conviction, yet impose a chilling of protected speech in the meantime. In *Osborne v. Ohio*, 495 U.S. 103 (1990), the Court distinguished *Stanley v. Georgia, supra,* from a state statute that prohibited the possession of material showing a minor in a state of nudity on the ground that the interests underlying prohibitions on child pornography were much greater than the interests involved in *Stanley*.

---

b. "Virtual" child pornography--

Ashcroft v. The Free Speech Coalition, 535 U.S. 234 (2002).

Facts. The Child Pornography Prevention Act of 1996 ("CPPA") expanded the federal prohibition of child pornography to include "virtual child pornography," which is sexually explicit images that appear to depict minors but are produced without using any real children, whether by using computer imaging or by using adults made to look like children. The CPPA did not require such pornography to be obscene under *Miller v. California, supra*, but prohibited all child pornography, real or virtual. The Free Speech Coalition (P), a trade association for the pornography or adult-entertainment industry, challenged the constitutionality of the CPPA. The district court granted summary judgment for Ashcroft (D), the U.S. Attorney General. The Ninth Circuit reversed, holding that pornography can be banned only if obscene under *Miller* or if it depicts actual children under *New York v. Ferber, supra*. The Supreme Court granted certiorari.

Issue. May Congress prohibit "virtual" child pornography?

Held. No. Judgment affirmed.

♦ Congress determined that children can be threatened by virtual pornography, even when they are not harmed in the production process, because pedophiles might use the materials to encourage children to participate in sexual activity. Virtual child pornography might also prompt the sexual appetites of pedophiles. The harm Congress identified flows from the content of the images, not from the means of production.

♦ Modern imaging technology also makes it harder to prosecute pornographers who use real minors. Innocent pictures of real children can be modified to make it appear that the children are engaged in sexual activity.

♦ The CPPA prohibits any depiction of sexually explicit activity, even if in a psychology manual or in a movie about the horrors of sexual abuse, and it applies to depictions of person under 18 years of age. However, teenage sexual activity has been the topic of countless literary works, from Shakespeare to acclaimed modern movies.

♦ Congress cannot prohibit speech that adults have a right to hear in an attempt to shield children from that speech. It also cannot prohibit otherwise protected speech because pedophiles might use it for illegal purposes. The tendency of speech to encourage unlawful acts is not a sufficient reason for banning it.

♦ D's argument that virtual pornography makes it difficult to prosecute actual child pornography is an argument that protected speech may be banned as a means to ban unprotected speech. However, D may not suppress lawful speech as the means to suppress unlawful speech. Protected speech does not become unprotected merely because it resembles unprotected speech.

Concurrence (Thomas, J.). If imaging technology develops to the point that the government cannot prove that child pornography depicts real children, it may be necessary to regulate virtual child pornography as long as there is an appropriate affirmative defense.

Concurrence and dissent (O'Connor, J., Rehnquist, C.J., Scalia, J.). Although the CPPA is overbroad, the prohibition of pornographic images that appear to be of minors is constitutional. D's concern about the advances in computer-graphics technology is reasonable.

Dissent (Rehnquist, C.J., Scalia, J.). Congress has a compelling interest in making it possible to enforce prohibitions of actual child pornography. The CPPA need not be interpreted so as to reach films or other literature that has literary or artistic value.

c.   **Sex discrimination and pornography--**

American Booksellers Association, Inc. v. Hudnut, 771 F.2d 323 (7th Cir. 1985), *aff'd mem.* 475 U.S. 1001 (1986).

Facts. American Booksellers Association, Inc. (P) sued Hudnut (D), the mayor of Indianapolis, to prevent enforcement of an ordinance that defined "pornography" as a practice that discriminates against women, subjecting it to regulation and remedies used for other forms of discrimination. The ordinance precludes trafficking in pornography, coercing others into performing in pornographic works, forcing pornography on a person, or assaulting anyone in a way that is directly caused by specific pornography, for which a right of action arises under the statute against pornography makers or sellers. The district court held that the ordinance was unconstitutional and prevented its enforcement. D appeals.

Issue. May the government restrict pornographic speech that conveys a message of discrimination against women?

Held. No. Judgment affirmed.

♦   D's ordinance does not judge the work as a whole, but focuses on particular depictions, so that it is irrelevant whether the work has literary, artistic, political, or scientific value. D notes that the ordinance is not intended to vindicate community standards of offensiveness, but to alter the socialization of men and women.

♦   There are many arguments for and against the ordinance, but basically the ordinance discriminates against expression on the ground of the content of the speech. Speech treating women in the approved way, with sexual encounters premised on equality, is lawful regardless of how sexually explicit, while speech treating women in an unapproved way is unlawful, regardless of the literary, artistic, or political qualities of the work taken as a whole.

♦   The First Amendment prevents the government from evaluating ideas and regulating based on content. Yet this statute expressly regulates speech based on its viewpoint. D claims that the regulation is justified because the prohibited form of pornography is not an idea but an injury because it does not persuade people but it changes them and socializes them by establishing what conduct is permissible.

♦   D's position demonstrates the power of pornography as speech. Its adverse effects depend on mental intermediation. This is also true of speech advocating racial bigotry, anti-Semitism, violence, and other undesirable social activity. Many types of speech have the effect of social conditioning, including religious ceremonies and school curriculum. If the government could regulate speech based on its effect on people, there would be no free speech.

♦ D argues that pornography is low value speech, similar to obscenity. But the Supreme Court's definition of obscenity is not based on the point of view of the particular work. D's approach focuses on the message of the speech and is therefore unconstitutional. Any rationale to support D's ordinance could not be limited to sex discrimination. There is no way to construe D's ordinance that would make it constitutional.

---

      d.   **Racist speech.** In *Collin v. Smith*, 578 F.2d 1197 (7th Cir. 1978), *cert. denied,* 439 U.S. 916 (1978), the court held that a city could not make it a misdemeanor to disseminate material promoting and inciting racial or religious hatred, such as Nazi swastikas and uniforms. The city had not acted to protect against physical violence, but to prevent the infliction of psychic trauma on resident holocaust survivors. The protection of such interests is indistinguishable from protection against speech that invites dispute or stirs people to anger, but the latter type of speech is clearly protected by the First Amendment. Public expression cannot be prohibited on the grounds that the ideas expressed are offensive to the hearers.

B. UNCONVENTIONAL FORMS OF COMMUNICATION

    1.   **Introduction.** The protection afforded unpopular words extends to symbolic conduct that can be considered expression; *i.e.,* conduct undertaken to communicate an idea. Not all such conduct is protected, however. If regulation of the conduct has only an incidental restriction on expression, the regulation may be permitted.

    2.   **Draft Card Burning--**

United States v. O'Brien, 391 U.S. 367 (1968).

Facts. O'Brien and others (Ds) publicly burned their draft cards, in violation of federal law. Ds claim their action was intended to influence others to adopt their antiwar beliefs. Ds were convicted, but the court of appeals held that the statute was an unconstitutional abridgment of freedom of speech. The Supreme Court granted review.

Issue. When conduct contains both "speech" and "nonspeech" elements, may an important governmental interest in regulating the nonspeech element justify incidental limitations on First Amendment freedoms?

Held. Yes. Judgment reversed.

- The statute on its face does not abridge free speech, but deals with conduct having no connection with speech, *i.e.,* destruction of draft cards. It is similar to a motor vehicle law prohibiting destruction of drivers' licenses.

- Although freedom of expression includes certain symbolic speech, it does not include any and all conduct intended to express an idea. Even conduct that contains a protected communicative element is not absolutely immune from government regulation. A sufficiently important governmental interest in regulating the nonspeech element of conduct can justify incidental limitations on the speech element.

- A government regulation is justified if: (i) it is within constitutional authority; (ii) it furthers an important governmental interest; (iii) the interest is unrelated to the suppression of free expression; and (iv) the incidental restriction on First Amendment freedoms is no greater than is essential to the furtherance of that interest.

- The draft card laws meet this test. Therefore, D may properly be prosecuted for his illegal activity.

Concurrence (Harlan, J.). This decision does not foreclose a First Amendment claim in those rare instances where a regulation would entirely prevent a speaker from lawfully conveying a message. D could have conveyed his message in many other ways.

Dissent (Douglas, J.). The underlying and basic question here is whether conscription is permissible in the absence of a declaration of war.

---

3. Flag Burning--

Texas v. Johnson, 491 U.S. 397 (1989).

Facts. During the 1984 Republican National Convention, Johnson (D) doused an American flag with kerosene and set it on fire, to chants of "America, the red, white, and blue, we spit on you." Several witnesses were seriously offended, but no one was physically injured or threatened with injury. D was convicted of desecration of the flag and sentenced to a year in prison and a $2,000 fine. The Texas Court of Criminal Appeals reversed. Texas (P) appeals.

Issue. May a state make it a criminal offense to burn the American flag?

Held. No. Judgment affirmed.

- D's burning the flag constitutes expressive, overtly political conduct, so he can invoke the First Amendment under *Spence v. Washington*, 418 U.S. 405 (1974). The government has greater latitude to regulate expressive conduct than written or spoken words, but it may not prohibit conduct because of the conduct's expressive elements.

♦ The standard established in *O'Brien, supra,* applies when the government interest in regulating conduct is unrelated to the suppression of expression. P here claims an interest in preventing breaches of the peace and in preserving the flag as a symbol of nationhood and national unity. On these facts, the first interest is not implicated, and the second is related to the suppression of expression. Accordingly, the *O'Brien* test does not apply.

♦ P's interest in preserving the symbolism of the flag is aimed not at the flag's physical integrity (because burning is a permitted means of disposing of an old flag), but at the likely offense D's conduct would cause. Because P's restriction is content-based, it is subject to the most exacting scrutiny.

♦ The government clearly may not prohibit the expression of an idea simply because society finds the idea offensive. No exceptions to this principle have ever been permitted. The government is not empowered to insure that a symbol be used to express only one view, nor does the Constitution recognize any special judicial category for the American flag. Therefore, the government may not criminally punish a person for burning the flag as a means of political protest.

Concurrence (Kennedy, J.). I agree that the flag holds a place of honor, but the Constitution guarantees D the right to this form of speech. Sometimes we must make decisions that we do not like because the law compels it.

Dissent (Rehnquist, C.J., White, O'Connor, JJ.). The American flag is not just another idea competing for recognition in the marketplace of ideas. The flag has a special status. D could have conveyed his message in any of a number of alternative ways. In fact, D's form of protest was relatively inarticulate, and he was punished not for the idea he sought to convey, but only for the use of this particular symbol.

Dissent (Stevens, J.). The flag symbolizes not just nationhood, but also freedom, equal opportunity, and other fundamental values. The government may protect the flag as much as it may protect the Washington Monument against even political graffiti. Sanctioning public desecration of the flag will tarnish its value. This case involves disagreeable conduct, not disagreeable ideas.

Comment. The same majority held unconstitutional a federal statute enacted by Congress in reaction to the *Johnson* case that was intended to prevent any mutilation, including burnings, of any flag of the United States except during proper disposal. [United States v. Eichman, 496 U.S. 310 (1990)]

4. Sleeping in Public Parks--

Clark v. Community for Creative Non-Violence, 468 U.S. 288 (1984).

Facts. The Community for Creative Non-Violence (P) obtained a permit from Clark (D), Secretary of the Interior, to conduct a wintertime demonstration in Lafayette Park and the Mall in Washington, D.C. The demonstration consisted of two symbolic tent cities, intended to show the plight of the homeless. However, D denied P's request that demonstrators be allowed to sleep in the tents. D's regulations prohibited camping in National Parks except in designated campgrounds. P sued to prevent application of the regulations to its demonstration. The district court granted D summary judgment, but the court of appeals reversed. D appeals.

Issue. May the federal government prevent demonstrators from sleeping in National Parks pursuant to general regulations when the sleeping is asserted to be expression?

Held. Yes. Judgment reversed.

◆　Assuming that overnight sleeping is expressive conduct, it is subject to reasonable time, place, and manner restrictions. In addition, symbolic expression may be regulated or forbidden if:

　　(i)　The regulation is narrowly drawn to further a substantial governmental interest; and

　　(ii)　The interest is unrelated to the suppression of free speech.

◆　D's regulations are defensible both as time, place, and manner restrictions on expressive conduct and as regulations of symbolic conduct. The regulation is clearly content-neutral. It narrowly focuses on D's interest in maintaining the parks in a suitable condition.

◆　Although D could have issued more restrictive regulations, these regulations are valid as reasonable as long as the parks would be more exposed to harm without the sleeping prohibition than with it. The court of appeals determined that other alternatives, less restrictive on speech, were available. This is a disagreement with D, but the judiciary does not manage the National Parks.

Concurrence (Burger, C.J.). Sleeping is conduct, not speech entitled to First Amendment protection.

Dissent (Marshall, Brennan, JJ.). The symbolic speech involved here is subject to reasonable time, place, and manner restrictions. D's regulations do not advance substantial government interests in this case. The Court has adopted a two-tiered approach to First Amendment cases. Once the regulation has been shown to be content-neutral, the Court applies a lower level of scrutiny, thus diminishing First Amendment protections.

5. **Building Closure.** In *Arcara v. Cloud Books, Inc.*, 478 U.S. 697 (1986), the Court held that a state may force the closure of a building for one year if it has been used for purposes of lewdness, assignation, or prostitution. This statute was applied to close an adult bookstore in which these activities had taken place, even though there was no claim that the books in the store were obscene. The Court noted that an incidental burden on expression is permissible, and that the sexual activity being regulated has no element of protected expression.

C. LESS PROTECTED SPEECH

1. Near Obscene Speech.

a. Zoning--

Young v. American Mini Theatres, Inc., 427 U.S. 50 (1976).

Facts. The city of Detroit (represented by Young (D)) adopted amendments to an "Anti-Skid Row" ordinance that regulated the locations of theaters showing sexually explicit "adult" movies. American Mini Theatres, Inc. (P) was denied use of its theaters because they violated D's location regulations. P sought declaratory and injunctive relief. The court of appeals held for P. D appeals.

Issue. May a city use exhibition of sexually explicit "adult" movies as a basis for statutory classification of theaters?

Held. Yes. Judgment reversed.

♦ The location regulations clearly are within D's police power and do not, by themselves, violate the First Amendment.

♦ The question whether speech is, or is not, protected by the First Amendment often depends on the content of the speech. Society's interest in protecting expression of erotic materials is wholly different, and lesser, than its interest in protecting political or philosophical discussion. Although the First Amendment does not permit total suppression of erotic material, it does permit the states to use their content as a basis for classification.

♦ The line drawn by D's regulation is reasonable in light of D's valid objectives.

Concurrence (Powell, J.). This is a case of an innovative land-use regulation, only incidentally affecting First Amendment rights. The regulation is not aimed at expression but at the quality of life in the city, and it does not offend the First Amendment.

Dissent (Stewart, Brennan, Marshall, Blackmun, JJ.). The Court's holding drastically departs from precedent in allowing D to use a system of prior restraints and criminal sanctions to enforce content-based restrictions on expression. The First Amendment prohibits selective interference with protected speech, even if distasteful.

---

b. Regulation of speech based on secondary effects--

Renton v. Playtime Theatres, Inc., 475 U.S. 41 (1986).

Facts. The city of Renton (D) adopted a zoning ordinance that prohibited adult motion picture theaters within 1,000 feet of any residential zone, single- or multiple-family dwelling, church, or park, or within one mile of a school. Subsequently, Playtime Theatres, Inc. (P) purchased two theaters within D's jurisdiction and within the prohibited areas. Desiring to use the theaters for adult films, P sought declaratory and injunctive relief against the ordinance. In the meantime, D added a statement of reasons for the ordinance and reduced the one-mile distance to 1,000 feet from a school. The district court granted summary judgment for D. The court of appeals reversed. The Supreme Court granted certiorari.

Issue. May a city prohibit the operation of adult movie theaters within 1,000 feet of residences, churches, parks, and schools?

Held. Yes. Judgment reversed.

♦ An ordinance similar to D's was approved in *Young, supra*. D's ordinance is not a total ban; it is a time, place, and manner regulation. It is neither explicitly content-based nor content-neutral. The ordinance is aimed at the secondary effects of such theaters; D's predominate concern was with protecting and preserving the quality of life in neighborhoods and commercial districts, not with suppressing unpopular views.

♦ Because D's ordinance is not content-based and is aimed at undesirable secondary effects, it must be reviewed under the standards applicable to content-neutral time, place, and manner regulations. As long as the ordinance is designed to serve a substantial governmental interest and allows for reasonable alternative avenues of communication, it is permissible.

♦ D relied on the experiences of the city of Seattle in determining the substantial governmental interest justifying its ordinance, and there is no requirement that a city produce new evidence when the experience of other cities is relevant. Nor does it matter that Seattle chose a different type of zoning.

♦ D's ordinance leaves open over 5% of the city's land area, or 520 acres, for P's use. It does not matter that there are no readily available adult theater sites in the 520 acres; there is no First Amendment protection against competition in the real estate market. D has not denied P a reasonable opportunity to open and operate an adult theater within the city.

Dissent (Brennan, Marshall, JJ.). The ordinance is clearly content-based. It is designed to suppress constitutionally protected expression. D has not shown that P's theaters will necessarily result in undesirable secondary effects that could not be effectively addressed by less intrusive restrictions. Nor does it leave open reasonable alternative avenues of communication, because the 520 acres is largely occupied or unsuited for movie theaters.

---

2. **Prohibition of Public Nudity--**

City of Erie v. Pap's A.M., 529 U.S. 277 (2000).

Facts. The city of Erie (D) made it an offense to knowingly or intentionally appear in public in a "state of nudity." Pap's A.M. (P) operated "Kandyland," which featured totally nude erotic dancing by women. Under D's ordinance, P's dancers had to wear "pasties" and a "G-string." P sued D seeking declaratory relief and a permanent injunction against enforcement of the ordinance. The trial court held the ordinance unconstitutional, and the Pennsylvania Supreme Court ultimately agreed, holding that because the ordinance was related to the suppression of expression and was not content-neutral, it was subject to strict scrutiny. The Supreme Court granted certiorari.

Issue. May a municipality ban appearing in public in a state of nudity?

Held. Yes. Judgment reversed and remanded.

♦   Government restrictions on public nudity such as D's ordinance should be evaluated under *United States v. O'Brien, supra*, for content-neutral restrictions on symbolic speech. Although being "in a state of nudity" is not an inherently expressive condition, nude dancing of the type at issue here is expressive conduct that falls within the outer ambit of the First Amendment's protection.

♦   The appropriate level of scrutiny depends on whether the ordinance is related to the suppression of expression. If the governmental purpose in enacting the ordinance is unrelated to such suppression, the ordinance need only satisfy the "less stringent," intermediate *O'Brien* standard. If the governmental interest is related to the expression's content, however, the ordinance falls outside *O'Brien* and must be justified under the more demanding, strict scrutiny standard.

♦   An almost identical public nudity ban was upheld under the First Amendment in *Barnes v. Glen Theatre, Inc.*, 501 U.S. 560 (1991). The ordinance in this case is a general prohibition on public nudity that regulates conduct alone. It does not target nudity that is accompanied by expressive activity, such as an erotic message. The Pennsylvania Supreme Court construed the ordinance's preamble to mean that one of its purposes was to combat negative secondary effects, such as crime, caused by the presence of adult entertainment establishments like Kandyland and not at suppressing the erotic message conveyed by this type of nude dancing.

◆ Courts should not strike down otherwise constitutional statutes on the basis of allegedly illicit motive. Even if D's public nudity ban has some minimal effect on the erotic message, P's dancers are free to perform wearing pasties and G-strings. Any effect on the overall expression is therefore *de minimis*. Thus, D's ordinance is valid if it satisfies the *O'Brien* test.

◆ D's ordinance satisfies *O'Brien*'s four-factor test. First, the ordinance is within D's police power to protect public health and safety. Second, the ordinance furthers the important government interests of regulating conduct through a public nudity ban and of combating the harmful secondary effects associated with nude dancing, as demonstrated in other cases. Although requiring dancers to wear pasties and G-strings may not greatly reduce these secondary effects, *O'Brien* requires only that the regulation further the interest in combating such effects.

◆ D's ordinance also satisfies *O'Brien*'s third factor, that the government interest is unrelated to the suppression of free expression. The fourth *O'Brien* factor— that the restriction is no greater than is essential to the furtherance of the government interest—is satisfied because the ordinance regulates conduct, and any incidental impact on the expressive element of nude dancing is *de minimis*. The pasties and G-string requirement is a minimal restriction in furtherance of the asserted government interests, and the restriction leaves ample capacity to convey the dancers' erotic message.

Concurrence (Scalia, Thomas, JJ.). D modeled its ordinance on the public nudity statute upheld in *Barnes*, which was upheld because, as a general law regulating conduct and not specifically directed at expression, it was not subject to First Amendment scrutiny at all. There is no need to identify "secondary effects" associated with nude dancing that Erie could properly seek to eliminate. The traditional power of government to foster good morals, and the acceptability of the traditional judgment that nude public dancing *itself* is immoral, have not been repealed by the First Amendment.

Concurrence and dissent (Souter, J.). The record in this case fails to reveal any evidence on which D may have relied, either for the seriousness of the threatened harm or for the efficacy of its chosen remedy. Under *O'Brien*, the incidental speech restriction must be no greater than essential to achieve the government's legitimate purpose. D might have been able to counter secondary effects by the significantly lesser restriction of zoning.

Dissent (Stevens, Ginsburg, JJ.). The Court today holds that secondary effects may justify the total suppression of protected speech and not merely the regulation of the location of indecent entertainment.

---

3. **Commercial Speech.**

    a. **Introduction.** Commercial speech is entitled to some degree of protection under the First Amendment, although subject to more stringent regulation than would be permissible with respect to noncommercial speech. In determining the degree of protection, the free speech interest in the contents of the speech must be weighed against the public interest served by the governmental regulation. (*See Bigelow v. Virginia*, 421 U.S. 809 (1975), which held that commercial speech merits some protection.)

    b. **Scope of protection--**

Virginia State Board of Pharmacy v. Virginia Citizens Consumer Council, 425 U.S. 748 (1976).

Facts. The Virginia State Board of Pharmacy (D) prohibited advertisement of the retail prices of prescription drugs by pharmacists. The Virginia Citizens Consumer Council (P), for itself and on behalf of users of prescription drugs, sought an injunction against the enforcement of D's rule. The three-judge district court granted the injunction. D appeals.

Issue. Is purely commercial speech wholly outside First Amendment protection?

Held. No. Judgment affirmed.

♦   First Amendment protection extends to the communication, to its source, and to its recipients. P, as a potential recipient of the advertising, has standing to bring this action.

♦   The speech in question, commercial advertising, is not disqualified from protection merely because the speaker's interest is purely economic. The particular consumer has a vital interest in the free flow of commercial information, possibly a greater interest than in current political debates, which are clearly protected.

♦   Society in general has a strong interest in the free flow of commercial information. Actually, such a free flow is essential to the proper functioning of our economic system. It is likely that no line can properly be drawn between "important," and hence protected, advertising and the opposite kind.

♦   D claims an interest in protecting the public from unscrupulous pharmacists who would use advertising to their own advantage and the public's detriment. But the choice between the dangers of suppressing information and the dangers of its misuse if it is freely available has been made by the First Amendment. Therefore, D cannot prohibit commercial advertising of the type involved here.

♦ Although commercial speech is protected, it remains subject to proper restrictions, *e.g.,* time, place, and manner restrictions; false and misleading advertising prohibitions; and prohibitions against advertising illegal transactions.

Concurrence (Burger, C.J.). The Court expresses no opinion as to regulation of advertising by other professionals, such as lawyers.

Concurrence (Stewart, J.). Commercial price and product advertising differs markedly from ideological expression because it is confined to the promotion of specific goods or services. Commercial expression is protected because of the information of potential interest and value conveyed, rather than because of any direct contribution to the interchange of ideas. Therefore, commercial speech is subject to proper regulation assuring its accuracy and reliability.

Dissent (Rehnquist, J.). The Court expands the standing requirements and extends First Amendment protection beyond what is necessary. This ruling prevents the states from protecting the public against dangers resulting from excessive promotion of drugs that should be used only with professional guidance.

Comment. The Court emphasized the importance of a free flow of information by invalidating an ordinance that prohibited the posting of "for sale" signs on real estate. The township had justified the ordinance as a means of preventing "white flight" from racially integrated neighborhoods, but this justification was inadequate. [*See* Linmark Associates, Inc. v. Township of Willingboro, 431 U.S. 85 (1977)]

---

c. **Attorney advertising--**

Ohralik v. Ohio State Bar Association, 436 U.S. 447 (1978).

Facts. Ohralik (P) solicited two clients in person after discovering they had been injured. When the clients later sought other counsel, P sued for breach of contract. The Ohio State Bar Association (D) suspended P indefinitely. P challenged the suspension, but the lower courts upheld D's action. P appeals.

Issue. May a state prohibit attorneys from soliciting clients in person for pecuniary gain?

Held. Yes. Judgment affirmed.

♦ Commercial speech is protected under the First Amendment, although the protection is limited as compared to noncommercial speech. A course of conduct may be prohibited even if it is carried out by means of language.

- P's solicitation was a business transaction. The state has a significant interest in regulating lawyers because of the role they play in society. Solicitation of clients has several evils, including stirring up litigation, possible misrepresentation, etc., which provide grounds for regulation. In-person solicitation is even more likely to pressure potential clients than mere advertising, which was permitted in *Bates v. State Bar*, 433 U.S. 350 (1977).

- Even though P claims no harm was done in this case, the state does not need to prove actual injury. The only witnesses to such solicitation are normally the attorney and the solicitee. The difficulty of proving what actually occurred should not immunize attorneys against improper solicitation.

Comment. The majority of the Court would uphold a restriction on commercial billboards to further the aesthetic and traffic safety interests of a city. [Metromedia, Inc. v. San Diego, 453 U.S. 490 (1981)]

---

d. **Four-part analysis of commercial speech.** In *Central Hudson Gas & Electric Corp. v. Public Service Commission*, 447 U.S. 557 (1980), the Court set forth a four-part analysis regarding commercial speech.

1) First, is the expression protected? If it concerns lawful activity and is not misleading, it generally is.

2) Second, is the asserted governmental interest in regulation substantial?

3) Third, does the regulation directly advance the governmental interest?

4) Fourth, is the regulation more extensive than necessary?

e. **Regulations on advertising and sale of tobacco products--**

Lorillard Tobacco Co. v. Reilly, 533 U.S. 525 (2001).

Facts. Reilly (D), the Attorney General of Massachusetts, promulgated comprehensive regulations on the advertising and sale of tobacco products. The regulations included a prohibition on outdoor advertising within 1,000 feet of a school or playground and a point-of-sale regulation that prohibited indoor advertising lower than five feet from the floor. Lorillard Tobacco Co. and other tobacco manufacturers and retailers (Ps) challenged the constitutionality of the regulations. The district court found the regulations valid, except for the point-of-sale regulation. The First Circuit reversed the ruling on the indoor advertising issue, but upheld the district court's decision that the regulations were not pre-empted by the Federal Cigarette Labeling and Advertising Act ("FCLAA"). The Supreme Court granted certiorari.

Issue. Does the First Amendment prohibit a state from placing comprehensive regulations on the advertising and sale of legal products, even if the purpose of the regulations is to prevent the use of the products by underage consumers?

Held. Yes. Judgment reversed in part.

♦ The FCLAA prevents states and localities from regulating the location of cigarette advertising. Consequently, D's regulations regarding outdoor and point-of-sale advertising of cigarettes are preempted. However, because this preemption applies only to cigarettes, we must consider the smokeless tobacco and cigar petitioners' First Amendment challenges to the outdoor and point-of-sale advertising regulations.

♦ The cigarette petitioners did not raise a preemption challenge to the sales practices regulations. Thus, we must consider the cigarette petitioners' claim, as well as the smokeless tobacco and cigar petitioners' claim, that certain sales practices regulations for tobacco products violate the First Amendment.

♦ The *Central Hudson* (*supra*) analysis applies to this case, but only the last two steps of the four-part analysis are at issue here.

♦ The third step of *Central Hudson* concerns the relationship between the harm that underlies the state's interest and the means identified by the state to advance that interest. The ban on outdoor advertising within a 1,000-foot radius of a school is supported by D's evidence of the problem with underage use of smokeless tobacco and cigars, as well as by evidence that limiting youth exposure to advertising will decrease such use. This satisfies the third step of *Central Hudson*.

♦ The fourth *Central Hudson* step requires narrowly tailored means to achieve the desired objective. The broad sweep of D's outdoor advertising regulations does not suggest careful calculation of the speech interests involved. Also, the effect of the regulations would vary throughout the state, depending on whether an area is rural, suburban, or urban. D's ban affects a substantial portion of the metropolitan areas in the state, and would constitute nearly a complete ban in some areas. While D has a compelling interest in preventing underage tobacco use, adult usage of these products is legal.

Concurrence (Kennedy, Scalia, JJ.). Because the outdoor advertising restrictions are overbroad and fail the fourth part of the *Central Hudson* test, I refrain from considering the third part of the test.

Concurrence (Thomas, J.). An asserted government interest in keeping people ignorant by suppressing expression can no more justify regulation of commercial speech than it can justify regulation of noncommercial speech. And it cannot be argued that

First Amendment principles should not apply to cigarette advertising because of the harm from smoking if alcohol and high-calorie, high-fat foods can advertise without similar restrictions. Even speech about an activity that legislatures regard as harmful is entitled to First Amendment protections.

Concurrence and dissent (Stevens, Ginsburg, Breyer, Souter, JJ.). The FCLAA does not preempt D's regulations. The case should be remanded for further fact-findings regarding the tailoring of D's regulations.

---

4.   **Private Speech and** *Gertz*--

Dun & Bradstreet, Inc. v. Greenmoss Builders, Inc., 472 U.S. 749 (1985).

Facts. Dun & Bradstreet, Inc. (D) was a credit reporting agency. D reported that Greenmoss Builders, Inc. (P) had filed for bankruptcy. The report was false and negligently prepared. P sued for defamation and recovered compensatory and punitive damages. The lower courts upheld the award. The Supreme Court granted certiorari.

Issue. May a defamed person recover presumed and punitive damages, even without proving actual malice, if the defamation was not speech on a public matter?

Held. Yes. Judgment affirmed.

♦   When defamatory statements involve no issue of public concern, the court must balance the state's interest in compensating injured parties against the First Amendment interest in protecting the expression. Speech on private matters does not merit the highest First Amendment protection; thus, there are fewer constitutional limits on state libel law in this area.

♦   Examination of D's credit report indicates it did not constitute speech on a public issue. It was intended only for the benefit of D and its business audience of five subscribers. The speech was wholly false and clearly damaging to P. Thus the speech merits little protection.

♦   There is little danger of chilling due to libel suits, because the market itself provides the incentive to be truthful.

Concurrence (White, J.). *Gertz* should be overruled, but at any rate this case does not involve a matter of public importance.

Dissent (Brennan, Marshall, Blackmun, Stevens, JJ.). The First Amendment applies equally to citizens and the institutional press. The Court gives no guidance as to what is a protected matter of public concern. Surely a company's filing for bankruptcy is a matter of public concern to the community where the company is located. Bankruptcy is a matter of public record. The speech here was not advertising; even if the credit report is commercial speech, the appropriate remedy should be actual damages, or, upon a showing of actual malice, presumed or punitive damages.

---

5. **Content of "Fighting Speech"--**

R.A.V. v. St. Paul, 505 U.S. 377 (1992).

Facts. R.A.V. (D) and several other teenagers assembled a cross from broken chair legs and burned it inside the fenced yard of a black family who lived across the street from D's current residence. The city of St. Paul, Minnesota (P) charged D with disorderly conduct pursuant to an ordinance that provided, "Whoever places on public or private property a symbol, object, appellation, characterization or graffiti, including, but not limited to, a burning cross or Nazi swastika, which one knows or has reasonable grounds to know arouses anger, alarm or resentment in others on the basis of race, color, creed, religion or gender commits disorderly conduct and shall be guilty of a misdemeanor." D moved to dismiss the charge on the ground that the ordinance was invalid under the First Amendment because it was overbroad and impermissibly content-based. The trial court granted D's motion, but the Minnesota Supreme Court reversed, construing the ordinance to apply only to conduct that amounts to "fighting words," *i.e.,* "conduct that itself inflicts injury or tends to incite immediate violence." The Supreme Court granted certiorari.

Issue. May the government regulate "fighting words" based on the subjects the speech addresses?

Held. No. Judgment reversed.

♦   Content-based speech regulations are presumptively invalid, but, as the Court held in *Chaplinsky, supra,* there are exceptions in a few limited areas that are "of such slight social value as a step to truth that any benefit that may be derived from them is clearly outweighed by the social interest in order and morality."

♦   Certain categories of expression are "not within the area of constitutionally protected speech" (*e.g.,* obscenity, defamation, etc.), which means that they may be regulated because of their constitutionally proscribable content. This does not mean they may be used to discriminate on the basis of content unrelated to their distinctively proscribable content; *i.e.,* although the government may proscribe libel, it cannot proscribe only libel that is critical of the government.

♦ The exclusion of "fighting words" from the scope of the First Amendment means that the unprotected features of the words are essentially a "nonspeech" element of communication. But there is a "content discrimination" limitation on the government's prohibition of proscribable speech; the government may not regulate use based on hostility or favoritism towards the underlying message expressed.

♦ When the basis for content discrimination entirely consists of the very reason the class of speech is proscribable, there is no significant danger of idea or viewpoint discrimination. The government may prohibit only the most patently offensive obscenity, but it cannot prohibit only obscenity that includes offensive political messages. Or, the government may regulate price advertising in one industry and not in others, because the risk of fraud is greater there, but it cannot prohibit only that commercial advertising that depicts men in a demeaning fashion.

♦ The government could properly give differential treatment to even a content-defined subclass of proscribable speech if the subclass is associated with particular "secondary effects" of the speech; *e.g.,* prohibiting only those obscene live performances that involve minors. And laws against conduct instead of speech may reach speech based on content, such as sexually derogatory "fighting words" that violate Title VII's prohibition against sexual discrimination. The key element is that the government does not target conduct on the basis of its expressive content.

♦ In this case, P's ordinance is facially unconstitutional because it applies only to "fighting words" that insult, or provoke violence, "on the basis of race, color, creed, religion or gender." It does not apply to abusive invectives on other topics, but singles out those speakers who express views on disfavored subjects. Instead of singling out a particularly offensive mode of expression, P has proscribed fighting words of whatever manner that communicate messages of racial, gender, or religious intolerance. This creates the possibility that P hopes to handicap the expression of certain ideas.

♦ P's content discrimination is not reasonably necessary to achieve P's compelling interests; an ordinance not limited to the favored topics would have precisely the same beneficial interest.

Concurrence (White, Blackmun, O'Connor, Stevens, JJ.).

♦ P's ordinance is overbroad because it criminalizes expression protected by the First Amendment as well as unprotected expression. The majority's rationale is a new doctrine that was not even briefed by the parties and is a departure from prior cases. The Court has long applied a categorical approach that identifies certain classifications of speech as unprotected by the First Amendment because the evil to be restricted so overwhelmingly outweighs the expressive interests, if any, at stake. The Court now holds that the First Amendment protects these categories to the extent that the government may not regulate some fighting words more strictly than others because of their content. Now, if the government decides to criminalize certain fighting words, it must criminalize all fighting words.

♦ The Court also refuses to sustain P's ordinance even though it would survive under the strict scrutiny applicable to other protected expression.

♦ Although the Court's analysis is flawed, the conclusion is correct because P's ordinance is overbroad. Even as construed by the Minnesota Supreme Court, the ordinance criminalizes a substantial amount of expression that is protected by the First Amendment. That court held that P may constitutionally prohibit expression that "by its very utterance" causes "anger, alarm or resentment," but such generalized reactions are not sufficient to strip expression of its constitutional protection.

Concurrence (Blackmun, J.). States should be able to regulate categories of speech that cause great harm. There is nothing unconstitutional about a law that prevents hoodlums from driving minorities out of their homes by cross burnings. However, I concur in the judgment because this particular ordinance is too broad.

Concurrence (Stevens, J.). P's ordinance regulates conduct that has some communicative content, and it raises two questions: Is it "overbroad" because it prohibits too much speech, and if not, is it "underbroad" because it does not prohibit enough speech? The majority and concurring opinions deal with the basic principles that (i) certain categories of expression are not protected and (ii) content-based regulations of expression are presumptively invalid. But both principles have exceptions. The majority applies the prohibition on content-based regulation to "fighting words"—speech that previously had been considered wholly "unprotected." Now, fighting words have greater protection than commercial speech, which is often regulated based on content. Assuming arguendo that the ordinance regulates only fighting words and is not overbroad, it regulates speech not on the basis of its subject matter or the viewpoint expressed, but rather on the basis of the harm the speech causes—injuries based on "race, color, creed, religion, or gender." It only bans a subcategory of the already narrow category of fighting words. It is not an unconstitutional content-based regulation of speech, and should be upheld, except that it is overbroad.

---

6. **Statutory Inference of Intent from Conduct Not Allowed--**

Virginia v. Black, 538 U.S. 343 (2003).

Facts. The state of Virginia enacted a statute prohibiting the burning of a cross with "an intent to intimidate a person or group of persons." Subsequently, Virginia added a provision that the public burning of a cross was prima facie evidence of an intent to intimidate. Black and others (Ds) were tried for violating the statute. At the trial, the jury was instructed that Ds' burning of the cross, by itself, was sufficient evidence from which the jury could infer the required intent to intimidate. Ds were convicted. The Virginia Supreme Court declared the statute unconstitutional. The Supreme Court granted certiorari.

Issue. May a criminal statute provide that the burning of a cross is prima facie evidence of an intent to intimidate when such an intention is one of the elements of the crime?

Held. No. Judgment affirmed in part, vacated in part, and case remanded.

♦ The government may regulate categories of expression, including fighting words and incitement, as well as true threats. Intimidation is a type of true threat, where the speaker directs a threat to a person with the intent of making the victim fear bodily harm or death. Some cross burnings fit within this definition of intimidating speech.

♦ Virginia may properly outlaw cross burnings done with the intent to intimidate because such activity is a particularly virulent form of intimidation, given its history as a signal of impending violence.

♦ However, the statute is unconstitutional because the prima facie evidence provision allows a conviction without proof of the very element that makes it constitutional for Virginia to ban cross burning—the intent to intimidate. Virginia could not ban cross burning alone, without the intimidation intent as an element of the offense, so it cannot simply provide that cross burning constitutes prima facie evidence of the required intent. The statute does not distinguish between cross burning with intent to intimidate and cross burning as a political statement not intended to intimidate.

Concurrence and dissent (Scalia, Thomas, JJ.). I agree that a state may constitutionally prohibit cross burning with the intent to intimidate, but I disagree with the majority's finding that the prima facie evidence part of the statute is unconstitutional. However, in this case, the jury was instructed that "[t]he burning of a cross, by itself, is sufficient evidence from which you may infer the required intent." This instruction makes it impossible to determine whether the jury based its verdict on all of the facts presented, including evidence rebutting intent, or chose to ignore such rebuttal and focused only on the fact that the defendant burned a cross.

Concurrence and dissent (Souter, Kennedy, Ginsburg, JJ.). I agree that the Virginia statute makes a content-based distinction within the category of punishable intimidating expression, which is unconstitutional. This content-based proscription of cross burning could be an effort to ban not only intimidation, but also the messages communicated by non-threatening cross burning. No content-based statute should survive under *R.A.V.* without a high probability that no official suppression of ideas is afoot.

Severance of the prima facie evidence provision of the statute would not eliminate the unconstitutionality of the whole statute.

Dissent (Thomas, J.). Whatever expressive value cross burning may have, the legislature wrote it out by banning only intimidating conduct undertaken by a particular means. The statute addressed conduct only, not speech, and should not fall within the First Amendment. Even if the statute did implicate the First Amendment, permitting a jury to draw an inference of intent to intimidate from the cross burning itself is permissible. The inference is rebuttable, and the jury still has to find the existence of each element of the offense beyond a reasonable doubt. The Court values physical safety less than the right to be free from unwanted communications.

D. PRIOR RESTRAINTS

1. **Early Cases.** Government normally cannot regulate in advance what expressions may or may not be uttered or published, even to guard against speech or ideas that, once published, would be constitutionally unprotected and subject to state punishment, such as defamatory speech. Individual as well as public rights are deemed sufficiently protected by the deterrent effect of such punishment. The further step of prior restraint would make the government a censor, thereby undermining the core of the First Amendment. The early cases in this area involved attempts at prior restraint through licensing requirements and court injunctions.

   a. **Licensing.**

      1) **Introduction.** A state cannot condition the right of a person to express her views publicly on obtaining a permit to do so from local authorities when such permits are given on a purely discretionary basis. There must be some reasonable standard established on which to decide who gets a permit, when, and why.

      2) **Permit to distribute circulars--**

Lovell v. Griffin, 303 U.S. 444 (1938).

Facts. The city of Griffin (P) enacted an ordinance requiring written permission from the city manager for the distribution of literature of any kind at any time, at any place, and in any manner. Lovell (D) was convicted of violating the statute by distributing religious literature without a permit. D appeals, claiming the ordinance violates both freedom of the press and of religion.

Issue. May government prohibit all distribution of all literature without prior approval of a government agent?

Held. No. Judgment reversed.

- ◆ The ordinance is invalid on its face. Freedom of the press includes a right to publish without a license.

- ◆ The ordinance is overbroad because it prohibits distribution that does not in any way interfere with proper government functions.

---

3) Permit for door-to-door advocacy--

Watchtower Bible and Tract Society of New York v. Village of Stratton, 536 U.S. 150 (2002).

Facts. The village of Stratton (D) adopted an ordinance that regulated uninvited peddling and solicitation on private property by requiring a permit from the mayor to engage in door-to-door advocacy. The Watchtower Bible and Tract Society of New York (P) coordinated preaching activities of Jehovah's Witnesses throughout the United States, including in Stratton. P sued D to get an injunction against enforcement of the ordinance, claiming that it violated the First Amendment. The district court upheld the ordinance. The Sixth Circuit affirmed. The Supreme Court granted certiorari.

Issue. May a city require people to get a permit before engaging in the door-to-door advocacy of a political or religious cause?

Held. No. Judgment reversed.

- ◆ To require a citizen to inform the government of his desire to speak to his neighbors and to obtain a permit to do so offends the values protected by the First Amendment and the very notion of a free society.

- ◆ Local governments such as D have an interest in some form of regulation to prevent fraud, such as where solicitation for money is involved, and to prevent crime such as burglary, but any regulation must balance these interests with the First Amendment rights.

- ◆ D asserts that its ordinance serves the proper governmental interests of preventing fraud, preventing crime, and protecting residents' privacy. However, the ordinance applies to promoters of any cause, not merely commercial activities and the solicitation of funds. As such, it applies to religious causes and political activity. D's ordinance is overbroad and is not tailored to D's stated interests.

- ◆ The lack of a permit would not preclude criminals from knocking on doors and engaging in conversations not covered by the ordinance, such as asking for directions or posing as census takers.

Concurrence (Breyer, Souter, Ginsburg, JJ.). D did not specifically state that preventing burglaries and violent crimes was an important justification for the ordinance.

Concurrence (Scalia, Thomas, JJ.). While the majority's rationale is largely acceptable, the fact that some people may have a religious objection to applying for a permit should not be a ground for finding D's ordinance invalid.

Dissent (Rehnquist, CJ.). The problem of crime has been associated with door-to-door canvassing for many years. The Court has long held that a town may require a permit for door-to-door canvassers, as long as no discretion is given to the issuing authority. D's ordinance should be upheld.

---

b.   **Injunctions--**

Near v. Minnesota, 283 U.S. 697 (1931).

Facts. Minnesota (P) enacted a statute that provided for the abatement, as a public nuisance, of a "malicious, scandalous and defamatory" publication. Near (D) published a periodical that criticized law enforcement officers. P brought an action seeking to suppress D's publication. The state courts granted P's request. D appeals.

Issue. May a state grant an injunction against publication of allegedly defamatory material?

Held. No. Judgment reversed.

♦   Permitting public authorities to suppress publication of scandalous matter relating to charges of official dereliction, restrained only by the publisher's ability to satisfy the judge that the charges are true, is the essence of censorship. Liberty of the press under the Constitution has meant, principally although not exclusively, immunity from previous restraints or censorship.

♦   The only permissible restraint is the deterrent effect of actions against defamatory publications arising after publication.

Dissent (Butler, J.). The previous restraints precluded by the First Amendment refer to subjection of the press to the arbitrary will of an administrative officer. There is no similarity between such impermissible previous restraint and the decree authorized by this statute to prevent further publication of defamatory articles, and the statute should be upheld.

---

2. **Obscenity and Commercial Speech.**

a. **Injunctions after a determination of obscenity.** The Court's reluctance to permit prior restraints reflects a concern to protect expressions that might turn out to be constitutionally protected. However, this concern does not apply where there has already been a judicial determination that the material is "obscene." Thus, in *Kingsley Books, Inc. v. Brown*, 354 U.S. 436 (1957), the Court approved a procedure whereby the state instigated civil suits to determine "obscenity," and upon a determination that a work was obscene, the state court could grant an injunction against publication. The Court contrasted this case with *Near*, which involved an injunction against future publications. In *Kingsley*, the state could not act upon matters not already published and not yet found to be offensive.

b. **Special rule for motion pictures--**

Times Film Corp. v. Chicago, 365 U.S. 43 (1961).

Facts. Times Film Corp. (P) owned the exclusive right to show a movie in Chicago. Chicago had an ordinance requiring submission of all motion pictures for examination before they were allowed a permit to be shown. P refused to submit a copy for examination, was refused a permit, and challenged the constitutionality of the ordinance as a prior restraint.

Issue. Does the Constitution guarantee complete freedom to show, at least once, every motion picture?

Held. No. Judgment affirmed.

♦ Exceptions to the privilege against prior restraint have been made in cases of obscene publications, for obscenity is not protected speech. It therefore follows that the protection against prior restraint is not absolute.

♦ Motion pictures are "different" from other forms of expression, and the time delay inherent in any censorship system is not as critical for films as for other means of expression. Accordingly, statutes requiring that motion pictures be submitted "for examination or censorship" prior to being shown locally are constitutionally permissible.

Dissent (Warren, C.J., Black, Douglas, Brennan, JJ.). The majority's opinion is overbroad. It allows censorship of all motion pictures to prevent exhibition of constitutionally unprotected films.

Comment. This case involved only the censor's basic authority, not the standards to be used in evaluating films. In *Freedman v. Maryland*, 380 U.S. 51 (1965), the Court set forth the minimum procedural requirements for film censorship, including a prompt final judicial decision, preceded by an adversarial proceeding in which the censor has the burden of proof that the film is unprotected.

---

    c.   **Informal sanctions.** "Informal" sanctions taken by state agencies may be held unconstitutional. In *Bantam Books, Inc. v. Sullivan*, 372 U.S. 58 (1963), a state juvenile delinquency commission was empowered to make "informal recommendations" to book distributors as to which publications were objectionable for sale to youths. The recommendations were followed up by threats of court action, visits from police, etc., and the distributors were given no notice of hearing before their publications were listed as objectionable. The Court held this procedure unconstitutional, since its effect was to censor, in advance, what could be published.

    d.   **Restrictions on commercial speech.** The Court has held that a state may prohibit commercial advertising of illegal matters. In *Pittsburgh Press Co. v. Human Relations*, 413 U.S. 376 (1973), the Court upheld an injunction against a newspaper's "male" or "female" help-wanted columns on grounds of illegal sex discrimination.

  3.   **Licensing "Professionals"--**

Lowe v. S.E.C., 472 U.S. 181 (1985).

Facts. Lowe (D) published financial newsletters that he offered to the general public through the mail on a regular schedule. The Investment Advisors Act of 1940 prohibited such use of the mails by investment advisors not registered with the Securities and Exchange Commission (P). The definition of "investment advisor" included one who advises others through publications as to investments in securities, but does not include a publisher of a bona fide financial publication of general and regular circulation. D's registration with P had been revoked due to D's convictions of various offenses. P sued to enjoin D from publishing his newsletter. The lower courts held for P. The Supreme Court granted certiorari.

Issue. May the government forbid publication and distribution to the general public of a regular newsletter if the publisher has been convicted of fraud-related crimes?

Held. No. Judgment reversed.

♦   The general policy against prior restraint and the doctrine of freedom of the press require that the exclusion for bona fide publishers be broadly construed. The purpose of the "bona fide" and "regular and general circulation" requirements is to eliminate hit-and-run tipsters and promotional material that could mislead investors. D's newsletters fall within this exclusion.

♦ The dangers of fraud, deception, and overreaching are present in personalized communications, but not in publicly offered publications. The former can create a fiduciary, personal relationship in which the dangers are present. The latter are impersonal and unlikely to result in the threatened harm.

Concurrence (White, J., Burger, C.J., Rehnquist, J.). The injunction P sought would violate the First Amendment. Government may regulate professions, even those that are practiced mainly through speech, such as the legal profession. Licensing professionals does not include licensing of speech per se, however. When the regulation of the profession extends to regulation of speech or of the press, it must pass First Amendment scrutiny. The line should be drawn where the speaker has no personal professional relationship with the receiver and does not purport to exercise judgment on behalf of any particular individual.

---

4.   **National Security.**

a.   **Prevention of publication of sensitive government documents--**

New York Times Co. v. United States [The Pentagon Papers Case], 403 U.S. 713 (1971).

Facts. The United States (P) sought to enjoin publication in the *New York Times* and *Washington Post* of a classified study known as the "Pentagon Papers." All federal courts involved except the court of appeals in the *New York Times* case held that P had not met its heavy burden of justification. The New York Times Company (D) appeals the judgment of the court of appeals in its case.

Issue. May the executive branch prevent publication of items that it considers to threaten grave and irreparable injury to the public interest?

Held. No. Judgment affirmed.

♦ The United States has failed to meet its heavy burden of showing justification for the enforcement of such a prior restraint.

Concurrence (Black, Douglas, JJ.). The injunctions should have been vacated and the cases dismissed without oral argument because it would be impossible to find that the President has "inherent power" to halt the publication of news by resorting to the courts.

Concurrence (Douglas, Black, JJ.). The only possible power possessed by the government to restrict publication by the press of sensitive material arises from its inherent power to wage war successfully. Congress has not declared war, so the government cannot exercise this power.

Concurrence (Brennan, J.). Courts cannot issue temporary stays and restraining orders to accommodate the government's desire to suppress freedom of the press without adequate proof of a direct, inevitable, and immediate serious adverse effect.

Concurrence (Stewart, White, JJ.). The executive branch has the duty to protect necessary confidentiality through executive regulations. The courts are limited to construing specific regulations and applying specific laws. Since the courts were asked to do neither here, they cannot act.

Concurrence (White, Stewart, JJ.). Some circumstances might justify an injunction as requested, but not these. Congress has relied on criminal sanctions and their deterrent effect to prevent unauthorized disclosures, and the courts should not go beyond the congressional determinations.

Concurrence (Marshall, J.). The Court would violate the concept of separation of powers by using its power to prevent behavior that Congress has specifically declined to prohibit.

Dissent (Burger, C.J.). The Court has not had sufficient time to gather and analyze the facts.

Dissent (Harlan, J., Burger, C.J., Blackmun, J.). Judicial review of executive action in foreign affairs is narrow. The Court should inquire only whether the subject matter is within the President's foreign relations power and whether the head of the department concerned has personally made the determination that disclosure would irreparably impair national security.

Dissent (Blackmun, J.). The case is too important to be handled in such haste and ought to be remanded.

---

b. **Injunction permitted.** Distinguishing *The Pentagon Papers Case*, a federal district court enjoined a magazine from publishing technical material on hydrogen bomb design, which was available in public documents. In exercising the first instance of prior restraint against a publication, the court cited the government's showing of the likelihood of injury to the nation and the fact that the suppression of the technical portions of the article would not impede the publication in its goal of stimulating public knowledge of nuclear armament and enlightened debate on national policy. [United States v. Progressive, Inc., 467 F. Supp. 990 (W.D. Wis. 1979)] An appeal in that case was dismissed after the government dropped its prosecution.

E. ADMINISTRATION OF JUSTICE

1. **Trial Publicity.** There is a strong policy against prior restraints of media reporting of criminal proceedings. Such reporting is a means of assuring a fair trial for the accused. On the other hand, there is a risk that media coverage could taint a trial by giving jurors evidence not properly admitted at trial or by creating an atmosphere that makes a fair trial impossible. Before an injunction against media reporting can be granted, the court must find that (i) there is a clear and present danger that pretrial publicity would (not merely could) threaten a fair trial, (ii) alternative measures are inadequate, and (iii) an injunction would effectively protect the accused.

   a. **Reasonable protections.** In *Sheppard v. Maxwell*, 384 U.S. 333 (1966), the Court agreed with the lower court's finding that the media had exceeded reasonable bounds in covering the accused's murder trial. The jurors, witnesses, and counsel were photographed as they came and went, and publicity contained information not presented at trial. The jury was sequestered only for deliberations. The Court, despite its reluctance to limit the media's freedom to report the public proceedings, set forth several means for trial judges to use to reasonably protect defendants, including sequestration of the jury at an early stage, transfer of the trial to another court, and a continuance.

   b. **Restriction on pretrial reporting--**

Nebraska Press Association v. Stuart, 427 U.S. 539 (1976).

Facts. Stuart (D), a state district judge, presided over the criminal trial involving a shocking multiple murder that had occurred in a small Nebraska town. To avoid the dangers that pretrial publicity would present to the fairness of the accused's trial, D entered a restrictive order that prohibited Nebraska Press Association (P) and others from reporting certain subjects relating to the trial. The order applied only until the jury was impaneled. On appeal, the Nebraska Supreme Court modified D's order to prohibit reporting only of any confessions made by the accused (except to members of the press) and other facts "strongly implicative" of the accused. P appeals.

Issue. Is a prior restraint on pretrial publicity, intended to ensure the fairness of a criminal defendant's trial, subject to a lesser standard of review than prior restraints generally?

Held. No. Judgment reversed.

♦ Generally, pretrial publicity does not threaten the right to a trial by an impartial jury because of the trial judge's control over proceedings (*e.g.,* change of venue, continuance, and sequestration of jury). However, in certain "sensational" cases, like the one here, the possibility arises that these normal means of preserving fairness are inadequate. Accordingly, resort is sometimes made to a restrictive order such as that used by D.

♦   Prior restraints on speech and publication pose the most serious and least tolerable infringements of First Amendment rights. The barriers to prior restraint may not be relaxed even where there is a possible conflict with an equally important constitutional right. The barrier may be breached only where "the gravity of the 'evil,' discounted by its improbability, justifies such invasion of free speech as is necessary to avoid the danger."

♦   The "evil" of an unfair trial is clearly great. However, the evidence here is insufficient to show that, except for the prior restraint imposed by D, the accused would certainly have had an unfair trial. Before any prior restraint is permissible, a court must find a clear and present danger that pretrial publicity would (not merely could) threaten a fair trial, that alternative measures would be inadequate, and that the prior restraint would actually protect the accused.

Concurrence (Brennan, Stewart, Marshall, JJ.). Resort to prior restraints on the freedom of the press is a constitutionally impermissible means of enforcing the right to a fair trial. Judges have less drastic means of ensuring fundamental fairness. There can be no prohibition on the publication by the press of any information pertaining to pending judicial proceedings or the operation of the criminal justice system, no matter how the information is obtained. There is no need to subordinate First or Sixth Amendment rights to one or the other.

----

2.   **Newsgathering.**

a.   **Reporter's testimonial privilege--**

Branzburg v. Hayes, 408 U.S. 665 (1972).

Facts. Branzburg (D), a reporter, observed illegal drug transactions that he used in a news article. D was subpoenaed to appear before a grand jury. D sought prohibition and mandamus to avoid having to reveal his confidential information, but the state courts denied his petition. D appeals. (Two other cases involving two similarly situated reporters were consolidated with this appeal.)

Issue. Does the First Amendment grant a special testimonial privilege to reporters, protecting them from being forced to divulge confidential information to a grand jury's investigation?

Held. No. Judgment affirmed.

- ◆ D claims that forcing reporters to reveal confidences to a grand jury will deter other confidential sources of information, thus curtailing the free flow of information protected by the First Amendment. However, journalists have no constitutional right of access to several types of events (*e.g.,* grand jury proceedings, meetings of private organizations and of official bodies gathered in executive sessions, etc.). Although these exclusions tend to hamper newsgathering, they are not unconstitutional.

- ◆ All citizens have an obligation to respond to a grand jury subpoena and to answer questions relevant to crime investigation. The only testimonial privilege for unofficial witnesses is the Fifth Amendment; there is no necessity to create a special privilege for journalists based on the First Amendment.

- ◆ The public interest in pursuing and prosecuting those crimes reported to the press by informants and thus deterring future commission of those crimes is not outweighed by the public interest in possible future news about crime from undisclosed, unverified sources.

- ◆ A judicially created journalist's privilege would necessarily involve significant practical and conceptual problems in its administration. However, Congress and the state legislatures are not precluded from fashioning whatever standards and rules they might deem proper if they choose to create a statutory journalist's privilege.

Concurrence (Powell, J.). Journalists are not without remedy in the face of a bad-faith investigation. Motions to quash and appropriate protective orders are available where the requested testimony is not within the legitimate hold of law enforcement.

Dissent (Douglas, J.). Journalists have an absolute privilege against appearing before a grand jury, unless personally implicated in a crime, in which case the Fifth Amendment immunity applies.

Dissent (Stewart, Brennan, Marshall, JJ.). The Court undermines the independence of the press by inviting authorities to annex the journalistic provision as an investigative arm of government. Exercise of the power to compel disclosure will lead to "self-censorship" and, as a consequence, significantly impair the free flow of information to the public. To force disclosure, the government must show:

(i)   Probable cause that the journalist has information clearly relevant to a specific probable violation of law;

(ii)   That there are no less obtrusive means of obtaining the information; and

(iii)   A compelling and overriding interest in the information.

b. Privilege against searches--

Zurcher v. Stanford Daily, 436 U.S. 547 (1978).

Facts. A staff member of the *Stanford Daily* (P), who was present when demonstrators assaulted police officers, took photographs of the protest and claimed he could have photographed the assault. The next day, the district attorney obtained a search warrant to search P's office for negatives, film, and pictures of the events. The police searched P's offices but found no photos not already published by P. P brought suit for declaratory judgment. The lower courts granted P relief. Zurcher (D) appeals.

Issue. Does the Constitution require any special considerations for searches of newspaper offices?

Held. No. Judgment reversed.

♦   P asserts several reasons why a third-party newspaper, not suspected of a crime, should be exempt from searches unless a subpoena duces tecum would be impracticable. However, the Fourth Amendment provides all the necessary protection. When the government seeks to seize presumptively protected materials, the warrant requirement should be administered to leave as little as possible to the discretion of the searching officer. The Fourth Amendment was aimed at general warrants, but no special provision for the press was included in the Constitution.

♦   If the requirements of specificity and reasonableness are properly applied, officers will not have an opportunity to rummage at large in newspaper files or interfere with the operation of the newspaper. The press is not easily intimidated.

Concurrence (Powell, J.). The dissent errs in creating a new and per se rule that any search of an entity protected by the Press Clause is unreasonable as long as a subpoena could be used as a substitute procedure.

Dissent (Stewart, Marshall, JJ.). The danger resulting from an unannounced police search of a newspaper office is the possibility of disclosure of confidential sources. Permitting the police to search such offices will deter such sources from working with the newspapers.

Comment. 42 U.S.C. sections 2000aa-2000aa-12, enacted in response to *Zurcher*, place limits on the power of government officials to search for publishers' work products.

---

c. Right of access to courtroom proceedings--

Richmond Newspapers, Inc. v. Virginia, 448 U.S. 555 (1980).

Facts. Early in the fourth criminal trial of the same defendant, the trial judge granted an uncontested closure motion made by the defendant. Later, reporters for Richmond Newspapers (P) sought a hearing on a motion to vacate the closure order; the hearing was granted, but the public was excluded from the hearing. At the hearing, the court denied the motion, considering the criminal defendant's interest paramount. The defendant was acquitted in the closed trial. P appealed from the trial court's closure order, but the state courts affirmed. P appeals.

Issue. Is the right of the public and press to attend criminal trials guaranteed by the Constitution?

Held. Yes. Judgment reversed.

♦ In *Gannett Co. v. DePasquale*, 443 U.S. 368 (1979), this Court held that neither the public nor the press has an enforceable right of access to a pretrial suppression hearing.

♦ Throughout the evolution of the trial procedure, the trial has been open to all who cared to observe. However, the Constitution contains no explicit provisions protecting the public from exclusion.

♦ The First Amendment protects freedom of speech and press, including expression regarding events at trials. These guaranteed rights would be meaningless if access to the trial could be foreclosed arbitrarily. Other constitutional rights, not explicitly established, have been recognized as implied. Clearly, the public interest in judicial functions and in freedom of speech requires open trials.

♦ In some circumstances, where an overriding interest is articulated in findings, a criminal trial may be closed to the public, but only where the common alternatives are insufficient (*e.g.,* jury sequestration, witness sequestration, etc.).

Concurrence (Brennan, Marshall, JJ.). Publicity is an important means of assuring the right to a fair trial. What happens in a courtroom is public property. The First Amendment requires open access, and agreement between the judge and the parties cannot override the First Amendment.

Concurrence (Stewart, J.). The First and Fourteenth Amendments give the press and the public a right of access to civil and criminal trials. A courtroom is a public place, even more so than city streets and parks. The right is not absolute, but in this case the judge gave no recognition to the right of the press and the public to be present.

Concurrence (White, J.). If *Gannett* had been decided correctly, this case would not have arisen.

Concurrence (Blackmun, J.). The Court does not apparently accept a Sixth Amendment right to a public trial, but at least it recognizes some protection for public access under the First Amendment.

Concurrence (Stevens, J.). This is the first time the Court has held that the acquisition of newsworthy matter has constitutional protection.

Dissent (Rehnquist, J.). There are no provisions in the Constitution that prohibit a state from denying public access to a trial when both the prosecution and the defense consent to the closure order.

————————————

F. GOVERNMENT PROPERTY AND THE PUBLIC FORUM

1. **The Traditional Public Forum.** Public streets and parks have traditionally been available for those who seek to express opinions or distribute literature. Such government property is considered a public forum for dissemination of information by citizens. However, use of such a forum is subject to reasonable restrictions.

    a. **Mandatory access to public forums.**

    1) **Distribution of literature.** An ordinance that bans the unlicensed communication of any views or the advocacy of any cause from door to door, and permits canvassing in public subject to the power of a police officer to determine, as a censor, what literature may be distributed from house to house and who may distribute it, has been held invalid. The claimed interest of the community in the prevention of littering the streets could be achieved by a statute specifically directed at that practice. [*See* Schneider v. Irvington, 308 U.S. 147 (1939)]

    2) **Permit to demonstrate.** A state statute prohibiting a parade or procession upon public streets without a special license specifying the day and hour of the procession, applied in a nondiscriminatory manner, was sustained based on the state's police power over traffic and safety. [*See* Cox. v. New Hampshire, 312 U.S. 569 (1941)]

    b. **Equal access.**

    1) **Introduction.** If a restriction on speech relies on the content of the speech, the Court will scrutinize it much more carefully than if the restriction is content-neutral.

2) Ban on labor picketing--

Chicago Police Department v. Mosley, 408 U.S. 92 (1972).

Facts. The city of Chicago passed an ordinance that prohibited picketing, except for peaceful labor picketing, near public schools at certain times. Mosley (P), who had picketed a certain school over several months, sought declaratory and injunctive relief in order to continue his picketing. The Chicago Police Department (D) appeals a judgment in favor of P.

Issue. May a government entity regulate picketing solely on the basis of subject matter?

Held. No. Judgment affirmed.

◆ Although picketing is protected by the First Amendment, reasonable "time, place, and manner" regulations are permitted to further significant governmental interests.

◆ D's ordinance, however, invalidates certain picketing solely in terms of subject matter, while permitting other picketing of the same time, place, and manner. This cannot be permitted in the absence of a showing that the regulation is narrowly tailored to a legitimate objective.

2. **New Forums.**

   a. **Access to government charity drive.** The President may exclude political activist organizations from eligibility for participation in a federal charitable campaign. [Cornelius v. NAACP Legal Defense & Education Fund, Inc., 473 U.S. 788 (1985)] Participation in the Combined Federal Campaign ("CFC") is a form of charitable solicitation of funds, which is protected speech. The Court held that the CFC was a nonpublic forum limited to charitable organizations.

   b. **Utility poles.** Los Angeles prohibited the posting of signs on public property. In *Los Angeles v. Taxpayers for Vincent*, 466 U.S. 789 (1984), the Court held that the city had a constitutional power to enhance its appearance, which justified the ordinance. The interest was unrelated to the suppression of ideas.

   c. **Airports--**

International Society for Krishna Consciousness, Inc. v. Lee, 505 U.S. 672 (1992).

Facts. Members of the International Society for Krishna Consciousness, Inc. (P) performed a religious ritual known as sankirtan, which consisted of going into public places, disseminating religious literature, and soliciting funds to support the religion. P desired to perform sankirtan at the airports in the New York City area. Lee (D) was the police superintendent of the airports and was responsible for enforcing a regulation that prohibited the repetitive sale of merchandise, the solicitation of money, or the distribution of literature within the interior areas of buildings at the airport. Such activities were permitted on the sidewalks outside the terminal buildings. P challenged the regulation. The district court granted P summary judgment. The court of appeals affirmed with regard to the ban on distributing, but reversed with regard to the ban on solicitation. The Supreme Court granted certiorari.

Issue. May an airport terminal operated by a public authority prohibit solicitation in the interior of its buildings?

Held. Yes. Judgment affirmed.

♦ Solicitation is clearly a form of protected speech, but the government need not permit all forms of speech on property it owns and controls. Prior cases reflect a "forum-based" approach to assess government restrictions on the use of its property. There are three categories of government property:

Traditional public fora—property that has traditionally been available for public expression. Regulation of speech on this type survives only if it is narrowly drawn to achieve a compelling state interest.

Designated public fora—property that the government has opened for expressive activity by part or all of the public. Regulation of speech on this type also survives only if it is narrowly drawn to achieve a compelling state interest.

All remaining public property. Regulation of speech on this type survives if it is reasonable, as long as the regulation is not an effort to suppress the speaker's activity due to disagreement with the speaker's views.

♦ A traditional public forum exists where the property has immemorially been held in trust for the use of the public and has been used for purposes of assembly, communicating thoughts between citizens, and discussing public questions. Examples include streets and parks. Designated public fora are areas that are intentionally dedicated for use in public discourse.

♦ Airports do not meet these requirements. For one thing, they have not been in existence for many years. For another, they have not historically been made available for speech activity, except when ordered to by the courts. Airports are not just "transportation nodes" like bus and rail terminals, but have special characteristics. The purpose of an airport is to facilitate travel and to make a regulated profit, not to promote expression.

♦ Because an airport is not a public forum, D's regulations are permissible as long as they are reasonable. P's proposed solicitation had a disruptive effect on airport travelers who are typically in a hurry and for whom a delay can mean a lost flight and severe inconvenience. Face-to-face solicitation presents a risk of duress and fraud that D can properly attempt to avoid. Therefore, D's ban on solicitation is sustained.

Concurrence (O'Connor, J.). An airport is clearly not a public forum. It could be closed to everyone except those who have legitimate business there, unlike public streets and parks, but government officials make airports open to the public as a convenience. The airport does contain restaurants, shops, newsstands, and other facilities not directly related to travel, but D's regulations are reasonably related to maintaining the multipurpose environment created by D. At the same time, the ban on leafleting cannot be upheld as reasonable, since distributing literature does not present the same problems as soliciting funds.

Concurrence (Kennedy, Blackmun, Stevens, Souter, JJ.). The areas of an airport that are outside the passenger security zones are public forums. The Court's categorical approach to classifying government property leaves no room for the development of new public forums without government approval. The traditional three-part analysis provides a better, more objective approach, based on the actual, physical characteristics and uses of the property. An airport, for example, is not much different from a street and sidewalk, since both have a principal purpose of facilitating transportation, not public discourse. As long as expressive activity would be appropriate and compatible with the actual uses of public property, the property should be considered a public forum. Under this analysis, passenger convenience would not be a sufficiently strong rationale for banning solicitation. The ban on solicitation and receipt of funds is nevertheless a proper time, place, and manner restriction. The ban does not prevent solicitation that does not involve the immediate receipt of money.

Concurrence and dissent (Souter, Blackmun, Stevens, JJ.). The traditional public forums are only "archetypes" of property from which the government may not exclude speech, and the airports involved in this case fit the archetype. The ban on solicitation is not sufficiently narrowly tailored to further a significant state interest and should not be sustained.

Comment. In *Lee v. International Society for Krishna Consciousness, Inc.*, 505 U.S. 830 (1992), the Court held that the ban on the distribution of literature was invalid.

---

3. Privacy and the Public Forum--

Hill v. Colorado, 530 U.S. 703 (2000).

Facts. Colorado Rev. Stat. section 18-9-122(3) made it unlawful for any person within 100 feet of a health care facility's entrance to "knowingly approach" within eight feet of another person, without that person's consent, in order to pass "a leaflet or handbill to, displa[y] a sign to, or engag[e] in oral protest, education, or counseling with [that] person . . . ." Hill and others (Ps) sought to enjoin enforcement of the statute, claiming it was facially invalid. The trial court dismissed the complaint, holding that the statute imposed content-neutral time, place, and manner restrictions narrowly tailored to serve a significant government interest. The court of appeals affirmed, and the state supreme court denied review. The United States Supreme Court remanded that judgment in light of its holding in *Schenck v. Pro-Choice Network of Western New York,* 519 U. S. 357, that the state could not create a speech-free floating buffer zone with a 15-foot radius. On remand, the state courts distinguished *Schenck,* concluding that the statute was narrowly drawn to further a significant government interest, rejecting Ps' overbreadth challenge, and concluding that ample alternative channels of communication remained open to Ps. The Supreme Court granted certiorari.

Issue. May a state restrict free speech rights within close proximity to the entrance of a health care facility?

Held. Yes. Judgment affirmed.

♦ Ps have clear and undisputed First Amendment interests. At the same time, D's police powers allow it to protect its citizens' health and safety, especially to protect access to health care facilities and to avoid potential trauma to patients associated with confrontational protests. The statute protects listeners from unwanted communication; it does not restrict a speaker's right to address a willing audience.

♦ Section 18-9-122(3) passes the content-neutrality test outlined in *Ward v. Rock Against Racism,* 491 U.S. 781 (1989), for three independent reasons. First, it is a regulation of places where some speech may occur, not a "regulation of speech." Second, it was not adopted to target any particular viewpoint, but is content-neutral. Third, D's interests are unrelated to the content of the demonstrators' speech.

♦ Ps claim that because the statute applies to those who "knowingly approach" within eight feet of another to engage in "oral protest, education, or counseling," it is "content-based" under *Carey v. Brown,* 447 U.S. 455 (1980) as it requires examination of the content of a speaker's comments. However, it is not improper to look at a statement's content to determine whether a rule of law applies to a course of conduct. Here, the state does not need to know the exact words spoken to know whether sidewalk counselors are engaging in oral protest, education, or counseling rather than social or random conversation. By contrast, *Carey* involved a statute that prohibited all picketing except for picketing of a place of employment in a labor dispute, thus preferring expression concerning one particular subject.

- The statute is also a valid time, place, and manner regulation under *Ward,* for it is "narrowly tailored" to serve the state's significant and legitimate governmental interests and it leaves open ample alternative communication channels. A content-neutral regulation need not be the least restrictive or intrusive means of serving the statutory goal if it does not entirely foreclose any means of communication. The eight-foot zone should not adversely impact a reader's ability to read demonstrators' signs.

- Unlike the "floating buffer zone" rejected in *Schenck*, D's zone in this case allows the speaker to communicate at a "normal conversational distance," and to remain in one place while other individuals pass within eight feet. The "knowing" requirement protects speakers who thought they were at the proscribed distance from inadvertently violating the statute. Whether the eight-foot interval is the best possible accommodation of the competing interests, deference must be accorded to the Colorado legislature's judgment. The burden on the distribution of handbills is more serious, but the statute does not prevent a leafletter from simply standing near the path of oncoming pedestrians and proffering the material, which pedestrians can accept or decline.

- The statute is not overbroad, because it does not ban any forms of communication, only the places where communication may occur. Nor is it unconstitutionally vague, since it requires scienter and the language of the statute is plain. It provides adequate guidance to law enforcement officials to prevent arbitrary enforcement.

Concurrence (Souter, O'Connor, Ginsburg, Breyer, JJ.). A restriction is content-based only if it is imposed because of the content of the speech and not because of offensive behavior identified with its delivery. If the ostensible reason for regulating is really something about the ideas, the regulation is invalid. In this case, the ostensible reason is the true reason. The regulation prohibits close encounters; it is the behavior of the protestors, not their anti-abortion message, that is regulated.

Dissent (Scalia, Thomas, JJ.). The Court has concluded that a regulation requiring speakers on the public thoroughfares bordering medical facilities to speak from a distance of eight feet is "not a 'regulation of speech,'" but "a regulation of the places where some speech may occur," and that a regulation directed to only certain categories of speech (protest, education, and counseling) is not "content-based." It then holds that the regulation survives the less rigorous scrutiny afforded content-neutral time, place, and manner restrictions because it is narrowly tailored to serve the government's interest in protecting citizens' "right to be let alone," even though such an interest is incompatible with the guarantees of the First Amendment. The Court applies this unusual analysis because the regulation in this case is directed against the opponents of abortion. Having deprived abortion opponents of the political right to persuade the electorate that abortion should be restricted by law, the Court now restricts their individual right to persuade women contemplating abortion that what they are doing is wrong. Because, like the rest of our abortion jurisprudence, today's decision is in stark contradiction of the constitutional principles we apply in all other contexts, I dissent.

Dissent (Kennedy, J.). The law here imposes a content-based restriction on speech and is intended to restrict only speakers who protest abortions. It creates a right for citizens to avoid unpopular speech in a public forum. This holding contradicts 50 years of First Amendment cases by approving a law that bars a private citizen from passing a message, in a peaceful manner and on a profound moral issue, to a fellow citizen on a public sidewalk. This holding will lead to the elimination of the proud tradition of free and open discourse in a public forum. There are less burdensome alternatives to address the law's purported concerns. In addition, the Court's decision conflicts with the essence of the joint opinion in *Planned Parenthood v. Casey, supra.*

G. GOVERNMENT SUPPORT OF SPEECH

1. Conditioning Federal Funds on Refraining from Speaking--

Rust v. Sullivan, 500 U.S. 173 (1991).

Facts. Congress enacted Title X of the Public Health Service Act that provided federal funding for family planning services, provided that none of the funds could be used in programs where abortion is a method of family planning. Sullivan (D), Secretary of the Department of Health and Human Services, promulgated new regulations that: (i) specified that a Title X project cannot provide counseling concerning abortion or referrals for abortion; (ii) prohibited a Title X project from engaging in activities that encourage, promote, or advocate abortion as a method of family planning; and (iii) required that Title X projects be physically and financially separate from prohibited abortion activities. Rust (P) challenged the facial validity of the regulations, claiming they violated the First and Fifth Amendments to the Constitution. The lower courts upheld the regulations. The Supreme Court granted certiorari.

Issue. May the federal government condition the acceptance of federal funds by a particular project on the project's agreement to refrain from promoting or even discussing abortion?

Held. Yes. Judgment affirmed.

♦ D's regulations do not exceed D's authority so long as they reflect a plausible construction of the plain language of the statute and do not otherwise conflict with Congress's expressed intent. The language of the statute is ambiguous and broad enough to allow D's interpretation. Courts normally must defer to the expertise of the agency charged with administering the law. The fact that the regulations are a change from the prior regulations is justified by D's experience under the prior policy.

♦ Ps claim that the regulations are discrimination based on viewpoint because they promote childbirth over abortion. But D has merely chosen to fund one activity to the exclusion of the other. The government has no obligation to subsidize counterpart rights once it decides to subsidize one protected right. D's regulations do not deny anyone a benefit, but merely require that public funds be spent for the purposes for which they were authorized. And they apply to the project, not to the grantee, who is left free to perform abortions and to advocate abortion in other contexts.

♦ Ps also claim that D's regulations violate a woman's Fifth Amendment right to choose whether to terminate her pregnancy. But Congress's refusal to fund abortion counseling and advocacy leaves a pregnant woman with the same choices as if Congress had chosen not to fund family planning services at all. D's regulations do not affect a doctor's ability to provide information about abortion outside the context of a Title X project.

Dissent (Blackmun, Marshall, Stevens, O'Connor, JJ.). D's regulations clearly constitute content-based regulation of speech aimed at suppressing "dangerous ideas." They are also viewpoint-based, since they prohibit abortion advocacy but do not regulate anti-abortion advocacy.

Comment. The Court noted that government funding is not always sufficient by itself to justify government control over the content of expression. For example, government ownership of real property does not justify restriction of speech in such areas if they have been traditionally open to the public for expressive activity, and government payments to universities do not justify control of speech there. In this case, D's regulations do not significantly impinge upon the doctor-patient relationship because they do not apply to post-conception medical care, and the doctor can make it clear that advice regarding abortion is beyond the scope of the Title X program.

---

2. **Decency Standards for Federal Spending--**

National Endowment for the Arts v. Finley, 524 U.S. 569 (1998).

Facts. The National Endowment for the Arts (D) was funded by Congress. Applications for funding by D were reviewed by advisory panels of experts who in turn reported to the national council, who then advised D's chairperson, who awarded the grants. After D funded some controversial projects, Congress amended the statute to require the chairperson to consider "general standards of decency and respect for the diverse beliefs and values of the American people" in establishing procedures to judge the artistic merit of grant applications. Finley and other artists (Ps) applied for grants before the amendment was adopted. Ps were denied funding, and they sued, claiming D denied their First Amendment rights by rejecting their applications on political grounds. The district court denied D's motion for judgment on the pleadings. The court granted summary judgment to Ps on their facial challenge to the amendment and enjoined D from enforcing it. The court of appeals affirmed. The Supreme Court granted certiorari.

Issue. May Congress impose decency standards on discretionary spending of federally-appropriated funds?

Held. Yes. Judgment reversed.

♦ The amendment, section 954(d)(1), does not impose a categorical requirement. It consists of advisory language only and is aimed at reforming procedures rather than precluding speech. There is no realistic danger that the provision will compromise First Amendment values.

♦ It is also unlikely that the provision will introduce any greater element of selectivity than the determination of "artistic excellence" itself. The nature of arts funding requires content-based considerations. Some constitutionally protected expression will be rejected regardless of the criteria used.

♦ In *Rosenberger v. Rector and Visitors of University of Virginia*, 515 U.S. 819 (1995), the Court held that a school could not exclude religious student publications when it encouraged a diversity of views from private speakers. In this case, however, D is not indiscriminately encouraging a diversity of views; it is trying to make aesthetic judgments on the content of submissions.

♦ The government may allocate competitive funding according to criteria that would be impermissible if it were directly regulating speech. It may selectively fund programs by making choices among the alternatives.

♦ The language of section 954(d)(1) is vague, but when the government acts as patron rather than as sovereign, the consequences of imprecision are not constitutionally severe. Thus, the amendment is not unconstitutionally vague. The provision simply adds some imprecise factors to an already subjective selection process.

Concurrence (Scalia, Thomas, JJ.). Section 954(d)(1) establishes content- and viewpoint-based criteria upon which D is to evaluate grant applications. This is not a categorical requirement, but a legitimate preference for speech that will help foster values such as decency and respect. Artists can get funds from sources other than the United States.

Dissent (Souter, J.). D has failed to show why the statute should be exempted from the fundamental rule of the First Amendment that viewpoint discrimination in the exercise of public authority over expressive activity is unconstitutional. Once the government decides to subsidize expressive conduct at large, it cannot discriminate on the basis of the content.

3. **Government as Educator and Editor.** Special problems arise with respect to speech in public schools. As an educator, the government must balance the competing interests of reasonable discipline necessary to facilitate learning and free expression. This balancing must also take into account the youthfulness of the student audience. The government may not compel attendance at public schools. [Pierce v. Society of Sisters, 268 U.S. 510 (1925)]

a. **Armbands in public schools--**

Tinker v. Des Moines School District, 393 U.S. 503 (1969).

Facts. Tinker and other students (Ps) wore black armbands to school to protest the Vietnam War, in spite of a school policy against such action. Ps were suspended and sought an injunction against the Des Moines School District (D) to prevent D from disciplining them. The lower courts upheld D's action as reasonable to maintain school discipline. Ps appeal.

Issue. May school officials ban a silent, peaceful expression of opinion, such as wearing an armband, and punish offenders?

Held. No. Judgment reversed.

◆ Wearing an armband is a symbolic act worthy of First Amendment protection. Constitutional rights are not abandoned at the schoolhouse gate. Yet school authorities may properly proscribe and control conduct in the schools.

◆ Ps' expression was silent and passive, unaccompanied by disorder or interference with the school's work. Prohibition of a particular expression of opinion is only justified by a showing that the expression would materially interfere with the school's discipline, which D has failed to show. Avoidance of the controversy attending unpopular opinion is an inadequate reason to ban expression of such opinions.

Concurrence (Stewart, J.). Children's First Amendment rights are not co-extensive with adults.

Dissent (Black, J.). The record shows that Ps' conduct was disruptive and distracting.

Dissent (Harlan, J.). Ds acted in good faith and their policy should be upheld.

b. **Student newspapers--**

Hazelwood School District v. Kuhlmeier, 484 U.S. 260 (1988).

Facts. Kuhlmeier and other students (Ps) were staff members of a high school newspaper. The principal of the school would review page proofs before the paper was published. The principal objected to two articles Ps wanted to publish: one dealing with three students' experiences with pregnancy, and the other with the impact of divorce on the students. The principal approved publication of the paper without the stories. Ps sued the Hazelwood School District (D) for an injunction and for damages for violation of their rights. The district court denied an injunction, but the court of appeals reversed. The Supreme Court granted certiorari.

Issue. May a high school exercise control over the content of a student-produced high school paper?

Held. Yes. Judgment affirmed.

◆ The newspaper was not a public forum unless the school had opened it for indiscriminate use by the general public or by some segment of the public. In this case, D supported the newspaper solely as part of the curriculum and for its educational benefits. Thus, D was entitled to regulate the contents of the paper in any reasonable manner.

◆ This case involves the question of whether the First Amendment requires a school affirmatively to promote particular student speech, a different question from that involved in *Tinker, supra*; *i.e.,* whether a school must tolerate particular student speech. Because the newspaper is school sponsored, the public might reasonably perceive it to bear the imprimatur of the school and educators may exercise greater control over this type of student expression to preserve its educational value as well as protect against attribution of the expression to the school. Judicial intervention would be appropriate only if the newspaper had no educational purpose.

◆ The principal in this case acted reasonably in deleting the specific articles involved.

Dissent (Brennan, Marshall, Blackmun, JJ.). This is the first case to distinguish between personal and school-sponsored speech. Under *Tinker*, official censorship intended to protect the audience or dissociate the sponsor from the expression is not permitted. Censorship does not further the curricular purposes of a student newspaper.

Comment. In *Bethel School District No. 403 v. Fraser*, 478 U.S. 675 (1986), the Court upheld the right of a school district to discipline a high school student who made a lewd speech at a school assembly. This speech was contrasted with the political message involved in *Tinker*.

---

c.   **Control over library material--**

Board of Education v. Pico, 457 U.S. 853 (1982).

Facts. The Board of Education (D) obtained a list of "objectionable" books and removed them from the high school library for review by board members. D appointed a committee to recommend whether the books should be retained in the library, then rejected the recommendations and returned only one of the removed books. D based its decision on the claim that the books were anti-American and that they presented moral danger to the students. Pico (P) challenged the decision in federal court. The district court granted summary judgment for D, but the court of appeals reversed and remanded for trial. D appeals.

Issue. Does the First Amendment impose limitations on a local school board's discretionary removal of books from a high school library?

Held. Yes. Judgment affirmed.

♦ This case does not involve the use of books in the classroom, but merely optional library books. Nor does it involve acquisition of books. Because of the procedural posture of the case, the judgment must be affirmed if there is any question of fact.

♦ Local school boards have discretion in managing school affairs. However, this discretion is subject to the First Amendment rights of the students. These rights may be impinged by the removal of books from a school library. D's discretion may not be exercised so as to deny students access to ideas with which the board members disagree, although they could remove books that were pervasively vulgar or educationally unsuitable.

♦ The evidence as to D's motive in removing the books is unclear. There is evidence that D acted out of disagreement with the ideas contained in the books. By disregarding the committee's recommendations, the board acted in an ad hoc manner. The case must be remanded for necessary fact findings.

Concurrence (Blackmun, J.). The state may not suppress exposure to ideas without a sufficiently compelling reason. And it may not deny access to an idea simply because state officials disapprove of or disagree with the idea. However, there is no right to receive ideas on the part of students. The determinative question is the motive of the school officials.

Concurrence (White, J.). There is no need to decide the question in the absence of a complete factual record.

Dissent (Burger, C.J., Powell, Rehnquist, O'Connor, JJ.). School boards, not judges and students, are charged with administering schools. Such boards are responsive to the voters and therefore reflect the views of the community. The values of morality, good taste, and relevance to education may properly be considered by elected officials in performing their duty.

Dissent (Powell, J.). Removal of nine vulgar or racist books from a high school library is not despotism or intolerance.

Dissent (Rehnquist, J., Burger, C.J., Powell, J.). D did not deprive the public generally of the ideas in the books. Education, especially short of the university level, is necessarily selective, and those charged with providing the education must be free to determine what is necessary and what is not. The First Amendment right to receive information does not apply to an institution that is necessarily selective in the ideas it may impart.

Dissent (O'Connor, J.). D has been deprived of one of the fundamental elements necessary to properly operate a school. It is D's responsibility, not ours, to decide what books to have in the library.

Comment. In *Southeastern Promotions, Ltd., v. Conrad,* 420 U.S. 546 (1975), the Court held that a municipal theater was a public forum, so that the directors could not refuse to permit the performance of the musical *Hair* on the grounds that the production was obscene. This was deemed to be an unconstitutional prior restraint.

---

d. Requiring Internet filters in government-supported libraries--

United States v. American Library Association, Inc., 539 U.S. 194 (2003).

Facts. After providing funding to help public libraries provide public Internet access, Congress became concerned that its programs were facilitating access to illegal and harmful pornography by minors. The Children's Internet Protection Act (CIPA) provided that a public library could not receive federal funds to provide Internet access unless the library installed filtering software to prevent minors from accessing harmful material and to block obscenity and child pornography. Although some libraries had begun installing blocking and filtering software prior to CIPA, the American Library Association, Inc. (P) challenged CIPA. The District Court held that the CIPA provisions were facially invalid because they induced public libraries to violate patrons' First Amendment rights. The Supreme Court granted certiorari.

Issue. May Congress require public libraries to limit Internet access to certain content as a condition for receiving public funds?

Held. Yes. Judgment reversed.

♦ Congress has wide latitude to attach conditions to the receipt of federal assistance in order to further its legitimate policy objectives. However, Congress cannot induce the recipient of funds to do something that is unconstitutional.

- A public forum analysis with heightened judicial scrutiny is incompatible with the broad discretion that public libraries must have when considering content in making collection decisions. Internet access in public libraries is neither a traditional nor a designated public forum. A public library does not provide Internet access to create a public forum for Web publishers to express themselves. Instead, it provides this access for the same reasons it provides other resources—to facilitate research, learning, and recreational pursuits.

- A library reviews and chooses to acquire every book in its collection, but it does not review every Web site that it makes available. However, this difference does not taint the judgments that a library does make regarding access to Internet material. Most libraries already exclude pornography from their print collections because they consider it inappropriate. These decisions are not subjected to heightened scrutiny, and libraries' decisions to block online pornography should not be treated differently. Furthermore, the vast amount of material on the Internet makes it impossible for libraries to review all of the material when deciding what to include in their collections.

- Even if filtering software can "overblock" by blocking access to constitutionally protected speech outside the categories intended to be blocked, patrons can have the software disabled for particular sites.

- Assuming that public libraries have First Amendment rights, Congress still has authority to define the limits of programs that it funds. The lack of a subsidy is not a penalty, so Congress is not penalizing libraries that choose not to install the filtering software.

Concurrence (Kennedy, J.). If, as the government maintains, a librarian will unblock filtered material or disable the filter on the request of an adult user without significant delay, there is little to this case.

Concurrence (Breyer, J.). The Act allows libraries to permit an adult patron access to "overblocked" material by merely asking the librarian to unblock the Web site or to disable the filter. This is a small burden for the patron. Any speech-related harm that CIPA may cause is not disproportionate when considered in relation to its legitimate objectives.

Dissent (Stevens, J.). CIPA is a blunt nationwide restraint on adult access to a large amount of constitutionally protected speech. Libraries should be allowed to exercise their discretion in this matter the same way they do when making other decisions about what to include in their collections.

Dissent (Souter, Ginsburg, JJ.). Internet blocking is not the same as the selective process of acquiring library materials. Internet access presents no issues of funding or space, because the blocking takes place after the money is spent on the Internet connection. Blocking Internet access in public libraries is like removing books from library shelves because of their content.

H. MASS MEDIA

1. **Access to the Mass Media.** The mass media presents difficult First Amendment problems because of its pervasiveness and the barriers to entry. There are a limited number of frequencies to be used by radio and television, and the government allocates these frequencies according to established procedures. Those who are permitted to broadcast have a special privilege. Government therefore also imposes a special responsibility to provide a range of programs that are in the public interest. Newspapers, which are also part of the mass media, do not of course operate on allocable frequencies. Yet some argue that the expense of establishing a significant newspaper is such that government should also regulate to some extent the content of newspapers, or at least assist the general public in gaining access to newspapers.

   a. **Access by statute.** In response to the problems of access to the media, some states and Congress itself have provided rights of access by statute. In assessing such statutes, the Court looks to the nature of the media involved. In this context, the First Amendment acts as a protection against government interference.

      1) **Access to newspapers--**

Miami Herald Publishing Co. v. Tornillo, 418 U.S. 241 (1974).

Facts. Tornillo (P) was a candidate for the Florida state legislature. The Miami Herald Publishing Company (D), a newspaper publisher, printed editorials critical of P's candidacy. P sued to force D to publish P's response under a Florida "right of reply" statute. The state supreme court reversed the lower court and held the statute constitutional. D appeals.

Issue. May the state require a newspaper to publish a candidate's reply to criticism made by the newspaper?

Held. No. Judgment reversed.

♦ P demonstrates the consolidation of control over the public media, and argues that an enforceable right of access is a necessary remedy to assure open public debate. However, such a right requires some mechanism, either governmental or consensual. If governmental, as here, the First Amendment protections are invoked.

♦ Although a responsible press is desirable, it is not mandated by the Constitution and, like many other virtues, cannot be legislated. P would use governmental coercion to compel D to publish material that D deems improper for publication. Such interference with editorial decisionmaking exceeds constitutional bounds.

♦ To uphold the state law would encourage editors to avoid controversial subjects, to the detriment of public discussion.

---

2) **Access to the electronic media.** The Court has indicated that a greater scope of regulation may be permissible as to radio and television broadcasting than as to the print media. For example, the Court has upheld orders by the Federal Communications Commission ("FCC") under a statutory "fairness doctrine" that requires broadcasters to provide broadcast time for discussion of public issues as well as fair coverage for each side of issues presented. In *Red Lion Broadcasting Co. v. FCC*, 395 U.S. 367 (1969), the Court upheld FCC orders that required a radio station to offer free broadcasting time to opponents of political candidates or views endorsed by the station, and to any person who has been personally attacked in the course of a broadcast, for reply to the attack. A broadcasting licensee has no right to monopolize a frequency to the exclusion of fellow citizens. The right of viewers and listeners is paramount to the right of the broadcaster. Broadcasters may be treated as proxies for the entire community, obligated to give suitable time and attention to matters of great public concern, including time to respond to personal attacks or political endorsements.

b. **Access by constitutional right--**

Columbia Broadcasting System, Inc. v. Democratic National Committee, 412 U.S. 94 (1973).

Facts. Radio station WTOP, owned by the Columbia Broadcasting System, Inc. (D), followed a policy of refusing to sell air time for spot announcements to individuals and groups who wished to express their views on controversial issues. The Democratic National Committee (P) sought a declaratory ruling that a broadcaster such as D could not as a general policy refuse to sell time to responsible parties for comment on public issues. The FCC rejected P's request, but the court of appeals reversed. D appeals.

Issue. May a government-regulated broadcaster refuse, as a general policy, to sell broadcast time to responsible parties for comment on public issues?

Held. Yes. Judgment reversed.

♦ The broadcast media are a unique vehicle of expression because physical limitations require allocation of frequencies among applicants. Such allocation is performed by the government, which accordingly seeks assurance that licensees operate in the public interest. In broadcasting, the rights of the viewers and listeners, not those of the broadcasters, are paramount. The scheme of broadcast regulation evinces an intent to preserve the widest journalistic freedom consistent with the public obligation. The fairness doctrine makes broadcasters responsible for providing the public with access to a balanced presentation of information on issues of public importance.

♦ The First Amendment restrains governmental, not private, action. Congress was careful to preserve the fullest journalistic independence possible for broadcast licensees. D's challenged policy was not mandated by the government but resulted from independent editorial decision. Thus, although government does regulate the broadcast media in various respects, D's policy is sufficiently removed from government interference as to fall beyond the First Amendment mandate.

♦ The system of broadcast regulation requires that licensees meet a "public interest" standard in their operation. This standard does not require licensees to accept editorial advertisements, nor, assuming governmental action, would the First Amendment. The FCC, charged with executing the statute, determined that such a requirement would undermine the public interest by favoring the ideas of those with access to greater wealth. The alternative would be heavier government involvement in the licensee's editorial decisionmaking, which would infringe the First Amendment.

Concurrence (Douglas, J.). The broadcast media are as protected by the First Amendment as are newspapers and magazines. The latter are in actuality as unavailable to the public as are the broadcast media. Although government properly regulates technical aspects of broadcasting, P has no place in editorial aspects; the fairness doctrine itself is excessive government interference.

Dissent (Brennan, Marshall, JJ.). The fairness doctrine, standing alone, is insufficient to provide the kind of broad interchange of ideas to which the public is entitled. The Court permits exclusions from a public forum based on content alone, contrary to our prior cases.

---

c. **"Must carry" requirements for cable television.** Congress adopted the Cable Television Act of 1992, sections 4 and 5 of which required cable operators to carry the signals of local broadcast television stations. The purpose was to counter the concentration of economic power in the cable industry, which Congress found was endangering the availability of free over-the-air broadcast television, especially for those consumers who did not have cable. In *Turner Broadcasting System, Inc. v. FCC*, 512 U.S. 622 (1994) (Turner I), Turner Broadcasting System, Inc. and others challenged the regulations. The Supreme Court held that the "must carry" provisions were subject to intermediate First

Amendment scrutiny under *United States v. O'Brien, supra*, so that a content-neutral regulation is sustained if it advances important governmental interests unrelated to the suppression of free speech and does not burden substantially more speech than necessary to further those interests. After remand for additional factfinding, the Court affirmed the prior result on the ground that Congress had substantial evidence for making the judgment it did and that the rules were substantially related to the important government interest in competition and diversity in programming. [Turner Broadcasting System, Inc. v. FCC, 520 U.S. 180 (1997) (Turner II)]

2. **Content Regulation.** Besides the fairness doctrine, the government may regulate the content of broadcasts when necessary to protect the public interest. This may include prohibitions against inappropriate content, such as indecent but not obscene speech. However, the government may not prohibit discussion of public issues that lie at the heart of the First Amendment protections.

   a.   **Indecent speech--**

FCC v. Pacifica Foundation, 438 U.S. 726 (1978).

Facts. A New York radio station owned by Pacifica Foundation (D) broadcast a monologue by George Carlin that contained several indecent words. A listener complained to the FCC (P), which issued a declaratory order finding the monologue indecent as broadcast and therefore subject to regulation. The district court reversed D's determination. P appeals.

Issue. Does the federal government have power to regulate a radio broadcast that is indecent but not obscene?

Held. Yes. Judgment reversed.

◆   The statute on which P based its power to regulate D's broadcast (18 U.S.C. section 1464) forbids the use of any "obscene, indecent, or profane" language. Because the disjunctive is used, each word has a separate meaning, and language need not be obscene to be indecent. D's words were admittedly not obscene, but P could still properly find them indecent.

◆   Broadcasting, of all forms of communication, has the most limited First Amendment protection because of its unique ability to penetrate privacy and its accessibility to children.

◆   The First Amendment does not prohibit all governmental regulation that depends on the content of speech. Nor is P's action invalidated by its possible deterrent effect on similar broadcasts.

Concurrence (Powell, Blackmun, JJ.). While P's finding does not violate the First Amendment, the Court should not decide on the basis of content which speech is less "valuable" and hence less deserving of protection.

Dissent (Brennan, Marshall, JJ.). The word "indecent" must be construed to prohibit only obscene speech. Since the broadcast was concededly not obscene, and since it does not fit within the other categories of speech that are totally without First Amendment protection, it should not be subject to government control. The government does not have a duty to protect its citizens from certain broadcasts merely because some citizens, even if a majority, object to the broadcast.

Dissent (Stewart, Brennan, White, Marshall, JJ.). P had no authority to ban D's broadcast.

---

b. **Publicly-funded broadcasting.** Congress cannot prohibit editorializing on the air by television and radio stations that accept federal subsidies. The Public Broadcasting Act of 1967 prohibited noncommercial educational stations that receive a grant from the Corporation for Public Broadcasting to "engage in editorializing." In *FCC v. League of Women Voters*, 468 U.S. 364 (1984), the Court held that provision unconstitutional. The government's interest in safeguarding the public's right to a balanced presentation of public issues, which justified the fairness doctrine in *Red Lion, supra*, was insufficient to justify the substantial abridgement of important journalistic freedoms that the ban imposed.

c. **Telephone messages.** In *Sable Communications v. FCC*, 492 U.S. 115 (1989), the Court distinguished *Pacifica, supra,* in refusing to uphold a federal statute that prohibited indecent interstate commercial telephone messages (so-called "dial-a-porn"). Unlike *Pacifica*, *Sable* involved a total ban on broadcasting, a non-captive audience, and no legislative findings that less restrictive means were unavailable.

d. **The Internet--**

Reno v. American Civil Liberties Union, 521 U.S. 844 (1997).

Facts. Certain provisions of the Communications Decency Act of 1996 ("CDA") prohibited the knowing transmission of obscene or indecent messages to any recipient under 18 years of age and the knowing sending or displaying of patently offensive messages in a manner that is available to a person under 18 years of age. These provisions were designed to prevent Internet obscenity. An affirmative defense was available for those who take good faith, reasonable, effective, and appropriate actions to restrict minor access to such material, or who require certain designated forms of age proof, such as a verified credit card or an adult identification number. The American Civil Liberties Union (P) challenged the Act. A three-judge district court enjoined enforcement of the Act, except with respect to obscenity and child pornography, on the ground that it violated freedom of speech. Reno (D), the United States Attorney General, appeals.

Issue. May Congress suppress certain types of Web pages to deny minors access to potentially harmful speech?

Held. No. Judgment affirmed.

♦ Previous cases do not support P's position. *Ginsberg v. New York*, 390 U.S. 629 (1968), upheld a New York prohibition on selling obscene material to minors, but this did not prohibit their parents from buying the material for their children, as does the CDA. The New York statute was also better defined and applied to persons under the age of 17. *Pacifica, supra*, applied to the timing of a radio broadcast and did not involve a criminal prosecution. *Renton, supra*, applied to a zoning ordinance that was aimed at "secondary effects," unlike the CDA, which is a content-based blanket speech restriction, not a time, place, and manner regulation.

♦ Previous cases have recognized special justifications for regulation of broadcast media that do not apply to other speakers. Broadcast media have a history of extensive government regulation, they have scarce available frequencies, and they are invasive in nature. The Internet, which does not have a history of government regulation, allows anyone to "publish" information, which is then accessible to anyone who accesses the Internet unless the publisher imposes restrictions; *i.e.*, there is no scarcity of broadcast spectrums. Unlike radio or television communications that can be received passively, Internet communications require deliberate effort on the part of the recipient. There are methods to allow parents to block access to undesired web sites.

♦ The CDA contains undefined terms and different phrases for different sections, raising uncertainty about how the two standards relate to each other. The vagueness of the CDA is of special concern because as a content-based regulation, it has a chilling effect on free speech. It is also a criminal statute. The CDA attempts to use just one of the three *Miller* prongs, but all three are necessary.

♦ The CDA also lacks the necessary precision required by a content regulation. To deny minors access to potentially harmful speech, the CDA suppresses a large amount of speech that adults have a constitutional right to receive. Such a broad content-based restriction on adult speech is unacceptable if less restrictive alternatives would be equally effective. Currently available user-based software is a reasonably effective method that parents can use to prevent their children from accessing inappropriate material.

◆ The CDA's severability clause allows deletion of the term "or indecent" such that knowing transmission of "obscene" messages to any recipient under 18 years of age may continue to be punishable.

Concurrence and dissent (O'Connor, J., Rehnquist, C.J.). The only way for a speaker to avoid liability under the CDA is to completely refrain from using indecent speech. The CDA should be construed to impose a knowledge requirement, which would make it constitutional as applied to a conversation involving only an adult and one or more minors. Restricting adult communication with minors does not restrict an adult's ability to communicate with other adults. Regarding minors, however, there is very little speech that is constitutionally protected as to minors but banned by the CDA. The Court should reject the argument that the CDA is facially overbroad because it substantially interferes with the First Amendment rights of minors. It does not burden a substantial amount of minors' constitutionally protected speech.

---

e. **Regulation of cable television--**

Denver Area Educational Telecommunications Consortium, Inc. v. FCC, 518 U.S. 727 (1996).

Facts. Congress adopted provisions in the 1992 Cable Television Act that, regulated the broadcasting of "patently offensive" sex-related material on cable television. The provisions applied only to two types of special cable channels. The first, "leased channels," are those that federal law requires a cable system operator to reserve by commercial lease by unaffiliated third parties. The second, "public access channels," are those that local governments have required cable system operators to set aside for public, educational, or governmental purposes. Until 1992, federal law prohibited cable system operators from exercising editorial control over the content of any program broadcast over either type of channel. In section 10(a) of the 1992 Act, Congress permitted a cable operator to prohibit programming on leased channels that the operator "reasonably believes describes or depicts sexual or excretory activities or organs in a patently offensive manner as measured by contemporary community standards." Section 10(b)(1) requires cable operators who decide not to prohibit such programming to segregate it to one channel and block it to all except those who make a written request for it. Section 10(c) required the FCC (D) to implement regulations that would allow cable operators to prohibit such material on public access channels. The Denver Area Educational Telecommunications Consortium, Inc. (P) challenged the three provisions. The D.C. circuit held that the provisions did not violate the First Amendment. The Supreme Court granted certiorari.

Issue. May the government require cable operators to segregate and block patently offensive sex-related material appearing on leased cable channels when it has no such requirement for non-leased channels?

Held. No. Judgment reversed in part.

- The First Amendment includes a commitment to protect speech from government regulation through close judicial scrutiny, but there are no rigid judicial formulas that can be applied to all media. The changes in the law, technology, and the industrial structure of telecommunications makes it unwise to pick a single analogy and apply it to this field. Instead, the challenged provisions may be scrutinized to assure that they properly address an extremely important problem without imposing, in light of the relevant interests, an unnecessarily great restriction on speech.

- Regarding section 10(a), the need to protect children from patently offensive sex-related material is an extremely important justification. It applies to a specific type of programming that would not be available without congressional action. The balance struck by Congress is similar to the balance approved by the Court in *Pacifica*. The permissive nature of section 10(a) gives cable operators appropriate flexibility. The definition of materials subject to the restriction is not too vague. For these reasons, the provision is not unconstitutional.

- Section 10(b)(1) is significantly different because it requires cable operators to restrict speech on leased channels, but not on other channels. The segregate and block requirements are not the least restrictive alternative. Federal law uses a variety of other means to protect children from patently offensive material broadcast on unleased cable channels, including the requirement that cable operators honor a subscriber's request to block any programs the subscriber does not want. There is no reason to believe that leased channels could not use these same restrictions to address the government's interest, so this section is unconstitutional.

- Section 10(c) is similar to 10(a) except that it applies to public access channels. These channels have no historical background of cable operators exercising editorial control. Public access channels are subject to a variety of supervisory controls, including input from the municipalities that establish the channels. These control systems would normally avoid, minimize, or eliminate patently offensive programming anyway. At the same time, the programming restriction would greatly increase the risk that certain categories of acceptable programming may not appear. Because the need for this provision is not obvious, it cannot withstand review.

Concurrence (Stevens, J.). Leased channels should not be considered public fora. Section 10(c) would make the federal government a censor and disable local governments from choosing what programs to carry.

Concurrence (Souter, J.). Our old standards may not suffice for new technology. We should take time to determine the final method of review for cases like this.

Concurrence and dissent (O'Connor, J.). Section 10(c) is not unconstitutional. Allowing the cable operator the option of prohibiting the transmission of indecent speech is a constitutionally permissible means of addressing the public interest in protecting children.

Concurrence and dissent (Kennedy, Ginsburg, JJ.). Section 10(a) shares a fundamental flaw with section 10(c)—in each, Congress has singled out one sort of speech to be vulnerable to private censorship in a context where content-based discrimination is not otherwise permitted. A public access channel is a public forum, and the leased access channels are comparable to common carriers. The Court should apply existing First Amendment jurisprudence to this case to address the basic issue, which is whether the government can deprive certain speakers, on the basis of the content of their speech, of protections afforded all others. The answer is simply no. All three of these provisions should be held unconstitutional.

Concurrence and dissent (Thomas, J., Rehnquist, C.J., Scalia, J.). None of these provisions should be held unconstitutional. Prior cases have allowed the government to require broadcast licensees to share frequencies and to conduct themselves as fiduciaries to give voice to representative views that would otherwise be barred from the airwaves. Cable operators have been treated more like nonbroadcast media than broadcast media. Both leased and public access channels have been created by the government at the expense of cable operators' editorial discretion. The First Amendment does not prohibit Congress from returning part of the operators' editorial discretion. Section 10(b)(1) does not ban indecent speech, but because it imposes content-based restrictions, it must be subjected to strict scrutiny. The Court finds the section unconstitutional because there are alternatives that the Court considers less restrictive. But the Court's alternatives still would not allow parents to simply block out certain channels at certain times, because the open nature of leased-access programming, coming from a variety of sources, can allow indecent programming at random times. Section 10(b) is narrowly tailored to further Congress's compelling interest.

---

f.   Regulation of time for cable programming--

United States v. Playboy Entertainment Group, Inc., 529 U.S. 803 (2000).

Facts. The Telecommunications Act of 1996 contained regulations regarding cable operators who provide sexually-oriented programming. Section 504 allows parents to tell cable operators to keep any channel out of their home. Section 505 requires cable operators to either fully scramble sexually-oriented channels or to limit their transmission to between 10 p.m. and 6 a.m. When signals are not fully scrambled, the signal can occasionally bleed through to the viewer, but the technology to fully scramble signals was expensive so most cable owners chose the limited transmission option. Playboy Entertainment Group, Inc. (P) challenged the regulations. The district court found that Section 505's content-based restriction on speech violated the First Amendment because the government might further its interests in less restrictive ways. The United States (D) appeals.

Issue. May Congress require cable operators to limit the transmission of sexually-oriented programming to nighttime hours?

Held. No. Judgment affirmed.

♦ The only reasonable way for many cable operators to comply with section 505 is to limit their broadcast to the eight specified nighttime hours, regardless of the wishes of the viewers. The record shows that as much as half of all adult programming is viewed by households prior to 10 p.m., so this regulation is a significant restriction of communication.

♦ Whether a regulation is a ban or a burden on speech, a content-based regulation must satisfy the same rigorous scrutiny. Because the statute is content-based, it must be narrowly tailored to promote a compelling government interest.

♦ The key difference between cable television and broadcasting media is that cable systems can block unwanted channels on a household-by-household basis. Targeted blocking is less restrictive than banning, so the government should not be allowed to ban speech if targeting blocking is reasonably available.

♦ Under Section 504, parents can request blocking of sexually-oriented programming to their homes. This approach is narrowly tailored to the government's goal of supporting parents who oppose this type of material. The government cannot impose a more burdensome restriction such as 505 without showing that the less restrictive alternative is ineffective to meet its goals.

Concurrence (Stevens, J.). Justice Scalia's approach would treat programs whose content is protected by the First Amendment as though they were obscene because of the way they are advertised. A deceptive ad cannot make the program obscene.

Dissent (Scalia, J.). The government has greater latitude to regulate advertising that emphasizes the sexually provocative aspects of nonobscene programming because neither the buyer nor the seller is interested in the work's literary, artistic, political, or scientific value. Section 505 regulates that type of business.

Dissent (Breyer, J., Rehnquist, C.J., O'Connor, J., Scalia, J.). Section 504's opt-out alternative may be less restrictive, but it is not similarly practical and effective as a way to protect children. Section 505 protects children against sexually-oriented programming where parents are unaware of what the children are watching, cannot supervise television viewing habits, or are simply unavailable at critical times.

Comment. The majority addressed the dissent by stating that even if the government has an interest in substituting itself for informed and empowered parents, its interest is not sufficiently compelling to justify a widespread restriction on speech.

---

g. **Restricting Internet speech to protect minors.** *Ashcroft v. American Civil Liberties Union*, 542 U.S. 656 (2004), involved the Child Online Protection Act ("COPA"), which imposed criminal penalties for knowingly posting on the World Wide Web, for commercial purposes, obscene or indecent messages to any recipient younger than 18 years of age. The Court held that the government may not restrict Internet speech to protect minors if there is a less restrictive means available, such as blocking and filtering software. Justice Breyer, joined by Chief Justice Rehnquist and Justice O'Connor, dissented, arguing that COPA's burden on protected speech was modest and that it applied only to material unprotected by the First Amendment, *i.e.*, legally obscene material. He contended that COPA did not censor even that material, but merely required providers to restrict minors' access to harmful material. Justice Scalia also dissented, asserting that COPA should not have been subjected to strict scrutiny because the First Amendment allows the government to entirely ban obscene material.

I. THE RIGHT NOT TO SPEAK AND FREEDOM OF ASSOCIATION

1. **Right to Refrain from Speaking.** The First Amendment incorporates the concept of individual freedom of mind. Thus it protects the right not to speak as well as the right to speak.

    a. **State-mandated speech.** In *Wooley v. Maynard*, 430 U.S. 705 (1977), the Court struck down a state law requiring display of auto license plates carrying the state motto, "Live Free or Die." The motto represented an ideological point of view that the challengers, members of Jehovah's Witnesses, found unacceptable. The Court failed to find any state interest sufficient to justify the infringement on the First Amendment right to refrain from speaking.

    b. **State-permitted speech on private property--**

PruneYard Shopping Center v. Robins, 447 U.S. 74 (1980).

Facts. Robins (P) set up a table inside the PruneYard Shopping Center (D) for the purpose of distributing pamphlets and seeking signatures. D had a policy to forbid such activity if not directly related to D's commercial purposes. P was asked to leave and did so. P then sued D to enjoin it from denying P access. The California Supreme Court held that the California Constitution protected P's reasonable speech, even in privately owned shopping centers. D appeals.

Issue. Does a state constitution that permits free speech on privately owned, publicly available shopping centers deny the owner's Fifth Amendment property rights or his First Amendment freedom of speech?

Held. No. Judgment affirmed.

♦ Although the United States Constitution does not grant P the right granted by the California Constitution, states may recognize more expansive rights than those existing under federal law. The limit on those rights is the extent to which they would impinge on another person's federal rights.

♦ The Fifth Amendment Taking Clause is violated where a state forces some people alone to bear public burdens that, in all fairness and justice, should be borne by the public as a whole. Here, D has realized no economic injury and retains power to establish reasonable time, place, and manner restrictions to minimize interference with its commercial function. Hence, there is no taking.

♦ D claims a right not to be forced by the state to use his property as a public forum. However, D has chosen to open his property to the public. P's message is not dictated by the state. D is free to disclaim association with P. Therefore, D's free speech rights are not impinged.

Concurrence (Powell, White, JJ.). This type of state action could raise serious First Amendment issues if the opinions expressed required rebuttal by the owner to remove mistaken impressions, which would impinge the owner's right to choose not to speak, or if the speakers used the owner's premises to propagate views morally repugnant to the owner.

---

c. **Access to a parade--**

Hurley v. Irish-American Gay, Lesbian and Bisexual Group of Boston, 515 U.S. 557 (1995).

Facts. The Irish-American Gay, Lesbian and Bisexual Group of Boston (P) sought to participate in the annual St. Patrick's Day parade organized by Hurley and other members of a privately-organized council (Ds). Ds annually applied for and received a parade permit. Ds allowed various groups to participate in the parade. When P sought to march in the parade to express pride in their Irish heritage as openly gay, lesbian, and bisexual individuals, Ds refused to grant P's application. P obtained an injunction and marched anyway. The next year, when Ds again refused to allow P to participate, P sued under a state law prohibiting any discrimination on the basis of sexual orientation relative to the admission to any place of public accommodation. The state courts held that the parade was a public accommodation, so that Ds had to allow P to participate. The state supreme court affirmed. The Supreme Court granted certiorari.

Issue. May a state require private citizens who organize a parade to include a group imparting a message the organizers do not wish to convey?

Held. No. Judgment reversed.

♦ Parades are forms of expression and are entitled to First Amendment protection. The protected expression is not limited to banners and songs, but includes the overall activity.

♦ Although Ds are lenient in admitting a variety of participants, a private speaker does not forfeit constitutional protection by combining various speakers. Newspapers consist of a compilation of numerous writers, and Ds' acceptance of a variety of groups is similar.

♦ Members of P's group were not excluded from participating on the same basis as other individuals. Ds simply did not want P's message to be part of Ds' parade. The state courts in effect required Ds to alter the expressive content of their parade, which violates a fundamental First Amendment principle that speakers may choose the content of their own messages. A speech restriction cannot be used to require expression of a government-approved message.

Comment. In *NAACP v. Claiborne Hardware Co.*, 458 U.S. 886 (1982), the Court held that a consumer boycott organized to force the white merchants who were being boycotted to make changes in racial practices was essentially political speech and therefore immune from government regulation. This type of boycott was distinguished from labor boycotts organized for economic objectives, which can be prohibited by the government.

————————————

d. **Compelled support of government speech.** *Johanns v. Livestock Marketing Association,* 544 U.S. 550 (2005), involved a First Amendment challenge to the Beef Promotion and Research Act, which established a federal policy of promoting and marketing beef products. Advertising was funded by an assessment collected from beef producers. Some of the beef producers sought declaratory and injunctive relief with respect to the compelled subsidy of the advertising. The Court held that compelled support of private speech may be challenged under the First Amendment, but compelled support of government speech is not susceptible to a First Amendment attack, regardless of whether the subsidy is through targeted assessments devoted exclusively to funding the program or through general taxes. The Court rejected the claim that the speech was not government speech because it was controlled by the Beef Board and its Operating Committee. The members of the Beef Board were appointed by the Secretary of Agriculture, and the Operating Committee was ancillary to the Beef Board. Moreover, the government controlled the program because Congress and the Secretary of Agriculture established the overall message.

2. Expressive Associations--

Roberts v. United States Jaycees, 468 U.S. 609 (1984).

Facts. The United States Jaycees (P), an organization dedicated to developing young men for activity in civic affairs, excluded men over 35 years old and all women from participation as regular members. These groups could participate as nonvoting, non-office-holding associate members, however. Two local chapters of P, located in Minnesota, violated P's national bylaws and admitted women as regular members. P's national president announced an intent to revoke the chapters' charters, and the local chapters filed charges of discrimination with the Minnesota Department of Human Rights. P sued Roberts and other state officials (Ds) for declaratory and injunctive relief. The district court found for Ds, but the court of appeals reversed. Ds appeal.

Issue. May a large organization that is basically unselective about membership exclude applicants solely on the basis of sex?

Held. No. Judgment reversed.

♦ "Freedom of association" comprehends two distinct types of association. There are certain intimate human relationships that the state cannot interfere with as a principle of fundamental personal liberty. There are also associations for the purpose of engaging in activities protected by the First Amendment such as speech and religion. The degree of protection given to association varies, depending on the type of liberty involved.

♦ Personal affiliations, such as family relationships, demand the fullest possible protection. They are characterized by small numbers, a high degree of selectivity, and seclusion from others in critical aspects of the relationship. On the other hand, large business enterprises, while in a sense associations, do not involve the concerns underlying the First Amendment protection.

♦ P in this case consists of local chapters of large and basically unselective groups. The evidence indicated that members were actively recruited, and applicants were never denied membership except for sex. Women were allowed to participate in P's functions.

♦ The state statute prohibiting sex discrimination may infringe in some hypothetical way P's freedom of expressive association, because women now are unable to vote or hold office. This interference with the internal organization, however, is justified by the state's compelling interest in eradicating discrimination against its female citizens. Besides, the impact is likely to be minimal because the state law does not change P's objective of promoting the interests of young men. The impact on P's protected speech is no greater than that necessary to accomplish the state's legitimate purpose.

Concurrence (O'Connor, J.). The Court's analysis is both overprotective of activities undeserving of constitutional shelter and underprotective of important First Amendment concerns. An association engaged exclusively in protected expression should be protected in its choice of members. On the other hand, there should be only minimal constitutional protection of the freedom of commercial association; regulation of commercial enterprises must only meet the rational basis test. P is a commercial association. The amount of expression it engages in is not enough to preclude state regulation of its commercial activities, including the commercial opportunity presented by regular membership.

---

3. Exclusive Membership Based on Sexual Orientation--

Boy Scouts of America v. Dale, 530 U.S. 640 (2000).

Facts. The Boy Scouts of America (D) is a private, not-for-profit organization that instills its system of values in young people, including its assertion that homosexuality is inconsistent with those values. Dale (P) was an adult leader within D. When a newspaper reported that P was co-president of the Lesbian/Gay Alliance at Rutgers University, D revoked P's adult membership in D. P sued in state court, alleging illegal discrimination. The trial court granted summary judgment for D, but the appellate division reversed in pertinent part and remanded. The state supreme court affirmed, holding that D violated the state's public accommodations law by revoking P's membership based on his avowed homosexuality and that P's reinstatement would not compel the Boy Scouts to express any message. The Supreme Court granted certiorari.

Issue. May the Boy Scouts of America prohibit participation by homosexuals?

Held. Yes. Judgment reversed.

- ◆ The application of New Jersey's public accommodations law to require D to admit P violates D's First Amendment right of expressive association. The government may not intrude into a group's internal affairs by forcing it to accept a member it does not desire if such forced membership affects in a significant way the group's ability to advocate public or private viewpoints.

- ◆ Under *Roberts, supra*, freedom of expressive association is not absolute, and it must yield to regulations adopted to serve compelling state interests, unrelated to the suppression of ideas, that cannot be achieved through means significantly less restrictive of associational freedoms. To determine whether a group is protected, the courts must determine whether the group engages in "expressive association." D clearly does so when its adult leaders inculcate its youth members with its value system.

♦ The next step is to determine whether forcing D to accept P would significantly affect D's ability to advocate public or private viewpoints. D asserts that homosexual conduct is inconsistent with the values embodied in the Scout Oath and Law, particularly those represented by the terms "morally straight" and "clean," and that D does not want to promote homosexual conduct as a legitimate form of behavior. P's presence as a leader within D's organization would significantly burden D's expression of its viewpoints by interfering with D's choice to not propound a viewpoint that is contrary to its beliefs.

♦ An association's expression may be protected whenever it engages in expressive activity that could be impaired. Expression need not be its only purpose. Application of the New Jersey public accommodation law to force D to accept P as a leader would violate D's First Amendment rights.

♦ The intermediate standard of review enunciated in *United States v. O'Brien* is inapplicable here. The appropriate level of analysis is found in *Hurley, supra*. The state interests embodied in New Jersey's public accommodations law do not justify the severe intrusion on D's freedom of expressive association that P's participation would present. It is not a question whether D's teachings with respect to homosexual conduct are right or wrong because public or judicial disapproval of an organization's expression does not justify the state's interference with a defendant's expressive message.

Dissent (Stevens, Souter, Ginsburg, Breyer, JJ.). The New Jersey Supreme Court provided an expansive coverage to the state's usage of the term "place of public accommodation." This expansive construction does not violate D's constitutional rights. The law does not impose any serious burdens on D's efforts to achieve its goals, and does not force D to communicate any message it does not want to endorse. D's policy statements are officially silent on homosexuality; D has simply adopted an exclusionary membership policy. P's participation did not send a cognizable message to D or to the world. The right of free speech is not effectively an unlimited right to exclude for every organization. The only rationale for this holding is that homosexuals are so different from the rest of society that their presence alone should be singled out for special First Amendment treatment.

---

4. **Freedom of Association and Employment.**

   a. **Political patronage--**

Elrod v. Burns, 427 U.S. 347 (1976).

Facts. A newly elected sheriff (D) sought to replace some nonpolicymaking and nonconfidential employees in the sheriff's office with members of his own party. The employees (Ps) brought suit alleging a violation of the First Amendment. The district court dismissed the complaint, but the court of appeals reversed. The United States Supreme Court granted certiorari.

Issue. May a nonpolicymaking and nonconfidential public employee be dismissed based solely on political party affiliation?

Held. No. Judgment affirmed.

♦ Dismissals from public employment based solely on beliefs and associations are violative of those rights as well as impose an unconstitutional burden on receipt of a public benefit. To be constitutional, such patronage must be the least restrictive means of achieving a vital government interest.

♦ None of the interests asserted here satisfy this test. First, there are other means available for dealing with poor job performance that are not based on patronage. For example, a politically-motivated, insubordinate employee can be dismissed for cause. Second, positions of policymaking or confidentiality in which party affiliation and beliefs would significantly affect the effectiveness and efficiency of the government are exempt from this holding. Finally, political parties existed before patronage and there is no evidence that patronage is necessary for their survival.

Concurrence (Stewart, Blackmun, JJ.). This holding does not apply to all types of patronage, only to the case of a nonpolicymaking, nonconfidential government employee, who is satisfactorily performing his job.

Dissent (Powell, J., Burger, C.J., Rehnquist, J.). Ps knowingly accepted the patronage system when they received their jobs, thus they should not be able to challenge the system when it is their turn to be replaced. This decision should be left to locally elected representatives.

Comment. In *Branti v. Finkel*, 445 U.S. 507 (1980), the Court held that a public defender may not discharge his assistants solely on political partisan grounds. An assistant public defender's duty is to represent individual citizens, not his superior; party affiliation is irrelevant to the performance of that duty. In *Rutan v. Republican Party of Illinois*, 497 U.S. 62 (1990), the Court extended *Elrod* and *Branti* to hiring decisions.

---

    b.   **Disclosures and disclaimers.** A government employer, just as any private employer, should have the power to inquire of its employees or potential employees about any matters that may prove relevant to their fitness for public employment. However, such inquiries may not impinge on freedom of speech. Thus, governments may not require an oath that the employee has not engaged, or will not engage, in protected speech activities. Oaths to support the Constitution or to oppose the overthrow of government by illegal means are permissible. Employees who refuse to take an oath to support the Constitution may be discharged or refused employment. [*See* Cole v. Richardson, 405 U.S. 676 (1972)]

c.   **Restriction of employee's speech--**

Connick v. Myers, 461 U.S. 138 (1983).

Facts. Myers (P) worked as assistant district attorney under Connick (D), the local district attorney. Despite her objections, P was to be transferred to another section. She prepared a questionnaire intended to solicit her fellow employees' opinions about transfer policy, office morale, the level of confidence in named supervisors, and pressure to work in political campaigns. D fired P for insubordination. P sued, claiming wrongful termination based on her exercise of free speech. The lower courts upheld P's claim. The Supreme Court granted certiorari.

Issue. Do the First and Fourteenth Amendments prohibit the discharge of a state employee for circulating a questionnaire concerning internal office affairs?

Held. No. Judgment reversed.

♦   Evaluation of a public employee's right to free speech involves a balance between the employee's interests as a citizen in commenting on matters of public concern and the state's interest as an employer in promoting the efficiency of the public services it provides through its employees.

♦   The focus of P's questionnaire is to gather ammunition for her controversy with D. Such speech dealing with matters of personal interest is normally not the type that federal courts should pass on as to whether the termination was unconstitutional. The matter of pressure to work on political campaigns does touch a public concern, though.

♦   The state's burden to justify a termination depends on the nature of the employee's speech. Here, P's limited First Amendment interest did not require D to tolerate disruptive activity. The evidence indicates that P's actions carried the potential to undermine office relations. Therefore, P's dismissal was not unconstitutional.

Dissent (Brennan, Marshall, Blackmun, Stevens, JJ.). P's questionnaire dealt with the manner in which the government is, or should be, operated. Such communication is essential for self-governance, which is a major basis for the First Amendment. The public interest of a statement does not depend on where it is said or why. The district court found that the questionnaire was not disruptive. The deference given by the majority to D's judgment is unjustified. The effect of the decision will be to deter public employees from speaking out.

Comment. In some circumstances, the government may condition benefits on a person's or group's restraint in exercising First Amendment rights. Thus, the IRS may withdraw the tax-exempt status of an organization that engages directly in lobbying. [Regan v. Taxation With Representation of Washington, 461 U.S. 540 (1983)]

J. WEALTH AND THE POLITICAL PROCESS

1. Campaign Expenditures.

a. Introduction. Although Congress has constitutional power to regulate federal elections, it may not unreasonably interfere with First Amendment freedoms when it regulates such elections. The Court attempted to strike a balance between these competing interests when it considered the 1974 amendments to the Federal Election Campaign Act of 1971 and the Internal Revenue Code of 1954. The opinion, *Buckley v. Valeo, infra,* consumed nearly 300 pages in the U.S. Reports. Basically, it held that Congress can limit the amounts individuals may contribute to federal political campaigns, but it may not limit expenditures by candidates.

b. Balancing approach to regulation of campaign financing--

Buckley v. Valeo, 424 U.S. 1 (1976).

Facts. Buckley and other candidates and groups (Ps) brought suit against Valeo (D) and other federal officials, seeking a declaration that the reporting and disclosure requirements of the Federal Election Campaign Act were unconstitutional. The requirements applied to all political committees and candidates and involved detailed reporting of contributors and amounts contributed. Ps also challenged the contribution and expenditure limitations, which included the following restrictions:

A $1,000 limit on individual and group contributions to a candidate or authorized campaign committee per election;

A $1,000 limit on expenditures relative to a clearly identified candidate;

An annual ceiling on a candidate's expenditures from personal or family resources; and

Public financing of presidential campaigns.

The court of appeals upheld the Act in its entirety. Ps appeal.

Issues.

(i)   May Congress impose contribution limitations on federal elections?

(ii)   May Congress impose expenditure limitations on federal elections?

(iii)   May Congress impose detailed reporting and disclosure requirements on political contribution activity?

(iv)   May Congress permit public financing of presidential campaigns?

Held. (i) Yes. (ii) No. (iii) Yes. (iv) Yes. Judgment affirmed in part and reversed in part.

♦   Congress may impose contribution limits on federal elections.

        The financial limitations imposed on political campaigns cannot be considered as regulation of conduct alone, since exercise of free speech depends largely on the ability to finance that speech. This is especially true when the electorate depends on the mass media for so much of its information.

        The $1,000 limit on campaign contributions has minimal effect on freedom of association or on the extent of political discussion. On the other hand, it deals directly with the sources of political corruption, or the appearances thereof, which are the statute's objective. It does not violate the First Amendment.

♦   Congress may not impose expenditure limitations on federal elections.

        Even though the expenditure limitations are content-neutral, they impose severe restrictions on freedom of political expression. Equalizing the relative ability of individuals and groups to influence elections is not a sufficient rationale to justify the infringement of First Amendment rights.

        The interest in avoiding the danger of candidate dependence on large contributions, which is asserted as a reason for limiting expenditures, is served by the contribution limits and disclosure requirements. It is not within the government's power to determine that spending to promote one's political views is wasteful, excessive, or unwise.

♦   Congress may impose detailed reporting and disclosure requirements on political contribution activity.

        The government interest in assuring the free functioning of our national institutions is served by the disclosure requirement. The electorate is provided with relevant information, thereby deterring corruption and facilitating enforcement of contribution limitations.

P claims the requirements are overbroad as applied to minor parties and independent candidates, but P has failed to show any actual harm to these groups. If such harm actually occurs, courts will be available to provide appropriate remedies, but a blanket exemption is unnecessary.

◆ Congress may permit public financing of presidential campaigns.

Public financing does not constitute invidious discrimination against minor and new parties in violation of the Fifth Amendment. Even though the scheme provides full funding only for major parties, it assists minor parties and does not limit the ability of minor party candidates to raise funds up to the applicable spending limit.

Dissent in part (Burger, C.J.). It is an improper intrusion on the First Amendment to limit contributions. It is inappropriate to subsidize presidential campaigns.

Dissent in part (White, J.). It is illogical to restrict contributions but permit unlimited expenditures.

---

2. **Campaign Finance Reform--**

McConnell v. Federal Election Commission, 540 U.S. 93 (2003).

Facts. The Bipartisan Campaign Reform Act of 2002 ("BCRA") amended the Federal Election Campaign Act of 1971 ("FECA"), which was designed to moderate the impact of wealth in the political process. FECA had imposed limitations only on "hard money" contributions, or money used to influence an election for federal office. BCRA restricted the use of soft money and issue ads. "Soft money," or money used for state or local elections and for issue ads, was unregulated under FECA. Among other things, BCRA: (i) prohibited national party committees from soliciting, receiving, directing, or spending any soft money; (ii) prevented state and local party committees from using soft money for activities that affect federal elections; (iii) prohibited the use of soft money by state and local party committees or candidates and officeholders for public communication supporting or attacking a federal candidate; (iv) imposed restrictions on candidates' use of soft money; (v) imposed restrictions on corporations and labor unions to prevent them from funding electioneering communications, defined as political broadcasts that refer to a clearly identified federal candidate that are made within 60 days before an election. Senator McConnell and others (Ps) challenged the law by suing the Federal Election Commission (D). The district court upheld part of the law and found some parts unconstitutional. The Supreme Court granted certiorari.

Issue. May Congress limit the use of soft money contributions and impose detailed restrictions on how organizations can influence elections?

Held. Yes. Affirmed in part and reversed in part.

♦ Soft money contributions have often been much larger than the contributions of hard money that FECA permits, and the largest corporate donors have often made substantial contributions to both parties. This indicates that many corporate contributions have been motivated by a desire for access to candidates, rather than by ideological support for the candidates and parties. There is a danger that officeholders will decide issues according to the wishes of those who have made large financial contributions, instead of according to the desires of their constituencies. Unlike straight cash-for-votes transactions, such corruption is neither easily detected nor practical to criminalize. The best means to prevent these abuses is to identify and remove the temptation.

♦ Mere political favoritism or opportunity for influence alone is insufficient to justify regulation; it is the manner in which parties have sold access to federal candidates and officeholders that has given rise to the appearance of undue influence and to the idea that money buys influence.

♦ The use of soft money by state and local parties and candidates for issue ads also has a dramatic effect on federal elections. Public communication that promotes or attacks a candidate for federal office directly affects the election in which he is participating.

♦ The soft money restrictions and contribution caps to public communications are closely drawn to match the important governmental interests of preventing corruption and the appearance of corruption.

Concurrence and dissent (Scalia, J.). Today the Court, which sternly disapproves of restrictions on pornography, approves of a law that cuts to the heart of the First Amendment—the right to criticize the government. BCRA basically prohibits the criticism of members of Congress by those entities most capable of criticizing effectively—the national political parties and corporations. Even though it also prohibits criticism of those candidates challenging members of Congress, such evenhandedness is not fairness. It favors incumbents, who typically raise about three times as much hard money as challengers. Regulation of money used for disseminating speech is equivalent to regulating the speech itself.

Concurrence and dissent (Thomas, Scalia, JJ.). Besides continuing the errors of *Buckley*, the Court now expands the anti-circumvention rationale beyond reason. The Court should require a showing of why bribery laws are insufficient to address the concerns asserted by Congress. The Court also continues to decrease the level of scrutiny applied to restrictions on core political speech.

Concurrence and dissent (Kennedy, Rehnquist, C.J., Scalia, Thomas, JJ.). The citizens have the right to judge for themselves the most effective means for expressing political views, and to decide for themselves whom to believe. BCRA is the codification of an assumption that the mainstream media alone can protect freedom of speech, and it is an effort by Congress to make sure that civic discourse takes place only through the modes of its own choosing. The Court has moved beyond the anti-corruption rationale of *Buckley* to allow regulation of any conduct that wins goodwill from or influences a member of Congress. Access, in itself, is not corruption. The new regulations impose far greater burdens on associational rights than do regulations that merely cap the amount of money a person can contribute to a political candidate or committee.

Dissent (Rehnquist, C.J., Scalia, Kennedy, JJ.). The issue under Title I is not whether Congress can permissibly regulate campaign contributions to candidates or attempt to eliminate corruption. Title I is regulation of much speech that has no plausible connection to either candidate contributions or corruption. It regulates all donations to national political committees, regardless of how the funds are used. As such, Title I is overinclusive. The Court should only permit regulation of financing that is closely linked to corruption or the appearance of corruption. In effect, the Court has eliminated the "closely drawn" tailoring requirement and meaningful judicial review.

IX. FREEDOM OF RELIGION

A. INTRODUCTION

The First Amendment provides that "Congress shall make no law respecting an establishment of religion, or prohibiting the free exercise thereof." These two clauses, the Establishment Clause and the Free Exercise Clause, have provided considerable grounds for litigation. One other reference to religion is found in the Constitution. Article VI provides that "no religious test shall ever be required as a qualification to any office or public trust under the United States."

B. ESTABLISHMENT CLAUSE

1. **Introduction.** The central purpose of the Establishment Clause is to insure governmental neutrality in matters of religion. "When government activities touch on the religious sphere, they must be secular in purpose, evenhanded in operation, and neutral in primary impact." [Gillette v. United States, 401 U.S. 437 (1971)] Many cases arising under the Establishment Clause have involved schools. As applied to schools, the clause prevents governments from enacting laws that further the religious training or doctrine of any sect.

2. **Aid to Religion.**

   a. **Basic test.** The Court has promulgated three guidelines for determining the validity of state statutes granting financial aid to church-related schools. To be valid, the statute must: (i) reflect a clearly secular purpose; (ii) have a primary effect that neither advances nor inhibits religion; and (iii) avoid "excessive government entanglement" with religion. [*See* Lemon v. Kurtzman, *infra*] The wall of separation between church and state works both ways. It prevents religion from seeping into the functions of government, and it also prevents government from encroaching on matters of religion.

   b. **Transportation--**

Everson v. Board of Education, 330 U.S. 1 (1947).

Facts. A local New Jersey board of education (D) authorized reimbursement to parents of the costs of using the public transportation system to send their children to school, whether public or parochial. Everson (P) challenged the scheme as an unconstitutional exercise of state power to support church schools. P appeals adverse lower court decisions.

Issue. May a state use public funds to assist student transportation to parochial, as well as public, schools?

Held. Yes. Judgment affirmed.

♦ The Establishment Clause was intended to erect a wall between church and state. It does not prohibit a state from extending its general benefits to all its citizens without regard to their religious belief.

♦ Reimbursement of transportation is intended solely to help children arrive safely at school, regardless of their religion. It does not support any schools, parochial or public. To invalidate D's system would handicap religion, which is no more permissible than favoring religion.

Dissent (Rutledge, Frankfurter, Jackson, Burton, JJ.). The Court should be as strict to prohibit use of public funds to aid religious schools as P is to prevent introduction of religious education into public schools.

---

c. **Tax exemptions--**

Walz v. Tax Commission, 397 U.S. 664 (1970).

Facts. Walz (P), a New York taxpayer, instituted a suit against the Tax Commission (D) to enjoin it from continuing to grant religious organizations tax-exempt status for property and income. P alleged that this favorable treatment violated the Establishment Clause in that it advanced the cause of religion and had no secular purpose.

Issue. Can a state maintain a neutral position with respect to religions if it grants them indirect aid such as a property tax exemption?

Held. Yes. Injunction denied.

♦ The Establishment Clause does not require the state to be hostile to religion. The tax exemption here is neither sponsorship nor hostility.

♦ The state statute authorizing the exemption grants favorable treatment to educational facilities and charities also, indicating that the state has made a value judgment that institutions dealing with moral or mental improvement (including religions) should be given favorable treatment.

♦ Since the state statute does not involve the state in impermissible entanglement in its administration, it cannot be set aside on this ground.

Concurrence (Brennan, J.). The tax exemptions are granted for secular purposes. Religions and other nonprofit organizations contribute to the well-being of the community. The state is not using its power to influence or inhibit religious participation.

Dissent (Douglas, J.). Economic aid to religions advances their cause by allowing them to obtain a vast amount of wealth and property without paying taxes. The tax exemption is an impermissible subsidy that aids religion, thereby violating the Establishment Clause.

---

d. Public aid to parochial schools--

Lemon v. Kurtzman, 403 U.S. 602 (1971).

Facts. Rhode Island and Pennsylvania provided for, respectively, salary supplements for nonpublic school teachers and reimbursement of nonpublic schools for certain expenditures. Both laws provided for comprehensive regulation, including auditing, to assure that the funds were used only for secular education and not for religious activity or instruction. The lower courts upheld the Pennsylvania law and declared the Rhode Island law unconstitutional.

Issue. May the state financially assist nonpublic schools if the use of funds is sufficiently regulated to assure their use for exclusively secular purposes?

Held. No. Judgment affirmed (Rhode Island) and reversed (Pennsylvania).

- ♦ Applying the three-part test, it is clear that these programs involve excessive government entanglement with religion. Earlier cases have allowed states to provide secular, neutral, or nonideological services, facilities, or materials such as bus transportation and textbooks. However, the effect of this type of aid on religion is easily ascertainable at the outset. A grant of funds differs from this type of assistance in that its effect can be determined only by continuing state surveillance, which requires the type of excessive entanglement dangerous both to church and to state.

- ♦ By bringing financial aid to nonpublic schools into the political arena, the states threaten to make religious preferences a significant political issue in the selection of public officials. These programs are subject to continual debate as funds are appropriated. This type of entanglement differs from the tax-exemption in *Walz*, *supra*, which is neutral because no continuing oversight is needed.

---

e. Loans to private secular schools--

Mitchell v. Helms, 530 U.S. 793 (2000).

Facts. Chapter 2 of the Education Consolidation and Improvement Act ("ECIA") provided for federal grants to local educational agencies ("LEAs"), which in turn loaned educational materials and equipment, including library and media materials and computer equipment, to public and private elementary and secondary schools to implement "secular, neutral, and nonideological" programs. In Jefferson Parish, Louisiana, about 30 percent of these funds were allocated for private schools, most of which were religiously affiliated. The amount of the grant was based solely on enrollment in each school. Helms (P) filed suit claiming that ECIA violated the First Amendment's Establishment Clause. The district court agreed with P. The district court judge was later replaced with another judge, who upheld the statute. During P's appeal, the Supreme Court decided *Agostini* v. *Felton*, 521 U.S. 203 (1997). The court of appeals held that *Agostini* had not rejected the distinction between textbooks and other in-kind aid and held that the statute was unconstitutional. The Supreme Court granted certiorari.

Issue. May the federal government provide funds to local educational agencies that loan educational materials, including books and computer equipment, to private secular schools, so long as the purpose is to implement secular, neutral, and nonideological programs?

Held. Yes. Judgment reversed.

♦ In *Agostini*, the Court modified the *Lemon* test by recasting the entanglement inquiry as simply one factor relevant to determining a statute's effect. Under *Agostini*, a court may determine that government aid has the effect of advancing religion if it (i) results in governmental indoctrination, (ii) defines its recipients by reference to religion, or (iii) creates an excessive entanglement. In this case, the district court held that Chapter 2 has a secular purpose and that it did not create an excessive entanglement. This leaves the first two *Agostini* criteria to consider.

♦ The first criterion is whether any indoctrination that occurs at the school could reasonably be attributed to governmental action. To determine whether indoctrination is attributable to the government, the Court applies the neutrality principle. Aid that is offered to a broad range of groups or persons without regard to their religion is permitted. If the government, seeking to further some legitimate secular purpose, offers aid on the same terms, without regard to religion, to all who adequately further that purpose, then any aid going to a religious recipient only has the effect of furthering that secular purpose.

♦ One factor that helps assure neutrality is whether any governmental aid that goes to a religious institution does so as a result of the genuinely independent and private choices of individuals. In this case, the grants were based on school enrollment, which reflects the private choices of students and their parents. This process makes it more difficult for a government to grant special favors that might lead to a religious establishment.

♦ *Agostini*'s second primary criterion—whether an aid program defines its recipients by reference to religion—is closely related to the first. It uses the same facts to answer a different question—whether the criteria for allocating the aid create a financial incentive to undertake religious indoctrination. Such an incentive is not present when the aid is allocated on the basis of neutral, secular criteria that neither favor nor disfavor religion, and is made available to both religious and secular beneficiaries on a nondiscriminatory basis.

♦   P claims that direct, nonincidental aid to religious schools is always impermissible, but such an approach is inconsistent with the Court's more recent cases. The purpose of the direct/indirect distinction is to prevent "subsidization" of religion, and the Court's more recent cases address this concern through the principle of private choice, as incorporated in the first *Agostini* criterion (*i.e.*, whether any indoctrination could be attributed to the government). If aid to schools, even "direct aid," is neutrally available and, before reaching or benefiting any religious school, first passes through the hands (literally or figuratively) of numerous private citizens who are free to direct the aid elsewhere, the government has not provided any "support of religion."

Concurrence (O'Connor, Breyer, JJ.). The plurality appears to treat neutrality as the most important factor in evaluating Establishment Clause challenges to school-aid programs. While neutrality is an important factor, it is not the only consideration. The per-capital aid program is not the same as the true private choice programs approved in prior cases. The Court should simply apply the *Agostini* criteria. Application of *Agostini* to these facts does demonstrate that the program is not unconstitutional. P would have to prove that the aid actually is, or has been, used for religious purposes. Although there may have been some minor use of government-loaned equipment for religious instruction, it was at best de minimis.

Dissent (Souter, Stevens, Ginsburg, JJ.). The First Amendment prohibits any government act favoring religion, a particular religion, or even irreligion. The Establishment Clause has been consistently applied to prohibit public aid to religion and to the religious mission of sectarian schools. Until now, the question has been whether the benefit was intended to aid in providing the religious element of the education and was likely to do so. The Court today changes this approach by applying an evenhandedness approach. It holds that there is nothing wrong with aiding a school's religious mission, so long as the religious teaching obtains its tax support under a formally evenhanded criterion of distribution.

---

f.   **Publicly financed school choice--**

Zelman v. Simmons-Harris, 536 U.S. 639 (2002).

Facts. The state of Ohio adopted a pilot program that gave financial assistance to families living in any Ohio school district that was under a federal court order to be supervised by the state education superintendent, Zelman (D). The Cleveland City School District, which included 75,000 children, was the only district in that category. The children in the Cleveland district were mostly from low-income and minority families. The pilot program provided tuition aid for students to attend a participating public or private school chosen by their parents instead of the one they would otherwise be assigned to. Any private school, religious or nonreligious, could participate in the program, but the school had to agree not to discriminate on the basis of race, religion, or ethnic background. Forty-six of the 56 participating private schools had a religious affiliation, and 96% of the students who participated in the program attended the religious schools. Simmons-Harris and other taxpayers (Ps) sought an injunction against the program. The district court granted Ps summary judgment. The court of appeals affirmed. The Supreme Court granted certiorari.

Issue. May a state provide tuition aid that enables students who would otherwise attend public schools to attend private religious schools?

Held. Yes. Judgment reversed.

♦ The state had a valid secular purpose for adopting the program—to provide educational assistance to poor children in a demonstrably failing public school system. The program would violate the Establishment Clause only if it has the forbidden effect of advancing or inhibiting religion.

♦ There is a clear distinction between government programs that provide aid directly to religious schools and programs that allow, through the exercise of true private choice, for government aid going to religious schools. In previous cases, the Court has upheld neutral government programs that provided aid directly to individuals who, through their own choice, directed the aid to religious schools.

♦ Funding programs based on choice might lead to the incidental advancement of a religious message, but that advancement is attributable to the individual recipient who makes the choice, not to the government. Ohio's program does not give rise to any reasonable inference that the government is endorsing religious schools in general.

♦ The program in this case actually gives more aid to participating public schools than it gives to private schools. Families who send their children to private schools must copay a portion of the school's tuition.

♦ The dissent notes that 96% of the children in private schools are enrolled in religious schools, but when all children enrolled in nontraditional schools are counted, that percentage drops to 20%.

♦ Unlike the program in *Committee for Public Education & Religious Liberty v. Nyquist*, 413 U.S. 756 (1973), cited by Ps, this program does not provide financial support exclusively to private schools and the parents of private school enrollees. *Nyquist* does not govern neutral educational assistance programs like the program in this case.

Concurrence (O'Connor, J.). Although a significant portion of the funds appropriated for the program reach religious schools with no restriction on the use of the funds, the total amount of $8.2 million that flows to religious schools in one year is small compared with the amount provided to religious institutions at all levels of government through tax credits and exemptions and other public benefit programs.

Concurrence (Thomas, J.). The Fourteenth Amendment was adopted to guarantee individual liberty and should not be used to prohibit the exercise of educational choice.

Dissent (Souter, Stevens, Ginsburg, Breyer, JJ.). Ohio's program allows the government to pay tuition at private religious schools to support the schools' religious missions. In *Everson, supra*, the Court held that no tax may be levied to support any religious activities or institutions. Ohio's program allows tax money to be used to teach religious doctrines in these schools. The Court is ignoring *Everson*. The facts that over 96% of the students attending private schools are in religious schools, and that most families did not choose the schools because of the religion taught there, demonstrate that the problem is a lack of sufficient nonreligious schools. Parents' choices are actually restricted to choosing which religious school to send their children to.

Dissent (Breyer, Stevens, Souter, JJ.). The Establishment Clause has permitted states to provide assistance to religious schools for such things as computers, secular textbooks, and transportation for students. However, voucher programs are different from assistance programs upheld in the past because they direct financing to the teaching of religion to children. Government funding for religious teaching is much more contentious than funding for secular textbooks and computers. And the "parental choice" of schools will not offset problems created by the program. It will not help the taxpayer who does not want to finance religious education nor the parent who has little real choice between inadequate public education and adequate education at a school with religious teaching contrary to his own beliefs.

———

3. **Religion and Public Schools.**

    a. **Introduction.** Apart from issues involving financial aid, the ability of public schools to accommodate religious activities requires a careful balancing of the competing interests. One common issue is accommodation of prayer.

    b. **Statutory requirement of period of silence in public schools for meditation or voluntary prayer--**

Wallace v. Jaffree, 472 U.S. 38 (1985).

Facts. The state of Alabama, of which Wallace (D) was governor, adopted a series of statutes relating to prayer in public schools. The 1978 statute permitted a one-minute period of silence in all public schools "for meditation." The 1981 statute authorized a period of silence "for meditation or voluntary prayer." The 1982 statute authorized teachers to lead willing students in a prescribed prayer. Jaffree (P), on behalf of his school-age children, sought an injunction enforcement of the statutes. The district court held that the 1978 statute was permissible, but that the latter two were attempts to encourage religious activity. Nevertheless, the court upheld all three statutes on the ground that a state can establish a state religion. The court of appeals held both the 1981 and 1982 statutes unconstitutional. The Supreme Court previously held the 1982 statute invalid. D appeals, claiming the 1981 statute is valid.

Issue. May a state authorize a period of silence in public schools for "meditation or voluntary prayer"?

Held. No. Judgment affirmed.

♦ It is clear that the Establishment Clause prohibits a state from establishing a state religion. Each citizen has the right to select any religious faith or none at all. Thus, the *Lemon v. Kurtzman*, *supra*, tests apply to this statute.

♦ Under the purpose test of *Lemon*, the court must determine whether the government's actual purpose is to endorse or disapprove of religion. In this case, the answer is clearly yes; indeed, the 1981 statute had no secular purpose. The sponsor of the bill in the state legislature indicated the purpose of the law was to return to voluntary prayer in public schools. The only addition to the existing statute was the words "or voluntary prayer."

♦ The effect of the statute was to have the state endorse prayer activities, even to favor such activities. This is inconsistent with the strict neutrality toward religion that government is supposed to maintain.

Concurrence (O'Connor, J.). A moment of silence is permissible, as it is not inherently religious. The problem is when the state conveys the message that the moment of silence should be used for prayer.

Dissent (Burger, C.J.). Hostility toward religion is as forbidden by the Constitution as an official establishment of religion. The purpose of this moment-of-silence statute was also to clear up the widespread misunderstanding that children are prohibited from engaging in silent individual prayer in school.

Dissent (Rehnquist, J.). Jefferson's famous statement that the Establishment Clause was intended to erect "a wall of separation between church and State" was made in a short courtesy note, 14 years after the Bill of Rights was adopted. He did not even participate in the adoption of the Bill of Rights, since he was in France at the time. By contrast, Madison played a significant role. He believed the amendment was intended to prevent the establishment of a national religion, and to prevent discrimination among sects. It was not intended to require neutrality by government between religion and irreligion. Surely, the Constitution was not intended to prevent a state from "endorsing" prayer.

---

c.   **Released-time programs--**

Zorach v. Clauson, 343 U.S. 306 (1952).

Facts. New York City established a released time program so that students whose parents so requested were permitted to leave the school grounds for religious instruction. Zorach (P), a parent whose children attended the New York public schools, challenged the program. The lower courts upheld it. P appeals.

Issue. May a state grant willing students permission to leave public school grounds during school hours in order to receive religious instruction elsewhere?

Held. Yes. Judgment affirmed.

♦   There is no evidence of coercion on the part of school officials. Only those students whose parents requested their release were permitted to participate.

♦   Although the First Amendment requires a separation of church and state, that separation is not absolute but well-defined. Otherwise, there would be hostility between the two, and religious groups would be unable to benefit from such basic government services as fire and police protection.

♦   Clearly students may be released from school to attend religious holidays or observances. This released time program is no different in character.

♦   Religion is an integral part of our society, and although the state may not coerce religious observances, it may make provision for those citizens desiring to retreat to a religious sanctuary for worship or instruction.

Dissent (Jackson, J.). Schooling is essentially suspended during the released time. The fatal defect of the state's plan is that it compels attendance at public school for those students who do not participate in the released time program and, thus, creates a "temporary jail" for pupils who will not attend services.

---

d.   **Secular purpose analysis and restrictions on teaching particular subjects.** While the state undoubtedly has the right to prescribe curriculum for the public schools, it does not have the right to forbid the teaching of any scientific theory, doctrine, or other subject merely because it may be contrary to some religious doctrine.

1) **Posting of the Ten Commandments.** The Court has held that a law requiring the posting of copies of the Ten Commandments in public school rooms clearly had no secular legislative purpose, even though the law required a statement on the copies explaining a secular application of the Commandments as the basis of the common law. [Stone v. Graham, 449 U.S. 39 (1980)]

2) **Prohibition on teaching evolution invalid.** The Court held that an Arkansas statute that forbade the teaching of evolution in public schools violated freedom of religion under the First and Fourteenth Amendments. The statute was not "religiously neutral"; it was aimed at one doctrine (evolution) that was offensive to certain fundamentalist religions. [*See* Epperson v. Arkansas, 393 U.S. 97 (1968)]

3) **Teaching of creation and evolution--**

Edwards v. Aguillard, 482 U.S. 578 (1987).

Facts. Louisiana enacted a law requiring "balanced treatment" of the theories of creation and evolution if the subject of the origin of man, life, Earth, or the universe was dealt with in public schools. Neither theory could be taught without the other, although neither had to be taught, and both were statutorily defined as science. The lower courts, including a sharply divided Fifth Circuit, held that the law was unconstitutional because the theory of creation is a religious belief.

Issue. May a state require its public schools to teach creation science if they teach evolution?

Held. No. Judgment affirmed.

♦ The first requirement under *Lemon* is that a statute must have been adopted with a secular purpose. The legislature here purportedly adopted this statute to protect academic freedom, but the public school teachers were not prohibited from teaching any particular scientific theory before the statute was adopted anyway. The legislative history indicates the statute was intended to eliminate the teaching of evolution, and the statute protects creationism and its proponents without protecting evolutionists.

♦ There is a well-known antagonism between the teachings of certain religions and the teaching of evolution. The clear purpose of the statute was to advance the religious viewpoint by restructuring the science curriculum. This does not mean that a variety of scientific theories may not be taught, but only that this

Act violated the Establishment Clause because it was intended to endorse a particular religious doctrine.

Dissent (Scalia, J., Rehnquist, C.J.). As long as there was a genuine secular purpose, the Act should not be invalidated. The secular purpose set forth in the Act should not be dismissed. In addition, the *Lemon* test is not based on the language of the Establishment Clause and leads to unpredictable decisions. The purpose test should be abandoned.

———————————

e. **Purpose.** In *Board of Education v. Mergens,* 496 U.S. 226 (1990), the Court held that Congress may prohibit public secondary schools that both receive federal financial assistance and give official recognition to noncurriculum-related student groups from denying equal access to student groups on the basis of the religious content of the speech at their meetings. The open forum policy in fact avoids entanglement with religion, and opening the school to all groups, including religious groups, conveys a message of neutrality, not endorsement of religion. The statute has a secular purpose of preventing discrimination against religious and other types of speech.

4. **Official Acknowledgment of Religion.**

a. **State-employed chaplains.** In *Marsh v. Chambers*, 463 U.S. 783 (1983), the Court upheld the practice of the Nebraska legislature of opening each day with a prayer by a chaplain paid by the state. The Court noted that the colonies, federal courts, and the Continental Congress itself followed such a practice. As deeply imbedded in history and tradition as such prayer is, it cannot be held to violate the First Amendment. The dissenting Justices noted that the practice does not pass any of the *Lemon* tests.

b. **Limitations on religious displays on government property--**

Allegheny County v. ACLU, 492 U.S. 573 (1989).

Facts. For many years, Allegheny County (D) permitted a Roman Catholic group to display a creche in the County Courthouse during the Christmas season. The creche was not accompanied with figures of Santa Claus or other nonsectarian decorations. A Christmas tree was also erected at the City-County Building a block away from the courthouse. An 18-foot Chanukah menorah was placed next to the tree, together with a sign saluting "Liberty." The ACLU (P) filed suit, seeking to enjoin the display of the creche and menorah. The district court denied P's request, but the court of appeal reversed. The Supreme Court granted certiorari.

Issue. May the government permit a religious group to display a Christmas creche at a courthouse during the Christmas season?

Held. No. Judgment affirmed in part.

♦ The Establishment Clause prevents the government from promoting or affiliating itself with any religions doctrine or organization, from discriminating among persons on the basis of their religious beliefs and practices, from delegating a governmental power to a religious institution, and from involving itself too deeply in a religious institution's affairs. Accordingly, the government may not display a copy of the Ten Commandments on the walls of public classrooms.

♦ In *Lynch v. Donnelly*, 465 U.S. 668 (1984), the Court held that a city can include a creche in its annual Christmas display located in a private park in a downtown shopping district. The rationale in *Lynch* was that inclusion of the creche was "no more an advancement or endorsement of religion" than had been permitted by the Court in the past, and that any benefit to religion from the display was "incidental." Justice O'Connor wrote a separate concurrence that rejected any toleration of government endorsement of religion and inquired into the message communicated by a government practice; *i.e.,* what was the context in which the contested religious object appeared. In *Lynch*, the creche was one of several displays, including a Santa Claus house, a Christmas tree, a wishing well, a miniature village, and various "cut-out" figures including a clown, dancing elephant, robot, and teddy bear. This context negated any message of endorsement of the Christian belief represented by the creche. The dissenters in *Lynch* agreed with the O'Connor approach, but simply disagreed with the conclusion that the display did not constitute an endorsement of religion.

♦ D's creche display in this case stands alone; nothing detracts from its religious message. In this setting and context, the display violates the Establishment Clause. The government may celebrate Christmas, but not in a way that endorses Christian doctrine.

♦ The display of the menorah is combined with a Christmas tree and a sign saluting liberty. This suggests not a simultaneous endorsement of both Christian and Jewish faith, but a secular celebration of Christmas coupled with an acknowledgment of Chanukah as a contemporaneous alternative tradition. Thus, it does not endorse religious faith.

Concurrence (O'Connor, Brennan, Stevens, JJ.). The display of a creche in the courthouse conveys a message to nonadherents of Christianity that they are not full members of the political community, while telling Christians that they are favored members of the political community. Justice Kennedy's reliance on historical practice is insufficient, because historical acceptance of a practice cannot validate that practice, any more than historical acceptance of racial or gender based discrimination is permissible under the Fourteenth Amendment. Display of the menorah is not unconstitutional because, when combined with the predominantly secular Christmas tree and liberty sign, it sends a message of pluralism and freedom to choose one's own beliefs, not an endorsement of Judaism.

Concurrence and dissent (Brennan, Marshall, Stevens, JJ.). The display of an object that retains a specifically religious meaning is incompatible with the separation of church and state, so the creche cannot be displayed. However, the menorah and Christmas tree display also shows favoritism toward Christianity and Judaism and should not be allowed.

Concurrence and dissent (Stevens, Brennan, Marshall, JJ.). The initial draft of the Establishment Clause prohibited only one national established church, not multiple establishments, but this draft was changed to broaden the scope of the clause. There is a strong presumption against the display of religious symbols on public property.

Concurrence and dissent (Kennedy, J., Rehnquist, C.J., White, Scalia, JJ.). The majority's approach reflects an unjustified hostility toward religion. The creche and menorah displays should both be allowed. Although the Establishment Clause doctrine represented by the *Lemon* test deserves revision, it is unnecessary to do so now because even under *Lemon*, the displays are not unconstitutional. The *Lemon* factor involved in this case is whether the "principal or primary effect" of the challenged government practice is one that neither advances nor inhibits religion. This does not require a relentless extirpation of all contact between government and religion, which would send a message of disapproval. The government may not establish a state religion or coerce anyone to support or participate in any religion, but it can accommodate religion. The government may participate in its citizens' celebration of a holiday that contains both a secular and a religious component by recognizing both components; to exclude only the religious component would represent callous indifference not required by our cases and traditions. The majority today has adopted the reasoning of a concurring opinion in *Lynch* instead of the reasoning of the *Lynch* majority opinion, which is contrary to the principle of stare decisis since the majority does not overrule *Lynch*. And the majority approach puts the Court in the position of a censor, determining what is orthodox (what the majority deems secular) and what every religious symbol means. Instead, the Court should allow local communities to make reasonable judgments respecting the accommodation or acknowledgment of holidays with both cultural and religious aspects.

Comment. In 2005, the Court reached opposite opinions in two cases involving the public display of the Ten Commandments. In *McCreary County v. ACLU*, 545 U.S. 844 (2005), the Court held that the Ten Commandments displays in two Kentucky courthouses were unconstitutional. The Court applied the purpose prong of the *Lemon* test and found that the displays did not reflect a predominantly secular purpose. In contrast, in *Van Orden v. Perry*, 545 U.S. 677 (2005), the Court upheld the display of a monument engraved with the Ten Commandments on the grounds of the Texas state capital. Here, instead of applying *Lemon*, the Court considered the "passive" nature of the monument and the historical meaning of the Ten Commandments and decided that merely having religious content or promoting a message consistent with a religious doctrine does not violate the Establishment Clause.

---

c.   **Prayer at graduation ceremonies--**

Lee v. Weisman, 505 U.S. 577 (1992).

Facts. Lee (D), the principal of a middle school, invited a rabbi to deliver prayers at a graduation exercise. He gave the rabbi a pamphlet containing guidelines that recommended public prayers be composed with "inclusiveness and sensitivity," and advised the rabbi that the prayers should be nonsectarian. Weisman (P), one of the students, objected to the prayers being part of the graduation ceremonies. The rabbi offered the prayers, which were nondenominational but did refer to and acknowledge God. P sued to enjoin school officials from inviting clergy members to deliver prayers at future graduations. The district court held that D's inclusion of prayers violated the Establishment Clause and granted the injunction because it violated the second *Lemon* test; *i.e.,* it did not have a primary effect that neither advances nor inhibits religion. The court of appeals affirmed. The Supreme Court granted certiorari.

Issue. May a public school invite members of the clergy to offer prayers at graduation ceremonies?

Held. No. Judgment affirmed.

♦   At a minimum, the Constitution guarantees that government may not coerce anyone to support or participate in religion or its exercise. In this case, D as a public official directed the performance of a formal religious exercise at a graduation ceremony for a public secondary school. Although attendance is not a condition for receipt of the diploma, students' attendance and participation is in a fair and real sense obligatory, even for students who object to the religious exercise. Including the prayer thus violated the Constitution.

♦   The government not only decided to include a prayer and chose the clergyman, but D advised the rabbi about the content of the prayer. This means that D directed and controlled the content of the prayer. But the Establishment Clause does not allow the government to compose official prayers to be recited as part of a religious program carried on by the government. The fact that D acted in good faith does not make its participation in the content of the prayer permissible.

♦   Religious beliefs and religious expression are too precious to be either proscribed or prescribed by the government. The government cannot choose to compose a nonsectarian prayer, even if it were possible to devise one that would be acceptable to members of all faiths.

♦ The First Amendment protects speech and religion differently. Speech is protected by insuring its full expression even when the government participates, since some of the most important speech is directed at the government, but in religious debate or expression, the government is not a prime participant. The Free Exercise Clause is similar to the Free Speech Clause, but the Establishment Clause prevents the government from intervening in religious affairs, a prohibition with no counterpart in the speech provisions.

♦ Prayer exercises in public schools carry a particular risk of indirect coercion, particularly in the elementary and secondary public schools. Even at the graduation ceremony, there is pressure to stand and remain silent during the prayer, signifying a degree of adherence or assent. The government may not exact religious conformity from a student as the price of attending her own school graduation.

Concurrence (Blackmun, Stevens, O'Connor, JJ.). The prayers offered at the graduation ceremonies in this case are prohibited by the Constitution. Even if no one is forced to participate, mixing government and religion threatens free government because it conveys a message of exclusion to all who do not adhere to the favored belief.

Concurrence (Souter, Stevens, O'Connor, JJ.). The Establishment Clause is just as applicable to governmental acts favoring religion generally as it is to acts favoring one religion over others. While the government must remain neutral in religious matters, nothing prevents it from ever taking religion into account by accommodating the free exercise of religion. But such accommodation must lift a discernible burden on free exercise. Students at P's school who see spiritual significance in their graduation are not burdened by excluding prayer; they may simply conduct their own private-sponsored exercises accompanied by like-minded students.

Dissent (Scalia, J., Rehnquist, C.J., White, Thomas, JJ.). The meaning of the Establishment Clause must be determined by reference to historical practices and understandings. Yet the majority ignores history in its holding. The tradition of invocations and benedictions at graduation ceremonies is as old as the ceremonies themselves. The Court's test of psychological coercion is boundless and boundlessly manipulable, and is based on facts that are not true in any relevant sense. Even if students were coerced to stand, which they were not, such an act does not establish a "participation" in a religious exercise. The Establishment Clause was aimed at coercion of religious orthodoxy and financial support by force of law and threat of penalty, but P in this case faced no threat of penalty or discipline. This situation is entirely different from daily prayers in classroom settings where parents are not present, which could raise concerns about state interference with the liberty of parents to direct the religious upbringing of their children. The Court has replaced the unfortunate *Lemon* test with its psycho-coercion test, which is not at all grounded in our people's historic practice. The Constitution must have deep foundations in the historic practices of our people, not the changeable philosophical predilections of the Justices of the Court.

d. **The Pledge of Allegiance.** In *Elk Grove Unified School District v. Newdow*, 542 U.S. 1 (2004), the father of an elementary student challenged the constitutionality of the school district's policy requiring elementary school classes to recite the Pledge of Allegiance, with the words "under God," each day. Although the Supreme Court held that the father did not have standing and reversed on procedural grounds, three concurring justices discussed the merits of the case. Chief Justice Rehnquist described the recitation of the Pledge as a patriotic exercise, not a religious one, and he concluded that the words "under God" do not make the Pledge a prayer or an endorsement of any religion. Justice O'Connor categorized the term "under God" as "ceremonial deism," which does not favor one religion over another and which allows the government to acknowledge the divine without violating the Constitution. Justice Thomas also found that the words "under God" do not violate the Establishment Clause, but he based his opinion on a rejection of *Lee*.

e. **Prayer at school functions--**

Santa Fe Independent School District v. Doe, 530 U.S. 290 (2000).

Facts. Before 1995, the Santa Fe Independent School District (D) allowed a student elected as Santa Fe High School's student council chaplain to give a prayer over the public address system before each home varsity football game. Two sets of current or former students and their mothers (Ps), one set Mormon and the other Catholic, sued anonymously as Doe for a restraining order to prevent D from violating the Establishment Clause at an upcoming graduation. Ps alleged that D had engaged in several proselytizing activities. The district court ordered that a student chosen by the graduating class could deliver a nondenominational prayer at the graduation. The text of the prayer would also be determined by the students without D's participation. In response, D adopted a policy that authorized two student elections, the first to determine whether "invocations" should be delivered at games, and the second to select the spokesperson to deliver them. D later adopted another policy requiring that invocations and benedictions be nonsectarian and nonproselytizing. The district court enjoined enforcement of the first, open-ended policy. Both parties appealed. The court of appeals agreed with Ps that both of D's policies violated the Establishment Clause. The Supreme Court granted certiorari.

Issue. May a public school district allow student-led, student-initiated prayer at high school football games?

Held. No. Judgment affirmed.

♦ In *Lee* v. *Weisman, supra,* the Court held that a school could not allow a prayer delivered by a rabbi at a graduation ceremony. The rationale was that the Establishment Clause guarantees that government may not coerce anyone to support or participate in religion or its exercise, or otherwise act in a way that establishes a state religion or religious faith, or tends to do so.

♦ D claims that *Lee* does not apply here because its policy resulted in messages that were private student speech, not public speech. However, the delivery of a message such as the invocation in this case—on school property, at school-sponsored events, over the school's public address system, by a speaker representing the student body, under the supervision of school faculty, and pursuant to a school policy that explicitly and implicitly encourages public prayer—is not properly characterized as "private" speech.

♦ D also claims that the school football game is a public forum, but this setting differs from a public forum in several ways. D does not open its ceremony to general use by the student body but only allows one student to give the invocation. The content of the invocation itself is subject to regulations regarding its content and topic. By making these a matter of vote, D guarantees that minority candidates cannot prevail and their views will be effectively silenced.

♦ D is closely involved with the message by facilitating it, by directing its performance, and by requiring that it be consistent with D's goals of solemnizing the event. The only type of message allowed by D's policy is an "invocation," suggesting a focused religious message. D's policy is obviously intended to preserve its traditional practice of prayer before football games, which is not private speech.

♦ *Lee* also noted that students could not be coerced into participating in religious observances. Yet the students were not unanimously in favor of the invocation. D was directly involved by holding the elections in the first place. While attendance at a football game may be voluntary for many students, for others, such as cheerleaders, band members, and team members, it may be part of their class requirements. There is also great social pressure on students to attend. Students cannot be forced to decide whether to attend or to risk facing a personally offensive religious ritual.

♦ D has subjected the issue of prayer to a majoritarian vote, thereby establishing a governmental mechanism that turns the public school into a forum for religious debate and empowers the majority of students to subject students of minority views to constitutionally improper messages. The award of that power alone violates the Constitution.

Dissent (Rehnquist, C.J., Scalia, Thomas, JJ.). Even if the *Lemon* test is appropriate to this case, it would not mean that D's student-message policy should be invalidated on its face. D's policy might result in a Christian prayer most of the time, and if the policy operates in that fashion, a record would be created that would help determine whether the policy, as applied, violated the Establishment Clause or unduly suppressed minority viewpoints. But possibly the students would vote not to have a pregame speaker, or the election might not focus on prayer. The policy has an expressed secular purpose that the Court does not defer to. The Court should await actual implementation of the policy before finding it unconstitutional.

- - -

  f. **Religious speech in public forums.** In *Capitol Square Review & Advisory Board v. Pinette*, 515 U.S. 753 (1995), the Court allowed the Ku Klux Klan to erect a cross on a public square where other unattended displays had been permitted, including a state-sponsored lighted tree during Christmas, a privately-sponsored menorah during Chanukah, and booths and exhibits during an arts festival. The Court held that the state did not sponsor the expression, which was made on government property open to the public for speech. A plurality held that there was no endorsement of religion, but three Justices believed there could be an endorsement where the government operates a public forum.

C. FREE EXERCISE CLAUSE

The Free Exercise Clause is designed to protect against governmental compulsion with regard to religious matters. It bars governmental acts that would regulate religious beliefs as such or interfere with the dissemination thereof, impede the observance of religious practices, or discriminate in favor of one religion over another, where such acts are not otherwise justifiable in terms of valid governmental aims.

1. **Conflict with State Regulation.**

  a. **Introduction.** Although the Free Exercise Clause prohibits any infringement of the freedom to believe, it does not constitute an absolute protection of all activity undertaken pursuant to religious beliefs. Such activity may be regulated or prohibited by the government if there is an important or compelling state interest that prevails when balanced against the infringement on religious freedoms.

  b. **Development of belief-action distinction.** The belief-action distinction arose in *Reynolds v. United States*, 98 U.S. 145 (1879), which upheld a law against bigamy aimed at stopping the practice of polygamy by Mormons. The Mormons practiced polygamy as a religious belief. The Court held that because polygamy was traditionally condemned, the practice could be outlawed. In *Cantwell v. Connecticut*, 310 U.S. 296 (1940), an action involving fund solicitation by a Jehovah's Witness, the Court abandoned the *Reynolds* ruling that conduct was outside the protection of the First Amendment. The Court found that the freedom to act under the Free Exercise Clause, although not absolute like the freedom to believe, could only be regulated without undue infringement of the freedom to believe.

c.   **Unemployment benefits--**

Hobbie v. Unemployment Appeals Commission, 480 U.S. 136 (1987).

Facts. Hobbie (P) was discharged when she refused to work on Saturday, which was the Sabbath day of the religion she converted to after she had begun working. The Unemployment Appeals Commission (D) denied P's application for unemployment compensation. P appeals.

Issue. May a state deny unemployment benefits to a person who is discharged for refusing to work on her Sabbath day?

Held. No. Judgment reversed.

♦   In *Sherbert v. Verner*, 374 U.S. 398 (1963), the Court held that disqualification for unemployment benefits of a person who refuses to work on the Sabbath forces the person to choose between following the precepts of her religion and abandoning those precepts to accept work. Government imposition of such a choice burdens free exercise of religion as much as would a fine imposed on Saturday worship.

♦   In *Thomas v. Review Board*, 450 U.S. 707 (1981), the Court held that a state could not deny unemployment benefits to a person who was transferred to a division that fabricated armaments and who refused to work because his religious beliefs forbade his participation in such production. The basic principle behind these cases is that the state may not burden religion by conditioning the receipt of an important benefit upon conduct proscribed by a religious faith, or by denying such a benefit because of conduct mandated by religious belief.

♦   The fact that in this case P was converted to her beliefs during the course of her employment, thereby creating a conflict between job and faith that had not previously existed, does not make any difference.

Dissent (Rehnquist, C.J.). There are few situations in which the Constitution requires special treatment on account of religion. This is not one of them.

---

d.   **Other cases.**

1)   **Exclusion of clergy from public office.** In *McDaniel v. Paty*, 435 U.S. 618 (1978), the Court overturned a state constitutional provision that prohibited ministers from serving as state legislators. The Court noted that experience had shown that clergymen were not less faithful to their oaths of civil office than unordained legislators, and that, applying a balancing test, the restriction violated the Free Exercise Clause.

2) Social Security payments. An employer may be required to pay Social Security on his employees' wages despite objections based on religious belief. [United States v. Lee, 455 U.S. 252 (1982)]

3) Conscientious objection. The Selective Service Act permitted exemption from the draft for those who, by reasons of religious belief, are conscientiously opposed to war in any form. This has been construed to apply only to persons opposed to all wars, not just to particular wars in which the United States is involved, such as the Vietnam War. [Gillette v. United States, *supra*]

4) Veterans preferences. The Court has upheld a federal law that grants educational benefits to veterans while denying the same benefits to conscientious objectors, even though the conscientious objectors performed the alternate civilian service required by the draft laws. The distinction was considered at most an incidental burden on the free exercise of religion and was justified by the need to raise and support armies. [Johnson v. Robison, 415 U.S. 361 (1974)]

5) Tax-exempt status. The IRS may deny tax-exempt status to religious schools that practice racial discrimination. [Bob Jones University v. United States, 461 U.S. 574 (1983)]

e. Limitation on required accommodation--

Employment Division v. Smith, 494 U.S. 872 (1990).

Facts. The state of Oregon made it a crime to use peyote. Smith (P) was dismissed from his job for using peyote as part of his religious ritual as a member of the Native American Church. P was denied unemployment benefits because his dismissal was due to misconduct. P sued the Employment Division (D), claiming that his use of peyote was inspired by religion and therefore was protected under the Free Exercise Clause of the First Amendment. The Oregon Supreme Court reversed, holding that the criminal sanction was unconstitutional as applied to the religious use of peyote, and ruled that P was entitled to unemployment benefits. The Supreme Court granted certiorari.

Issue. May a state make criminal certain conduct that is part of a religious organization's ritual?

Held. Yes. Judgment reversed.

♦ P relies on *Sherbert, supra*, that held that a state could not condition the availability of unemployment insurance on an applicant's willingness to forego conduct required by his religion. In that case, however, the conduct was not prohibited by law; in this case, peyote use was prohibited by law.

◆ The states cannot ban acts or abstentions only when they are engaged in for religious reasons, or only because of the religious belief they display, because this would constitute a prohibition of the free exercise of religion. This does not mean that a religious motivation for illegal conduct exempts the actor from the law. If prohibiting the exercise of religion is merely an incidental effect of a generally applicable and otherwise valid law, the First Amendment is not implicated.

◆ In some cases, such as *Wisconsin v. Yoder*, 406 U.S. 205 (1972), the First Amendment may prevent application of a neutral, generally applicable law to religiously motivated action, but these cases involve the Free Exercise Clause in connection with other constitutional protections, such as parents' right to direct the education of their children.

◆ P argues that the *Sherbert* test should be applied, but this test has never invalidated governmental action except the denial of unemployment compensation, and should not be extended beyond that field to require exemptions from a generally applicable criminal law. In the unemployment cases, the test is applied to prevent a state from refusing to extend religious hardship cases to a system of individual exemptions.

◆ If the compelling interest requirement were applied to religion cases such as this, many laws would not satisfy the test, and the result would approach anarchy, particularly in a society such as ours that contains a diversity of religious beliefs. This alternative would raise a presumption of invalidity, as applied to the religious objector, of every regulation of conduct that does not protect an interest of the highest order. The states are free, as many have, to exempt from their drug laws the use of peyote in sacramental services, but the states are not constitutionally required to do so.

Concurrence in part (O'Connor, Brennan, Marshall, Blackmun, JJ.). A law that prohibits religiously motivated conduct implicates First Amendment concerns, even if it is generally applicable. The First Amendment does not distinguish between laws that are generally applicable and laws that target particular religious practices; it applies to generally applicable laws that have the effect of significantly burdening a religious practice. The balance between the First Amendment and the government's legitimate interest in regulating conduct is struck by applying the compelling interest test. To be sustained, a law that burdens the free exercise of religion must either be essential to accomplish an overriding governmental interest or represent the least restrictive means of achieving some compelling state interest. In this case, the prohibition on use of peyote does satisfy the compelling state interest test.

Dissent (Blackmun, Brennan, Marshall, JJ.). The state's broad interest in fighting the war on drugs is not the interest involved in this case; the interest is the state's refusal to make an exception for the religious, ceremonial use of peyote. There is no evidence that the religious use of peyote ever harmed anyone, and 23 other states have adopted exemptions for the religious use of peyote. The assertion that requiring the state to make an exemption in this case would open the government to anarchy is speculative; such a danger is addressed through the compelling state interest test.

Comment. If the purpose of a statute or other governmental action is to single out religion for adverse treatment, it violates the Free Exercise Clause unless it is narrowly tailored to advance a compelling state interest. [*See* Church of the Lukumi Babalu Aye, Inc. v. City of Hialeah, 508 U.S. 520 (1993)—a city ordinance barring ritual animal sacrifice practiced by particular religion violated the Free Exercise Clause because its purpose was to suppress that religion]

---

f. Excluding the study of religion from public scholarships--

Locke v. Davey, 540 U.S. 712 (2004).

Facts. Davey (P) received a Promise Scholarship under a program funded by the state of Washington. Recipients were prohibited from using the scholarship at an institution where they would pursue a degree in devotional theology. P wanted to attend a private Christian college to become a church pastor. When P learned that he could not use his scholarship to pursue his desired degree, he sued Locke (D), the governor of Washington, for damages and injunctive relief. The District Court granted D summary judgment. The Ninth Circuit reversed on the ground that D had singled out religion for unfavorable treatment, contrary to *Church of Lukumi Babalu Aye, Inc. v. City of Hialeah, supra*. The Supreme Court granted certiorari.

Issue. May a state prohibit recipients of state-financed scholarships from using the money to pursue a degree in devotional theology?

Held. Yes. Judgment reversed.

♦   States may take actions that are permitted by the Establishment Clause but not required by the Free Exercise Clause. In this case, D could have permitted Promise Scholars to pursue a degree in devotional theology without violating the Establishment Clause.

♦   P claims that, under *Lukumi*, D's program is presumptively unconstitutional because it is not facially neutral with respect to religion. But *Lukumi* involved sanctions on a type of religious service or rite, whereas D's scholarship program merely chooses not to fund a distinct category of instruction.

♦   Training someone to become a minister is an essentially religious endeavor and is distinct from other academic pursuits. D has a substantial interest in not establishing religion. States even included provisions in their constitutions to exclude the ministry from receiving state funding. D's scholarship program does allow attendance at religious schools and covers theology courses. It merely denies funding for vocational religious instruction.

Dissent (Scalia, Thomas, JJ.). D's exclusion of religion from a public benefit generally available violates the Free Exercise Clause as much as would a special tax on vocational religious instruction. No field of study but religion is singled out for disfavor.

---

2. **Unusual Religious Beliefs and Practices.** The definition of "religion" for purposes of the First Amendment has not yet been definitively determined. The Court has set forth certain parameters, however.

   a. **Inquiry into truth of religious precepts forbidden.** In *United States v. Ballard*, 322 U.S. 78 (1944), the Court articulated its position that, under the First Amendment, submission to a jury of the truth of a party's religious beliefs is barred because of the subjective nature of such proof. "Men may believe what they cannot prove," so the truth or reasonableness of a belief cannot be questioned by a court.

   b. **Belief in God.** Belief in God may not be used as an essential qualification for office. When Maryland denied a commission as a notary public to an otherwise qualified appointee because he refused to declare his belief in the existence of God (as required by the Maryland Constitution for those who seek to qualify for "any office or profit or trust"), the Court held that such a "religious test for public office" imposed a burden on the applicant's freedom of belief and religion. [Torcaso v. Watkins, 367 U.S. 488 (1961)]

   c. **Draft-exemption definition.** In a draft case turning on whether a person was exempt as a conscientious objector by virtue of his "religious training and belief" (a requirement of the Selective Service Act, not a constitutional issue), the Court held:

      1) "Religious" belief is something more than essentially sociological, philosophical, economic, or political views.

      2) It does not require belief in any particular dogma, or in any supernatural force or Supreme Being.

      3) It must, however, be sincere and meaningful and occupy a place in the life of its possessor parallel to that filled by the orthodox belief in God of those who are customarily regarded as "religious" persons. [United States v. Seeger, 380 U.S. 163 (1965)]

D. PREFERENCE AMONG RELIGIONS

1. **Introduction.** The Establishment Clause was intended to avoid creation of a state religion and therefore bars government sponsorship or financial support of religion and any active involvement of government in religious activities. Perhaps most importantly, the clause prohibits any official preference for one religion over another.

2. **Religious Gerrymandering--**

Board of Education of Kiryas Joel v. Grumet, 512 U.S. 687 (1994).

Facts. The New York state legislature created a special separate school district and authorized its board of education, the Board of Education of Kiryas Joel Village School District (D), to open and close schools, hire teachers, etc. D's jurisdiction was limited to the Village of Kiryas Joel, which had been founded by, and was inhabited exclusively by, Satmar Hasidim, who were practitioners of a strict form of Judaism. The Satmars sought to avoid assimilation into the modern world and educated their children in private religious schools. D's only program was a special education program for handicapped Satmar children, although it also provided transportation and health and welfare services for the parochial schools. Grumet and others (Ps) challenged the constitutionality of the creation of D. The state courts held for Ps. The Supreme Court granted certiorari.

Issue. May a state create a separate school district, the boundaries of which are determined by the boundaries of a village inhabited exclusively by a distinct religious group?

Held. No. Judgment affirmed.

♦ In this case, the state has delegated civic power to the voters of the village, instead of specifically to religious authorities or only to adherents of a particular religion. However, in the context of this case, the recipients of governmental authority were in effect determined by reference to doctrinal adherence. D is the only district that the legislature carved from a single existing school district to serve local residents. Application of neutral principles would not have produced the same boundaries.

♦ There is no assurance that the next similarly situated group seeking a school district of its own will receive one. Even though the benefit was given only to a single small religious group, there is no less a constitutional problem than if it had been given to a larger group or even a particular religion as a whole.

Concurrence (Kennedy, J.). The real problem with D is that the state created it by drawing political boundaries on the basis of religion. Such religious gerrymandering violates the First Amendment.

Dissent (Scalia, J., Rehnquist, C.J., Thomas, J.). This case involves a public school whose students all share the same religion. There is nothing wrong with that. D was created for secular reasons (cultural alienation of students), which is permissible.

Comment. In *Larkin v. Grendel's Den, Inc.,* 459 U.S. 116 (1982), the Court held invalid a statute that granted religious bodies veto power over applications for liquor licenses that would be located within 500 feet of a church or synagogue. This fusion of governmental and religious functions had a primary and principal effect of advancing religion.

---

3. Litigation of Religious Disputes--

Jones v. Wolf, 443 U.S. 595 (1979).

Facts. A local congregation of the Presbyterian Church in the United States ("PCUS") voted to separate from PCUS. The majority faction, represented by Wolf (D), continued to use the local church property. The minority faction, represented by Jones (P), was ruled the true congregation by a PCUS commission and sued to retain the property. The Supreme Court of Georgia rejected the minority's challenge, applying "neutral principles" of property and trust law. P appeals.

Issue. In a dispute over ownership of church property, may civil courts resolve the dispute by applying "neutral principles of law?"

Held. Yes. Judgment vacated and remanded.

- ◆ Civil courts may not resolve church disputes if resolution requires court consideration of whether a particular faction has "departed from doctrine." Recognizing this, the state court correctly applied neutral principles of property and trust law to hold that legal title to the property was vested in the local congregation.

- ◆ The state court decreed that D, not P, represented the vested local congregation but failed to articulate the reasons. The decision is remanded to be reconsidered under the following principles.

- ◆ A civil court may, consistent with the neutral principles analysis, adopt a presumptive rule of majority representation, defeasible by a showing that the identity of the local church is to be determined by some other means, as provided by a corporate charter or church constitution.

Dissent (Powell, J., Burger, C.J., Stewart, White, JJ.). Civil courts ought to give full effect to the decisions of the church government agreed upon by the members before the dispute arose, even as to property ownership. Furthermore, in this case PCUS did officially determine the true representatives of the local congregation, and this determination should not be overruled by the majority rule.

---

4. Fundraising--

Larson v. Valente, 456 U.S. 228 (1982).

Facts. To protect the public against fraudulent practices, Minnesota provided for a system of registration and disclosure of charitable organizations. Religious organizations were exempt until 1978, when the state began to exempt only those religious organizations that received more than half of their total contributions from members of affiliated organizations. Valente and others (Ps) claimed that the 50% rule violated the Establishment Clause because their church, the Unification Church, did not satisfy the 50% requirement. The lower courts upheld Ps' challenge, and Larson (D) appeals.

Issue. May a state regulate religious organizations based on the manner in which they raise funds?

Held. No. Judgment affirmed.

♦　　The Establishment Clause clearly prohibits government preference for one denomination over another. Free exercise of religion is guaranteed only when legislators and voters must give other religions the same treatment they give their own. Any state law granting a denominational preference must be subject to strict scrutiny.

♦　　The 50% rule here clearly grants denominational preferences. Surely Minnesota has a significant interest in protecting the public from abusive or fraudulent solicitations by charities. This is a valid secular purpose, but the 50% rule is not narrowly drawn to achieve that purpose. The premises behind the rule are not supported in the record. The statute places burdens on selected denominations only; and the legislative history indicates that the law was directed at religious groups that raise funds by directly soliciting the public.

Dissent (White, Rehnquist, JJ.). The law does not name any churches or denominations. It does not distinguish among religions by belief. The only distinctions drawn are the source of contributions. Given the secular purpose for the law, the legislature's drawing of the line at one-half of contributions is not impermissible.

E. CONFLICT BETWEEN THE CLAUSES

1. Permissible Accommodation--

Corporation of the Presiding Bishop of the Church of Jesus Christ of Latter-Day Saints v. Amos, 483 U.S. 327 (1987).

Facts. The Corporation of the Presiding Bishop of the Church of Jesus Christ of Latter-Day Saints (D) operated the nonprofit Deseret Gymnasium. Amos (P) was a janitor at the gym. P did not qualify for a temple recommend, which required observance of D's standards including church attendance; tithing; and abstinence from coffee, tea, alcohol, and tobacco. P was fired. 42 U.S.C. section 2000e-1 exempts religious organizations such as D from the general prohibition against employment discrimination on the basis of religion. P sued, claiming the exemption should not apply to secular nonprofit activities of religious organizations. The district court and court of appeals upheld P's claim. D appeals.

Issue. May Congress accommodate religious practices by permitting religious organizations to discriminate in employment on the basis of religion even in secular nonprofit activities?

Held. Yes. Judgment reversed.

♦ Governmental accommodation of religious practices does not necessarily violate the Establishment Clause. Such benevolent neutrality permits free exercise of religion without either sponsorship or interference.

♦ The three-part *Lemon*, *supra*, analysis of religion cases may be applied to accommodation cases. The first requirement, that the challenged law serve a secular legislative purpose, is intended to prevent Congress from abandoning neutrality and acting to promote a particular point of view in religious matters. A legislative purpose to alleviate significant governmental interference with a religious group's ability to exercise its religion is a permissible purpose.

♦ Congress amended the Civil Rights Act to extend the exemption to secular nonprofit activities of religious organizations because the exemption previously applied only to religious activities. The exemption acted to minimize governmental interference with the decisionmaking process in religious groups, which is a permitted purpose.

♦ The second *Lemon* requirement is that the law have a principal effect that neither advances nor inhibits religion. A law may permit churches to advance religion; the prohibition is only against governmental advancement, through its own activities and influence, of religion. Any advancement of religion that D might achieve through its gymnasium cannot be fairly attributed to the government, as opposed to D.

♦ The third requirement is that Congress must have chosen a rational classification to further a legitimate end. Section 702 is rationally related to the legitimate purpose of alleviating significant governmental interference with the ability of religious organizations to define and carry out their religious missions.

Concurrence (Brennan, Marshall, JJ.). The exemption from Title VII's prohibition of religious discrimination burdens the religious liberty of employees such as P. However, religious organizations such as D have an interest in autonomy in ordering their internal affairs, including defining the religious community. While individual interests in religious freedom would only permit an exemption for religious activities, a case-by-case determination of which nonprofit activities are religious and which are not would involve unacceptable entanglement with religion and a chill on religious expression, and the balance between these interests must fall in favor of the broader exception relied on by D.

Concurrence (O'Connor, J.). Judicial deference to all legislation that purports to facilitate the free exercise of religion would vitiate the Establishment Clause. The Court suggests that the "effects" prong of the *Lemon* test is not implicated if the government action merely "allows" religious organizations to advance religion. A better approach is to recognize that by exempting religious organizations from a generally applicable regulatory burden, the government does advance religion; it only remains to be determined whether the benefit accommodates free exercise or unjustifiably awards assistance to religion. The probability that a nonprofit activity is involved in the organization's religious mission is sufficient to justify a conclusion that the government action exempting such activities is an accommodation, not a government endorsement, of religion.

――――――――――――

2. **Sales Tax Exemption.** In *Texas Monthly, Inc. v. Bullock*, 489 U.S. 1 (1989), the Court held that a statute exempting religious publications from a state sales tax was unconstitutional. The exemption had insufficient breadth of coverage; it did not apply to nonreligious publications that contributed to the community's cultural, intellectual, and moral betterment. Hence, it constituted an unjustifiable award of assistance to religious organizations and conveyed a message of endorsement. The dissent argued that breadth of coverage was not relevant unless the state asserted purely secular grounds for the exemption. When religion was singled out, particularly for an exemption from a tax that could be construed as an unconstitutional burden on religion, the exemption should be construed as an accommodation.

3. **Day of Worship.** Sunday closing laws have been upheld against attack by Sabbatarians (*e.g.*, Orthodox Jews). Such laws do not promote or discourage any religious beliefs, but simply make the practice of certain beliefs more expensive. [Braunfeld v. Brown, 366 U.S. 599 (1961)] However, the state

may not punish a person for worshipping on a day other than Sunday. [Sherbert v. Verner, *supra*] On the other hand, a state may not establish an obligation to give a day off to the employees choosing to worship. [Thornton v. Caldor, Inc., 472 U.S. 703 (1985)]

X. EQUAL PROTECTION

A. TRADITIONAL APPROACH

1. **Introduction.** The Fourteenth Amendment provides that no state may deny to any person within its jurisdiction the equal protection of the laws. Although no comparable provision expressly limits acts by the federal government, the guarantee of equal protection is implicit in the concept of Fifth Amendment due process. Basically, "equal protection" is a limitation on the exercise of government power that means that government regulation cannot be "arbitrarily discriminatory." All laws are to some extent inherently unequal, because part of the purpose of legislation is to distinguish among citizens. For example, tax laws vary depending on the individual's sources and uses of income, and criminal sanctions apply only to those convicted of crimes. Thus, equal protection does not require that all persons be treated equally under the law at all times, but that whatever classifications are made in a statute must be reasonable.

2. **Standards of Review.**

   a. **Development of equal protection doctrine.**

      1) **Traditional approach.** At one time, courts used equal protection only to insure that the legislative means were reasonably related to the legislative purpose; *i.e.,* that the regulation had a rational basis. This approach supported only minimal judicial intervention. This traditional approach is characterized by the following three requirements:

         a) The first requirement that must be established under the traditional equal protection test is that any statutory classification be "rational," or based on factors (*e.g.,* economic, social, historic, geographic, etc.) that justify disparate treatment. This requirement is generally satisfied as long as the classifications are not patently arbitrary.

         b) The second requirement is that the classification (the disparate treatment) rationally promotes a proper governmental purpose.

         c) Assuming that the classification drawn in the statute meets the first two requirements, it is also required that all persons affected by the classification be treated equally.

      2) **The Warren Court's "new" equal protection.** The Warren Court utilized the traditional equal protection analysis in most areas of

economic and social regulation. However, it also articulated a new, higher level of scrutiny applicable when legislation affected one of two areas: a "suspect classification" or a "fundamental right" or interest.

a) **Old standard.** In the absence of a suspect classification or fundamental right, equal protection requires that the legislative means must be "reasonably" related to "legitimate" state ends. This is also called the "rational basis" standard.

b) **New standard.** When a suspect classification, such as race, or a fundamental interest, such as voting, is involved, the legislative means must be "necessary" to achieve "compelling" state interests. This standard of review—also called "strict scrutiny"—has resulted in significant judicial intervention in assessing the constitutionality of legislation.

c) **Characteristics.** Common to most classifications that demand heightened scrutiny are the following characteristics: historical lack of political power; history of discrimination; immutableness of classification; irrelevance to performance; and obviousness (the basis for classification acts as a badge).

3) **The Burger and Rehnquist Courts.** The Burger and Rehnquist Courts have generally accepted the old and new standards of equal protection, although they have given greater effect to the old standard than the Warren Court did. The Court has also added a third, intermediate tier of scrutiny for certain classifications, including those based on sex, alienage, and illegitimacy. The new intermediate standard requires that the legislative means be "substantially related" to "important" governmental objectives. In actuality, the whole equal protection jurisprudence is confusing and at times inconsistent. The Court has never expressly adopted the "sliding scale" approach suggested by Justice Marshall, but clearly there are no rigid guidelines with which to decide every equal protection case.

b. **Types of classifications.** If ☐ represents the evil being proscribed, ///// represents people who threaten the evil, and +++++ represents people who do not threaten the evil, then the following types of classifications are possible:

1) ☐///// The statute covers all of those who threaten the evil.

2) ☐ //// The statute covers none of those who threaten the evil.

3) ☐/// /// The statute covers only a few. This is an under-inclusive classification.

4) $\boxed{+++///}$ The statute covers the target population but also inno-cent persons. This is an over-inclusive classification.

5) $\boxed{+++//}$ //   The statute is both under- and over-inclusive.

3.   Practical Considerations--

Railway Express Agency v. New York, 336 U.S. 106 (1949).

Facts. The city of New York (P) passed a traffic regulation that prohibited advertising on vehicles except for "business notices upon business delivery vehicles," or, in other words, owner advertising. Railway Express Agency (D), a nationwide express busi-ness, sold the space on its trucks for advertising by other businesses and was convicted for violation of P's regulation. The trial court found a reasonable basis for the regula-tion and upheld the conviction. D appeals.

Issue. May a local business regulation make distinctions based on practical consider-ations even though the distinctions are conceptually discriminatory?

Held. Yes. Judgment affirmed.

♦   D's equal protection argument is based on the allegedly irrational distinction between allowing owner advertising but banning advertising for hire. How-ever, P may have concluded that the former type of advertising is less distract-ing and possibly necessary for business.

♦   Equal protection questions are answered by such practical considerations based on experience rather than purely theoretical inconsistencies.

Concurrence (Jackson, J.). The Equal Protection Clause is properly invoked as the best measure to assure just laws.

Comment. The level of scrutiny applied to economic and business regulation has var-ied over recent years, resulting in an almost ad hoc approach.

4.   State Economic Regulation--

New Orleans v. Dukes, 427 U.S. 297 (1976).

Facts. New Orleans (D) passed an ordinance prohibiting street vendors from operating in the French Quarter, with an exception for vendors who had continually operated for eight years prior to the effective date of the ordinance. Dukes (P) had been a street vendor for two years and challenged the grandfather clause as a denial of equal protection. The district court granted D summary judgment. The court of appeals reversed. D appeals.

Issue. Are state economic regulations subject to strict judicial scrutiny?

Held. No. Judgment reversed and case remanded.

♦   States are accorded wide latitude in the regulation of their local economies under their police powers. Where local economic regulation neither affects fundamental rights nor involves suspect classifications, only wholly arbitrary acts are unconstitutional.

♦   Here, D has sought to preserve the appearance and customs that are attractive to tourists, and the ordinance rationally pursues this goal. That the statute only gradually works to eliminate vendors does not make it violative of due process.

Comment. In *New York City Transit Authority v. Beazer*, 440 U.S. 568 (1979), the Court upheld the city's exclusion of all methadone users from any employment by the Transit Authority. Even though this may exclude methadone users who are actually qualified to work, the classification serves the general objectives of safety and efficiency and does not define a class based on an unpopular trait or affiliation. Thus, it was of no constitutional significance that the degree of rationality is not as great with respect to certain subparts of the class as it was with respect to the class as a whole.

---

5.   **Extent of Deference Accorded--**

United States Railroad Retirement Board v. Fritz, 449 U.S. 166 (1980).

Facts. In 1974, Congress fundamentally altered the railroad retirement system that had been in effect since 1937. Essentially, Congress acted to place the system on a sound financial basis by eliminating future accruals of "windfall" benefits, resulting from concurrent qualification for railroad retirement and Social Security. The new system established several classes of employees whose benefits would be computed differently. Fritz (P) represented a class of employees who had between 10 and 25 years of railroad industry employment but who would be denied "windfall" benefits because they had no "current connection" with the railroad industry in 1974 or as of the date of retirement. P claimed the new system denied equal protection. The district court agreed, and the United States Railroad Retirement Board (D) appeals.

Issue. May legislation be upheld if there is a plausible reason for the classification made based on the plain language of the statute, regardless of the actual reason for which the statute was enacted?

Held. Yes. Judgment reversed.

- The district court held that a differentiation based on whether an employee was "active" in the railroad business in 1974 was not "rationally related" to the congressional purposes of insuring the solvency of the railroad retirement system and protecting vested benefits. However, in recent years we have refused to invalidate economic legislation on equal protection grounds just because it was unwise or inartfully drawn.

- Congress could have eliminated "windfall" benefits entirely, so it is not improper for it to draw lines to phase out such benefits.

- D has advanced plausible reasons for Congress's action. Thus, this Court's inquiry is at its end. It is constitutionally irrelevant whether this reasoning in fact underlays the legislative decision. We cannot say that Congress was unaware of what it accomplished or that it was misled by the groups that appeared before it.

Dissent (Brennan, Marshall, JJ.).

- The Court's approach here virtually immunizes social and economic legislative classifications from judicial review. The rational basis standard is not "toothless." The test requires examination of both the purposes of the statute and the relationship of the classification to that purpose. The classification here is not only rationally unrelated to the congressional purpose; it is inimical to it.

- The Court avoids serious analysis by, first, assuming purpose from result (Congress intended to do what it did do); second, by disregarding Congress's actual stated purpose for an unsupported justification that conflicts with the stated purpose; and third, by failing to ascertain whether the classification is rationally related to the identified purpose.

- Application of the Court's new analysis will mean that in future cases, we will defer not to the considered judgment of Congress, but to the arguments of skilled government litigators.

B. RACE AND ETHNIC ANCESTRY

1. Historical Background--

Dred Scott v. Sandford, 60 U.S. (19 How.) 393 (1857).

Facts. Dred Scott (P) was born a slave in Virginia but his master took him from Missouri (a slave state) to Illinois, a free state, and Wisconsin, a free territory. P and his owner returned to Missouri, where P was sold to Sandford (D), a New York resident. Subsequently, P sued D for trespass, claiming he had attained his freedom under Illinois and Wisconsin law. D claimed that P was not a citizen of Missouri, so there was no federal diversity of citizenship jurisdiction. D also claimed that P was not free.

Issue. May a black man be deemed a citizen of the United States capable of invoking federal jurisdiction based on diversity of citizenship?

Held. No. Case dismissed.

♦ It is clear from the language of the Constitution that the slaves were not to be regarded as citizens but as beings of inferior order. Changes in public opinion should not induce the Court to give the words of the Constitution a more liberal construction than they were intended to bear when the instrument was framed and adopted.

♦ Under the Constitution, the citizens of the United States have the power to conduct the government through their representatives and are thus the sovereign people. This status was not accorded to persons imported as slaves, or their descendants, whether free or not.

♦ Even though Congress has declared that slavery is prohibited in federal territories, Congress does not have power under the Constitution to deprive a citizen of his liberty or property merely because he brings the property into a particular territory of the United States. The Constitution expressly upholds the right of property in a slave. Accordingly, the law that prohibits a slave owner from owning slaves in federal territories is unconstitutional, and P was not made free by virtue of being taken to the territory by his owner.

♦ Although P was taken to Illinois, a free state, his current status is governed by Missouri law, not Illinois law. Under Missouri law, P is still a slave.

---

2. **Discrimination Against Racial and Ethnic Minorities.** Because racial discrimination prompted adoption of the Fourteenth Amendment, racial classifications are "suspect," meaning they invite the strictest judicial scrutiny. There are numerous types of discrimination based on race. The government may place unequal burdens on persons because of their race, restrict interaction among people of different races, or gather and disseminate racial information. Discrimination may be expressly stated, or it may consist of discriminatory enforcement of an ostensibly neutral law. It may also arise when the adoption of a neutral law is motivated by racial considerations. These situations present difficult issues for the courts.

a. **Use of Fourteenth Amendment.** In *Strauder v. West Virginia*, 100 U.S. 303 (1880), the Court used the Fourteenth Amendment to invalidate a state statute that permitted only white persons to serve on juries.

The Court noted that the amendment was aimed against discrimination because of race or color.

b. Separate but equal doctrine--

Plessy v. Ferguson, 163 U.S. 537 (1896).

Facts. Plessy (P), who was seven-eighths white and one-eighth black, refused to comply with a demand that he sit in the black railway carriage rather than the one for whites. P was convicted of violation of a state statute providing for separate railway carriages for the white and black races. P challenged the law but lost. P appeals.

Issue. May a state require that separate railway carriages be provided for black citizens and white citizens?

Held. Yes. Judgment affirmed.

♦   The law does not imply the inferiority of one race or the other. The only proper restraint on the exercise of state police power is that it be reasonable and intended for the promotion of the general good. The state legislature may properly have concluded that the law would preserve the public peace and good order.

♦   It certainly is no more obnoxious to the Fourteenth Amendment than laws requiring separate schools, which are universally accepted. Legislation cannot overcome social prejudices; the attempt to do so can only result in accentuating difficulties. The Constitution can act to equate civil and political rights of the two races, but cannot affect social standing.

Dissent (Harlan, J.). No legislature or court may properly regard the race of citizens where civil rights are involved. Every citizen, regardless of color, has a right to occupy the public transportation of his choice; governmental infringement of that right is unconstitutional. Our Constitution is color-blind, and neither knows nor tolerates classes among citizens. Any evils resulting from commingling of the races are less than those resulting from curtailment of civil rights upon the basis of race.

c. Proper distinction based on race--

Korematsu v. United States, 323 U.S. 214 (1944).

Facts. Korematsu (D) was convicted of remaining in a "military area" in violation of an Army command that all persons of Japanese ancestry be excluded from certain areas for national defense reasons. D was not accused of disloyalty. D appeals, claiming denial of equal protection.

Issue. May race be used as a criterion for curtailing civil rights in a time of grave threats to national security?

Held. Yes. Judgment affirmed.

♦ Legal restrictions that curtail the civil rights of a single racial group are subject to the most rigid judicial scrutiny, but are not per se unconstitutional. Although never justified by racial antagonism, they may be permitted in times of pressing public necessity.

♦ Here, military authorities determined that the existence of Japanese sympathizers was a threat. Espionage and sabotage must be deterred even at great cost. Under war emergency, nothing less than exclusion of the entire group would solve the problem of guarding against disloyalty. The power to protect must be commensurate with the threatened danger.

♦ In light of the totality of the circumstances, the exclusion order cannot be held to be unjustified.

Concurrence (Frankfurter, J.). The Court does not approve of the action, but defers to Congress and the executive branch because the action is not prohibited by the Constitution.

Dissent (Murphy, J.). The exclusion exceeds the brink of constitutional power. The exigencies were not so great as to preclude hearings for the persons involved, and there is no basis for the assumption that this racial group had distinct dangerous tendencies toward disloyalty.

Dissent (Jackson, J.). The Court permits an inference of inheritable guilt, contrary to the fundamental assumption of our system. A civil court is not competent to determine whether a military command is reasonable, and should not attempt to justify one as the Court has done here.

Comment. *Korematsu* was the Court's last decision upholding overt racial discrimination.

———————

d. **School desegregation and repudiation of the separate but equal doctrine.** Even after the Thirteenth Amendment was ratified, several southern states adopted racially discriminatory statutes, referred to as the "Black Codes." These were designed to keep blacks in an inferior position socially, politically, and economically. The Civil Rights Act of 1866 and the Fourteenth Amendment were intended to counter this official discrimination, although apparently they were not originally supposed to insure full protection of civil rights for all races. For nearly 100 years, states followed a "separate but equal" doctrine, whereby state facilities, including public schools, could be racially segregated as long as they provided "equal" services. The doctrine was successfully challenged beginning in 1938 in cases involving state law schools. The most significant case, however, involved secondary and primary schools.

e. **Application to secondary and primary schools--**

Brown v. Board of Education (Brown I), 347 U.S. 483 (1954).

Facts. Brown (P) and other black schoolchildren (the opinion consolidates appeals from four states) were denied admission to schools attended by white children under laws requiring or permitting segregation based on race. P challenged the law but was denied relief under the "separate but equal" doctrine. (In the Delaware case, the plaintiff was admitted solely because the white school was superior; *i.e.,* separate was not equal.) P appeals.

Issue. May children be segregated in essentially "equal" public schools solely on the basis of race?

Held. No. Judgments vacated and reargument on the issue of appropriate relief ordered.

- ◆ The circumstances surrounding adoption of the Fourteenth Amendment are not determinative, especially here where public education, which barely existed then, is at issue. The effect of segregation on public education in its current setting is therefore determinative.

- ◆ Granting that black and white schools are substantially "equal" in tangible factors, there yet exists an invidious effect when black and white children are segregated. Namely, segregation creates a feeling of inferiority that may significantly affect a child's motivation to learn. Separate educational facilities are therefore inherently unequal, and their maintenance by government authority denies equal protection of the law.

f. **Implementation of desegregation--**

Brown v. Board of Education (Brown II), 349 U.S. 294 (1955).

Facts. *See Brown v. Board of Education (Brown I)* above. The Court initially permitted gradual integration of public schools in recognition of the difficulties inherent in school desegregation. This opinion addresses the relief granted in *Brown I*.

Issue. In what matter is relief to be accorded?

Held.

♦ The full implementation of the constitutional principles requires solution of various local school problems, to be solved by school authorities and reviewed by the courts to assure good faith compliance.

♦ The cases are remanded to the lower courts, who are to be guided by equitable principles in fashioning decrees. The competing interests involve Ps' rights to admission at the earliest date and the need for systematic, effective, and orderly removal of obstacles to full integration.

Comment. The Court emphasized its determination that all public schools be integrated by holding that threats of violence resulting from state actions against desegregation would not justify failure to integrate. [Cooper v. Aaron, 358 U.S. 1 (1958)] All nine Justices delivered the opinion to emphasize their unity.

———————————

g. **Blatant racial classifications.**

1) **Equal application to all races.** An early case, *Pace v. Alabama*, 106 U.S. 583 (1883), upheld a theory of "equal application," whereby a statute that created racial classes was upheld as long as it applied to all races equally.

2) **More than equal application required--**

Loving v. Virginia, 388 U.S. 1 (1967).

Facts. Loving (D), a white man, married a black woman in violation of a Virginia (P) antimiscegenation statute. D was convicted. The state courts upheld the conviction. D appeals.

Issue. May a state prevent marriages between persons solely because they are of different races?

Held. No. Judgment reversed.

◊ The state claims that equal protection is afforded when any penalties due to interracial elements of an offense are applied equally to members of both races. However, equal protection means more than mere "equal application."

◊ Courts must consider whether statutory classifications constitute arbitrary and invidious discrimination. Racial classifications, especially in criminal statutes, are subject to the most rigid scrutiny and must be essential to the accomplishment of some permissible state objective to be permitted.

♦ The state has failed to show any legitimate overriding purpose for the distinction between one-race and interracial marriages other than invidious racial discrimination, and the statute cannot be upheld.

Concurrence (Stewart, J.). A state law that makes the criminality of an act depend on the race of the actor cannot be constitutional.

---

h. **Racial identification and classification.** In invalidating a state requirement that a candidate's race appear on the ballot, the Court held that even though the requirement applied to all candidates, by directing the citizen's attention to the single consideration of race or color the state was indicating that race or color was an important consideration that may influence the citizen to cast his ballot along color lines. [Anderson v. Martin, 375 U.S. 399 (1964)] However, the Court did permit a state to require that every divorce decree specify the race of the spouses. [*See* Tancil v. Woolls, 379 U.S. 19 (1964)]

i. **Judicial consideration of private bias in making child custody determinations.** In *Palmore v. Sidoti*, 466 U.S. 429 (1984), the Court held that a mother cannot be divested of the custody of her child merely because of her remarriage to a person of a different race. The Court noted that even if the child may suffer from social stigmatization because of the racially mixed household, such private biases are not permissible considerations under the Constitution. Private biases may be beyond the reach of the law, but the law cannot give them effect.

3. **De Jure and De Facto Discrimination.**

a. **Introduction.** "De jure" discrimination exists where the statute explicitly discriminates or where the law, although neutral on its face, is deliberately administered in a discriminatory way. "De facto" discrimination exists where an otherwise neutral law and administration nevertheless results in discrimination. Also, if the law was enacted with a discriminatory motive, it is de jure discrimination.

b. **Discriminatory administration of law--**

Yick Wo v. Hopkins, 118 U.S. 356 (1886).

Facts. San Francisco passed an ordinance requiring that all laundries housed in wooden buildings be licensed before operating. Yick Wo (P), a Chinese citizen, was convicted and imprisoned for violation of the ordinance. P petitioned for a writ of habeas corpus, proving that his equipment was not a fire hazard and that, while he and 200 other Chinese laundrymen had been denied permits, virtually all non-Chinese who made application received permits. P's petition was denied by the state court; P appeals.

Issue. Does discriminatory application of a statute that is fair and impartial on its face constitute denial of equal protection under the Fourteenth Amendment?

Held. Yes. Judgment reversed and remanded, with directions to discharge P from imprisonment.

♦   The Fourteenth Amendment equal protection provisions apply to all persons, whether or not citizens of the United States.

♦   The statute appears fair and impartial on its face, but its administration makes illegal and unjust discriminations of a material character among people in similar circumstances. Discriminatory application such as this denies P equal protection of the law and cannot be sanctioned. P is therefore illegally imprisoned.

---

c.   **Relevance of discriminatory impact in finding a discriminatory purpose.**

1)   **General rule.** Laws or other official actions that are racially neutral on their face and that rationally serve a permissible governmental end do not violate equal protection simply because they have a racially discriminatory impact (*i.e.,* affect minorities more adversely than whites). A violation requires that the governmental action have a discriminatory purpose (intentional or deliberate discrimination).

2)   **Qualification test--**

Washington v. Davis, 426 U.S. 229 (1976).

Facts. Davis (P), a black police officer, challenged the promotion policies and recruiting practices of the District of Columbia Police Department. P filed for partial summary judgment on the recruiting question, specifically challenging a qualification test that allegedly discriminated against blacks in violation of the Fifth Amendment Due Process Clause. The district court denied P's motions; the court of appeals reversed. Washington (D) appeals.

Issue. Does a qualification test that has not been established as a reliable measure of job performance and that fails a higher percentage of blacks than whites violate the Fifth Amendment Due Process Clause?

Held. No. Judgment reversed.

♦   A disproportionate impact on different races resulting from a general qualification test does not, by itself and independent of any discriminatory purpose, establish a constitutional violation. Government action is not unconstitutional solely because it has a racially disproportionate impact; there must be a racially discriminatory purpose to justify invalidation. The purpose need not be express, but it must exist, whether on the face of the statute or in its application.

♦   When a disproportionate racial impact is proven, the government must show that the law is neutral on its face and serves proper governmental ends, but the burden is not high. The test involved here has a reasonable relation to the need for competent police officers. Additionally, D has made affirmative efforts to recruit black officers, indicating a lack of intent to discriminate.

♦   Even though the test was not shown to relate directly to eventual job performance, it is closely related to the requirements of the training program for new recruits.

Concurrence (Stevens, J.). The line between discriminatory purpose and impact is not bright and not determinative since dramatic discriminatory impact is unacceptable.

---

d.   Adverse effect alone not a violation--

Memphis v. Greene, 451 U.S. 100 (1981).

Facts. The city of Memphis (D) closed the north end of a primarily residential street that traverses a white residential community. Greene (P), a resident of a predominantly black area to the north, customarily used the street to reach southern destinations. P claimed the closing violated the Civil Rights Act of 1866 and the Thirteenth Amendment. Reversing the district court, the court of appeals held the street closing invalid because it adversely affected P's ability to hold and enjoy his property. The Court granted certiorari.

Issue. Is state action that adversely affects members of a minority race but that is undertaken for a legitimate purpose unconstitutional?

Held. No. Judgment reversed.

♦   The record indicates that the closing was motivated by D's interest in protecting the residential neighborhood's safety and tranquility. The decisionmaking procedures were fair, and there is no indication that D would not confer a comparable benefit upon black residents. The value of P's property was not affected, although the closing did cause some inconvenience.

♦   The only injury to P is that he must choose an alternate route. This suffices neither as a violation of the Civil Rights Act nor as a "badge of slavery" under the Thirteenth Amendment. The inconvenience to P is a function of where he lives, not his race. The impact P suffers is a routine burden of citizenship and does not reflect a violation of the Thirteenth Amendment.

Dissent (Marshall, Blackmun, Brennan, JJ.). Neither the Constitution nor federal law permits a city to carve out racial enclaves. The reality here is that white citizens have taken legal measures to keep out "undesirable" traffic. Where the government takes action with full knowledge of its enormously disproportionate racial impact, the Civil Rights Act requires it to carry a heavy burden to justify its action.

---

e.   **Disproportionate impact based on sex--**

Personnel Administrator v. Feeney, 442 U.S. 256 (1979).

Facts. Feeney (P), a woman and nonveteran, challenged a Massachusetts statute that gave veterans an "absolute lifetime preference" for consideration for state civil service positions. Veterans with passing scores were automatically ranked above all other candidates. Ninety-eight percent of veterans were male. P claimed this system discriminated against women and denied P equal protection. The federal court invalidated the law. The Personnel Administrator of Massachusetts (D) appeals.

Issue. Does a veteran's preference program that does not specifically favor males, but in reality benefits males almost exclusively, deny equal protection to women?

Held. No. Judgment reversed.

♦   Although a neutral law may have a disparate impact upon a group, the Fourteenth Amendment guarantees equal laws, not equal results. Thus, a two-part inquiry is needed. First, is the classification really neutral, *i.e.*, not gender-based? If so, does the adverse effect on the group reflect invidious discrimination? If so, the law is invalid, because purposeful discrimination is the condition that offends the Constitution.

♦   The statute is neutral on its face. Many men are nonveterans and are thus also excluded from preference. And some women are veterans. The distinction is clearly between veterans and nonveterans, not between men and women.

♦   Although the legislature was certainly aware that most veterans are male, "discriminatory purpose" implies more than intent as awareness of consequences. It implies action taken "because of," not merely "in spite of," its effect. Nothing indicates that the legislature acted in order to prevent women from getting these jobs. Instead, the record shows a valid interest in assisting veterans.

Concurrence (Stevens, White, JJ.). The number of males disadvantaged is sufficiently large to refute P's claim.

Dissent (Marshall, Brennan, JJ.). Because of the disproportionate impact, D should have the burden to affirmatively prove that sex-based considerations played no part in the adoption of this scheme.

---

f.   **Standard procedures resulting in disproportionate impact--**

Arlington Heights v. Metropolitan Housing Development Corp., 429 U.S. 252 (1977).

Facts. Metropolitan Housing Development Corporation (P) applied to the village of Arlington Heights (D) for rezoning in order to build units for low-income tenants, many of whom would be racial minorities. When denied the application, P sued, claiming the denial was racially discriminatory. The district court found for D, but the court of appeals reversed. D appeals.

Issue. Does the Constitution prohibit a denial of a zoning change request when the denial impacts disproportionately on certain racial groups but was made pursuant to standard procedures?

Held. No. Judgment reversed.

♦   The *Davis* case reaffirmed the requirement that governmental action having a racially disproportionate impact also have a discriminatory purpose in order to justify judicial invalidation. However, the challenged action need not rest solely on such a racially discriminatory purpose. It is enough to show that such a purpose was a motivating factor in the decision.

♦   Sensitive inquiry into relevant evidence concerning intent is necessary. Such inquiry here fails to reveal any such intent on D's part. D's zoning plan and policies existed long before P's application, and other proposals, not involving racial minorities, have been rejected in the same manner as P's. Without proof of improper intent, mere showing of disproportionate impact on a racial minority is inadequate to the constitutional question.

---

4.   **Remedying Segregation.**

a.   **Introduction.** The significance of disproportionate impact has been articulated most fully in school desegregation cases. The Court has adopted a bifurcated approach to school desegregation problems. "De facto" segregation is nondeliberate segregation. If an official segregation policy existed as of 1954, there could not be de facto segregation in the school system. Thus, in the South, most school systems were characterized by "de jure" or deliberate segregation. The Court faced three alternatives in fashioning guidelines for remedying segregation:

1) Prohibit only activity that results in segregation; *i.e.,* require desegregation only (the emphasis is on process).

2) Hold that any racially imbalanced school system is by itself a violation; *i.e.,* require integration (the emphasis is on results).

3) Hold that, once de jure segregation is shown (process), integration is required (results). This is the approach the Court currently applies.

b. Early judicial remedies. After *Brown I, supra*, the Court decided several cases involving judicial responses to segregation.

1) Public schools. In *Griffin v. County School Board*, 377 U.S. 218 (1964), the Court ordered the reopening of a public school system that the school board had closed because of court-ordered integration. The record showed that the schools were closed to perpetuate segregation; the state and county were providing financial assistance to the remaining private schools, which were segregated.

2) Acceleration of desegregation. In *Green v. County School Board*, 391 U.S. 430 (1968), the Court held that school boards had an affirmative duty to take immediate steps to desegregate schools.

c. Authority of district courts to order desegregation in southern metropolitan areas--

Swann v. Charlotte-Mecklenburg Board of Education, 402 U.S. 1 (1971).

Facts. The Board of Education (D) had a long history of maintaining a dual set of schools in a single system in order to perpetrate discrimination in spite of *Brown I, supra*. Swann (P) brought suit to force desegregation. The district court ordered D to establish a plan, which it did, but the court rejected the plan and instead adopted a plan created by a court-appointed master. The Supreme Court granted certiorari.

Issue. Are district courts justified in ordering compliance with their own desegregation plans when the local school authorities fail to desegregate voluntarily?

Held. Yes. Judgment affirmed.

♦ The objective of the federal courts from *Brown I* to the present has been to eliminate all vestiges of state-imposed segregation in the public schools. Judicial authority to remedy violations expands when local authority defaults.

♦ The central problems here involve student assignment, and these problems are separated into four categories. The first is the extent to which racial quotas may be used to correct a segregation system. A remedial plan is judged by its effectiveness. Awareness of the racial composition of a school system is a useful starting point in shaping an effective remedy, and limited use of mathematical ratios is permissible. The guiding principle is that no pupil should be excluded from any school on account of race, but every school need not always reflect the racial composition of the school system as a whole.

♦ The remaining categories are elimination of one-race schools, remedial altering of attendance zones, and transportation of students in order to dismantle the dual school system. Demographic factors may result in virtually or completely one-race schools; these are not certain indications of imposed segregation. However, gerrymandering of school districts and attendance zones and provision for optional transfer of students to other schools is useful, and, to be effective, must grant free transportation and assurance of a place in the desired school.

---

d. **Judicial remedies for northern schools.**

1) **All minorities.** In determining whether a school is "segregated," the courts must consider the number of all minority groups (not just blacks) who have suffered unequal treatment in education.

2) **Presumption.** A finding that school authorities intentionally segregated—or delayed integrating—any significant portion of the school district creates a presumption that the entire school district is being operated on a segregated basis. This is because of the "substantial reciprocal effect" that segregation of some schools may have on others.

a) This presumption is not rebutted or satisfactorily explained merely by showing that the board had adopted a "neighborhood school policy" (assigning students to the schools closest to their homes), even though such policy on its face appears to be racially neutral.

b) But the presumption may be rebutted by a showing that because of natural geographic boundaries, the school district is in fact divided into clearly unrelated areas, which require separate treatment. But the burden of proving this is on the school board.

3) Prima facie case--

Keyes v. School District, 413 U.S. 189 (1973).

Facts. Keyes (P) challenged certain actions taken by School District No. 1 of Denver (D) that allegedly were intended to create or maintain segregated schools. No law supported such segregation; the Colorado Constitution expressly prohibited it. The district court held that blacks and Hispanics must be counted separately for purposes of defining a "segregated" school. P appeals.

Issue. Must courts consider the number of all minority groups (not just blacks) who have suffered unequal treatment in education when determining whether a school is segregated?

Held. Yes. Judgment modified and remanded.

♦ When a school district does not have a history of legally imposed segregation, a plaintiff must show intentional acts by school authorities intended to segregate schools and actual existence of currently segregated schools. If a plaintiff shows that such acts were taken in one portion of a school system, he has made a prima facie case of unlawful segregation intent for all segregated schooling within the system.

♦ For purposes of determining whether a school is segregated, it is improper to separate minorities who are subject to similar disadvantages. The lower court erred in not combining proportions of blacks and Hispanic students for this purpose.

♦ When the plaintiff has made a prima facie case, the defendant must rebut by showing that no segregative intent even partially motivated their actions. Alternatively, the defendant could show that a lesser degree of segregation would not have resulted even if the defendant had not acted as it did; *i.e.*, the defendant may rebut the plaintiff's claim by showing that its past segregative acts did not create or contribute to the current segregated condition of the core city schools.

Comment. Permissible judicial remedies include designating the location of new schools and abandonment of old schools so as not to perpetuate segregation; gerrymandering school districts and attendance zones, even if the result is that the new districts and zones are neither compact nor contiguous; and assigning students, faculty, and staff to schools in ratios substantially the same as in the community.

---

e.   Type of proof needed--

Columbus Board of Education v. Penick, 443 U.S. 449 (1979).

Facts. The public schools in Columbus, Ohio, were highly segregated. Although there was no statutory requirement or authorization to operate segregated schools, the Columbus Board of Education (D), as of 1954, had operated schools under a systematic program of segregation. D had failed to disestablish its dual system in the intervening years. In addition, D had taken actions that aggravated, not alleviated, racial segregation. In response, the district court imposed a system-wide remedy, which the court of appeals upheld. D appeals, claiming there was no showing of discriminatory purpose.

Issue. Is proof of purposeful and effective maintenance of separate black schools in a substantial part of a school system sufficient, by itself, to establish a prima facie case of an unconstitutional dual system?

Held. Yes. Judgment affirmed.

◆   D failed to rebut the inference of segregative intent based on 1954 segregation, failure to affirmatively desegregate, and adoption of policies that did not promote integration.

◆   Disparate impact and foreseeable consequences of D's actions, without more, do not establish improper motive, but are relevant evidence.

◆   The trial court found that D's practices had current, system-wide impact. This finding is supported by the record and is not rebutted by D. Therefore, a system-wide remedy is appropriate.

Dissent (Rehnquist, Powell, JJ.). The Court has adopted a policy either of almost total deference to the trial court, thus undermining local autonomy in educational matters, or of requiring system-wide remedies whenever racial imbalance is found if the Court can find some evidence of pre-1954 discriminatory purpose, regardless of any causal relationships. Both approaches are erroneous. The Court now requires local school boards to exploit all integrative opportunities that might come along; integration has become the controlling educational consideration in school board decisionmaking. The system-wide remedy upheld here cannot be properly considered without inquiring into causality and purpose. The result is that 30-year-old violations with respect to five schools, only three of which still exist, are used to justify a remedy involving 172 schools, most of which did not even exist 30 years ago.

f.   **Limits on remedies.** A federal court may not order busing of students between or among school districts to remedy de jure segregation in only one of the districts, unless the discriminatory acts of one school district have been a substantial cause of interdistrict segregation; *e.g.,* the district boundaries were drawn so as to foster such segregation, or one district had engaged in racial discrimination that caused the segregation to exist in the other district. [Milliken v. Bradley, 418 U.S. 717 (1974)]

1) The impact is that federal courts cannot achieve desegregation of urban schools by ordering the children bused to suburban school districts (and vice versa), as long as the suburban school districts had nothing to do with causing the segregation that exists in the city school districts (*i.e.,* no interdistrict remedies).

2) However, a metropolitan-area remedy for public housing segregation may be imposed even though the segregation took place only within the city, if (i) the government agency that engaged in segregation can act outside city boundaries, and (ii) the remedy does not "impermissibly interfere" with innocent suburban governmental units. [*See* Hills v. Gautreaux, 425 U.S. 284 (1976)—the Court ordered the Department of Housing and Urban Development to correct segregation in metropolitan Chicago]

g. **Incremental relinquishment of court control.** In *Freeman v. Pitts,* 503 U.S. 467 (1992), the Court held that a federal court in a school desegregation case may relinquish supervision and control in incremental stages with respect to discrete categories in which the school district has achieved compliance with a court-ordered desegregation plan before full compliance has been achieved in every area. Factors that a court must consider include: (i) whether there has been full and satisfactory compliance with the court's desegregation decree in those areas where supervision is to be withdrawn; (ii) whether retention of judicial control is necessary or practicable to achieve compliance with the decree in other facets of the school system; and (iii) whether the school system has demonstrated its good-faith commitment to the whole of the court's decree.

5. **Repeals of Remedies and Structurings of the Political Process that Burden Minorities.** Significant public discontent with the various remedies for de facto segregation resulted in attempts to repeal such remedies.

a. **Removal of authority from school district.** In *Washington v. Seattle School District,* 458 U.S. 457 (1982), the voters had approved Initiative 350, which prohibited school boards from requiring any student to attend a school other than the geographically closest school. The Court held that the initiative violated equal protection because it restructured the political process so as to make it more difficult for minorities to achieve favorable legislation. The initiative was drawn for racial purposes, despite its facial neutrality. After the initiative, only statewide elections could result in adoption of a remedial busing plan. The dissent noted that states are under no constitutional duty to adopt integration programs when no prior constitutional violation exists. The school districts themselves could have canceled the busing plans. The effect of the majority's ruling is that neither the legislature nor the people can alter the decision of a local school district, thus allowing the school district to forever preempt the state.

b.   **Constitutional amendment--**

Crawford v. Los Angeles Board of Education, 458 U.S. 527 (1982).

Facts. The California Supreme Court held that the state constitution required state school boards to alleviate both de facto and de jure segregation. Three years later, the voters ratified Proposition 1, which amended the constitution to permit state courts to order busing only where federal courts could do so under the Fourteenth Amendment. The California courts rejected Crawford's (P's) challenge of the proposition, and the Supreme Court granted certiorari.

Issue. After a state grants its courts broader authority to order busing to stop discrimination than is required by federal law, may it then limit such power to the requirements of federal law?

Held. Yes. Judgment affirmed.

♦   California could not have violated the Equal Protection Clause by simply adopting it as its own. Besides, the school districts still have a duty to desegregate on their own, and they can adopt busing plans to do so.

♦   Proposition 1 does not use racial classifications; it is racially neutral. The fact that California at one time exceeded the federal requirement does not prevent it from returning to the generally prevailing standard. There is no reason to conclude that the voters acted for a discriminatory purpose.

Concurrence (Blackmun, Brennan, JJ.). This case did not involve a distortion of the political process. The rights enforced by the courts originate elsewhere, as in state laws and constitutions. Repeal of a statute or a constitutional provision does not change the structure of the political process; it just repeals the rights to invoke a judicial busing remedy.

Dissent (Marshall, J.). This case is not different from an attempt to remove authority from local school boards.

---

6. **Affirmative Action and Benign Discrimination.**

   a. **Introduction.** Attempts to remedy adverse effects of past discrimination have resulted in various means such as affirmative action, quotas, and minority preferences, which in effect discriminate in favor of minorities. Such means do not violate equal protection if they fall within certain constitutional parameters.

   b. **Special state school admissions program for minorities--**

Regents of the University of California v. Bakke, 438 U.S. 265 (1978).

Facts. Bakke (P) was denied admission to the medical school of the University of California at Davis in two consecutive years. The Regents of the University of California (Ds) maintained both a regular admissions system and a special admissions program intended to assist disadvantaged minorities in getting admitted. P claimed that because he was white, he was denied consideration for the places reserved for minorities in the special program, denying him equal protection and violating Title VI of the 1964 Civil Rights Act. The California Supreme Court altered lower decisions and found that Ds' admissions program was illegal, that P must be admitted to the medical school, and that Ds may not accord any consideration to race in the admissions process. Ds appeal.

Issue. May a state school use race as a factor in its admissions process?

Held. Yes. Judgment affirmed in part and reversed in part.

♦   Title VI of the Civil Rights Act of 1964 must be held to proscribe only those racial classifications that would violate the Equal Protection Clause of the Fifth Amendment.

♦   Ds claim that since their procedure does not disadvantage minorities, it should not be subject to strict judicial review. However, Ds do disadvantage a specific race—whites. Equal protection requires that racial and ethnic distinctions of any sort be examined by the most exacting judicial scrutiny. It is incorrect to assert that the Fourteenth Amendment justifies "benign" preference for one race over another due to past discrimination, since its language is inconsistent with such an interpretation, and the kind of variable sociological and political analysis necessary to produce and enforce such rankings is beyond judicial competence. Such an interpretation would be manifestly unjust. The Court has approved preferential classifications in some instances (*e.g.,* school desegregation, employment discrimination), but only after proof of constitutional or statutory violations, absent here, and only when the remedy was closely related to the violation.

♦   The use of a suspect classification may be justified if the state can show that its purpose or interest is both constitutionally permissible and substantial, and that its use of the classification is necessary to the accomplishment of its purpose or the safeguarding of its interest. Ds' reasons for using their special admissions process are inadequate under this standard. Although Ds do have a valid interest in seeking diversity among the student body, their program, focusing as it does solely on ethnic diversity, hinders rather than promotes genuine diversity. An admissions process seeking diversity may properly consider race as one of many characteristics of an applicant that are compared with those of all other applicants to decide who is to be admitted, such as the procedure used at Harvard. But reservation of a fixed number of seats to a minority group unnecessarily denies other persons of an equal chance to be considered, and is therefore unconstitutional.

♦ The California court's judgment that Ds' special admission program is unlawful and that P must be admitted is affirmed. Its judgment that Ds be enjoined from any consideration of race in their admissions process is reversed.

Concurrence and dissent (Brennan, White, Marshall, Blackmun, JJ.).

♦ The central meaning of the decision is that the government may take race into account when it acts not to demean or insult any racial group but to remedy disadvantages caused by past discrimination, when supported by appropriate findings.

♦ Ds' affirmative action program is constitutional. Congress has enacted legislation under Title VI incorporating racial quotas. Prior decisions of this Court suggest that remedial use of race is permissible. Ds' goal of admitting minority students disadvantaged by the effects of past discrimination is sufficiently important to justify use of race-conscious admissions criteria. Ds should not be forced to abandon their reasonable and effective procedure.

Concurrence and dissent (Marshall, J.). For several hundred years, blacks have suffered discrimination, yet the Court is unwilling to hold that a class-based remedy for that discrimination is permissible. It is difficult for me to accept that blacks cannot now be afforded greater protection to remedy the effects of past discrimination.

Concurrence and dissent (Blackmun, J.). It is ironic that we are so disturbed over using race as an element when schools have conceded preferences for athletes, children of alumni, the affluent, etc.

Concurrence and dissent (Stevens, J., Burger, C.J., Stewart, Rehnquist, JJ.). The California court judgment should be affirmed in its entirety based on the plain language of Title VI of the Civil Rights Act, which specifies that "No person . . . on the ground of race, color, or national origin, be excluded from participation in . . . any program . . . receiving federal assistance." There is no need to reach the constitutional issues.

Comment. The holding and effect of *Bakke* can be illustrated by the following table:

	Specific System Was Unconstitutional	States Can Consider Race as a Factor
J. Brennan and three others	No	Yes
J. Powell	Yes	Yes
J. Stevens and three others	Yes	No

In summary, the less formal and specific the admissions system, the more likely it will be constitutional.

---

    c.   **Post-*Bakke* university admissions policies**. In response to *Bakke*, state schools modified their admissions policies to avoid racial quotas. This did not eliminate the use of race as a factor in deciding whether to admit individual students, however. The Court has recognized that diversity is a legitimate basis for considering race, but not if the admissions policy is in effect a quota.

    d.   **Race as a factor for law school admission--**

Grutter v. Bollinger, 539 U.S. 306 (2003).

Facts. Grutter (P), who was white, applied for admission to the University of Michigan Law School. P had a 3.8 grade point average and an LSAT score of 161. P was denied admission. P sued Bollinger (D), the President of the University, and other officials, claiming that their admissions policy discriminated against her on the basis of race. D's admissions policy sought to achieve diversity in the student body and therefore enrolled a "critical mass" of minority students, including African-Americans, Hispanics, and Native Americans. The district court found that D's use of race as a factor in admissions decisions was unlawful, but the court of appeals reversed. The Supreme Court granted certiorari.

Issue. Does a state university have a compelling state interest in obtaining the educational benefits that flow from a diverse student body, sufficient to justify the use of race as a factor in admissions criteria?

Held. Yes. Judgment affirmed.

♦   Under the Equal Protection Clause, a racial classification must survive strict scrutiny review. Justice Powell's decision in *Bakke* recognized that student body diversity is a compelling state interest that can justify the use of race in university admissions.

♦   The Court has never held that only remedial objectives can provide a basis for consideration of race. D in this case was not seeking to remedy past discrimination, but was seeking diversity in its student body, which D considers essential to its educational mission.

♦   Given the important purpose of public education and the expansive freedoms of speech and thought associated with the university environment, universities have a special niche under the Constitution. D's consideration of race is not simply to assure racial balancing, which is patently unconstitutional, but instead focuses on the educational benefits that diversity produces. In addition, law schools are the training ground for a large number of civil leaders. To cultivate a set of leaders that the citizens deem legitimate, the path to leadership must be open to talented and qualified individuals of every race and ethnicity.

♦   D's admissions policy is narrowly tailored to further the compelling state interest. There is no quota. Admissions decisions are based on individual considerations. Race is considered as a "plus" factor during consideration of each individual candidate. Race is not the defining feature of an application. There are many other diversity considerations, including living or traveling abroad, speaking other languages, etc. At the same time, D's program does not unduly burden individuals who are not members of the favored racial and ethnic groups.

♦   D's race-conscious admissions program must be limited in time, however. In 25 years, racial preferences will likely be unnecessary to further the diversity interest.

Concurrence (Ginsburg, Breyer, JJ.). Minority students still encounter inadequate and unequal educational opportunities, which hopefully will be remedied within the next generation.

Dissent (Renhquist, C.J., Scalia, Kennedy, Thomas, JJ.). D's admissions program is not narrowly tailored to the interest D asserts. Over five years, D has admitted 91 to 108 African-Americans to achieve "critical mass," so that members of that race would not feel isolated or like spokespersons for their race. During the same time, D admitted 13 to 19 Native Americans and between 47 and 56 Hispanics. D offers no explanation why fewer Hispanics and Native Americans are needed to achieve "critical mass." It turns out that the percentage of students admitted in each of these groups corresponds very closely to the percentage of applicants who were in the same groups. This is the type of racial balancing that is not permissible.

Dissent (Kennedy, J.). Justice Powell's approach in *Bakke* is the correct approach to this case. A university admissions program may take account of race as one nonpredominant factor in a system that considers each applicant as an individual, but the program must satisfy strict scrutiny. The majority here has distorted the strict scrutiny test. D's pursuit of critical mass has mutated into the equivalent of a quota. To be constitutional, a university's compelling interest in a diverse student body must be achieved while safeguarding individual assessment throughout the process.

Concurrence and dissent (Scalia, Thomas, JJ.). The Court invites further litigation about the scope of a "good faith effort" and the extent of the permissible "critical mass." The government simply should not discriminate on the basis of race.

Concurrence and dissent (Thomas, Scalia, JJ.). Minorities can achieve in every avenue of American life without the meddling of university administrators. The Court has deferred to D in an unprecedented way that is inconsistent with the concept of "strict scrutiny." I do not agree that the law school's discrimination benefits those who are admitted as a result of it. The school tantalizes unprepared students with the promise of the opportunities that a University of Michigan degree offers. These overmatched students take the bait, only to find that they cannot succeed because of the competition. Although they may graduate with law degrees, there is no evidence that they have received a better legal education than if they had gone to a less "elite" law school for which they were better prepared.

---

  e. **Race as a preferential factor for undergraduate admission--**

Gratz v. Bollinger, 539 U.S. 244 (2003).

Facts. Gratz (P) was a Caucasian resident of Michigan who was denied admission to the University of Michigan as an undergraduate. She filed suit, challenging the constitutionality of the school's undergraduate affirmative action policy. Under the university's policy, an applicant needed 100 points to guarantee admission. Applicants who were members of underrepresented racial or ethnic minority groups automatically received 20 points. The district court granted summary judgment on the basis that D's policy was the equivalent of a quota. While the case was under appeal, the Sixth Circuit decided *Grutter, supra*. The Supreme Court granted certiorari in both cases, even though the Sixth Circuit had not rendered a judgment in *Gratz*.

Issue. May an undergraduate university automatically confer 20 points, out of the 100 needed to guarantee admission, to every applicant who is a member of a specified race?

Held. No. Judgment affirmed.

- D's policy grants preferences to every minority applicant, solely on the basis of race. This policy is not narrowly tailored to achieve the interest in educational diversity that D claims as justification.

- Under Justice Powell's *Bakke* opinion, each applicant should be assessed as an individual. No single characteristic automatically ensures a specific and identifiable contribution to a university's diversity. D's policy does not include such individualized consideration.

- Although D's policy may be easier to administer than an individualized consideration process, administrative challenges cannot make constitutional an otherwise problematic system.

Concurrence (O'Connor, Breyer, JJ.). D's policy also awarded points for other diversity contributions, including high school leadership, but these awards were capped at a level much lower than 20 points. D's policy is in sharp contrast to the law school admissions program in *Grutter*, which did allow admissions officers to make individualized judgments.

Concurrence (Thomas, J.). Any use of racial discrimination in higher education admissions is unconstitutional.

Concurrence (Breyer, J.). Although I concur, I agree with Justice Ginsberg that government decisionmakers may distinguish between policies of inclusion and exclusion because the former are more likely to be consistent with the basic constitutional obligation that the law respect each individual equally.

Dissent (Stevens, Souter, JJ.). This case should be dismissed for lack of standing.

Dissent (Souter, Ginsburg, JJ.). D's policy is closer to *Grutter* than to what *Bakke* prohibits. There is no quota, and the 20 points does not convert race into a decisive factor comparable to reserving minority places as prohibited by *Bakke*.

Dissent (Ginsburg, Souter, JJ.). D's policy was designed to help achieve equality in light of the history of discrimination against these minorities. D has not limited or decreased enrollment by any particular racial or ethnic group, and it has not reserved places on the basis of race.

---

7. **Affirmative Action in Employment and Government Contracts.**

   a. **Teacher layoffs.** In *Wygant v. Jackson Board of Education*, 476 U.S. 267 (1986), the Court considered a collective bargaining agreement that limited the percentage of minority personnel laid off to the percentage of minorities employed at the time of the layoff. The effect was to protect recently hired minority teachers at the expense of more senior white teachers. The Court held that the provision was unconstitutional because it was not related to specific prior discrimination by the government unit involved and did not necessarily bear a relationship to the harm caused by prior discriminatory hiring practices.

b. **Public contracts.** In *Fullilove v. Klutznick*, 448 U.S. 448 (1980), the Court held that Congress may affirmatively require a minimum minority participation as a condition of the expenditure of federal funds. Congress had enacted a statute that required that federal grants to local governments for local public work projects be awarded only to applicants who assure that at least 10% of the grant will be spent for minority business enterprises. The Court held that the objective of the legislation—to prohibit traditional procurement practices that perpetuate the effects of prior discrimination—was within the constitutional scope of congressional power. It primarily regulates state action in the use of federal funds. The means used, involving as they do racial criteria, must be narrowly tailored to achievement of the permissible objectives. Congress, of all parts of government, possesses the broadest remedial powers. The set-aside program was clearly remedial, and its adverse effect on non-qualifying parties is incidental. The administrative scheme, containing provisions for waiver, provides reasonable assurance that the application of racial criteria will be limited to accomplishing the proper objectives.

c. **Rejection of state and local set-aside programs absent evidence of direct discrimination--**

Richmond v. J.A. Croson Co., 488 U.S. 469 (1989).

Facts. Citing the authority of the *Fullilove* opinion, *supra*, the city of Richmond (P) required prime contractors on city projects to set aside at least 30% of its subcontracts to minority business enterprises, using the *Fullilove* definition of minority group members. The program was adopted based on evidence that minority businesses had received a significantly lower percentage of contracts (.67%) than the percentage of minorities living in the city (50%). However, there was no evidence of racial discrimination on P's part or on the part of any of P's prime contractors. P brought suit against J.A. Croson Company (D) to enforce the rule. The district court found for P. The court of appeals reversed. P appeals.

Issue. May a city adopt a set-aside program favoring minority-owned contractors on city projects when there is no evidence of direct discrimination on the part of the city or its prime contractors?

Held. No. Judgment affirmed.

♦ P notes that under *Fullilove*, Congress was not required to make specific findings of discrimination to engage in race-conscious relief. P asserts that if the federal government could do this, a city such as P can as well. However, unlike the states and their subdivisions, such as P, Congress has a specific constitutional mandate to enforce the Fourteenth Amendment.

♦ To enable states to use racial classifications merely by reciting a benign or compensatory purpose would be to give them the full power of Congress under section 5 of the Fourteenth Amendment, and to insulate their actions from judicial scrutiny under section 1. However, the objective of the Fourteenth Amendment was to limit the states' use of race as a criterion for legislative action and to empower the federal courts to enforce those limitations.

♦ Under the Equal Protection Clause, a state or its subdivisions may eradicate the effects of private discrimination within its own legislative jurisdiction, but this requires that the discrimination be identified with the particularity required by the Fourteenth Amendment. P would have to show it had become a "passive participant" in a system of racial exclusion practiced by elements of the local construction industry, but it failed to do so.

♦ The Equal Protection Clause protects individual persons; P's plan denied certain citizens the opportunity to compete for a fixed percentage of public contracts based solely on their race, and thereby implicates the personal rights of the excluded persons. Such race-based regulations are subject to strict scrutiny, regardless of the race of those burdened or benefited by the classification. [Wygant, *supra*]

♦ P's factual predicate for its plan consists of a generalized assertion that there has been past discrimination in the "construction industry," attributable to a series of racial as well as nonracial factors. P can do no more than speculate as to how many minority firms would exist absent past discrimination. It cannot show how many minority members are qualified to act as contractors, or how many minority members are eligible for membership in contractors' associations. All P can show is that minority businesses received less than 1% of prime contracts, even though its minority population is 50%, but statistical generalizations cannot substitute for evidence of discrimination. Permitting a racial classification on such generalizations would enable local governments to create a patchwork of racial preferences without ascertainable limit on size or duration.

♦ P's plan covers Spanish-speaking, Oriental, Indian, Eskimo, and Aleut persons, against whom there is no evidence of discrimination in P's construction industry. This suggests that P's purpose was not to remedy past discrimination.

♦ A court cannot assess whether P's plan is narrowly tailored to remedy prior discrimination because it is not linked to identified discrimination. There is no indication that P considered race-neutral means to increase minority participation in the construction industry. The quota's only goal appears to be racial balancing. But unlike the plan upheld in *Fullilove*, P's plan does not provide for a waiver of the set-aside provision where the minority contractor's higher price was not attributable to the effects of past discrimination. P evaluates bids on a case-by-case basis, and can investigate the need for remedial action in particular cases as appropriate; P cannot use broad statistical requirements simply to minimize the administrative burdens of remedying specific prior discrimination.

Concurrence (Stevens, J.). Unlike the plan in *Wygant*, which was intended to improve education by assuring an integrated faculty, P's plan has no objective to increase efficient performance of its construction contracts. P's plan was formulated by a legislative body, instead of a court, which is better equipped to identify past wrongdoers and to fashion appropriate remedies. P's plan does not address the specific characteristics of the racial groups involved; it relies merely on a stereotypical analysis that cannot be condoned under the Equal Protection Clause.

Concurrence (Kennedy, J.). The driving force of the Equal Protection Clause is the moral imperative of racial neutrality. Justice Scalia's proposed rule of automatic invalidity would reduce caseloads but is a break from our precedents. The majority's strict scrutiny standard will generally accomplish the same objective while being consistent with our precedents.

Concurrence (Scalia, J.). There are no situations in which state and local governments may discriminate on the basis of race (except a social emergency, such as a prison race riot, or when necessary to undo the effects of their own unlawful racial classifications), because a solution to past discrimination that consists of aggravating present discrimination is no solution. The federal government is uniquely capable of dealing with past racial discrimination because racial discrimination finds more ready expression at the state and local levels than it does at the federal level. P's plan is an example of local racial classification; it directly benefits the dominant political group, which is also the dominant racial group. P is free to give a contracting preference to identified victims of discrimination, but this could apply to whites as well as blacks; it would be race neutral. Remedies must address discrimination against individuals; a past injustice to a black man cannot be compensated for by discriminating against a white man.

Dissent (Marshall, Brennan, Blackmun, JJ.). P's plan was patterned after, and is indistinguishable from, the *Fullilove* plan. The majority is unpersuaded by P's factual findings, but it should not second-guess the judgment of the former capital of the Confederacy, which found that its local construction industry did not deviate from the national pattern Congress found as set forth in *Fullilove*. P has a compelling interest other than remedying past discrimination; it has an interest in preventing its own spending decision from furthering racial discrimination. P's plan is substantially related to these interests and is appropriately limited to five years in duration, has a waiver provision, and has a minimal impact on innocent third parties, since it only affects 3% of overall contracting in P's area. The majority also for the first time introduces strict scrutiny of race-conscious remedial remedies as if racial discrimination and its vestiges have been eradicated in the United States. It also imposes a difficult factual standard of proof of a prima facie case of a constitutional or statutory violation before states and localities can act to remedy racial discrimination. This decision marks a full-scale retreat from the Court's long-standing solicitude to race-conscious remedial efforts.

Comment. The plurality, that stated that race-based regulations are subject to strict scrutiny in all cases, noted that while Justice Marshall's approach would apply a relaxed standard of review to race-conscious classifications designed to further remedial goals, in this case the majority of P's city council, and about half of P's population, were black. Under this view, if the level of scrutiny varied according to the ability of different groups to defend their interests in the representative process, the plurality argued that heightened scrutiny would be appropriate in this case, because the classification was to the advantage of the racial group that had a political majority. Justice Marshall noted that numerical inferiority is but one of several factors to be considered.

---

     d.   **Congressional authority to order remedial programs.** *Metro Broadcasting, Inc. v. FCC*, 497 U.S. 547 (1990), involved FCC policies for granting broadcast licenses. Minority ownership both constituted a positive factor in deciding whether to grant an applicant a license, and qualified for an exception to the general rule against receiving an assignment of a license that is being challenged before the FCC. The policies were not justified as remedial compensation to victims of past discrimination, but merely reflected the fact that minorities were inadequately represented in broadcasting. The Court, in a five to four decision, upheld the policies as having been approved by Congress and having met the requirements of serving important governmental objectives and being substantially related to the achievement of those objectives. Congress could adopt a policy of minority ownership as a means of achieving greater programming diversity. The dissent argued that the government may not allocate benefits and burdens among individuals based on the assumption that race determines how they think, and that the majority wrongly departed from the traditional requirement that racial classifications may be used only if necessary and narrowly tailored to achieve a compelling result.

     e.   **Strict scrutiny of affirmative action--**

Adarand Constructors, Inc. v. Pena, 515 U.S. 200 (1995).

Facts. Adarand Constructors, Inc. (P) submitted the low bid for a guardrail subcontract on a federal road project. The prime contract's terms provided for additional compensation if subcontractors were hired who were certified as small businesses controlled by "socially and economically disadvantaged individuals." P's competitor,

Gonzales Construction Company, certified as such a business and received the sub-contract, although its bid was higher than P's. Under federal law, general contractors must presume that socially and economically disadvantaged individuals include specified racial minorities. P sued Pena (D), Secretary of Transportation, claiming that P was deprived of property without due process of law under the Fifth Amendment. The court of appeals upheld the law. P appeals.

Issue. Is the federal government's use of race-based classifications subject to strict scrutiny even for affirmative action?

Held. Yes. Judgment reversed and case remanded.

♦ The Fifth Amendment protects against arbitrary treatment by the federal government, but it does not guarantee equal treatment.

♦ In *Croson, supra,* the Court held that the Fourteenth Amendment requires strict scrutiny of all race-based action by state and local governments. Thus, any person, of whatever race, has the right to demand that the government justify any racial classification subjecting that person to unequal treatment under the strictest judicial scrutiny.

♦ In *Metro Broadcasting, supra,* the Court held that "benign" racial classifications required only intermediate scrutiny. This holding undermined the basic principle that the Fifth and Fourteenth Amendments protect persons, not groups. Group classifications must be subject to detailed inquiry to assure that the personal right to equal protection has not been infringed. Therefore, it is inconsistent to treat "benign" racial classifications differently from other types of racial classifications, and all racial classifications shall now be subject to strict scrutiny.

♦ This holding does not preclude the government from acting in response to the lingering effects of racial discrimination. When race-based action is necessary to further a compelling interest, it is permitted as long as it satisfies the "narrow tailoring" test of strict scrutiny.

Concurrence (Scalia, J.). There can never be a compelling interest in discriminating on the basis of race to compensate for past racial discrimination in the opposite direction. Under the Constitution, there can be neither a creditor nor a debtor race.

Concurrence (Thomas, J.). The government may not make distinctions on the basis of race, whether the objectives are to oppress a race or to help a race. Affirmative action programs undermine the moral basis of the equal protection principle and arouse resentment in those not benefited. The targeted minorities are stamped with a badge of inferiority and are prompted to develop dependencies or an attitude that they are "entitled" to preferences.

Dissent (Stevens, Ginsburg, JJ.). There is a clear distinction between policies designed to oppress minorities and policies designed to eradicate racial subordination.

Dissent (Souter, Ginsburg, Breyer, JJ.). Stare decisis compels the application of *Fullilove* to this case. Although *Fullilove* was not doctrinally consistent, its holding has been generally accepted.

Dissent (Ginsburg, Breyer, JJ.). The judiciary should defer to Congress, as the political branches are better suited to respond to changing conditions.

C. DISCRIMINATIONS BASED ON GENDER

1. **Introduction.** Although early decisions dealt with gender-based classifications under the traditional equal protection tests, more recent cases have judged gender-based classifications under a higher standard, but not so high a test as would apply to the inherently suspect classes. The Court declined to make gender a suspect classification in *Reed v. Reed*, 404 U.S. 71 (1971). However, it did hold that a state could not prefer men over women in appointing estate administrators simply to reduce the work load of probate courts. *Reed* was the first decision to hold that sex discrimination violated the Equal Protection Clause and was based on the arbitrary nature of the legislative choice favoring men.

2. **Development of the Intermediate Standard.** As late as 1961, the Court based a decision that generally excluded women from jury duty on the role of the woman as the center of home and family life. [Hoyt v. Florida, 368 U.S. 57 (1961)] After *Reed*, the Court began developing an intermediate standard of review for gender classifications.

   a. **Military benefits--**

Frontiero v. Richardson, 411 U.S. 677 (1973).

Facts. Frontiero (P), a female officer in the Air Force, sought to claim her husband as a "dependent" in order to receive the additional benefits attached to such a claim. Male members of the armed forces could claim their wives as dependents without any showing, but women in the service had to show that their spouses were actually dependent on them for over one-half of their support. P claimed that the distinctions violated the Due Process Clause. The district court upheld the statutes making the distinction. P appeals.

Issue. May the military require that servicewomen but not servicemen make a showing that their spouses are actually dependent before claiming them as "dependents"?

Held. No. Judgment reversed.

- Classifications based upon sex are included among those that are inherently suspect and therefore subject to close judicial scrutiny.

- This statute cannot withstand such scrutiny. Its sole justification lies in administrative convenience, which, though important in some circumstances, is hardly a significant governmental interest closely and reasonably related to the classification. The statutes involve arbitrary discrimination and deny due process.

Concurrence (Powell, J., Burger, C.J., Blackmun, J.). The statutes are unconstitutional under *Reed*. There is no need to go further and characterize sex as a suspect classification. To do so unnecessarily preempts the prescribed constitutional processes of amending the Constitution, which at this time is dealing with this very issue in the guise of the Equal Rights Amendment.

---

b. **Liquor regulation--**

Craig v. Boren, 429 U.S. 190 (1976).

Facts. Craig (P), a male, challenged an Oklahoma statute that denied beer sales to males under age 21 and females under age 18. The three-judge district court dismissed P's action. P appeals.

Issue. May a state properly impose gender-based differentials in regulating sales of alcoholic drinks?

Held. No. Judgment reversed.

- To withstand constitutional challenge, classifications by gender must serve important governmental objectives and must be substantially related to the achievement of those objectives. The state objective here—enhancement of traffic safety—is clearly important. However, the relation between this objective and the challenged statute is based on statistical evidence fraught with shortcomings and is inadequate to show that sex represents a legitimate, accurate proxy for the regulation of drinking and driving.

- Failure to show a substantial relation between the gender-based classification and achievement of the state's objectives requires that the statute be invalidated as unconstitutional. The operation of the Twenty-First Amendment, limited as it is when applied outside Commerce Clause issues, does not alter application of the equal protection standards that govern here.

Concurrence (Powell, J.). The Court has added confusion to the appropriate standard for equal protection analysis. The statistics do tend to support the state's view but are inadequate to support the classification.

Concurrence (Stevens, J.). The classification here is not totally irrational, but it is unacceptable because it has little relation to traffic safety. It prohibits only sales of beer, not consumption, which is the real threat to traffic. The law punishes all males for the abuses of only 2% of their class.

Dissent (Rehnquist, J., Burger, C.J.).

♦   Men challenging a gender-based statute unfavorable to themselves should not be able to invoke a more stringent standard of review than normally pertains to most other types of classifications, since men, as a group, have not suffered the type of prior discrimination that has always supported a standard of special scrutiny. Nor is the interest involved here—beer purchasing—"fundamental" in the constitutional sense of invoking strict scrutiny.

♦   The Court has added a new standard to the norm of "rational basis" and the "compelling state interest" required where a "suspect classification" is involved—that of the "important governmental objectives" and "substantial relation to achievement of those objectives." This new standard is unnecessary and invites judicial confusion and interference into the proper roles of the legislature.

♦   The correct standard here is the rational basis test, under which a classification is invalid only if it rests on grounds wholly irrelevant to the achievement of the state's objective. The state has provided sufficient evidence to show a rational basis, and the statute should be upheld.

---

   c.   **Single-sex military school--**

United States v. Virginia, 518 U.S. 515 (1996).

Facts. The Virginia Military Institute ("VMI") was founded in 1839 and at the time of the litigation was the only single-sex school among Virginia's (D's) public schools of higher learning. VMI's mission was to produce "citizen-soldiers" who are prepared for leadership in civilian and military life. The school's training used an "adversative method" designed to instill physical and mental discipline in its cadets. This involves complete lack of privacy, wearing uniforms, and eating and living together, all in a high-pressure environment comparable to Marine Corps boot camp. VMI excluded women from its program, although neither the school's goals nor teaching methodologies were inherently unsuitable for women. When one woman complained about being denied admission, the United States (P) sued, alleging that D's single-sex policy violated equal protection. In response to an earlier remand from the federal court of appeals, D proposed a separate but parallel program for women, called Virginia Women's Institute for Leadership ("VWIL"), which would have a goal of producing "citizen-soldiers" but still differ significantly from VMI's program. The court of appeals approved this approach, and the Supreme Court granted both parties' petitions for certiorari.

Issue. If a state-sponsored single-sex school denies equal protection, may the state offer a parallel program for the opposite sex while retaining the single-sex status of the school?

Held. No. Judgment reversed.

♦ Under *J.E.B. v. Alabama ex. rel. T.B., infra,* and *Mississippi University for Women v. Hogan, infra,* those who seek to defend gender-based government action must demonstrate an "exceedingly persuasive justification" for that action. Gender classifications have not been equated with racial or national origin classifications for all purposes, but official action that denies opportunities to an individual because of gender must be carefully inspected by the courts. Gender is not a proscribed classification; physical differences between men and women are enduring. These differences may not be used to denigrate the members of either sex or to artificially constrain their opportunities.

♦ To prevail against a challenge, D must show that the classification serves "important governmental objectives" and that the discriminatory means used are "substantially related" to the achievement of those objectives. In this case, D has shown no "exceedingly persuasive justification" for its exclusion of all women from VMI. D claims the single-sex education contributes to diversity in education. While that may be true, diversity was not the reason VMI excluded women. D's plan to provide a unique educational benefit only to males is not equal protection when there is no corresponding plan for females.

♦ D also claims that VMI's adversative method of training provides educational benefits that cannot be made available to women without modification. To accommodate women, VMI claims it would have to "destroy" its program. In fact, the VMI methodology could be used for some women, and the only accommodation necessary would be in housing assignments and physical training programs for female cadets. But while most women may not choose VMI's adversative method, most men would also not choose it. The state simply cannot constitutionally deny entrance to women who have the will and capacity to attend VMI.

♦ Establishment of a comparable school for women would not remedy the constitutional problem. D's separate program does not include the rigorous military training found at VMI. D claims that the methodological differences between the institutions are based on "real" differences between men and women, but again this is based on estimates of what is appropriate for most women. Such generalizations fail to recognize that some women do well under the adversative method and want to attend VMI. D's alternative program for women is simply not the equal of VMI.

Concurrence (Rehnquist, C.J.). The Court should continue to follow the *Craig* approach and not introduce new terminology such as "exceedingly persuasive justification." The true constitutional violation was not the exclusion of women, but the maintenance of an all-men school without providing a comparable institution for women.

Dissent (Scalia, J.). VMI existed for over 150 years. The tradition of having government-funded military schools for men has not been unconstitutional over those years. Changes such as the one the Court imposes should be brought about through democratic means, not by the courts. The Court now holds that a sex-based classification is invalid unless it relates to characteristics that hold true in every instance. In so doing, it has executed a *de facto* abandonment of the intermediate scrutiny that should be applied to gender-based classifications. The facts in this case show that D's real options were an adversative method that excludes women or no adversative method at all. The courts below found that VMI would be fundamentally changed if it admitted women.

---

3.   **Differences.**

    a.   **Disability insurance.** A state law that excluded from state disability insurance benefits "disabilities arising from normal pregnancy and childbirth" has been upheld. This provision did not violate the Equal Protection Clause because it furthered the state policy of making the disability insurance program self-supporting by excluding certain physical conditions from coverage thereunder. The fact that this particular condition (pregnancy) happens to apply to only one sex does not render the exclusion invalid. [Geduldig v. Aiello, 417 U.S. 484 (1974)]

    b.   **Statutory rape--**

Michael M. v. Superior Court, 450 U.S. 464 (1981).

Facts. California's statutory rape law makes men alone criminally liable for the act of sexual intercourse. Michael M. (D) was prosecuted under the statute and challenged it as an unlawful discrimination on the basis of gender. The California Supreme Court upheld the law, and D appeals.

Issue. May a state's statutory rape law permit prosecution only against members of one sex?

Held. Yes. Judgment affirmed.

♦   A legislature may not make overbroad generalizations based on sex that are entirely unrelated to any differences between men and women or that demean the ability or social status of the affected class. However, legislation may realistically reflect the fact that the sexes are not similarly situated in certain circumstances.

♦ The asserted purpose of the statute is to prevent illegitimate pregnancy and its attendant social harms, a valid state purpose. The question is whether a state may attack the problem directly by prohibiting a male from having sexual intercourse with a minor female. We hold that such a statute is sufficiently related to the state's objectives to pass constitutional muster.

♦ D claims that the statute is under-inclusive since a gender-neutral statute would serve the state's goal equally well. We do not sit to redraw constitutionally permissible lines, and even if we were so inclined we cannot say that a gender-neutral statute, attended by increased enforcement difficulties, would be equally effective.

Concurrence (Blackmun, J.) This statute is a sufficiently reasoned and constitutional effort to control the problem at its inception. It does not implicate the serious questions arising when the state seeks to regulate a woman's dealing with pregnancy once it has become a reality.

Dissent (Brennan, White, Marshall, JJ.). While the desirability of achieving the state's asserted statutory goal is unquestionable, this statute is not substantially related to success. California has failed to prove that its gender-based law is more successful than would be a gender-neutral law.

Dissent (Stevens, J.). The validity of a total ban is not an adequate justification for a selective prohibition. A rule that authorizes punishment of only one of two equally guilty wrongdoers violates the essence of the constitutional requirement that the sovereign must govern impartially.

---

c. **Draft registration--**

Rostker v. Goldberg, 453 U.S. 57 (1981).

Facts. The Military Selective Service Act permitted the registration and conscription only of men. A lawsuit initiated earlier by Goldberg (P), challenging the draft as improperly gender-based, was revived, and the district court held the Act unconstitutional.

Issue. May Congress restrict draft registration to males?

Held. Yes. Judgment reversed.

◆ Congress specifically considered the constitutionality of the Act and explicitly relied on its "broad constitutional power" to raise and regulate armies and navies. Thus, the courts must decide whether Congress has transgressed an explicit guarantee of individual rights that limit the specific authority relied on.

◆ Congress determined that the purpose of registration was to prepare for a draft of combat troops. Women are not eligible for combat. Thus, the exemption of women from registration is not only sufficiently but also closely related to Congress's purpose in authorizing registration. Since men and women are not similarly situated with respect to combat, the classification challenged does not violate the United States Constitution.

Dissent (Marshall, Brennan, JJ.). This statute excludes women from a fundamental civic obligation. It is not a conscription statute, as the majority seems to believe, but merely a registration statute. D has failed to carry its burden of showing that completely excluding women advances important governmental objectives.

---

d. **Peremptory challenges.** In *J.E.B. v. Alabama ex rel. T.B.*, 511 U.S. 127 (1994), the Court held that gender-based peremptory challenges were unconstitutional. The concurring opinions noted the reality of different life experiences and perceptions affected by gender, so that while gender makes no difference as a matter of law, it may make a difference as a matter of fact.

4. **Remedial Discrimination.**

a. **Widows' tax benefits.** In *Kahn v. Shevin*, 416 U.S. 351 (1974), the Court upheld a property tax exemption for widows that did not apply to widowers. The law was reasonably designed to assist the sex for whom the loss of a spouse is a disproportionately heavy burden. The classification was not a mere administrative convenience as in *Frontiero*.

b. **Military career regulations.** The Court upheld a federal law that gave women more time to get promoted in the Navy because of the restricted sea and combat duty available to women. [Schlesinger v. Ballard, 419 U.S. 498 (1975)]

c. **Social Security survivors' benefits.** The Court struck down a provision in the Social Security Act that granted "survivors' benefits" to widows, but not widowers, while they care for minor children of the deceased wage earner. The disqualification of widowers was held "irrational," since the purpose of the benefits was to enable the surviving parent to stay at home and care for the children. The classification thus discriminated against the children, based on the gender of the surviving parent. [Weinberger v. Wiesenfeld, 420 U.S. 636 (1975)]

    d.   **Proof of dependency requirement.** In *Califano v. Goldfarb*, 430 U.S. 199 (1977), the plurality held that *Wiesenfeld* applied to a requirement that a widower, but not a widow, must prove dependency on the deceased spouse in order to collect benefits. The dissent distinguished *Wiesenfeld* on the grounds that the statute did not totally foreclose widowers and that favoring aged widows was not invidious discrimination.

    e.   **Social Security benefits--**

Califano v. Webster, 430 U.S. 313 (1977).

Facts. Webster (P), an old-age insurance benefits recipient, challenged the statutory scheme for computing those benefits. The scheme effectively gave women fewer elapsed years from which to exclude lower earnings years in order to increase the average monthly wage. As a result, women were able to generally compute a higher average monthly wage than similarly situated men. A lower court held the scheme unconstitutionally discriminatory. Califano (D), Secretary of Health, Education, and Welfare, appeals.

Issue. May Congress discriminate between men and women in order to compensate women for adverse past discrimination?

Held. Yes. Judgment reversed.

♦   Reduction of the disparity in economic condition between men and women caused by the long history of discrimination against women has been recognized as an important governmental objective.

♦   This scheme is substantially related to achievement of that proper objective. The level of benefits is directly related to the level of past earnings. If women's past earnings were comparatively low because of discrimination, it is proper to correspondingly increase their benefits.

Concurrence (Burger, C.J., Stewart, Blackmun, Rehnquist, JJ.). Certainty in the law is not achieved by allowing five Justices to determine if a law is "offensive" or "benign." Favoring aged widows is not invidious discrimination.

    f.   **Women's college--**

Mississippi University for Women v. Hogan, 458 U.S. 718 (1982).

Facts. The Mississippi University for Women (D) was a state school that excluded males. D established a school of nursing. Hogan (P), a male registered nurse, applied for admission to D, the only state school in the city, to obtain a degree. P was denied admission but was allowed to audit classes. P sued in federal court, claiming that D's policy violated the Equal Protection Clause. The district court denied preliminary injunctive relief, but the court of appeals reversed. The Supreme Court granted certiorari.

Issue. May a state exclude males from enrolling in a state-supported professional nursing school?

Held. No. Judgment affirmed.

♦ Because D's policy discriminates on the basis of gender, it is subject to strict equal protection scrutiny. D must show that the classification serves important governmental objectives and that the discriminatory means employed are substantially related to the achievement of those objectives.

♦ D claims that its policy compensates for discrimination against women and is educational affirmative action. While a compensatory purpose may justify an otherwise discriminatory classification in some situations, this argument is unpersuasive with respect to the nursing school. Women have earned the large majority of nursing degrees in the state, and in the nation as a whole. The actual effect of D's policy is to perpetuate the stereotyped view of nursing as a woman's job.

♦ D has also failed to show that the classification is substantially and directly related to its compensatory objective. D allows men to audit classes and to participate in continuing education classes. Women must not therefore be adversely affected by the presence of men.

Dissent (Burger, C.J.). The opinion is limited to professional nursing schools.

Dissent (Powell, Rehnquist, JJ.). Women's colleges have been an element of diversity that has enriched American life. The majority errs by assuming the equal protection standard is appropriate here, where the intent was to expand women's choices. P's only real claim is that the colleges open to him are located at inconvenient distances and that he has a right to attend a college in his home city.

D. SPECIAL SCRUTINY FOR OTHER CLASSIFICATIONS

1. **Introduction.** Because racial discrimination prompted adoption of the Fourteenth Amendment, racial classifications are clearly "suspect," meaning they invite the strictest judicial scrutiny. The Fourteenth Amendment was not phrased solely in terms of race, however. Other classifications may invite heightened scrutiny not reaching the strictest levels. Common to most of these classifications are the following characteristics: historical lack of po-

litical power; history of discrimination; immutability of the basis for classification; irrelevance to performance; and obviousness (the basis for classification acts as a badge).

2. Illegitimacy.

    a. Introduction. The Court's analysis of classifications based on illegitimacy has been erratic, but the level of scrutiny falls between the rational basis standard and the standard for gender-based classifications. Illegitimacy classifications have often been held unconstitutional. The appropriate level of equal protection analysis depends upon whom the legislation was intended to affect and whether its effect is sufficient to treat it as discrimination against illegitimate children.

    b. Social Security benefits--

Mathews v. Lucas, 427 U.S. 495 (1976).

Facts. Lucas (P) filed an application for Social Security benefits for her two children following the death of their father, whom P had never married and from whom P had been separated for two years prior to his death. Her application was denied because it contained no proof of her children's actual dependency on the deceased. The children were unable to meet any of the statutory classifications that relieve class members from the individualized burden of proof of dependency. Among these classes is simple legitimacy. P claimed these classifications denied due process and discriminated against illegitimate children. The district court ordered the government, represented by Mathews (D), to pay the benefits. D appeals.

Issue. Does a classification that presumes dependency for legitimate children unconstitutionally deny due process to illegitimate children, who must prove actual dependency?

Held. No. Judgment reversed.

♦   The district court erroneously concluded that legislation treating legitimate and illegitimate offspring differently is constitutionally suspect. The statute involved here was intended merely to replace support lost by a child when his father dies and not to grant welfare benefits to certain legitimate or otherwise "approved" children.

♦   The presumptions of dependency are administrative aids; although they approximate rather than precisely mirror the results that case-by-case adjudication would show, they are reasonably related to the likelihood of dependency at death and therefore are permissible under the Fifth Amendment. P is free to prove actual dependency. Failure to extend any presumption of dependency to P's children does not impermissibly discriminate against them.

Dissent (Stevens, Brennan, Marshall, JJ.). The holding in effect adds to the burdens acquired by illegitimate children at birth. Such children should not be punished for conditions over which they have no control. Fair evaluation of the competing interests would result in affirming the lower decision.

Comment. In *Miller v. Albright*, 523 U.S. 420 (1998), the Court upheld a provision of federal naturalization law that distinguishes between out-of-wedlock children born outside the country to a citizen father and those born to a citizen mother. A child of a citizen mother becomes a citizen if the mother has physically been in the United States for one year. A child of a citizen father can be a United States citizen only if the child obtains formal proof of paternity before the age of 18. The plurality opinion provided various rationales, but focused on the different situations of the unmarried fathers and mothers.

---

    c.   **Other benefits.** A state may not provide welfare benefits to legitimate children while denying the same benefits to illegitimate children. [New Jersey Welfare Rights Organization v. Cahill, 411 U.S. 619 (1973)] Also, in *Weber v. Aetna Casualty & Surety Co.*, 406 U.S. 164 (1972), the Court held that a state may not deny to illegitimate children workers' compensation benefits granted to legitimate children upon the death of their parent. Likewise, illegitimate children are entitled to bring wrongful death actions and suits for support from their natural father, the same as legitimate children.

3.   **Sexual Orientation.**

    a.   **Introduction.** The legal treatment of sexual orientation has raised many issues. The courts have reached a variety of conclusions about what is appropriate and what is required under the Constitution.

    b.   **States cannot prohibit protection of homosexuality--**

Romer v. Evans, 517 U.S. 620 (1996).

Facts. Colorado voters adopted an amendment to the Colorado Constitution that prohibited all legislative, executive, or judicial action at any level of state or local government designed to confer a protected status upon, or to allow claims of discrimination by, any person based on homosexual, lesbian, or bisexual orientation. Evans (P) initiated litigation to have the amendment declared unconstitutional. The Colorado Supreme Court held that the amendment was subject to strict scrutiny because it infringed the fundamental right of homosexuals to participate in the political process, and, after remand to the trial court, held the amendment unconstitutional. The Supreme Court granted certiorari.

Issue. May a state prohibit governmental action that confers a protected status upon, or allows claims of discrimination by, any person based on homosexual, lesbian, or bisexual orientation?

Held. No. Judgment affirmed.

♦   D claims that the amendment simply puts homosexuals in the same position as all other persons; *i.e.*, it does no more than deny homosexuals special rights. However, the actual effect of the amendment is to put homosexuals in a solitary class with respect to transactions and relations in both the private and governmental spheres. It imposes a special disability upon these persons by forbidding them to seek or enjoy the safeguards against discrimination that other groups can enjoy.

♦   To reconcile the Equal Protection Clause with the reality that most legislation creates classes, the Court has held that legislation that neither burdens a fundamental right nor targets a suspect class will be upheld so long as the classification bears a rational relation to some legitimate end. The amendment in this case has the peculiar property of imposing a broad and undifferentiated disability on a single named group, and its breadth is so discontinuous with the purported reasons for it that it cannot be explained by anything but animus toward homosexuals. As such, it lacks a rational relationship to legitimate state interests.

♦   Animus toward a politically unpopular group cannot constitute a legitimate state interest. The interest asserted is respect for other citizens' freedom of association, such as the liberties of employers or landlords who oppose homosexuality. But the breadth of the amendment is so far removed from these justifications that they cannot reasonably be deemed the true legitimate purpose of the amendment.

Dissent (Scalia, J., Rehnquist, C.J., Thomas, J.). This amendment is a modest attempt to preserve traditional sexual mores against the efforts of a politically powerful minority to revise those mores through the use of the laws. The majority has made the Court accept the proposition that opposition to homosexuality is as reprehensible as racial or religious bias. But the Constitution says nothing about the subject, and the resolution of such public values should be left to the democratic processes, not the courts. The only denial of equal treatment articulated by the Court is that homosexuals may not obtain preferential treatment without modifying the state constitution. Furthermore, there was a legitimate rational basis for the amendment. In *Bowers v. Hardwick*, 478 U.S. 186 (1986), the Court held that the Constitution does not prohibit making homosexual conduct a crime. If a state may make homosexual conduct criminal, it should be allowed to enact laws disfavoring homosexual conduct; and if so, it should certainly be allowed to adopt a provision that does not even disfavor homosexual conduct but merely prohibits special protections for homosexuals. The animus toward homosexuals—moral disapproval of homosexual conduct—is the same "animus" that for centuries led to criminalization of homosexual conduct. Congress itself required the states of Arizona,

New Mexico, Oklahoma, and Utah to adopt a ban against polygamy as a condition of statehood. The Court has approved this criminalization of polygamy; thus the Court has today concluded that the perceived social harm of polygamy is a legitimate concern of government, and the perceived social harm of homosexuality is not. The amendment is simply designed to prevent piecemeal deterioration of the sexual morality favored by a majority of Coloradoans and should be upheld.

Comment. In *Lawrence v. Texas, supra*, the majority characterized an equal protection argument under *Romer* as tenable but did not discuss it. Justice O'Connor would have decided the case solely on equal protection grounds, and concluded that the sodomy law was directed toward gay persons as a class. Justice Scalia, joined by Chief Justice Rehnquist and Justice Thomas, rejected the equal protection argument, contending that the law applied equally to all persons. They found that the statute had no purpose to discriminate against men or women as a class, so rational basis review should apply.

———————————

4. **Alienage.**

   a. **Introduction.** Under the Constitution, Congress has plenary power over admission or exclusion of aliens, so the courts normally defer to federal law even when it draws distinctions based on alienage. State laws discriminating against aliens once admitted are inherently suspect, however. Most such laws are not upheld. The only significant exception permits such discrimination in situations involving state government functions. For example, a state may categorically exclude aliens from its police force [Foley v. Connelie, 435 U.S. 291 (1978)], but it cannot exclude aliens from all civil service jobs [Sugarman v. Dougall, 413 U.S. 634 (1973)], nor make citizenship a requirement for the practice of law [*In re* Griffiths, 413 U.S. 717 (1973)]. The exception applies if a two-part test is satisfied:

      1) The classification must be specific, neither over-inclusive nor under-inclusive; and

      2) The classification must be applied only to those public officers who participate directly in the formulation, execution, or review of broad public policy and hence perform functions that go right to the heart of representative government.

   b. **Control over employment of aliens--**

   Ambach v. Norwick, 441 U.S. 68 (1979).

Facts. The state of New York, represented by Ambach, Commissioner of Education (D), forbade certification as a public schoolteacher of any non-United States citizen, except when the applicant intended to apply for citizenship. Norwick (P), a citizen of Great Britain but a United States resident for 15 years, sought certification. P was qualified in all ways but her citizenship, and challenged that requirement. A three-judge district court held that the statute violated the Equal Protection Clause. D appeals.

Issue. May a state include citizenship, or at least an intention to become a citizen, as an essential qualification for certification as a public schoolteacher?

Held. Yes. Judgment reversed.

♦   State regulation of alien employment is limited by constitutional considerations, but states have greater latitude when excluding aliens from public employment. Some state functions are so closely related to the operation of the state as a governmental entity that persons who have not become part of the process of self-government may be excluded from those functions. Examples include state elective and important nonelective positions that are essential to representative government.

♦   The distinction between citizens and aliens is fundamental to the definition and government of a state and is recognized in the United States Constitution. Public education is one of the most important functions of local government; teachers significantly influence their students, and the state may properly determine that citizenship is an essential qualification for participation in this important function. D's statute bears a rational relationship to this interest and is therefore valid.

Dissent (Blackmun, Brennan, Marshall, Stevens, JJ.). The statute permits noncitizens to teach in private schools, indicating that the state interest is not all that strong. It irrationally excludes persons whose foreign experience may be a valuable asset. If noncitizens may practice law [*see In re* Griffiths, *supra*], they should be allowed to teach school.

Comment. In *Bernal v. Fainter*, 467 U.S. 216 (1984), the Court held that a state may not include citizenship as an essential qualification for becoming a notary public. A notary's duties, though important, do not go to the heart of representative government. They are essentially clerical and ministerial. If the political function exception does not apply to attorneys, it should not apply to notaries public. The state's justifications for the discrimination—that notaries should be familiar with state law and available to testify to acts they have performed—are not shown by the evidence to be compelling. The state requires no proficiency tests of notary applicants and has not shown that the unavailability of notaries' testimony presents a real problem.

c.   **Federal restrictions on aliens.** The federal government has power over immigration and naturalization, and Congress regularly makes rules applicable to aliens that would be unacceptable if applied to citizens. In *Mathews v. Diaz*, 426 U.S. 67 (1976), the Court upheld the limitation of federal Medicare benefits to aliens who had been admitted for permanent residence and who had lived in the United States continuously for five years. The Court deferred to congressional judgment that the distinctions drawn within the class of aliens were appropriate.

5.   **Mental Retardation--**

Cleburne v. Cleburne Living Center, Inc., 473 U.S. 432 (1985).

Facts. Under a city zoning ordinance, group homes for the mentally retarded may operate only with a special permit that requires the signatures of property owners within 200 feet of the property to be used. The applicants were unable to obtain the required signatures in a residential neighborhood. The lower courts held the ordinance unconstitutional. The Court granted certiorari.

Issue. Is mental retardation a suspect class for equal protection analysis?

Held. No. Judgment affirmed on other grounds.

♦   Generally, under the Equal Protection Clause, legislation is presumed valid and will be upheld if the classification drawn by the statute is rationally related to a legitimate state interest. Certain types of classifications are subject to strict scrutiny, others to heightened scrutiny.

♦   The court of appeals held that mental retardation is a quasi-suspect classification. However, the legislature has a legitimate interest in providing for the various problems of the mentally retarded, and courts are ill-equipped to make substantive judgment about legislative decisions in this area. Legislatures have addressed the problems of the mentally retarded and need the flexibility of the rational basis test to be effective.

♦   Under the rational basis test, however, the ordinance is defective. It does not apply to nursing homes for the aged or convalescents, apartment houses, sanitariums, or boarding houses. Nothing in the record explains how the permit requirement for only facilities for the mentally retarded is rationally related to any governmental purpose.

Concurrence (Stevens, J., Burger, C.J.). The mentally retarded have historically been subject to mistreatment. This ordinance reflects the irrational fears of neighboring property owners, not a concern for the welfare of the mentally retarded.

Concurrence and dissent (Marshall, Brennan, Blackmun, JJ.). The Court has created a "second order" rational basis review. Normally under the rational basis test, the legislature does not have to address all ills at once. Thus, zoning plans based on fears of proximity to a high school, location in a flood plain, and crowded living conditions or increased congestion are perfectly valid, even if applied one step at a time. However, the class of mentally retarded persons deserves heightened scrutiny, and the Court reaches the correct result.

---

6. **Other Challenged Bases for Discrimination.**

    a. **Age.** In *Massachusetts Board of Retirement v. Murgia*, 427 U.S. 307 (1976), the Court rejected a police officer's challenge to mandatory retirement at age 50. The Court explained that strict scrutiny is required only when a classification impermissibly interferes with the exercise of fundamental rights or operates to disadvantage a suspect class. Age is not a suspect class nor is a right to continued governmental employment a fundamental right.

    b. **Wealth.** For many years, the Court suggested that the government could not discriminate on account of poverty any more than it could on grounds of religion or race. However, in more recent years, the Court has stated that financial need alone does not identify a suspect class for purposes of equal protection analysis. In *James v. Valtierra*, 402 U.S. 137 (1971), the Court upheld a requirement for local referendum approval before low-rent housing projects could be developed.

E. FUNDAMENTAL RIGHTS

1. **The Right to Vote.** Several constitutional provisions relate to voting and elections. The Fourteenth Amendment Equal Protection Clause has been applied to the right to vote. The Fifteenth Amendment forbids denial or abridgment of the right to vote on account of race, color, or previous condition of servitude, and the Nineteenth Amendment grants the franchise to women. The Twenty-Fourth Amendment abolishes the poll tax for federal elections. The Twenty-Sixth Amendment grants the right to vote in state and federal elections to 18-year-olds.

    a. **Denial or qualification of the right to vote.**

        1) **Impact of a poll tax--**

Harper v. Virginia Board of Elections, 383 U.S. 663 (1966).

Facts. Harper (P) and other Virginia residents brought suit to have Virginia's poll tax declared unconstitutional. The district court, under *Breedlove v. Suttles*, 302 U.S. 277 (1937), dismissed P's complaint. P appeals.

Issue. May a state exact a poll tax as a condition for exercise of the right to vote?

Held. No. Judgment reversed.

♦ Once the franchise is granted to the electorate, lines may not be drawn that are inconsistent with the Equal Protection Clause of the Fourteenth Amendment.

♦ Lines drawn by the affluence of the voter or by the payment of any fee violate equal protection. Undoubtedly, states may impose reasonable voter qualifications, but these must pass careful scrutiny because the franchise is preservative of other basic civil and political rights. Wealth or payment of a fee is an irrelevant factor in measuring a voter's qualifications.

♦ Notions of what constitutes equal treatment for purposes of the Equal Protection Clause do change, and *Breedlove* is overruled.

Dissent (Black, J.). Poll taxes can rationally further a state's interest without an invidious purpose.

Dissent (Harlan, Stewart, JJ.). In the past it was accepted that property owners have a deeper stake in community affairs and are more responsible, educated, and knowledgeable. We should not strike down a law just because a different theory is popular now.

---

2) Voter qualifications not based on wealth--

Kramer v. Union Free School District, 395 U.S. 621 (1969).

Facts. Kramer (P) challenged a state law that restricted eligibility to vote in certain school district elections to those who either own or lease taxable real property within the district, or who are parents (or have custody) of children enrolled in the local public schools. The lower courts upheld the law. P appeals.

Issue. May a state restrict the franchise for limited purpose elections merely on a showing of a rational basis for the restrictions?

Held. No. Judgment reversed.

♦ Statutes denying some residents the right to vote impinge on one of the most fundamental rights of a democratic society. Accordingly, such exclusions must be necessary to promote a compelling state interest.

♦ Even if the state interests here are substantial enough to justify limiting the exercise of the franchise to those "primarily interested" or "primarily affected" (which is not decided), this statute is not narrowly drawn to effectuate that purpose. It is both under-inclusive and over-inclusive. Therefore, it cannot stand.

Dissent (Stewart, Black, Harlan, JJ.). If a state may impose valid restrictions based on residence, literacy, and age, it ought to be able to impose these requirements, which are rational. The Court should apply only the traditional equal protection standard.

---

3) **Additional restrictions on the franchise.**

    a) **Special purpose elections.** In *Cipriano v. Houma*, 395 U.S. 701 (1969), a state law granted only property taxpayers the right to vote in elections to approve municipal utility bonds. The Court held the restriction invalid since all citizens have an interest in the quality of utility services and rates. In *Phoenix v. Kolodziejski*, 399 U.S. 204 (1970), the Court held that a statute limiting the vote for the issuance of general obligation bonds to real property owners was unconstitutional even though only property taxes would pay for the improvements, since all residents were said to have a substantial interest in the municipal improvements to be made. But in *Salyer Land Co. v. Tulare Lake Basin Water Storage District*, 410 U.S. 719 (1973), the Court upheld an election scheme in which only landowners could vote for the members of the district board, because costs were assessed against land benefited. The board had a special limited purpose, and its activities disproportionately affected landowners as a group.

    b) **Disenfranchisement of felons.** In *Richardson v. Ramirez*, 418 U.S. 24 (1974), the Court held that the states may disenfranchise convicted felons because Section 2 of the Fourteenth Amendment specifically permits such a limitation on the right to vote.

    c) **Ballot access.** The Court has looked closely at attempts to impede ballot access by independent candidates and fringe political parties. Most of these are defended as attempts to maintain the integrity of the political process, and this is a legitimate state interest. But the states may not be unduly restrictive. In *Anderson v. Celebrezze*, 460 U.S. 780 (1983), the Court specifically relied on the First Amendment instead of equal protection to invalidate an early filing deadline that applied to independents but not the nominees of political parties. The Court articulated a balancing test, comparing the restriction's injury to First Amendment rights with the justifications asserted by the state.

b. Dilution through apportionment.

1) Federal versus state apportionment. In early decisions, the Supreme Court consistently refused to review questions arising from a state's distribution of electoral strength among its political or geographical subdivisions. In *Baker v. Carr, supra*, the Court decided that federal courts had jurisdiction over challenges to apportionment plans. The modern approach to federal elections requires that representation must reflect the total population as precisely as possible. More flexibility is permitted in apportionment of state legislatures, but grossly disproportionate districts are not allowed. State apportionment may not be used to further discrimination, but numerical deviations resulting from political considerations may be allowed.

2) Justiciability of apportionment challenges. The courts' jurisdiction over constitutional challenges to a legislative apportionment were discussed in *Baker v. Carr, supra*.

3) Constitutional standards--

Reynolds v. Sims, 377 U.S. 533 (1964).

Facts. Sims (P) and others challenged the apportionment of the Alabama legislature, which was based on the 1900 federal census and thus seriously discriminated against voters who lived in an area where the population had grown disproportionately in the intervening years. The district court ordered temporary reapportionment; Reynolds (D) and other state officials appeal.

Issue. Must a state apportion its legislative districts on the basis of population?

Held. Yes. Judgment affirmed.

♦ The right to vote is essential to a democratic society and is denied by abasement or dilution of a citizen's vote just as effectively as by wholly prohibiting the free exercise of the franchise. The fundamental principle of representative government is one of equal representation for equal numbers of people, regardless of race, sex, economic status, or place of residence within a state.

♦ The Equal Protection Clause guarantees the opportunity for equal participation by all voters in the election of state legislators. Therefore, votes cannot be weighed differently on the basis of where the voters happen to reside. This applies whether the state legislature is unicameral or bicameral.

♦ The federal Congress cannot be taken as a guide for state legislative district apportionment because it arose from unique historical circumstances and represents a union of sovereigns. Political subdivisions of states never have been sovereign entities in that sense.

♦ Each state district must contain as nearly an equal population as possible, although precision, being impossible, is not required. Substantial equality of population must be the overriding objective. States need not perpetually update their apportionment plans, but there must be a reasonable plan for periodic readjustment.

Dissent (Stewart, Clark, JJ.). A state's plan for legislative apportionment must be rational and not permit the systematic frustration of the will of a majority of the electorate. So long as a plan achieves effective and balanced representation of the variety of social and economic interests of the state, it cannot be considered irrational.

Dissent (Harlan, J.). The history of the adoption of the Fourteenth Amendment shows that the Equal Protection Clause was not meant to limit the power of the states to apportion their legislatures as they saw fit.

Comment. In one of the five companion cases to *Reynolds*, *Lucas v. Forty-Fourth General Assembly*, 377 U.S. 713 (1964), involving the Colorado apportionment scheme, the Court held that the fact that a scheme had been approved by the state's voters is without constitutional significance.

---

4) **Super majorities.** *Gordon v. Lance*, 403 U.S. 1 (1971), held that state requirements of more than a majority (in this case 60%) for various kinds of law enactment—whether in the legislature or by referendum—do not violate equal protection as long as such provisions do not discriminate against or authorize discrimination against any identifiable class. The Court reasoned that the Constitution does not require that a majority always prevail on every issue. It did not pass on (i) a requirement of unanimity or giving a veto power to a very small group, or (ii) one requiring extraordinary majorities for the election of public officers.

5) **Permissible deviation.** In *Karcher v. Daggett*, 462 U.S. 725 (1983), which involved congressional districting, the Court disapproved a plan that had a maximum population difference of .694% because an alternative plan had a difference of only .4514% and the larger deviation was not shown to be necessary. In contrast, in *Gaffney v. Cummings*, 412 U.S. 735 (1973), the Court upheld a maximum deviation of 7.38%. An even greater deviation occurred in *Mahan v. Howell*, 410 U.S. 315 (1973), in which the Court approved a 16.4% variance in the redistricting of a state legislature, stating that greater flexibility is constitutionally permissible with respect

to state legislature reapportionment than in congressional redistricting because of the interest in the normal functioning of state and local governments.

c. **Dilution through gerrymanders.**

1) **Political gerrymandering--**

Davis v. Bandemer, 478 U.S. 109 (1986).

Facts. Indiana's 1981 state apportionment was enacted by the Republican-controlled state legislature and signed by the Republican governor. Bandemer (P) claimed that the apportionment was a gerrymander intended to disadvantage Democrats on a state-wide basis. The lower courts agreed. Davis (D) appeals.

Issue. Is a political gerrymandering claim justiciable?

Held. Yes. Judgment affirmed on this issue.

♦ Both *Baker* and *Reynolds* held that claims regarding the adequacy of state representation in state legislatures are justiciable. *Mobile* and subsequent cases held that racial gerrymandering is justiciable under the Equal Protection Clause. Political gerrymandering is also justiciable, although the Constitution does not require proportional representation or a reapportioning that allocates seats among contending parties in proportion to what their anticipated statewide vote will be.

♦ In order to state a justiciable claim, P had to prove (i) intentional discrimination against an identifiable political group and (ii) an actual discriminatory effect on that group. Unconstitutional discrimination arises from an arrangement of the electoral system such that the voters' influence on the political process as a whole is consistently degraded. The fact that an apportionment scheme makes winning elections more difficult is insufficient.

♦ A challenge to a specific district requires examination of the opportunity members of the group have to participate in candidate selection, registration, and voting. A challenge to an entire statewide reapportionment plan requires examination of the voters' direct or indirect influence on the elections of the legislature as a whole.

♦ In this case, the evidence supports a finding that the plan was adopted with the purpose of discriminating against Democratic voters, but there was insufficient proof that Ps' voting strength was diluted statewide.

Concurrence and dissent (Powell, Stevens, JJ.). District lines should be drawn pursuant to neutral and legitimate criteria, without regard to the voters' political beliefs or party affiliation. The plurality does not set forth any standards to guide legislatures and courts in the future. In this specific case, the evidence of discriminatory impact is clear, and there is no sufficient justification (rational basis) founded on permissible neutral criteria.

Concurrence (O'Connor, J., Burger, C.J., Rehnquist, J.). Apportionment is fundamentally a political process, and a challenge to an apportionment plan, brought by a political party responsible for the process, is clearly a political question. Members of the major political parties are not a discrete and insular group vulnerable to exclusion from the political process by a dominant group. A partisan gerrymander does not affect individuals differently than a bipartisan gerrymander such as was approved in *Gaffney*. The consequence of this holding is that political parties may dilute the vote of individuals through bipartisan gerrymander, but only as long as the parties themselves are not deprived of their group voting strength. Political gerrymandering should not be justiciable.

---

2) *Bandemer* called into doubt--

Vieth v. Jubelirer, 541 U.S. 267 (2004).

Facts. The 2000 census resulted in a decrease of Pennsylvania's Congressional delegation from 21 Representatives to 19. Consequently, the Republican-controlled Pennsylvania legislature adopted, and the Republican governor signed into law, a redistricting plan that benefited Republicans. Vieth and other Democratic voters (Ps) challenged the redistricting, claiming that it was an unconstitutional political gerrymander. The United States District Court dismissed Ps' claim. Ps appeal.

Issue. Are political gerrymandering claims justiciable?

Held. No. Judgment affirmed.

♦ In *Davis v. Bandemer, supra*, the Court held that political gerrymandering claims are justiciable, but the Court could not agree on a standard to adjudicate them. *Bandemer* should be overruled because political gerrymandering claims are nonjusticiable; there are no judicially discernible and manageable standards for adjudicating such claims.

♦ Political gerrymanders existed before the Constitution was framed, and the Constitution provides a remedy for potential problems by giving Congress power to "make or alter" federal election districts drawn by state legislatures. *Bandemer* extended that control to the courts, but nothing in the Constitution establishes a judicially enforceable limit on the political considerations that the state legislatures and Congress may use in districting.

◆ Eighteen years of experience with the *Bandemer* ruling has left the courts without any judiciable standards to apply. After considering several *Bandemer* claims, the lower courts have consistently refused judicial intervention even under *Bandemer*. There is no reason to retain *Bandemer*.

◆ The dissenters have come up with three different standards for adjudicating political gerrymandering claims, each with serious unresolved problems.

◆ Justice Kennedy concurs in the judgment and recognizes that there are no existing manageable standards for adjudicating political gerrymandering claims. However, he would have the courts continue to adjudicate such claims because such a standard may one day be discovered. We suggest that the lower courts treat this as a reluctant vote against justiciability at district and statewide levels.

Concurrence (Kennedy, J.). No adequate standard for adjudicating political gerrymandering claims has emerged in this case, but this does not prove that none will emerge in the future.

Dissent (Stevens, J.). Five members of the Court believe that political gerrymandering claims are justiciable, although for different reasons. I would consider whether a legislature allowed partisan considerations to dominate and control redistricting. If no neutral criterion can be identified, and if the only possible explanation for district lines is a desire to increase partisan strength, then there is no rational basis to save the district from an equal protection challenge.

Dissent (Souter, Ginsburg, JJ.). A plaintiff should have a case if he is able to show: (i) his membership in a cohesive political group or party; (ii) a disregard for traditional districting principles in the district of his residence; (iii) specific correlations between that disregard and the distribution of the population of the plaintiff's group; (iv) the existence of a hypothetical district that deviates less from traditional districting principles; and (v) intentional action by the defendants to adversely affect the plaintiff's group. After the plaintiff shows a prima facie case, the defendants would be required to justify their decision by referring to objectives other than pure partisan advantage.

Dissent (Breyer, J.). Normally, the legislature does not violate the Equal Protection Clause when drawing districting lines. However, the use of purely political boundary-drawing factors that entrench a minority in power can amount to a serious and remediable abuse.

---

d. **Dilution and race.**

1) **At-large system--**

Mobile v. Bolden, 446 U.S. 55 (1980).

Facts. The city of Mobile (D) was governed by a three-member city commission, elected at large. Bolden (P), a black Mobile voter, challenged this system as unfairly diluting the black vote. The district court found for P and ordered D to institute a mayor-council system, elected from single-member districts. The court of appeals affirmed. D appeals.

Issue. Does an at-large system of municipal elections not motivated by a discriminatory purpose violate the rights of a minority group constituting about one-third of the population?

Held. No. Judgment reversed.

♦   D's system is a common one in our nation. State action that is neutral on its face, like D's, violates the Fifteenth Amendment only if motivated by a discriminatory purpose. There is no right to have black or other minority candidates elected. The Fifteenth Amendment prohibits only the denial or abridgment of the freedom to vote, which P does not allege here.

♦   At-large electoral schemes are subject to challenge under the Fourteenth Amendment Equal Protection Clause when they are intended to result in a lack of representation of racial or ethnic minorities.

♦   There must be proof of official discrimination. [*See* White v. Regester, 412 U.S. 755 (1973)] Failure to elect proportional numbers of minority representatives is not sufficient proof. Here, P has failed to show the fatal purpose. D's system is readily explained on grounds apart from race.

♦   The dissent would find a substantive right of proportional representation, but no such right exists.

Concurrence (Blackmun, J.). The relief accorded was excessive; the case should be remanded for reconsideration of an appropriate remedy.

Concurrence (Stevens, J.). There is a distinction between state action that inhibits the right to vote, which is subject to strict scrutiny, and action affecting group political strength, which is judged by a standard that allows effective functioning of the political process. The proper test is the objective results of the state action, not the subjective motivation behind it. Under that test, D's plan is permissible.

Dissent (Brennan, J.). Proof of discretionary impact is sufficient. Even if it were not, P has adequately proven discriminatory purpose.

Dissent (White, J.). Invidious discriminatory purpose can be inferred from objective factors. The lower courts' findings were based on such a reasonable inference and should not be discarded.

Dissent (Marshall, J.). The plurality concludes that, absent proof of intentional state discrimination, the right to vote is meaningless for the politically impotent. There is a substantive constitutional right to equal participation in the electoral process that D denies P. There is no right to proportional representation per se, but the Court must affirmatively protect minorities such as P from vote dilution.

---

2) Subjective evidence of discriminatory intent--

Rogers v. Lodge, 458 U.S. 613 (1982).

Facts. Lodge and other black citizens of Burke County, Georgia (Ps), brought suit against Rogers and the other four county commissioners (Ds), challenging Ds' system of at-large elections. The majority of the county population was black, but because the white population was older, a slight majority of the voting population was white. About 38% of the registered voters were black. Ds were elected by majority vote, in runoff elections if necessary. No black person had ever been elected to the commission. The trial court found that the election system was racially neutral when adopted but was being maintained for invidious purposes, and ordered that the county be divided into five districts for purposes of electing commissioners. The court of appeals affirmed. Ds appeal.

Issue. May sociological evidence be used to prove a discriminatory intent behind an at-large voting system?

Held. Yes. Judgment affirmed.

♦ At-large voting systems are not per se unconstitutional, although they tend to minimize the voting strength of minority groups by allowing the political majority to elect all representatives of the district. To prove a violation of the Equal Protection Clause, Ps must trace the invidious quality of the law to a racially discriminatory purpose. This requires inquiry into the available circumstantial and direct evidence of intent.

♦ In *Mobile v. Bolden*, *supra*, the Court held that the presence of a discriminatory effect is insufficient; there must be a finding of discriminatory purpose. This case differs from *Mobile* because the district court below considered the relevant proof and concluded that Ds' scheme is being maintained for invidious purposes. It did not stop at finding the existence of a discriminatory effect.

♦ The evidence of bloc voting along racial lines, and the fact that no black has ever been elected to the commission, is insufficient by itself to prove purposeful discrimination. However, the trial court also considered the impact of past discrimination, which resulted in low black voter registration and absence of blacks in various governmental positions. Ds' voting scheme has served to maintain the status quo.

♦ There is no reason to overturn the district court's order to utilize single-member districts.

Dissent (Powell, Rehnquist, JJ.). The largely sociological evidence relied on by the Court is the same type of evidence that was insufficient in *Mobile*. Under the majority opinion, the district courts must assess at-large voting systems free from any standards. They must make subjective inquiries into the motivations of local officials in structuring local governments. Courts should instead focus on objective factors that are direct, reliable, and unambiguous indices of discriminatory intent.

---

3) State redistricting plan designed only to separate voters on the basis of race--

---

Shaw v. Reno, 509 U.S. 630 (1993).

Facts. After the 1990 census, North Carolina became entitled to a 12th congressional seat. Forty of the state's 100 counties were covered by the Voting Rights Act, which required approval from a federal court or from Reno (D), the United States Attorney General, for any changes to voting districts. Black persons made up 20% of the state's population and were the majority in five of the counties. The state legislature submitted a redistricting plan that included one majority-black congressional district. After D objected to the plan, the legislature enacted a revised plan that had two majority-black districts. To include sufficient black citizens to fill the district, the second district was 160 miles long and, for much of its length, was only as wide as the freeway corridor it followed from black neighborhood to black neighborhood. Shaw (P) challenged the redistricting, claiming that the deliberate segregation of voters into separate districts on the basis of race violated the right to vote in an electoral process not tainted by racial discrimination. The district court held that P did not state a claim under the Equal Protection Clause. P appeals.

Issue. May a state legislature create a voting district that is so irrational on its face that it can be understood only as an effort to segregate voters into separate voting districts because of their race?

Held. No. Judgment reversed.

♦ Redistricting legislation that is so bizarre on its face that it is unexplainable on grounds other than race requires close scrutiny. A reapportionment plan that includes groups who have little or nothing in common other than their race has the appearance of political apartheid. It reinforces the stereotype that all members of a particular racial group think alike and vote alike.

♦ When a district is created solely to create a majority of one racial group, the representative from that district may believe that the primary objective is to represent only the members of that group instead of their entire constituency. Accordingly, the courts should recognize an equal protection claim such as P's challenging the intentional creation of a majority-minority district that has no nonracial justifications.

♦ D claims that a jurisdiction covered by the Voting Rights Act may have a compelling interest in creating majority-minority districts. These states may have a strong interest in creating these districts, but they are still subject to constitutional challenges such as P's. Racial classifications of any type pose the risk of long-term harm to society by reinforcing the belief that citizens should be judged by the color of their skin.

Dissent (Blackmun, J.). It is ironic that the case in which the majority chooses to abandon settled law is a challenge by white voters to a plan under which North Carolina has sent black representatives to Congress for the first time since Reconstruction.

Dissent (Stevens, J.). There is no constitutional requirement of compactness or contiguity in a voting district. Equal protection is violated when a state creates an uncouth district for the sole purpose of making it more difficult for minorities to win an election, but it is not violated when the majority acts to facilitate the election of a member of a group that lacks power because it remains underrepresented in the state legislature. If it is permissible to draw districts to provide adequate representation for rural voters, union members, Hasidic Jews, Polish Americans, or Republicans, it is permissible to do the same thing for the very minority group whose history gave birth to equal protection.

Dissent (Souter, J.). There is no justification to depart from our prior decisions; we can have one equal protection analysis for electoral districting and another for most other types of state governmental decisions. Electoral districting in a mixed race area necessarily calls for decisions that require some consideration of race. Also, the mere placement of an individual in one district instead of another does not deny another individual of a right or benefit. Only if a cognizable harm such as vote dilution or the abridgement of the right to participate in the electoral process is shown is there a violation of equal protection.

---

4) **Race as a primary factor--**

Miller v. Johnson, 515 U.S. 900 (1995).

Facts. Twenty-seven percent of Georgia's population is black. The 1990 census gave Georgia an 11th congressional district. Previously, the state had one majority-black district. After two redistricting plans were rejected by the United States Attorney General, the state legislature adopted one that included three majority-minority districts.

One of these used narrow corridors to connect two cities containing black neighborhoods. Miller (P) challenged the reapportionment. The district court held that race was the predominant, overriding factor in designing the plan and granted relief. Johnson (D) appeals.

Issue. May a state use race as the primary factor in designing reapportionment districts?

Held. No. Judgment affirmed.

♦ The claim in *Shaw* was not a vote dilution claim, but an equal protection claim based on allegations that the state has used race as a basis for separating voters into districts. A state may not separate its citizens into different voting districts on the basis of race any more than it may separate them on the basis of race in its parks, buses, golf courses, etc.

♦ *Shaw* does not require that the challenged district be bizarre on its face. Shape is merely circumstantial evidence of intent to use race for its own sake. The state may not apply the stereotype that persons of the same or a particular race share a single political interest.

♦ The distinction between being aware of racial considerations and being motivated by them can be difficult to make, and federal courts must be careful to not improperly intrude upon districting legislation. Thus, a plaintiff has the burden to show that race was the predominant factor motivating the legislature's decision to place a significant number of voters within or without a particular district. This means showing that the traditional race-neutral districting principles such as compactness, contiguity, etc., were subordinated to racial considerations.

♦ The state's claim that it had a compelling interest in complying with the Attorney General's requirements is not acceptable to the extent that the Attorney General required more than is required by the Voting Rights Act. In this case, the Attorney General's objective was to maximize majority-black districts, which is not required by federal law. The Attorney General used the Voting Rights Act to demand the very kind of racial stereotyping forbidden by the Fourteenth Amendment.

Concurrence (O'Connor, J.). This does not call into doubt the vast majority of districts, which are drawn in accordance with customary districting principles, even if race is considered in the process. Only extreme cases of gerrymandering are subject to meaningful judicial review.

Dissent (Ginsburg, Stevens, Souter, Breyer, JJ.). The *Shaw* plan was not a problem because race was a factor, but because nonracial factors were virtually excluded. In this case, race did not overwhelm the other factors. The plan in this case did group people according to ethnicity, but that is a common factor for districting plans. In *Bush* *v. Vera*, 517 U.S. 952 (1996), the Court struck down a Texas redistricting plan after finding that race was the predominant factor in the new district lines. The decision indicated that strict scrutiny does not apply to all cases of intentional creation of majority-minority districts, but it is applicable upon proof that other legitimate districting principles (*e.g.*, compactness) are subordinated to race.

---

e. **Equality in counting votes--**

Bush v. Gore, 531 U.S. 98 (2000).

Facts. Authorities in Florida conducted a machine count and recount of the ballots cast in Florida in the 2000 Florida presidential election. Bush (P) led Gore (D) by fewer than 1,000 votes out of millions cast. Nationally, the race was close enough that the Florida winner would win the election in the electoral college. D sought further manual recounts in selected, heavily Democratic counties. The Florida Supreme Court extended the recount deadline established by the Florida secretary of state, but the United States Supreme Court vacated that order so that the deadline for recounts passed with only one county having completed the recounts. D then contested the election, and the Florida Supreme Court ordered a manual recount of the "undervotes," the ballots for which the machine counts failed to record any presidential choice. This occurred when the voter did not make a full perforation of the punchcard. The Florida Supreme Court's order left it to the discretion of the election officials to determine how to discern the "will of the voter" in cases where the punch stylus had produced "dimples" or hanging "chads" without making a complete perforation. P brought a federal action seeking a stay of the Florida ruling as a violation of the Constitution, which directs that the choice of presidential electors should be determined as the state legislature determines, and as a violation of due process and equal protection because the undefined "will of the voter" standard would produce unjustified disparities. The Supreme Court stayed the recount order on December 9, heard oral argument on December 11, and issued its decision on December 12.

Issue. May a state order a recount of ballots in a presidential election when the only standard to be used is for local officials to discern the "will of the voter" by examining ballots manually?

Held. No. Judgment reversed.

♦ The people have a fundamental right to vote as the legislature has prescribed, and each vote is entitled to equal weight. Equal protection applies not only to the right to vote but also to the manner of exercising that right. The state has an obligation to avoid arbitrary and disparate treatment of the voters.

◆ The recount mechanisms implemented in Florida in response to the state supreme court's orders do not satisfy the minimum requirement for non-arbitrary treatment of voters necessary to secure the fundamental right to vote. The objective of considering the "intent of the voter" is not objectionable as an abstract proposition, but the absence of specific standards to ensure its equal application makes the procedure improper.

◆ Under the Florida Supreme Court's order, the standards for accepting or rejecting contested ballots may vary from county to county, or even within a single county from one recount team to another. The recount procedure did not involve "overvotes" and did not specify who would recount the ballots.

◆ The Florida Supreme Court had power to assure uniformity in the statewide recount, but failed to provide adequate assurances that the rudimentary requirements of equal treatment and fundamental fairness were satisfied.

◆ The Florida Supreme Court also said that the recount had to be completed by December 12, but there is no satisfactory recount procedure in place to allow compliance with that date. Therefore, the recount cannot proceed.

Concurrence (Rehnquist, C.J., Scalia, Thomas, JJ.). The Florida Supreme Court violated Article II of the Constitution by not following the requirements set forth by the Florida legislature.

Dissent (Stevens, Ginsburg, Breyer, JJ.). The Court has previously found equal protection violation when individual votes within the same state were weighted unequally, but has never addressed the standards by which a state determines whether a vote has been legally cast. There is no reason to conclude that the "intent of the voter" standard is any less sufficient than the constitutionally acceptable standards used in courtrooms on a daily basis. Assuming that the Florida Supreme Court and the election officials are impartial, the court's decision does not raise a federal question. P's case is based on a lack of confidence in the impartiality of the state judges. The loser of this year's presidential election is the nation's confidence in the judge as an impartial guardian of the rule of law.

Dissent (Souter, Breyer, JJ.). The case should be remanded to the Florida courts with instructions to establish uniform standards for evaluating the ballots.

Dissent (Ginsburg, Stevens, JJ.). This case arises in an imperfect world in which thousands of votes have not been counted. The recount ordered by the Florida court, flawed as it may be, would not yield a result any less fair or precise than the certification that preceded the recount.

Dissent (Breyer, Stevens, Souter, Ginsburg, JJ.). By halting the manual recount so that uncounted legal votes will not be counted under any standard, the Court has created a remedy out of proportion to the asserted harm. The counties already use different types of voting systems, so voters inherently have an unequal chance that their votes will be counted. The recount order helped to redress this inequity and its deficiencies could easily be remedied.

---

2. **The Right to Travel.**

    a. **Introduction.** A citizen has a constitutional right to travel freely from state to state. State durational residence requirements that would impair this right must be justified by a "compelling" state interest, at least where they affect the citizen's right to receive some vital government benefit or service. However, states may apply a requirement of residency at the time of (and during) receipt of governmental benefits, subject only to the "traditional" test.

    b. **State welfare--**

Shapiro v. Thompson, 394 U.S. 618 (1969).

Facts. The Thompsons (Ps) were denied welfare benefits solely because they had not been residents of Connecticut for one full year prior to filing their applications. Two similar cases were joined before the Supreme Court. In all three instances, the district courts found that the state's denial of benefits to otherwise eligible residents of less than one year constituted an invidious discrimination denying the plaintiffs equal protection of the laws. Shapiro (D), representing Connecticut, appeals.

Issue. May a state create a one-year residency requirement as a condition for receiving state welfare assistance?

Held. No. Judgment affirmed.

♦   D argues that the statute preserves the fiscal integrity of state public assistance programs, which it clearly does, but only by discouraging the influx of poor families needing assistance. However, a state purpose of inhibiting immigration by needy persons is constitutionally impermissible as a burden on the right to travel. Any law that has the sole purpose of chilling the exercise of constitutional rights is invalid. D's argument that the statute intends to discourage immigration of needy people seeking solely to obtain larger benefits does not save it from this constitutional defect, since in such circumstances it still infringes on those persons' right to travel.

♦   States may not withhold welfare benefits from short-term residents who have contributed through taxes any more than they may restrict state services such as fire and police protection to long-term residents.

♦   Because the classification here touches on a fundamental constitutional right, it must be judged under the strict standard of whether it promotes a compelling state interest. D's assertion that other administrative objectives are served by the one-year requirement falls short of satisfying this standard. D claims that the statutes are approved by federal legislation. Even if true, it is the state statutes, by themselves, which must be examined for constitutional defects. Congress cannot authorize the states to deny equal protection.

♦ The state statutes violate the Equal Protection Clause and are therefore invalid.

Dissent (Warren, C.J., Black, J.). Congress has the power both to impose minimal nationwide residence requirements and to authorize the states to do so. Since the states here acted pursuant to congressional authorization, the statutes should be upheld.

Dissent (Harlan, J.). The compelling interest doctrine should be applied only to racial classifications and not to the enlarged list of suspect criteria that includes classifications based on recent interstate movement and perhaps the exercise of any constitutional right. In addition, when a statute affects only matters not mentioned in the Constitution and is not arbitrary or irrational, the Court should not characterize these matters as affecting fundamental rights, thereby giving them the added protection of an unusually stringent equal protection test. Applying the rationality standard, a welfare residence requirement has valid governmental objectives and has advantages not shared by other methods.

Comment. In *McCarthy v. Philadelphia Civil Service Commission*, 424 U.S. 645 (1976), the Court held that requiring personal residence at the place of governmental employment does not violate the right to travel.

---

      c.   **Durational residence requirements for voting.** State residence requirements for voting have been held to violate equal protection because they divide voters into two classes—old and new residents—and discriminate against the latter. [*See* Dunn v. Blumstein, 405 U.S. 330 (1972)—the Court used the burden on the right to travel, as well as the burden on the right to vote, to invalidate such state residence requirements] However, the Court has recognized the need for some registration requirements, and upheld a 50-day residency and registration requirement where necessary to prepare voters' lists, etc. [*See* Marston v. Lewis, 410 U.S. 679 (1973)]

      d.   **Duration of residency and distribution of state resources--**

Zobel v. Williams, 457 U.S. 55 (1982).

Facts. Alaska enacted a statute by which dividends from the state's permanent fund derived from mineral royalties would be distributed to the state's adult residents depending on how long they were residents of the state. Each resident would receive one dividend unit for each year of residency. Zobel (P), a relatively recent Alaska resident, challenged the statute on equal protection grounds. The Alaska courts upheld the plan. P appeals.

Issue. May a state distribute income derived from its natural resources to the citizens of the state in amounts depending on the length of the individual citizen's residency?

Held. No. Judgment reversed.

♦ The Equal Protection Clause applies whenever a state distributes benefits unequally. The asserted state purposes here are:

(i) A financial incentive for citizens to maintain residence in Alaska;

(ii) Incentive for prudent management of the fund; and

(iii) Recognition of the contributions made by citizens over the years.

♦ The first two purposes are not rationally related to the distinctions made. The third is not a legitimate state purpose. Governmental services and benefits may not be apportioned according to past taxes or other contributions of the citizens involved, nor may a state favor established residents over new residents. Therefore, the statute denies equal protection.

Concurrence (Brennan, Marshall, Blackmun, Powell, JJ.). Distinctions must be based on relevant characteristics. Length of residence does not necessarily reflect the value of contributions made to the state.

Concurrence (O'Connor, J.). A state may recognize the past contributions of its citizens. However, it must comply with the protections of the Privileges and Immunities Clause.

Dissent (Rehnquist, J.). As this is essentially economic regulation, the proper analysis is the rational basis approach. This scheme has a rational basis; the state is merely recognizing the contributions made by its residents.

_____

e.   **Reconsideration of** *Shapiro*--

Saenz v. Roe, 526 U.S. 489 (1999).

Facts. In response to high welfare benefit payments, California began limiting welfare benefits, for the first 12 months of a new citizen's residency in the state, to the level received by the individual in his previous state of residence. This change was apparently permitted by Congress in a statute titled Temporary Assistance to Needy Families ("TANF"). Roe and others (Ps) challenged the California statute. The lower courts held the California statute unconstitutional. The Supreme Court granted certiorari.

Issue. May a state limit the welfare benefits of a new citizen to the amount the new citizen would have received in his previous state of residency?

Held. No. Judgment affirmed.

♦ D claims that unlike the law in *Shapiro, supra,* the California statute here does not penalize the right of travel because new arrivals are not ineligible for benefits.

♦ The right to travel includes at least three components:

    (i)   The right to enter and leave another state;

    (ii)   The right to be treated as a welcome visitor; and

    (iii)   The right to elect to become a permanent resident and to be treated like other citizens of the new state.

♦ The statute in this case does not directly impair the right to free interstate movement. As for visitor status, there are some situations in which a noncitizen may be treated differently from a citizen, such as in tuition fees for a state university. But this case involves the third aspect of the right to travel, since Ps became residents of the state.

♦ The Privileges and Immunities Clause of the Fourteenth Amendment protects the third element of the right to travel. Under that clause, a United States citizen can become a citizen of any state by a bona fide residence therein, with the same rights as other citizens of that state. The right to travel includes the citizen's right to be treated equally in the new state of residence, so the discriminatory classification is itself a penalty. The Citizenship Clause expressly equates citizenship with residence and does not allow for degrees of citizenship based on length of residence. California has created a hierarchy of subclasses based on the original state from which the immigrants came. Yet neither the duration of Ps' California residence, nor the identity of their prior states of residence, has any relevance to their need for benefits.

♦ D claims that the statute will save the state approximately $11 million per year, but the state's legitimate interest in saving money does not justify discrimination among equally eligible citizens.

♦ The fact that Congress approved the durational residence requirements is not sufficient to make the law valid because Congress cannot authorize the states to violate the Fourteenth Amendment.

Dissent (Rehnquist, C.J., Thomas, J.). The right to travel is distinct from the right to become a citizen. In fact, Ps had to stop traveling to become citizens of California. The Court has confused the right to travel with the right to enjoy the privileges of citizenship. The Court has ignored the state's need to assure that only persons who establish a bona fide residence receive the benefits provided to current residents of the state. States cannot determine an individual's subjective intent, so the Court has allowed states to impose durational residence requirements to test intention. States can impose a residence requirement prior to granting the right to educational benefits, the right to terminate a marriage, or the right to vote in primary elections, and they should be able to do the same for welfare benefits.

Dissent (Thomas, J., Rehnquist, C.J.). The Court's reliance on the Privileges and Immunities Clause is surprising because that clause had been drained of meaning by the *Slaughter-House Cases*. The Court should consider how the clause relates to equal protection and substantive due process.

---

3. **Access to the Courts.**

    a. **Administration of criminal justice.** The Court has shown sensitivity to burdens placed on the access of litigants, particularly criminal defendants, to the courts. Both procedural due process and equal protection have been invoked for analysis.

        1) **Right to a record on appeal.** In *Griffin v. Illinois*, 351 U.S. 12 (1956), the Supreme Court relied on equal protection to hold that in a state prosecution where no appeal was possible without a transcript from the trial court, the state must provide indigent defendants a free transcript in all felony criminal cases. The rationale is that in criminal prosecutions (where the defendant is involuntarily involved), matters of "justice" are charged with too much social interest to be decided on the basis of some defendants being poor and others being rich. The dissent argued that due process did not require this result, since there is no constitutional right to an appeal, and equal protection was not applicable because the state was treating everyone in the same manner.

        2) **Right to counsel on appeal--**

Douglas v. California, 372 U.S. 353 (1963).

Facts. California (P) permitted one appeal as of right. Douglas (D), an indigent who had been convicted, sought appointed counsel to represent him in his appeal. The appellate court, after reviewing the transcript and determining that it would assist neither

D nor the court to have counsel appointed, denied D's request. The Supreme Court granted certiorari.

Issue. Must a state provide counsel for indigent criminal defendants to pursue an initial appeal?

Held. Yes. Judgment reversed.

♦ Denial of counsel in this situation is the same kind of invidious discrimination against indigents as was involved in *Griffin*.

♦ While absolute equality between rich and poor may not be required, the merits of the one and only appeal to which a person is entitled are too important to allow a decision without benefit of counsel just because the appellant is indigent.

Dissent (Harlan, Stewart, JJ.). Equal protection does not impose on the states an affirmative duty to lift the handicaps flowing from differences in economic circumstances. The only relevant constitutional provision is due process, and the state's rules are not so arbitrary or unreasonable that they deny due process.

Comment. In *Ross v. Moffit*, 417 U.S. 600 (1974), the Court refused to extend the *Douglas* approach to discretionary appeals.

———————

b. Civil litigation. In many of the cases dealing with civil litigation there is disagreement as to whether due process or equal protection should apply.

1) **Divorce fee.** In *Boddie v. Connecticut*, 401 U.S. 371 (1971), the Court used the Due Process Clause to hold that states may not require indigents to pay court fees as a condition for judicial dissolution of marriage. The Court limited the scope of the decision by noting (i) the basic position of the "marriage relationship" in society and (ii) the "state monopolization of the means for legally dissolving this relationship." It reasoned that due process requires that "absent a countervailing state interest of overriding significance, persons forced to settle their claims . . . through the judicial process must be given a meaningful opportunity to be heard."

2) **Bankruptcy.** The Court has given *Boddie* a narrow construction in other contexts. In *United States v. Kras*, 409 U.S. 434 (1973), the Court held that the Bankruptcy Act filing fee requirement as a condition for discharge is "rational" and does not violate equal protection as applied to indigent persons who seek voluntary bank-

ruptcy. The right to bankruptcy is not a "fundamental" interest but is in the "area of economics and social welfare."

3) Termination of parental rights--

M.L.B. v. S.L.J., 519 U.S. 102 (1996).

Facts. The state of Mississippi granted S.L.J.'s (P's) petition to have the parental rights of M.L.B. (D) terminated as to their two children. D filed an appeal, but was unable to pay the required transcript fees. The state supreme court denied her application to appeal in forma pauperis, and the United States Supreme Court granted certiorari.

Issue. May a state preclude a person from appealing a decree terminating parental rights solely because the person cannot pay the fees for preparing a transcript?

Held. No. Judgment reversed and remanded.

♦ There is a narrow category of civil cases in which a state must provide access to judicial process without regard to a party's ability to pay fees. A family association "of basic importance in our society" is at stake here. The termination order describes no evidence as to why D is unfit. Only a transcript can reveal the sufficiency or insufficiency of the evidence.

♦ Ordinarily a state's need for revenue to offset costs justifies fee requirements for transcripts. However, there are exceptions to this rule, such as when a proceeding is criminal or quasi-criminal in nature. Decrees that forever terminate parental rights are among the most severe forms of state action. In contrast to a loss of custody, the termination of parental rights is irreversible. Thus we place such decrees in the category of cases in which the state may not "bolt the door to equal justice."

Dissent (Thomas, J., Rehnquist, C.J., Scalia, J.). I would overrule *Griffin*, or at least not extend it to civil cases.

---

4. **Welfare.**

    a. **Introduction.** The Court has limited the fundamental rights approach by refusing to extend it to certain areas. Certain opinions written by the Warren Court indicated that classifications based on wealth might be suspect, and hence that there may be a fundamental right to economic benefits. Since then, the Court has held that there is no constitutional right to receive public welfare. Welfare classifications are subject only to the traditional equal protection test, unless they affect a "fundamental" right other than mere receipt of public assistance.

b.   Family size and public assistance--

Dandridge v. Williams, 397 U.S. 471 (1970).

Facts. Maryland imposed an upper limit of $250 per month per family for federal aid to families with dependent children ("AFDC"). Williams (P) challenged the statute as denying equal protection since large families received less aid per child than small families. The lower court held the statute invalid. Dandridge (D) appeals.

Issue. Does imposition of a ceiling on welfare benefits deny equal protection to large families, which receive less assistance per family member than do smaller families?

Held. No. Judgment reversed.

♦   No fundamental right is at stake here. In areas of economics and social welfare, a state does not deny equal protection merely because the classifications made by its laws are unequal.

♦   The Fourteenth Amendment does not grant federal courts power to set economic or social policy on the states. It is enough that the state's action be rationally based and free from invidious discrimination. This statute, intended to encourage gainful employment, meets that test.

Dissent (Marshall, Brennan, JJ.). A state may not, in the provision of important services or the distribution of governmental payments, supply benefits to some individuals while denying them to others who are similarly situated. This case illustrates the impropriety of the abstract dichotomy between the "traditional test" and the "strict scrutiny test." The Court equates the interest of these needy children with the interests of utilities and other corporations by classifying their interests as "economic."

---

c.   Housing. The right to housing is not guaranteed by the Constitution. State classifications in housing laws are subject only to the traditional test of reasonableness. Thus, a state may permit landlords to bring summary actions to evict tenants from rented premises, but cannot require posting of a bond for twice the amount of rent in order to appeal. [Lindsey v. Normet, 405 U.S. 56 (1972)]

5.   Education. Because there is no constitutional right to education, regulation of education is judged only by the traditional (rational basis) test.

a.   State spending for education--

San Antonio Independent School District v. Rodriguez, 411 U.S. 1 (1973).

Facts. Rodriguez (P), a Mexican-American, challenged the Texas system of financing public education. The system involved a combination of state, local, and federal funding, and was operated so that state and local expenditures per pupil varied according to the market value of taxable property per pupil within the various districts. P claimed that the system denied equal protection by invidiously discriminating against the poor. The district court found the system unconstitutional. The San Antonio Independent School District (D) appeals.

Issue. Is a state system of financing public education that closely correlates spending per pupil and the value of local taxable property subject to strict judicial scrutiny?

Held. No. Judgment reversed.

♦ D's system might be regarded as discriminating against functionally indigent persons, persons relatively poorer than others, or all who, regardless of their personal incomes, happen to reside in relatively poorer school districts. However, there is no evidence to support a finding that any persons in the first two groups are discriminated against, and the third group clearly cannot fit the traditional definition of a suspect class.

♦ Although the system does not operate to the peculiar disadvantage of any suspect class, strict review is still required where the state's action impermissibly interferes with the exercise of a "fundamental" right, which P claims includes education. Although education is an important state service, that importance is not determinative of equal protection examination. Only those rights explicitly or implicitly guaranteed by the Constitution are "fundamental" for purposes of equal protection.

♦ Education is neither explicitly nor implicitly guaranteed. Additionally, D's system was implemented to extend public education, not to interfere with any rights. Finally, courts should not interfere with state fiscal policies unless necessary. Therefore, D's system is not subject to strict judicial scrutiny.

Dissent (Brennan, J.). This scheme is devoid of any rational basis. Also, I disagree that a right may be deemed "fundamental" only if it is "explicitly or implicitly guaranteed by the Constitution."

Dissent (White, Douglas, Brennan, JJ.). The Court merely requires D to establish that unequal treatment is in furtherance of a permissible goal, but it should also require D to show that the means chosen to effectuate that goal are rationally related to its achievement.

Dissent (Marshall, Douglas, JJ.). The Court appears to find only two standards of equal protection review—strict scrutiny or mere rationality. In reality, there is a wide spectrum of review, depending on the constitutional and societal importance of the interest adversely affected and the recognized invidiousness of the classification. The amount of review accorded to nonconstitutional rights or interests varies according to the nexus between those rights and specific constitutional guarantees. Discrimination on the basis of group wealth in this case calls for careful judicial scrutiny.

---

b. Education of children of illegal aliens--

Plyler v. Doe, 457 U.S. 202 (1982).

Facts. Texas enacted a statute that withheld state funds for the education of illegal alien children and that allowed local school districts to deny enrollment to such children. Doe (P) challenged the constitutionality of the statute. The lower courts found the law unconstitutional. Plyler (D) appeals.

Issue. May a state deny the free public education to undocumented school-age children that it provides to citizens and legally admitted aliens?

Held. No. Judgment affirmed.

♦ The Fourteenth Amendment guarantees equal protection and due process to "any person within [a state's] jurisdiction." Even illegal aliens are entitled to this protection.

♦ Equal protection analysis does not require that illegal aliens be treated as a suspect class just because their illegal presence is not a constitutional irrelevancy. Education is not a fundamental right, although it is more than a mere government benefit. However, this case presents another consideration. The statute imposes a lifetime stigma on children who are not accountable for their disabling status. Therefore, the discrimination cannot be allowed unless it fulfills a substantial state purpose.

♦ Although national policy does not support unrestricted immigration, no policy exists that would deny these children an elementary education. The state interests—protection against excessive illegal immigration, avoidance of the special burden of educating such children, and the likelihood that the children will not remain in the state—are not furthered by the means chosen, even assuming the policies are legitimate. Because no showing of furthering a state interest was made, the statutory discrimination is unconstitutional.

Concurrence (Blackmun, J.). I believe *Rodriguez* uses the correct approach. A complete denial of education involves the state in the creation of permanent class distinctions, and thus strikes at the heart of equal protection.

Concurrence (Powell, J.). The children discriminated against here are innocent with respect to their status. The legislative classification threatens the creation of an underclass of future residents. Therefore, the state must show a fair and substantial relation to substantial interests. This D has failed to do.

Dissent (Burger, C.J., White, Rehnquist, O'Connor, JJ.). Although it is foolish and wrong to create an illiterate segment of society in the manner at issue here, the courts were never intended to set policy. The only issue here is whether Texas has a legitimate reason to distinguish between legal and illegal residents. The state purpose of preserving its limited resources for school financing is rationally related to the legislative classification. The majority admits that traditional equal protection analysis does not require a different result. Instead, the majority decided what the best result should be and then created an analysis to reach that result.

----

6. **Medical Care: Abortions.** The equal protection aspects of the right to an abortion were discussed in *Maher v. Roe, supra*, which held that a state practice of giving Medicaid for childbirth but not for nontherapeutic abortions did not violate equal protection.

XI. THE CONCEPT OF STATE ACTION

A. INTRODUCTION TO THE STATE ACTION DOCTRINE

1. **Basic Issue.** Both the Fourteenth and Fifteenth Amendments prohibit certain "state action" as opposed to private, nongovernmental action. The determinative question is whether any particular conduct is state action. The response to that question has changed over the years. Early cases held that these amendments did not apply to private acts of discrimination. Distinguishing between public and private conduct became increasingly difficult as the government became more intimately involved in regulating and even participating in the private sector, as will be seen in the more modern cases.

2. **Approach of the Nineteenth Century--**

The Civil Rights Cases, 109 U.S. 3 (1883).

Facts. The Civil Rights Act of 1875 made it unlawful for anyone to deny a person the enjoyment of accommodations at inns, on public transportation, etc., on the basis of race. Certain black persons (Ps) were excluded from inns, theaters, and a railroad in five separate states. The cases were consolidated before the Supreme Court.

Issue. May Congress prohibit private discriminatory actions by facilities generally open to the public?

Held. No. The Civil Rights Act is unconstitutional.

♦ The Fourteenth Amendment permits Congress to take corrective action only against state laws or acts done under state authority. The Civil Rights Act is directed toward acts by individuals and cannot be upheld under the Fourteenth Amendment.

♦ The Thirteenth Amendment permits direct as opposed to merely corrective legislation, but it only covers slavery or involuntary servitude, or the lingering badges of such. Refusing accommodation to a black person does not impose any badge of slavery or servitude. Mere racial discrimination is not a badge of slavery.

♦ Congress has no power to pass the Civil Rights Act, and Ps must seek a remedy under state law for any cause of action against private individuals or corporations that are discriminating.

Dissent (Harlan, J.). The Court has ignored the substance and spirit of these amendments. Freedom includes immunity from and protection against racial discrimination, particularly in the use of public, albeit privately owned, accommodations and facilities licensed by the state.

Comment. The common law of all states at the time of the Civil Rights Act of 1875 held that it was unlawful to deny facilities, such as inns and carriers, to any person. Therefore, Ps did have a remedy in state law. However, this case illustrates the approach to state action that permitted individuals to discriminate freely if they wanted to.

———

B. GOVERNMENT FUNCTION

1. **Introduction.** Some activity undertaken by private individuals or organizations replaces traditionally exclusive prerogatives of the state. In these situations, the private activity may be treated as state action on the grounds that it is a public or governmental function.

2. **The Conduct of Elections.** In a series of cases called the *White Primary Cases*, the Court has held that the conduct of elections is an exclusively public function. Therefore, state attempts to vest in private boards or political parties any effective control over the selection of candidates or the exercise of voting rights are not valid. The Court has invalidated such state action as:

    a. Giving authority to a political party to determine who can vote in primary elections from which the party nominee for the general election is chosen [Smith v. Allwright, 321 U.S. 649 (1944)]; and

    b. Structuring the state's electoral apparatus to vest in a political party the power to hold a primary from which black persons are excluded, or to determine who shall run in the party primary in which black persons are permitted to participate [*see* Terry v. Adams, 345 U.S. 461 (1953)].

3. **Private Company Towns.** In *Marsh v. Alabama*, 326 U.S. 501 (1946), a private corporation owned a town and posted signs prohibiting peddlers. Marsh, a Jehovah's Witness, distributed religious literature on the streets of the company town and was convicted of violating a state trespass law that made it a crime "to enter or remain on the premises of another" after being warned not to do so. The conviction was reversed because the town's streets, although privately owned, were in effect a public place. The Court held that neither the state nor any private owner can totally ban freedom of expression in public places; nor can state trespass laws be applied to enforce such a ban. Ownership does not "always mean absolute dominion. The more an owner opens up his property for use by the public in general, the more do his rights become circumscribed by the statutory and constitutional rights of those who

use it." This case shows that state action includes not only any action taken directly by the state executive, legislative, or judicial branches, but also any such action taken indirectly by delegating public functions to private organizations or by controlling, affirming, or to some extent becoming involved in that private action.

4. **Shopping Centers.** The Court has held that the "company town" rationale of *Marsh v. Alabama,* above, does not extend to the passageways in a privately owned shopping center. [Hudgens v. NLRB, 424 U.S. 507 (1976), *overruling* Amalgamated Food Employees Union v. Logan Valley Plaza, 391 U.S. 308 (1968)]

5. **Public Parks--**

Evans v. Newton, 382 U.S. 296 (1966).

Facts. In 1911, United States Senator Bacon had willed a tract of land to the city of Macon, Georgia, for use as a park for white persons only. Eventually, the city permitted black persons to use it, and Newton (P) and other park managers sued to have the city removed as trustee. Evans (D) and other black citizens intervened. The city resigned as trustee, and the state courts approved the appointment of new trustees who pursued the segregation policy. D appeals.

Issue. May private property that assumes a public character be used to promote racial segregation?

Held. No. Judgment reversed.

♦ The reach of the Fourteenth Amendment can be determined only by sifting facts and weighing circumstances. This park originated as a private grant of private property, but it gradually acquired character as a public facility when it was maintained by the city.

♦ Once the tradition of municipal control had become firmly established, mere substitution of trustees cannot instantly transfer the park from the public to the private sector. This is particularly true where, as here, the property provides a service that is essentially municipal in character. Therefore, the park must comply with Fourteenth Amendment mandates regardless of who has title under state law.

Dissent (Harlan, Stewart, JJ.). Private parks should be treated like private schools. Both serve an important public purpose and there is a tradition of public control in both areas. Private schools can limit admission to certain people and there are alternative schools available for others.

---

6.   Business Regulation--

Jackson v. Metropolitan Edison Co., 419 U.S. 345 (1974).

Facts. Metropolitan Edison Company (D), a state regulated private utility, terminated Jackson's (P's) electric service for nonpayment before affording P notice, hearing, and an opportunity to pay. P sued, contending that D's action constituted state action depriving her of property without due process of law. The lower courts dismissed P's complaint. P appeals.

Issue. Does termination of service by a heavily regulated private utility, using procedures permitted by state law, constitute state action?

Held. No. Judgment affirmed.

♦   State regulation of a private business, even if extensive and detailed, does not by itself convert private action into state action for Fourteenth Amendment purposes. There must be a close nexus between the state and the actual activity of the regulated entity. D's monopoly status, by itself, fails to show such a nexus. Nor is D's service a public function, since the state has no obligation to furnish such service. The limited notion that businesses "affected with a public interest" are state actors cannot be expanded to include private utilities.

♦   The state concededly approved D's termination procedures, but not upon consideration of a specific case. The state's approval amounts merely to a finding that the procedures are permissible under state law. For these reasons, D's actions cannot be considered to be state actions.

Dissent (Marshall, J.). The essential nature of D's service requires that D be subject to the same standards as other governmental entities. The interests of diversity and flexibility that favor protection of private entities from constitutional standards are irrelevant in monopoly situations like D's. Finally, the majority's opinion would appear to apply to a broad range of claimed constitutional violations by the company, including racial discrimination.

C. STATE INVOLVEMENT OR ENCOURAGEMENT

1.   **Introduction.** Private activity may also be treated as state action when the government requires, significantly encourages, or profits from the activity. This does not mean that the government's mere failure to forbid private discrimination is a constitutional violation, but if the government is closely involved in private discrimination in some way, the private discrimination is state action.

2. Enforcement of Private Contracts--

Shelley v. Kraemer, 334 U.S. 1 (1948).

Facts. Shelley (D), a black person, purchased residential property that, unknown to D, was encumbered by a restrictive agreement that prevented ownership or occupancy of the property by non-Caucasians. Kraemer (P), a neighbor and owner of other property subject to the restriction, brought suit to restrain D from possessing the property and to divest title out of D. The trial court denied relief, but the Missouri Supreme Court reversed. D appeals.

Issue. Does the Fourteenth Amendment Equal Protection Clause prohibit judicial enforcement by state courts of restrictive covenants based on race or color?

Held. Yes. Judgment reversed.

♦ Property rights clearly are among those civil rights protected from discriminatory state action by the Fourteenth Amendment. Early decisions invalidated any government restrictions on residency based on race. Here, the restrictions are purely private and, standing alone, are not precluded by the Fourteenth Amendment.

♦ Actions of state courts are state actions within the meaning of the Fourteenth Amendment. Judicial enforcement of these private racial restrictions constitutes state discrimination contrary to the Fourteenth Amendment, and denies D equal protection.

Comment. *Shelley* and other cases indicate that what is essentially a private act of discrimination may become illegal state action if the state or its officers are in any way involved in carrying out the private action. Possibly any private action that gets into court may then amount to state action.

---

3. Additional Cases.

a. **Civil damages.** In *Barrows v. Jackson*, 346 U.S. 249 (1953), a case involving a damages action against a co-covenantor, the Court applied the *Shelley, supra*, reasoning to block enforcement of the restrictive covenant. The Court stated that it would not require a state to coerce a covenantor to respond in damages for failure to observe a covenant that the state would have no right to enforce.

b. **Will provisions.** In *Evans v. Abney*, 396 U.S. 435 (1970), the Court affirmed the Georgia courts' decisions that Senator Bacon's will (involved in *Evans v. Newton, supra*) required reversion to his heirs because the terms could not be amended to strike the racial restrictions. The dissent felt that, contrary to *Shelley*, this action constituted court enforcement of a racial restriction to prevent willing parties from dealing with one another.

c. **Trespass.** In a three-to-three decision rendered in a case involving a restaurant sit-in, the Court reversed a trespass conviction on the basis of *Shelley*. The Court stated that the discrimination was done for business reasons and the property was associated with serving the public. The dissent, construing Section 1 of the Fourteenth Amendment more narrowly, argued that without cooperative state action, no property owner was forbidden from banning people from his premises, even if the owner was acting with racial prejudice. [Bell v. Maryland, 378 U.S. 226 (1964)]

4. **State Authorization of Discrimination--**

Reitman v. Mulkey, 387 U.S. 369 (1967).

Facts. Reitman (D) refused to rent to Mulkey (P), who was black, solely because of P's race. P sued for an injunction and damages under the California Civil Code. D claimed those provisions were null and void as a result of adoption of a state constitutional provision that assured persons of the right to decline to rent residential property to any person, based on personal discretion. The trial court granted D summary judgment, but the state supreme court reversed, finding the state constitutional provision violative of the Fourteenth Amendment. D appeals.

Issue. Does a state constitutional provision that mandates state neutrality in private residential discrimination matters deny due process?

Held. Yes. Judgment affirmed.

♦ The California Supreme Court determined that the immediate design and intent of the state constitutional provision was to repeal state laws preventing private discrimination and that the provision invalidly involved the state in racial discrimination in the housing market by effectively encouraging discrimination.

♦ The right to discriminate, by being included in the state constitution, would be a basic state policy. The California Supreme Court's decision that this violates the Fourteenth Amendment is correct.

Dissent (Harlan, Black, Clark, Stewart, JJ.). The provision merely assures state neutrality on the issue, and no more violates the Fourteenth Amendment than failure to pass antidiscrimination statutes in the first place would have. The California court made conclusions of law, not findings of fact, and its decision does not merit the high degree of deference accorded by the majority. The decision will hamper efforts in other states to enact what must now appear to be unrepealable antidiscrimination statutes.

5.   State Licensing--

Moose Lodge v. Irvis, 407 U.S. 163 (1972).

Facts. Irvis (P), a black person, was refused service by Moose Lodge No. 107 (D). P claimed that D's action was a state action because D was licensed by the state liquor board to sell alcoholic beverages. A three-judge district court held for P on the merits. D appeals.

Issue. Does state alcoholic licensing of a private club constitute sufficient state action to require that the club observe Fourteenth Amendment prohibitions against discrimination?

Held. No. Judgment reversed.

♦   A private entity is not covered by the Fourteenth Amendment when it merely receives any sort of benefit or service at all from the state, or if subject to any state regulation. Otherwise, the distinction between private and public would be meaningless. If the impetus for the discrimination is private, state involvement must be significant to implicate constitutional standards.

♦   Here, the state's liquor regulation in no way fostered or encouraged racial discrimination. However, those regulations did require that licensed clubs must adhere to their own constitutions and bylaws. States may not use sanctions to enforce segregative rules, and P is entitled to an injunction against the enforcement of the state regulation that would require D to enforce its own discriminatory rules.

Dissent (Douglas, Marshall, JJ.). The state's licensing scheme includes a complex quota system. The quota in D's area has been full for many years; no more club licenses may be issued in the city. Since private clubs are the only places that serve liquor for significant portions of each week, the state has restricted access by black persons to liquor by granting a license to D instead of to a nondiscriminatory club.

Dissent (Brennan, Marshall, JJ.). The state has become an active participant in the operation of D's bar through its detailed regulatory scheme, and D should be required to observe Fourteenth Amendment standards.

6. **Private Use of Government Property.** In *Burton v. Wilmington Parking Authority*, 365 U.S. 715 (1961), the Court held that a private lessee of state property is required to comply with the Fourteenth Amendment if the lease furthers state interests and forms an integral part of a state operation. In that case, Burton, a black person, was denied service at a private restaurant, the Eagle, located within a building owned and operated by the Wilmington Parking Authority, a state agency. In *Norwood v. Harrison*, 413 U.S. 455 (1973), the Court held that a state may not lend textbooks to students in racially segregated private schools because this would constitute state support for discrimination. The Court remanded *Gilmore v. Montgomery*, 417 U.S. 556 (1974), an action involving a federal injunction barring a city from permitting private segregated school groups and racially discriminatory nonschool groups from using its recreational facilities. The Court held that although exclusive temporary use interfered with a school desegregation order, the lower court's ruling against nonexclusive use by the groups, especially the private nonschool groups, was invalid without a proper finding of state action.

D. LATER DEVELOPMENTS

1. Publicly Funded Private School--

Rendell-Baker v. Kohn, 457 U.S. 830 (1982).

Facts. Rendell-Baker was a vocational counselor at a private school that specialized in assisting students who could not complete public high school. The school was funded primarily by the state and was subject to various state administrative regulations, including mandatory written job descriptions and personnel standards and procedures. The state used the school to fulfill a statutory requirement to assist students needing special help. Rendell-Baker and five teachers (Ps) were discharged by the school for supporting certain student grievances regarding school policies. Ps sued under 42 U.S.C. section 1983. The lower courts denied relief. The Supreme Court granted certiorari.

Issue. Does action taken by a private school used by the state to fulfill a legislative requirement constitute state action?

Held. No. Judgment affirmed.

- ◆ Under *Blum v. Yaretsky*, 457 U.S. 991 (1982), actions by a private facility may be considered state action depending on four factors: source of funding, extent of government regulation, exclusivity of the government function, and existence of a symbiotic relationship.

- ◆ The fact that the school depended on government funds to operate is not determinative, for all private contractors that perform government contracts depend on public funds.

- The school was subject to government regulation in some areas, but its decision to discharge Ps was not compelled or even influenced by state regulation. Even though a government committee approved hirees, the decision to discharge Ps was made solely by private management.

- Operation of a school is not an exclusive public function. Service to the public interest does not render private activity state action. Nor is there a symbiotic relationship because the government does not profit from the school's activity any more than it does from any contractor's performance of a public contract.

Dissent (Marshall, Brennan, JJ.). The school's very survival depends on the state, and the state depends on the school to perform its statutory duty. A closer relationship between government and private enterprise is difficult to imagine.

2. **Warehouseman's Lien--**

Flagg Brothers, Inc. v. Brooks, 436 U.S. 149 (1978).

Facts. Brooks (P) was evicted and her possessions stored by Flagg Brothers, Inc. (D). When P failed to pay storage charges, D threatened to sell P's possessions, pursuant to procedures established by the New York Uniform Commercial Code ("U.C.C."). P brought an action seeking damages, an injunction, and declaratory relief that the U.C.C. provision was unconstitutional. The district court dismissed the complaint, but the court of appeals reversed, finding state involvement in D's action sufficient to invoke constitutional protections. D appeals.

Issue. Does a warehouseman's sale of goods entrusted to him for storage constitute state action because it is permitted by state law?

Held. No. Judgment reversed.

- P claims that the state delegated to D a power traditionally held only by the state. While many functions have been traditionally performed by governments, very few have been exclusively reserved to the states. The settlement of disputes between debtors and creditors is not a traditionally exclusive public function, so D's action is not state action.

- P also claims that D's action is state action because the state has authorized and encouraged it by enacting the U.C.C. While private action compelled by a state is properly attributable to the state, mere acquiescence by the state is insufficient. The state here has merely refused to provide P a remedy for D's private deprivation of P's property. Therefore, D's action is not state action.

Dissent (Stevens, White, Marshall, JJ.). The question is whether a state statute that authorizes a private party to deprive a person of her property without her consent must satisfy due process requirements. Clearly, it should. Permitting only state delegation of exclusively sovereign functions to bring private actions within constitutional bounds is inconsistent with prior decisions. P should be permitted to challenge the state procedure permitted by state law.

---

3. **Government's Failure to Act--**

DeShaney v. Winnebago Department of Social Services, 489 U.S. 189 (1989).

Facts. DeShaney (P), a two-year-old child, had been the victim of child abuse by his father. The incidents were reported to the Winnebago Department of Social Services (D), which investigated but took no action. One year later, after P was treated at a hospital for further abuse, D required P's father to undergo counseling and to have his girlfriend move out, but the father never fully complied with these requirements. During the next year, D's caseworker recorded additional incidents of abuse, but took no action. P's father finally beat P so badly that he suffered permanent brain damage. P sued D, claiming D had deprived him of his liberty without due process of law. The lower courts granted judgment for D. The Supreme Court granted certiorari.

Issue. May the government's failure to protect a child from his parent's abuse constitute a violation of substantive due process?

Held. No. Judgment affirmed.

♦   Nothing in the Due Process Clause requires the state to protect the life, liberty, and property of citizens against invasion by private actors. The clause protects people from the state; it does not require the state to protect citizens from each other.

♦   The Due Process Clause does not confer an affirmative right to governmental aid, even when necessary to secure life, liberty, or property interests. Because the clause does not impose such an obligation, the state cannot be held liable under the clause for injuries that could have been avoided had the state assumed the obligation. There is no special relationship between P and D that arose merely because D knew P was in danger. If any such relationship is desired, the people may, through their legislatures, adopt a tort law remedy.

Dissent (Brennan, Marshall, Blackmun, JJ.). D in effect cut off private sources of help by preempting them. When D refused to help itself, it should not be permitted to avoid responsibility for the harm that resulted from its refusal.

Dissent (Blackmun, J.). I would adopt a "sympathetic" reading of our Fourteenth Amendment precedents, one that comports with the dictates of fundamental justice.

———

XII. CONGRESSIONAL ENFORCE-MENT OF CIVIL RIGHTS

A. INTRODUCTION

Each of the Civil War Amendments prohibits specified conduct even without any legislation. But each amendment also gives Congress authority to enforce its provisions by "appropriate" legislation. This allows Congress to remedy state discrimination it deems unconstitutional even if the Supreme Court would not have found the state action unconstitutional. The scope of this authority, particularly when used to revise judicial constitutional interpretation, remains controversial.

1. **Statutes.** Beginning with the Civil Rights Act of 1866, Congress has enacted civil and criminal statutes aimed at preventing private interference with constitutional rights. 42 U.S.C. sections 1981 and 1982 provide for equal rights to all citizens. The other basic statutes that prohibit deprivation of civil rights may be kept straight by referring to the following table:

Deprivation through:	Criminal sanctions	Civil sanctions
Color of law	18 U.S.C. §242	42 U.S.C.§1983
Conspiracy	18 U.S.C. §241	42 U.S.C. §1985(c)

2. **Case Law.** The Court has held that although the Fourteenth and Fifteenth Amendments only bar state action, Congress can protect against violation of personal constitutional and statutory rights by private action, as it did in 18 U.S.C. section 241. These include the right to vote, assemble, and travel. [United States v. Williams, 341 U.S. 70 (1951)] 18 U.S.C. section 242 is not impermissibly vague because it requires proof of a purpose to deprive a person of a specific constitutional right. [Screws v. United States, 325 U.S. 91 (1945)]

B. REGULATION OF PRIVATE PERSONS

1. **Private Conduct Under the Thirteenth Amendment--**

Jones v. Alfred H. Mayer Co., 392 U.S. 409 (1968).

Facts. Alfred H. Mayer Company (D) refused to sell a home to Jones (P), solely because P was black. P sued for injunctive and other relief under 42 U.S.C. section 1982. The lower courts dismissed P's complaint, concluding that section 1982 applies only to state action and does not reach private refusals to sell. P appeals.

Issue. Does the authority of Congress to enforce the Thirteenth Amendment "by appropriate legislation" include the power to eliminate all racial barriers, including private actions, to the acquisition of real and personal property?

Held. Yes. Judgment reversed.

♦　　The plain language of section 1982 appears to prohibit all discrimination, private and public, against black persons in the sale or rental of property.

♦　　The Thirteenth Amendment authorizes Congress to enact appropriate legislation to abolish all badges and incidents of slavery, and such laws may operate upon the unofficial acts of private individuals. Congress has determined that free exercise of property rights is essential to abolition of all badges and incidents of slavery. Therefore, section 1982 may properly act upon conduct of private individuals such as D.

♦　　Were Congress denied the power to enforce the Thirteenth Amendment to this extent, that amendment would constitute a promise that the nation could not keep.

Dissent (Harlan, White, JJ.). This case is unimportant in light of the recently passed Fair Housing Act, and the Court should have dismissed P's writ as improvidently granted.

―――――――

C.　REGULATION OF STATE ACTORS

1.　**The Right to Vote.** The right to vote for federal, state, and local officials is protected by the Fifteenth and Nineteenth Amendments. The Twenty-Fourth Amendment protects the right to vote in federal elections free from poll or other taxes imposed by either state or federal governments. Section 2 of the Fifteenth Amendment provides that "Congress shall have power to enforce this article by appropriate legislation." Thus, Congress was to be chiefly responsible for implementing the rights created in Section 1. The question in several cases was whether this power is remedial or substantive; *i.e.,* is Congress limited to remedying what the Court finds unconstitutional, or may it remedy what it itself deems unconstitutional?

2.　**Constitutionality of the Voting Rights Act of 1965--**

South Carolina v. Katzenbach, 383 U.S. 301 (1966).

Facts. In response to continued racial discrimination in voting, Congress enacted the Voting Rights Act of 1965. The Act included a scheme of remedies aimed at those areas of the country where voting discrimination had been the most flagrant, which were defined through a formula set forth in the statute. The remedies included: (i) suspension of literacy tests for five years from the last occurrence of substantial voting discrimination; (ii) suspension of all new voting regulations pending review by federal authorities to determine whether their use would perpetrate voting discrimination; and (iii) the assignment of federal examiners to list applicants who are entitled to vote in all elections. South Carolina (P), one of the states affected by the Act, brought suit in the Supreme Court seeking declaratory and injunctive relief against enforcement of the Act by Katzenbach (D), the United States Attorney General. The Court has original jurisdiction under Article III, Section 2.

Issue. May Congress interfere with the voter qualification procedures of specified states in order to remedy voting discrimination?

Held. Yes. Judgment for D.

♦ The language and purpose of the Fifteenth Amendment, as well as case law and the general doctrines of constitutional interpretation, all show that as against the reserved powers of the states, Congress may use any rational means to effectuate the constitutional prohibition of racial discrimination in voting. The test of such congressional action is the same as that applied to any exercise of the express powers of Congress, as set forth in *McCulloch v. Maryland, supra.*

♦ The remedies in the Act take effect without prior adjudication and apply to a small number of state and local governments. This approach is rational in light of Congress's finding that case-by-case litigation is inadequate to combat widespread discrimination, and that the identified governmental units had the problems sought to be remedied. The coverage formula is based on the use of tests for voter registration and a voting rate in the 1964 presidential election at least 12 points below the national average. This is rational in theory and practice. Besides, Congress established a procedure for termination of special statutory coverage in appropriate cases.

Concurrence and dissent (Black, J.). The Act is constitutional except where it requires the states to obtain federal approval of their voting regulations.

---

3.   **Congressional Control over State Voting Requirements--**

Katzenbach v. Morgan, 384 U.S. 641 (1966).

Facts. Morgan (P), a registered voter in the city of New York, challenged section 4(e) of the Voting Rights Act of 1965, which provides that any person who has successfully completed sixth grade in an accredited school in Puerto Rico cannot be denied the right to vote because of lack of English proficiency. P claims that the law pro tanto prohibits enforcement of New York election laws based on English proficiency. A three-judge district court granted P relief. Katzenbach (D), the United States Attorney General, appeals.

Issue. May Congress prohibit enforcement of a state English-literacy voting requirement by legislating under Section 5 of the Fourteenth Amendment, regardless of whether the judiciary would find such a requirement unconstitutional?

Held. Yes. Judgment reversed.

♦ Congress need not wait for a judicial determination of unconstitutionality before prohibiting the enforcement of a state law. Congress may enact any legislation that is appropriate.

♦ The test for appropriateness is whether (i) the end is legitimate and (ii) the means are not prohibited by and are consistent with the letter and spirit of the Constitution.

♦ Section 4(e) is plainly adapted to the legitimate end of assuring equal protection to all, including non-English-speaking citizens. D claims section 4(e) works an invidious discrimination in violation of the Fifth Amendment by failing to include persons attending schools not covered by the law. But section 4(e) extends the franchise and does not restrict or deny P. The fact that Congress went no further than it did does not constitute a constitutional violation.

Dissent (Harlan, Stewart, JJ.). The Court has confused the issue of the extent of the Section 5 enforcement power with the distinct issue of what questions are better resolved by the judiciary than by the legislature. Congress should not be permitted to enact remedial legislation where there is no constitutional infringement to be remedied, and the judiciary alone ultimately determines whether a practice or statute is unconstitutional. This Court has previously held that a state English-literacy test is permissible. Here, the Court grants Congress authority to override that judicial determination and define the substantive scope of the Fourteenth Amendment.

Comment. This decision is a far-reaching decision that may exempt the Fourteenth Amendment from the principle of Court and Congress relationships set forth in *Marbury v. Madison*, *supra* (*i.e.*, that the judiciary is the final arbiter of the Constitution). This would allow Congress to act independently. Another view is that Congress was merely acting to strengthen the judicially declared right of equal access to government services.

4.   **Limits on Congressional Enforcement Power--**

Boerne v. Flores, 521 U.S. 507 (1997).

Facts. In *Employment Division v. Smith, supra,* the Court held that, except in special circumstances, the Free Exercise Clause was not violated by a facially neutral and secular law, drafted without legislative animus, that had the effect of interfering with a given religious practice. In that case, Smith had been denied unemployment benefits because he had used peyote in a sacramental ceremony. The Court rejected application of the *Sherbert v. Verner, supra,* balancing test. In response, Congress passed the Religious Freedom Restoration Act of 1993 ("RFRA"), which required courts to apply the balancing test. Under RFRA, courts would have to determine whether a statute substantially burdened a religious practice, and if it did, whether the burden was justified by a compelling government interest. The city of Boerne (D) denied a building permit to enlarge a church, based on an ordinance governing historic preservation in the area. Flores (P), the Archbishop of San Antonio, challenged the denial under RFRA. The district court held that in enacting RFRA, Congress exceeded the scope of its Section 5 enforcement power under the Fourteenth Amendment. The fifth circuit reversed. The Supreme Court granted certiorari.

Issue. May Congress impose a rule of constitutional interpretation on the Supreme Court through its enforcement of the Fourteenth Amendment?

Held. No. Judgment reversed.

♦   Congress relied on the Fourteenth Amendment to impose the RFRA requirements on the states. Section 5 of the Fourteenth Amendment gives Congress power to enforce the constitutional guarantee that no state shall deprive any person of "life, liberty, or property, without due process of law"; nor deny any person "equal protection of the laws." In enacting RFRA, Congress sought to protect the free exercise of religion.

♦   While congressional authority under the Fourteenth Amendment is broad, it is not unlimited. Congress does have the power to enforce the constitutional right to the free exercise of religion, since the First Amendment liberties are included within the Due Process Clause of the Fourteenth Amendment. This power extends only to enforcement, however. It does not extend to changing or defining what the right of free exercise is. There is a distinction between enforcement and changing governing law.

♦   The power to interpret the Constitution in a case or controversy is in the judiciary, not in Congress. Congress does not have a substantive, nonremedial power under the Fourteenth Amendment. If Congress could define its own powers by altering the meaning of the Fourteenth Amendment, the Constitution would no longer be a superior paramount law that cannot be changed by ordinary means.

♦   Preventive rules may sometimes be appropriate remedial measures, but the means must be appropriate to the ends to be achieved. In this case, there was no record of generally applicable laws that were passed because of religious bigotry. The provisions of RFRA are so out of proportion to a supposed remedial objective that it cannot be treated as responsive to unconstitutional behavior. RFRA is applicable to all state and federal law, whenever enacted. The substantial costs RFRA imposes on government far exceed any pattern or practice of unconstitutional conduct under the Free Exercise Clause as interpreted by *Smith*.

♦ Each branch of the government must respect both the Constitution and the proper determination of the other branches. RFRA was designed to control cases and controversies, but it is the interpretation of the Constitution that must govern cases and controversies, not RFRA.

Concurrence (Stevens, J.). RFRA is actually a law respecting an establishment of religion in violation of the First Amendment. It gives churches a preference that other organizations do not enjoy.

Dissent (O'Connor, Breyer, JJ.). The Court should reexamine the *Smith* holding, which was incorrect. That holding allows the government to prohibit, without justification, conduct mandated by an individual's religious beliefs, so long as the prohibition is generally applicable. In so doing, *Smith* harmed religious liberty. If the Court corrected the misinterpretation of the Free Exercise Clause in *Smith*, we could then review RFRA in light of a proper interpretation. But the Court does correctly hold that Congress cannot independently define or expand the scope of constitutional rights by statute.

Dissent (Souter, J.). The Court cannot soundly decide this case without reexamining the free-exercise standard of *Smith*. The writ of certiorari should be dismissed.

Comment. It could be argued that since Congress is specifically mentioned in the Fourteenth Amendment, it does have special authority to determine what rights to enforce. It has such authority under the Thirteenth Amendment.

---

5. **Further Restrictions.**

a. **State employees unable to recover for ADEA violations.** In *Kimel v. Florida Board of Regents*, 528 U.S. 62 (2000), the Court addressed the Age Discrimination in Employment Act ("ADEA"), in which Congress sought to make states subject to federal court actions for violations. The Court held that age is not a suspect classification, so states may draw lines on the basis of age when they have a rational basis for doing so. The ADEA covered too much conduct that was not unconstitutional because it broadly restricted the use of age as a discriminating factor, more so than the Constitution does. Congress has power under Section 5 to enact reasonable legislation to enforce the Constitution, but it cannot substantively redefine the states' legal obligations with respect to age discrimination.

b. **State employees unable to recover for ADA Title I violations.** In *Board of Trustees of the University of Alabama v. Garrett*, 531 U.S.

356 (2001), the Court held that state employees may not recover damages for the state's failure to comply with Title I of the Americans with Disabilities Act ("ADA"). The Court noted that under *Cleburne v. Cleburne Living Center, supra*, the Fourteenth Amendment does not require a state to make special accommodations for the disabled as long as the state's action toward such individuals is rational. Such action need only satisfy rational-basis scrutiny. Congress has authority under Section 5 to respond only to state transgressions, not to those of local governments. However, Congress must identify a history and pattern of unconstitutional employment discrimination by the states against the disabled to legitimately make the ADA apply to the states. Congress assembled only a few incidents of unconstitutional state discrimination in employment against the disabled, which does not rise to a pattern of unconstitutional state behavior. Even if it did, the ADA creates rights and remedies that fail the *Boerne* test, *supra*, of congruence and proportionality.

c.   **State employees can recover under FMLA.** In *Nevada Department of Human Resources v. Hibbs*, 538 U.S. 721 (2003), the Court upheld the abrogation of state sovereign immunity under the Family Medical Leave Act ("FMLA"), which allows eligible employees to take up to 12 work weeks of unpaid leave to care for family members. The FMLA creates a private right of action against any employer, including a public agency, that interferes with FMLA rights. Congress enacted the FMLA in reliance on its power under Section 5 of the Fourteenth Amendment, which authorizes Congress to abrogate the states' Eleventh Amendment sovereign immunity. The FMLA protects the right to be free from gender-based discrimination in the workplace. The Court stated that stereotypes about women's domestic roles created a cycle of discrimination that forced women to continue to assume the role of primary family caregiver and fostered employers' stereotypical views about women's commitment to work and their value as employees. The Court found that Congress had created a legislative record that demonstrated widespread gender-based unconstitutional discrimination by the states that justified a private damages remedy.

d.   **States not subject to federal court actions for patent infringement.** In *Florida Prepaid Postsecondary Education Expense Board v. College Savings Bank*, 527 U.S. 627 (1999), the Court held that Congress could not make states subject to federal court actions for patent infringement because the lack of evidentiary support that states were depriving owners of their interest in patents made the law out of proportion to the supposed remedial object.

e.   **Recovery under ADA Title II.** *Tennessee v. Lane*, 541 U.S. 509 (2004) concerned the abrogation of state sovereign immunity under Title II of the ADA. Title II prohibits a public entity from denying the benefits of its services, programs, or activities to disabled persons. The Court held that Congress may abrogate state immunity from suits brought under Title II for denial of public services to disabled individuals. The Court noted that, unlike Title I, Title II involves rights of access to the courts that are protected by the Due Process Clause, as well as the Confrontation Clause of the Sixth Amendment. The Court concluded that Title II is an appropriate response to the history and pattern of unequal treatment because its requirement of program accessibility is congruent and proportional to its object of enforcing the right of access to the courts.

f. **No civil remedy under Violence Against Women Act.** In *United States v. Morrison*, *supra*, the Court held that Congress has no power under Section 5 to grant a civil remedy to victims of gender-motivated violence under the Violence Against Women Act. The civil remedy in this case was not aimed at proscribing discrimination by state officials, but at individuals.

XIII. LIMITATIONS ON JUDICIAL POWER AND REVIEW

A. CASE OR CONTROVERSY

1. Advisory Opinions.

a. **Introduction.** In addition to the congressional power over Supreme Court jurisdiction, the Court has itself imposed certain limits on the exercise of federal jurisdiction to avoid nonessential interpretation of the Constitution.

1) **Cases and controversies.** Article III, Section 2 limits the jurisdiction of all federal courts to "cases and controversies," requiring federal courts to deal only with real and substantial disputes that affect the legal rights and obligations of parties having adverse interests, and that allow specific relief through a conclusive judicial decree.

2) **Justiciability.** Justiciability is the term of art expressing this limitation placed on federal courts by the case and controversy doctrine. Justiciability is a highly flexible concept, construed narrowly by activist courts, broadly by more conservative courts. The limits of justiciability also preclude rendering advisory opinions (opinions based on assumed or hypothetical facts that are not part of an existing, actual controversy), deciding moot cases (ones already decided) or collusive or friendly suits, or adjudicating purely political questions.

3) **Common scenarios.** Problems of case and controversy and justiciability arise most frequently when a plaintiff seeks an injunction or a declaratory judgment as to the constitutionality of a statute.

2. Strict Necessity.
From its earliest days, the Court has followed a policy of "strict necessity" in disposing of constitutional issues, and has developed certain rules under which it has avoided decision of many constitutional questions presented to it. These rules go beyond mere jurisdictional requirements. They are intended to preserve the unique judicial function in a constitutional government. Even when the Court has jurisdiction, constitutional cases affecting legislation will not be determined:

a. In friendly, nonadversary proceedings;

b. In advance of the necessity of deciding them;

c. In broader terms than are required by the precise facts to which the ruling is to be applied;

d. If the record presents some other ground upon which the case may be disposed of; and

e. At the instance of one who fails to show that he is injured by the statute's operation, or who has availed himself of its benefits.

B. STANDING

1. **Introduction.** The Supreme Court articulated the standing requirement in constitutional cases as follows: the plaintiff must have "alleged such a personal stake in the outcome of the controversy as to assure that concrete adverseness which sharpens the presentation of issues upon which the court so largely depends for illumination of difficult constitutional issues." [Baker v. Carr, *supra*] The personal stake must be a distinct and palpable injury that has a causal connection with the challenged conduct. Standing cannot be predicated upon an injury that is common to all members of the public. This protects against the courts becoming general policymakers.

2. **Lack of Direct Personal Injury--**

Allen v. Wright, 468 U.S. 737 (1984).

Facts. The Wrights (Ps) brought a class action on behalf of black public school children, claiming that the failure of the Internal Revenue Service ("IRS") to deny tax-exempt status to private schools that practice racial discrimination constituted federal support for such schools and interfered with efforts to desegregate public schools. Ps sought declaratory and injunctive relief to force the IRS to deny tax exemptions to discriminatory private schools. The court of appeals held for Ps. The Supreme Court granted certiorari.

Issue. Does a private person have standing to force the government to comply with the law when the person can show no direct personal injury resulting from the alleged failure of the government to obey the law?

Held. No. Judgment reversed.

♦ Under Article III, Ps must have standing in order to obtain their requested relief. The standing requirement prevents a litigant from raising another person's legal rights, prevents adjudication in courts of generalized grievances better suited to representative branches, and precludes consideration of complaints that do not fall within the zone of interests protected by the law invoked.

◆ Although the standing doctrine may not be precisely defined, it fundamentally requires a plaintiff to allege personal injuries fairly traceable to the defendant's allegedly unlawful conduct and likely to be redressed by the requested relief. The injury must be distinct and palpable. It cannot be abstract or hypothetical.

◆ The first injury alleged by Ps is that of direct injury due to the mere fact of government financial assistance to racially discriminatory private schools. To the extent this claim is for a violation of the right to have the government abide by its laws, the claim is not sufficient to confer jurisdiction on the federal courts. To the extent the claim is for the stigma of being a member of a group that is discriminated against, the claim is cognizable only as to those persons who are personally discriminated against. However, Ps were not personally victims of discrimination.

◆ The second injury Ps alleged is that the federal tax exemptions granted to racially discriminatory private schools make desegregation of public schools more difficult and thus give their children a diminished ability to receive an education in a racially integrated school. This type of injury is serious. However, the injury is not fairly traceable to the government conduct that Ps challenge.

◆ The only way the tax exemptions could possibly cause the harm Ps complain of would be if there were enough racially discriminatory private schools receiving the exemptions in Ps' community that withdrawal of the exemptions would make an appreciable difference in public school integration. Ps have not alleged such a causal connection, and there is no evidence of the number of such schools in Ps' community. One can only speculate whether withdrawal of the exemption would cause a school to change its policies, whether parents would transfer their children to public school as a result of those changes, or whether enough private schools and parents would react to make a difference. Because Ps' claimed injury cannot be fairly traced to the challenged action, Ps have no standing.

Dissent (Brennan, J.). Ps' injury is clear, and the causal connection they allege is sufficient. They have identified 14 elementary schools in their own community that receive the tax exemption despite racially discriminatory policies.

Dissent (Stevens, Blackmun, JJ.). The actual wrong of which Ps complain is that the government subsidizes the exodus of white children from public schools that would otherwise be racially integrated. Clearly, D's tax exemption policy causes the wrong complained of. The standing requirement measures the plaintiff's stake in the outcome, not whether the court is authorized to provide the plaintiff with the outcome sought. The Court should examine the justiciability of Ps' case, not their standing.

---

3. **Congressional Power to Create Standing.** The Court has approved of a statutory trend to permit challenges to federal action (effectively granting

standing) on the basis of something other than economic harm. However, the requirement of personal injury must still be met. In *Sierra Club v. Morton*, 405 U.S. 727 (1972), the Court held that the Sierra Club did not have standing to challenge construction of a recreation area in a national forest because it failed to allege that it or its members used the site in question. A wide variety of injuries might justify standing under certain federal statutes, *e.g.*, "social benefits" and "embarrassment" [Trafficante v. Metropolitan Life Insurance Co., 409 U.S. 205 (1972)], or the possibility of increased refuse in national parks [United States v. SCRAP, 412 U.S. 669 (1973)].

4. **Injury Must Result from Unconstitutionality.** A party may not challenge the constitutionality of a statute or executive act unless (i) she is among the class of persons as to whom the statute (or act) is unconstitutional and (ii) she has suffered individual injury, as a direct result of the allegedly unconstitutional feature, that is likely to be redressed by judicial intervention. A plaintiff's injury must likewise be traceable to, and flow from, the unconstitutional conduct of the defendant. Thus, injuries from the independent action of a third party not before the court do not give the plaintiff standing—even where such injuries are encouraged by the defendant's conduct. [*See* Simon v. Eastern Kentucky Welfare Rights Organization, 426 U.S. 26 (1976)—the denial of hospital services was held not traceable to an IRS Revenue Ruling that allegedly "encouraged" denial of such service to indigents]

5. **Requirement of Cause and Effect.** The injury must result from the unconstitutionality of the challenged statute or conduct, such that judicial relief may prevent or redress the injury.

6. **Taxpayer Standing.** The Court in early decisions determined that a federal taxpayer's interest in federal spending or appropriation measures was simply "too remote and indefinite" to allow her to attack such measures. Now, however, the Court has found standing for taxpayers who can establish a "nexus" between their taxpayer status and the claim sought to be adjudicated sufficient to insure the personal stake in the outcome that is essential to standing. The taxpayer must show that the challenged measure was enacted under Congress's taxing and spending powers and that it exceeds some specific limitation on those powers.

   a. **Historical approach--**

Frothingham v. Mellon, 262 U.S. 447 (1923).

Facts. The Maternity Act appropriated money for use by whatever states complied with its provisions for reducing maternal and infant mortality. Frothingham (P), a taxpayer, claimed that the Act would take her money, through taxation, without due process of law. The lower courts dismissed P's claim.

Issue. May a taxpayer challenge a congressional appropriation on the ground that it is illegal?

Held. No. Case dismissed.

♦ P's interest as a federal taxpayer is comparatively minute and indeterminable, and much unlike the interest of a municipal taxpayer, who can prevent misuse of tax money by the municipality. The federal government's funds come partly from taxes and partly from other sources. P's interest is shared with millions of other taxpayers. The effect the Act will have on future taxation is too remote to afford a basis for exercise of equitable powers.

♦ The administration of a law that may impose some indefinite increased taxation on a vast number of taxpayers is a matter of public, not individual, concern. To permit one taxpayer to litigate a challenge to such a law would be to permit any, or all, taxpayers to challenge any or all appropriation acts. Such a suit cannot be maintained.

♦ P is essentially claiming that the executive branch is executing an Act that is allegedly unconstitutional. For the Court to prevent such action, it would have to assume power over another co-equal branch, power the Court has not been granted.

---

b.   **Adequate nexus showing--**

Flast v. Cohen, 392 U.S. 83 (1968).

Facts. Flast (P), a taxpayer, sought to enjoin expenditure of federal funds by Cohen (D), an administrator of the Elementary and Secondary Education Act of 1965. P claimed that funds appropriated under the Act were being used to finance instruction and buy books for religious schools, in contravention of the Establishment and Free Exercise Clauses of the First Amendment. A three-judge court ruled that P lacked standing, based on *Frothingham, supra.* P appeals.

Issue. Can a taxpayer be denied standing when he alleges that congressional action under the Taxing and Spending Clause (Article I, Section 8) is in derogation of those constitutional provisions that operate to restrict the exercise of the Taxing and Spending Clause?

Held. No. Judgment reversed. Standing is granted to invoke a federal court's jurisdiction for an adjudication on the merits.

♦ The emphasis in standing problems is on whether the party invoking federal court jurisdiction has a personal stake in the outcome of the controversy and whether the dispute touches upon the legal relations of parties having adverse legal interests. Article III contains no absolute bar to suits by federal taxpayers challenging allegedly unconstitutional federal taxing and spending programs.

♦ Federal taxpayers must establish a logical nexus between their status and the type of legislative enactment attacked. An enactment under Article I, Section 8, and not an incidental expenditure of tax funds, is properly subject to a challenge by a taxpayer.

♦ P must also establish a link between his taxpayer status and the precise nature of the constitutional infringement alleged. Here the Establishment Clause does specifically limit the taxing and spending powers conferred on Congress, so the link is adequate.

♦ In effect, P is claiming violation of the constitutional protection against being taxed to support establishment of religion, and should have standing.

Dissent (Harlan, J.). The Court should grant standing to representatives of public interests only when Congress has appropriately authorized such suits.

Comment. In *United States v. Richardson*, 418 U.S. 166 (1974), the Court denied standing to a taxpayer who challenged a statute permitting the Central Intelligence Agency to avoid public accounting of its expenditures as a violation of Article I, Section 9, Clause 7. The challenged statute was not enacted under Article I, Section 8, showing a lack of nexus to the taxpayer's status. Furthermore, no claim of a violation of a specific constitutional limitation on such powers was made.

---

c. Citizens' standing--

Valley Forge Christian College v. Americans United for Separation of Church and State, Inc., 454 U.S. 464 (1982).

Facts. Pursuant to a federal statute, the federal government transferred excess federal property to Valley Forge College (D), a Christian school, without cost because of the public benefit expected. Americans United for Separation of Church and State, Inc. (P) challenged the action as a violation of the First Amendment. The district court dismissed the suit on the ground that P lacked standing as a taxpayer. The court of appeals reversed, not on the ground of taxpayer standing but on the ground of "citizen" standing to seek relief for injury to the right not to have the government establish a religion. The Supreme Court granted certiorari.

Issue. Is the fact of citizenship sufficient to give standing to challenge a governmental action that allegedly violates the Constitution?

Held. No. Judgment reversed.

♦ Article III requires at least some personal injury or threat of injury traced to the challenged action that can be redressed by judicial action. The cases and controversies language prevents the courts from becoming publicly funded forums for the ventilation of public grievances.

♦ The lower courts properly held that P has no standing as a taxpayer. However, P cannot acquire standing by merely asserting a right to a particular kind of government conduct that the government allegedly violated. P has not alleged any injury. To grant standing in this case would remove the case and controversy requirement from the Constitution.

Dissent (Brennan, Marshall, Blackmun, JJ.). The case and controversy requirement does not override all other provisions of the Constitution. A complaint under the Establishment Clause justifies standing because use of tax funds to establish religion is specifically prohibited and constitutes a direct injury on P.

Comment. The Court denied standing in part because the transfer was done by an agency, not Congress, and in part because the property transfer was not an exercise of authority granted by the Taxing and Spending Clause.

———————

d. **Third-party standing.**

1) **Basic rule.** Normally, a person does not have standing to assert the rights of third parties who are injured by an allegedly unconstitutional act. There are two reasons for this rule.

a) **Need.** Courts should not adjudicate constitutional rights unnecessarily, and a third party may not want to assert his own rights or may not be able to enjoy them regardless of the outcome of the suit.

b) **Advocacy.** The third parties themselves are usually the best advocates of their own rights and normally would prefer direct involvement because of stare decisis.

2) **Exception.** Third-party standing may be permitted when the plaintiff has herself suffered injury and the third persons in question would find it difficult or impossible to vindicate their own rights, or where the plaintiff's injury adversely affects her relationship with the third parties.

7. **Public Interest Not Enough--**

———————

Lujan v. Defenders of Wildlife, 504 U.S. 555 (1992).

Facts. Section 7(a)(2) of the Endangered Species Act ("ESA") requires federal agencies to insure, in consultation with the Secretary of the Interior, that any action carried out by such agency is not likely to jeopardize the continued existence of any endangered or threatened species. The Fish and Wildlife Service and National Marine Fisheries Service promulgated a joint regulation stating that section 7(a)(2) extended to actions taken in foreign nations, but the regulation was later modified to require consultations only for actions taken in the United States or on the high seas. The ESA also provided that "any person may commence a civil suit on his behalf" to enjoin a government agency who is alleged to be in violation of the Act. The Defenders of Wildlife (P) brought suit against Lujan (D), the Secretary of the Interior, seeking a declaratory judgment that the more recent regulation incorrectly interpreted the ESA. Both parties moved for summary judgment. The district court granted P's motion. The court of appeals affirmed. The Supreme Court granted certiorari.

Issue. May Congress convert the public interest in proper administration of the laws into an individual right such that all citizens may have standing to sue?

Held. No. Judgment reversed.

♦   Neither P nor any of its members had any injury in fact. P's standing, if any, depends on the validity of the "citizen-suit" provision of the ESA. The court of appeals held that this provision created a "procedural right" to inter-agency consultation in all persons, so that anyone can file suit to challenge D's failure to follow the allegedly correct consultative procedure, even if there is no discrete injury resulting from that failure. In effect, the court held that the injury-in-fact requirement under Article III has been satisfied by congressional conferral upon all persons of an abstract, self-contained "right" to have the executive branch observe the procedures required by law.

♦   Article III confers jurisdiction on the federal courts only where there is a case or controversy. This requirement is not met by a plaintiff raising only a generally available grievance about the government, where the harm is only to the interest of all citizens in proper application of the Constitution and laws. Hence, a taxpayer does not have standing to challenge alleged violations of the Constitution by the executive or legislative branches where the violations would adversely affect only the generalized interest of all citizens in constitutional governance. The federal courts may only decide on the rights of individuals. Vindicating the public interest is the function of Congress and the President.

♦   If Congress could convert the undifferentiated public interest in an executive that complies with the law into an "individual right" to be vindicated in the courts, Congress could transfer from the President to the courts the Chief Executive's most important constitutional duty, to "take Care that the Laws be faithfully executed."

♦   The fact that Congress may not eliminate the requirement of a concrete personal injury does not preclude Congress from creating legal rights, the invasion of which creates standing.

Concurrence (Kennedy, Souter, JJ.). Congress may define injuries and articulate chains of causation that give rise to a case or controversy where none existed before, but at a minimum, Congress must identify the injury it seeks to vindicate and relate the injury to the class of persons entitled to bring suit. The citizen-suit provisions of the ESA do not establish that there is an injury in any person by virtue of any violation. The case and controversy requirement assures both that the parties have an actual stake in the outcome and that the legal questions presented will be resolved in a concrete factual context conducive to a realistic appreciation of the consequences of judicial action. The public is entitled to know what persons invoke the judicial power, their reasons, and whether their claims are vindicated or denied.

Concurrence (Stevens, J.). P does not lack standing, but Congress did not intend section 7(a)(2) to apply to activities in foreign countries.

Dissent (Blackmun, O'Connor, JJ.). Congress granted considerable discretion to the executive branch to determine how best to attain the goals of the ESA, constrained by specific procedural requirements. This does not constitute a violation of the separation of powers; nor should the separation of powers be deemed violated when Congress requires the federal courts to enforce the procedures. The citizen-suit provisions of the ESA were based on the same understanding that arose from earlier cases in which the Court justified a relaxed review of congressional delegation to the executive branch because Congress provided for judicial review of the exercise of that power. [*See* Immigration & Naturalization Service v. Chadha, *supra*]

C. TIMING OF ADJUDICATION

1. **Mootness.** The usual rule in federal cases is that an actual controversy must exist at all stages of appellate or certiorari review, and not simply at the date the action is initiated.

    a. **Capable of repetition.** Issues involving events of short duration (*e.g.,* pregnancy, elections, economic strikes) are not necessarily moot if the issues are "capable of repetition, yet evading review." For example, in *Sosna v. Iowa*, 419 U.S. 393 (1975), a class action was used to challenge a state residency requirement for divorce jurisdiction. By the time the case reached the Supreme Court, the plaintiff had satisfied the residency requirement, so the suit would have been moot, but the controversy was still alive as to other class members. A class action does not always work, however. *Hall v. Beals*, 396 U.S. 45 (1969), involved a challenge to a six-month residency requirement for voting. By the time the case reached the Supreme Court, the state had reduced the residency requirement to two months, so the law affected a different class of voters, and the case was moot.

b.   **Criminal cases.** A criminal case is not moot, even though a defendant has served his sentence or paid his fine, if there are any collateral consequences of the conviction, *e.g.,* loss of civil rights or damage to reputation.

c.   **Admission procedures--**

DeFunis v. Odegaard, 416 U.S. 312 (1974).

Facts. DeFunis's (P's) application for admission to the University of Washington Law School was denied. P brought suit, claiming that the school's admissions procedures invidiously discriminated against him on account of his race. The trial court granted a mandatory injunction, and P was admitted. The Washington Supreme Court reversed, but Justice Douglas stayed that judgment pending final disposition of the case by the United States Supreme Court. When the Court first considered P's case, P was in the first term of his third year, and the Court requested the parties to brief the issue of mootness. Both sides contended the case was not moot, and the case was orally argued during P's last term in school.

Issue. When mootness is not compelled by the record and there is a likelihood of repetitious litigation, must the court find mootness when it can no longer affect a party's rights by its decision?

Held. Yes. The case is moot.

♦   Federal courts are without power to decide questions that cannot affect the rights of litigants in the case before them, because the Constitution requires an actual case or controversy.

♦   Although under Washington law the case would be saved from mootness, it is a federal question that must be resolved before a federal court assumes jurisdiction.

♦   P is entitled to complete his legal studies regardless of the Court's decision and never will again seek admission. Therefore, the case is not "capable of repetition, yet evading review." If necessary, the issues can be raised again by other parties, should the same event recur.

Dissent (Brennan, Douglas, White, Marshall, JJ.). The issues raised will surely return to the Court. Because avoidance of repetitious litigation serves the public interest, that inevitability counsels against mootness determinations, as here, not compelled by the record. The Court should not transform principles of avoidance of constitutional decisions into devices for sidestepping resolution of difficult cases.

2. **Ripeness.** The timing of adjudication is critical; the Court will decide only those issues that are "ripe" for adjudication. It will not anticipate a question of constitutional law prior to the necessity of deciding it or pass upon issues that may or may not arise sometime in the future. These problems generally arise in suits for injunctions and declaratory judgments.

   a. **Possible threats are not sufficient--**

United Public Workers v. Mitchell, 330 U.S. 75 (1947).

Facts. A group of federal civil service employees (Ps) challenged an aspect of the Hatch Act as preventing them from exercising their First Amendment right to participate in political campaigns. One of the plaintiffs, Poole, alleged that action under the Hatch Act was being taken against him for his political activity. The remaining Ps had not violated the Act, but argued that they desired to take part in political campaigns.

Issue. Have Ps presented a case that is ripe for adjudication?

Held. Only Poole's case is ripe.

♦ Constitutional issues cannot be adjudicated until they present "concrete legal issues, presented in actual cases, not abstractions." In this case, all Ps, with the exception of Poole, are plainly seeking advisory opinions on the political expediency of the Hatch Act rather than the resolution of legal issues. Courts do not have the power to render advisory opinions.

♦ Courts may pass upon the constitutionality of congressional acts only when the litigants' interests need to be protected against actual interference. The threat to all Ps except Poole is merely hypothetical; Ps allege no actual harm. Poole, on the other hand, does face actual harm, as he has violated the Act and action against him is imminent. Only Poole presents a ripe controversy.

Dissent (Douglas, J.). If Ps participate in political campaigns as they desire, action will be taken against them under the Act. This threat is "real not fanciful, immediate not remote."

---

   b. **The importance of a constitutional determination.** In *Adler v. Board of Education*, 342 U.S. 485 (1952), Adler and others sought a judgment declaring unconstitutional a state law requiring the discharge of teachers who belonged to allegedly subversive organizations. The trial court granted a judgment on the pleadings, in effect finding that there could be no constitutional applications of the statute. On appeal, the state courts reversed. The Supreme Court affirmed. The question did not turn on particular conduct of the plaintiffs but solely on the statute. In addition, the case came up through the state courts, giving the Supreme Court jurisdiction by appeal. Had the Court decided against ripeness or concreteness, it would have left undisturbed the state court determination of federal constitutional law.

TABLE OF CASES
(Page numbers of briefed cases in bold)

Abrams v. United States - 155

Adair v. United States - 94

Adams v. Tanner - 94

Adarand Constructors, Inc. v. Pena - **304**

Adkins v. Children's Hospital - 94

Adler v. Board of Education - 376

Agostini v. Felton - 248, 249

Akron v. Akron Center for Reproductive Health - 123

Alberts v. California - **168**

Allegheny County v. ACLU - **255**

Allen v. Wright - **367**

Allgeyer v. Louisiana - 92

Allied Structural Steel Co. v. Spannaus - **110**, 111

Amalgamated Food Employees Union v. Logan Valley Plaza - 349

Ambach v. Norwick - **318**

American Booksellers Association, Inc. v. Hudnut - **178**

American Library Association, Inc., United States v. - **220**

Anderson v. Celebrezze - 323

Anderson v. Martin - 284

Aptheker v. Secretary of State - 141

Arcara v. Cloud Books, Inc. - 183

Arlington Heights v. Metropolitan Housing Development Corp. - **288**

Arnett v. Kennedy - 149

Ashcroft v. American Civil Liberties Union - 232

Ashcroft v. The Free Speech Coalition - **176**

Associated Press v. Walker - 162

Atkins v. Virginia - 146, 147

Bailey v. Drexel Furniture Co. (The Child Labor Tax Case) - **27**, 28

Baker v. Carr - 7, 8, 324, 326, 367

Baldwin v. Montana Fish and Game Commission - 82

Baldwin v. G.A.F. Seelig, Inc. - **64**

Ballard, United States v. - 267

Bantam Books, Inc. v. Sullivan - 200

Barnes v. Glen Theatre, Inc. - 185

Barron v. Mayor & City Council of Baltimore - **89**

Bartnicki v. Vopper - 167

Barrows v. Jackson - 351

Bates v. State Bar - 189

Beal v. Doe - 120

Beauharnais v. Illinois - **159**

Bell v. Burson - 148

Bell v. Maryland - 352

Bendix Autolite Corp. v. Midwesco Enterprises, Inc. - 75

Berman v. Parker - **96**

Bernal v. Fainter - 319

Bethel School District No. 403 v. Fraser - 218

Bibb v. Navajo Freight Lines - 79

Bigelow v. Virginia - 187

Bishop v. Wood - 149

Blum v. Yaretsky - 354

Board of Education v. Mergens - 255

Board of Education v. Pico - **219**

Board of Education of Kiryas Joel v. Grumet - **268**

Board of Regents of State Colleges v. Roth - 149

Board of Trustees of the University of Alabama v. Garrett - 363

Bob Jones University v. United States - 264

Boddie v. Connecticut - 341

Boerne v. Flores - **361**, 364

Bowers v. Hardwick - **137**, 139, 140, 317

Bowsher v. Synar - **52**, 55

Boy Scouts of America v. Dale - **236**

Bradley v. Public Utilities Commission - 76

Brandenburg v. Ohio - **158**, 159

Branti v. Finkel - 238

Branzburg v. Hayes - **204**

Braunfeld v. Brown - 272

Breard v. Alexandria - **66**

Breedlove v. Suttles - 321, 322

Breithaupt v. Abram - 113

Brown v. Board of Education (Brown I) - **282**, 289, 290

Brown v. Board of Education (Brown II) - **282**

Buck v. Kuykendall - 76

Buckley v. Valeo - 52, **240**, 243, 244

Bunting v. Oregon - 94

Burton v. Wilmington Parking Authority - 354

Bush v. Gore - 5, **334**

Bush v. Vera - 333

Butler, United States v. - **29**

C & A Carbone, Inc. v. Clarkstown - **72**

CTS Corp. v. Dynamics Corp. - **74**

Calder v. Bull - 89

Califano v. Goldfarb - 313

Califano v. Webster - **313**

Campbell v. Clinton - **44**

Cantwell v. Connecticut - 262

Capitol Square Review & Advisory Board v. Pinette - 262

Carey v. Brown - 212, 214

Carey v. Population Services International - 118

Carolene Products Co., United States v. - 95

Carter v. Carter Coal Co. - 21

Central Hudson Gas & Electric Corp. v. Public Service Commission - 189, 190

Champion v. Ames (The Lottery Case) - **17**, 20, 22

Chaplinsky v. New Hampshire - 172, 192

Chicago Police Department v. Mosley - **209**

Church of the Lukumi Babalu Aye, Inc. v. City of Hialeah -266

Cipriano v. Houma - 323

Cities Service Gas Co. v. Peerless Oil & Gas Co. - 70

Civil Rights Cases, The - **347**

Clark v. Community for Creative Non-Violence - **182**

Cleburne v. Cleburne Living Center, Inc. - **320**, 364

Cleveland Board of Education v. Loudermill - 150

Clinton v. Jones - **59**

Clinton v. New York - **50**

Cohen v. California - **173**

Cohens v. Virginia - 6

Cole v. Richardson - 239

Collector v. Day - 34

Collin v. Smith - 179

Columbia Broadcasting System, Inc. v. Democratic National Committee - **223**

Columbus Board of Education v. Penick - **292**

Committee for Public Education & Religious Liberty v. Nyquist - 250

Commonwealth Edison Co. v. Montana - **86**

Complete Auto Transit, Inc. v. Brady - **85**, 86

Connick v. Myers - **239**

Container Corp. v. Franchise Tax Board - **87**

Cooley v. Board of Wardens - **61**

Cooper v. Aaron - 5, 283

Coppage v. Kansas - 94

Cornelius v. NAACP Legal Defense & Education Fund, Inc. - 209

Corporation of the Presiding Bishop of the Church of Jesus Christ of Latter-Day Saints v. Amos - **271**

Cox v. New Hampshire - 208

Craig v. Boren - **307**, 310

Crawford v. Los Angeles Board of Education - **294**

Cruzan v. Director, Missouri Department of Health - **134**, 135, 137

Curtis Publishing Co. v. Butts - 161, 162

Curtiss-Wright Export Corp., United States v. - **43**

Dames & Moore v. Regan - **41**

Dandridge v. Williams - **343**

Darby, United States v. - **21**

Davis v. Bandemer - **326**, 327, 328

Dean Milk Co. v. Madison - 64, **65**, 66, 68, 72

Debs v. United States - **153**

DeFunis v. Odegaard - **375**

Dennis v. United States - **157**, 159

Denver Area Educational Telecommunications Consortium, Inc. v. FCC - **228**

DeShaney v. Winnebago Department of Social Services - **356**

Doe v. Bolton - **119**

Dolan v. City of Tigard - **105**

Douglas v. California - **340**

Dred Scott v. Sandford - 129, **278**
Dun & Bradstreet, Inc. v. Greenmoss Builders, Inc. - 162, **191**
Duncan v. Louisiana - 112
Dunn v. Blumstein - 337

Eastern Enterprises v. Apfel - 106
Eddings v. Oklahoma - 145
Edgar v. Mite Corp. - 75
Edwards v. Aguillard - **254**
Eichman, United States v. - 181
Eisenstadt v. Baird - 117, 133
Elk Grove Unified School District v. Newdow - 260
Elrod v. Burns - **237**, 238
Employment Division v. Smith - **264**, 362, 363
Energy Reserves Group v. Kansas Power & Light Co. - 111
Epperson v. Arkansas - 254
Erie, City of v. Pap's A.M. - **185**
Evans v. Abney - 351
Evans v. Newton - **349**, 351
Everson v. Board of Education - **245**, 251
Exxon Corp. v. Eagerton - 111

FCC v. League of Women Voters - 226
FCC v. Pacifica Foundation - **225**, 226, 227, 229
Feiner v. New York - **173**
Ferguson v. Skrupa - 96
Field v. Clark - 51
Flagg Bros., Inc. v. Brooks - **355**
Flast v. Cohen - **370**
Florida Prepaid Postsecondary Education Expense Board v. College Savings Bank - 364
Florida Star v. B.J.F. - **166**
Foley v. Connelie - 318
Francis v. Reseweber - 142
Freedman v. Maryland - 199
Freeman v. Pitts - 293
Frontiero v. Richardson - **306**, 312
Frothingham v. Mellon - **369**, 370
Full Crew Cases - 77
Fullilove v. Klutznick - 301, 302, 303, 306
Furman v. Georgia - **142**, 143, 144, 145

Gaffney v. Cummings - 325, 327
Gannett Co. v. DePasquale - 207
Garcia v. San Antonio Metropolitan Transit Authority - **35**
Geduldig v. Aiello - 310
Geer v. Connecticut - 73
Gertz v. Robert Welch, Inc. - **162**, 164, 191
Gibbons v. Ogden - **16**, 17, 61
Gideon v. Wainwright - 114
Gilbert v. California - 115
Gillette v. United States - 245, 264
Gilmore v. Montgomery - 354
Ginsberg v. New York - 227
Gitlow v. New York - **155**
Goldberg v. Kelly - 149, 150
Gonzales v. Raich - 26
Gooding v. Wilson - 174
Gordon v. Lance - 325
Goss v. Lopez - 148
Gratz v. Bollinger - **299**
Graves v. New York *ex rel.* O'Keefe - 34
Green v. County School Board - 289
Gregg v. Georgia - **143**
Griffin v. California - 115
Griffin v. County School Board - 289
Griffin v. Illinois - 340, 341, 342
Griffiths, *In re* - 318, 319
Griswold v. Connecticut - **116**, 123, 133
Grutter v. Bollinger - **297**, 299, 300

H.P. Hood & Sons, Inc. v. Du Mond - **68**
Haig v. Agee - **141**
Hall v. Beals - 374
Hammer v. Dagenhart - **19**, 27
Hamdi v. Rumsfeld - **45**
Hannibal & St. Joseph Railroad v. Husen - 63
Harlow v. Fitzgerald - 60
Harper v. Virginia Board of Elections - **321**
Harper & Row v. Nation Enterprises - **174**
Harris v. McRae - **121**, 122
Hawaii Housing Authority v. Midkiff - 97
Hazelwood School District v. Kuhlmeier - **217**
Heart of Atlanta Motel, Inc. v. United States - **23**
Helvering v. Davis - 29
Helvering v. Gerhardt - 34

Henneford v. Silas Mason Co. - 65

Hess v. Indiana - 159

Hicklin v. Orbeck - 82

Hill v. Colorado - **211**

Hills v. Gautreaux - 293

Hobbie v. Unemployment Appeals Commission - **263**

Hodel v. Indiana - 25

Hodel v. Virginia Surface Mining & Reclamation Association - 25, 35, 36

Hodgson v. Minnesota - 123

Home Building & Loan Association v. Blaisdell - **108**, 110

Houston, East & West Texas Railway v. United States (The Shreveport Case) - **18**, 19

Hoyt v. Florida - 306

Hudgens v. NLRB - 349

Hughes v. Alexandria Scrap Corp. - 79, 80

Hughes v. Oklahoma - **73**

Hunt v. Washington State Apple Advertising Commission - **66**

Hurley v. Irish-American Gay, Lesbian and Bisexual Group of Boston - **233**, 237

Hustler Magazine v. Falwell - **165**

Immigration & Naturalization Service v. Chadha - **48**, 374

International Society for Krishna Consciousness, Inc. v. Lee - **209**

J.E.B. v. Alabama *ex rel.* T.B. - 309, 312

Jackson v. Metropolitan Edison Co. - **350**

James v. Valtierra - 321

Johanns v. Livestock Marketing Association - 234

Johnson v. Robison - 264

Jones v. Alfred H. Mayer Co. - **358**

Jones v. United States - 27

Jones v. Wolf - **269**

Kahn v. Shevin - 312

Kahriger, United States v. - 28

Karcher v. Daggett - 325

Kassel v. Consolidated Freightways Corp. - **78**

Katzenbach v. McClung - **24**

Katzenbach v. Morgan - **360**

Kelo v. New London - **97**

Keyes v. School District - **291**

Keystone Bituminous Coal Association v. DeBenedictis - **100**

Kimel v. Florida Board of Regents - 363

Kingsley Books, Inc. v. Brown - 199

Kingsley International Pictures Corp. v. Regents - 168

Korematsu v. United States - 129, **280**, 281

Kramer v. Union Free School District - **322**

Kras, United States v. - 341

Larkin v. Grendel's Den, Inc. - 269

Larson v. Valente - **270**

Lassiter v. Department of Social Services - 151

Lawrence v. Texas - **139**, 140, 147, 318

Lee v. International Society for Krishna Consciousness, Inc. - 211

Lee v. Weisman - **258**, 260, 261

Lee, United States v. - 264

Leisy v. Hardin - 62

Lemon v. Kurtzman - 245, **247**, 248, 252, 254, 255, 257, 258, 259, 261, 271, 272

Lincoln Federal Labor Union v. Northwestern Iron & Metal Co. - 96

Lindsey v. Normet - 343

Linmark Associates, Inc. v. Township of Willingboro - 188

Lochner v. New York - 92, **93**, 94, 95

Locke v. Davey - **266**

Lockett v. Ohio - 145

Logan v. Zimmerman Brush Co. - 150

Lopez, United States v. - 25, 26

Loretto v. Teleprompter Manhattan CATV Corp. - 102, 103

Lorillard Tobacco Co. v. Reilly - **189**

Los Angeles v. Taxpayers for Vincent - 209

Lovell v. Griffin - **196**

Loving v. Virginia - **283**

Lowe v. S.E.C. - **200**

Lucas v. Forty-Fourth General Assembly - 325

Lucas v. South Carolina Coastal Council - **102**, 106

Lujan v. Defenders of Wildlife - **372**

Lynch v. Donnelly - 256, 257
Lynch v. United States - 107

M.L.B. v. S.L.J. - **342**
Mahan v. Howell - 325
Maher v. Roe - 120, 121, 346
Maine v. Taylor -73
Mapp v. Ohio - 114
Marbury v. Madison - **4**, 361
Marsh v. Alabama - 348, 349
Marsh v. Chambers - 255
Marston v. Lewis - 337
Martin v. Hunter's Lessee - **5**, 6
Maryland v. Baltimore Radio Show, Inc. -
    11
Massachusetts Board of Retirement v. Murgia
    - 321
Massachusetts v. Oakes - 176
Massachusetts v. United States - 34
Masses Publishing Co. v. Patten - **154**
Mathews v. Diaz - 320
Mathews v. Eldridge - 151
Mathews v. Lucas - **315**
McCardle, *Ex parte* - **9**, 10
McCarthy v. Philadelphia Civil Service Com-
    mission - 337
McCleskey v. Kemp - **145**
McConnell v. Federal Election Commission -
    242
McCreary County v. ACLU - 257
McCulloch v. Maryland - **13**, 15, **33**, 360
McDaniel v. Paty - 263
McDermott v. Wisconsin - 23
Memoirs v. Massachusetts - 170, 171
Memphis v. Greene - **286**
Memphis Light, Gas & Water Division v. Craft
    - 148
Metro Broadcasting, Inc. v. FCC - 304, 305
Metromedia, Inc. v. San Diego - 189
Meyer v. Nebraska - 115, 116
Miami Herald Publishing Co. v. Tornillo - **222**
Michael H. v. Gerald D. - **132**
Michael M. v. Superior Court - **310**
Michigan v. Long - 11
Milk Control Board v. Eisenberg Farm Prod-
    ucts - 69

Miller v. Albright - 316
Miller v. California - 168, 170, **171**, 176, 227
Miller v. Johnson - **332**
Milliken v. Bradley - 293
Minnesota v. Barber - 64
Minnesota v. Clover Leaf Creamery Co. - **71**
Mintz v. Baldwin - 63
Miranda v. Arizona - 10, 115
Mississippi University for Women v. Hogan -
    309, **313**
Missouri v. Holland - **32**, 33
Mistretta v. United States - 48, 56
Mitchell v. Helms - **247**
Mobile v. Bolden - 326, **328**, 330, 331
Moore v. East Cleveland - **130**
Moose Lodge v. Irvis - **353**
Morrison v. Olson - **53**
Morrison, United States v. - **25**, 26, 365
Muller v. Oregon - 94
Munn v. Illinois - 92

NAACP v. Claiborne Hardware Co. - 234
National Endowment for the Arts v. Finley -
    215
National League of Cities v. Usery - 35, 36,
    37
Near v. Minnesota - **198**, 199
Nebbia v. New York - **95**
Nebraska Press Association v. Stuart - **203**
Neveda Department of Human Resources v.
    Hibbs - 364
New Jersey Welfare Rights Organization v.
    Cahill - 316
New Orleans v. Dukes - **276**
New State Ice Co. v. Liebmann - 94
New York v. Ferber - **175**, 176
New York v. United States - 34, 37, 38
New York City Transit Authority v. Beazer -
    277
New York Times Co. v. Sullivan - **161**, 162,
    163, 164, 165
New York Times Co. v. United States [The
    Pentagon Papers Case] - **201**, 202
Nixon v. Administrator of General Services -
    57
Nixon v. Fitzgerald - 58

Nixon v. United States - **7**
Nixon, United States v. - **56**
NLRB v. Jones & Laughlin Steel Corp. - 21
Nollan v. California Coastal Commission - **104**, 106
North Dakota State Board v. Snyders' Drug Stores, Inc. - 96
Norwood v. Harrison - 354
Noto v. United States - 158

O'Brien, United States v. - **179**, 181, 185, 186, 225, 237
Ohralik v. Ohio State Bar Association - **188**
Osborne v. Ohio - 176

Pace v. Alabama - 283
Pacific States Telephone & Telegraph Co. v. Oregon - 7
Palazzolo v. Rhode Island - 106
Palmore v. Sidoti - 284
Parham v. J.R. - 151
Paris Adult Theatre I v. Slaton - **169**
Parker v. Brown - 69
Paul v. Davis - 149
Paul v. Virginia - 62
Penn Central Transportation Co. v. New York City - **101**, 106
Pennsylvania Coal Co. v. Mahon - **99**, 100, 101, 102
Perez v. United States - 22
Personnel Administrator v. Feeney - **287**
Philadelphia v. New Jersey - **70**
Phillips v. Washington Legal Foundation - 107
Phoenix v. Kolodziejski - 323
Pierce v. Society of Sisters - 115, 116, 217
Pike v. Bruce Church, Inc. - 64, 70
Pittsburgh Press Co. v. Human Relations - 200
Planned Parenthood v. Ashcroft - 122
Planned Parenthood v. Danforth - 122
Planned Parenthood of Southeastern Pennsylvania v. Casey - **124**, 127, 129, 130, 214
Playboy Entertainment Group, Inc., United States v. - **230**
Plessy v. Ferguson - **280**
Plyler v. Doe - **345**
Poe v. Ullman - 117

Poelker v. Doe - 120
Powell v. McCormack - 15
Printz v. United States - **38**
Prize Cases, The - 45
Progressive, Inc., United States v. - 202
Prudential Insurance Co. v. Benjamin - 63
PruneYard Shopping Center v. Robins - **232**

R.A.V. v. St. Paul - **192**, 195
Railroad Retirement Board v. Alton Railroad - 21
Railway Express Agency v. New York - **276**
Raymond Motor Transportation, Inc. v. Rice - 78, 79
Rasul v. Bush - 47
Red Lion Broadcasting Co. v. FCC - 223, 226
Reed v. Reed - 306, 307
Reeves, Inc. v. Stake - **79**, 81
Regan v. Taxation With Representation of Washington - 240
Regents of the University of California v. Bakke - **295**, 297, 298, 299, 300
Reid v. Covert - 33
Reidel, United States v. - 169
Reitman v. Mulkey - **352**
Rendell-Baker v. Kohn - **354**
Reno v. American Civil Liberties Union - **226**
Reno v. Condon - 39
Renton v. Playtime Theatres, Inc. - **184**, 227
Reynolds v. Sims - **324**, 325, 326
Reynolds v. United States - 262
Richardson v. Ramirez - 323
Richardson, United States v. - 371
Richmond v. J.A. Croson Co. - **301**, 305
Richmond Newspapers, Inc. v. Virginia - **207**
Roberts (Stanislaus) v. Louisiana - 144
Roberts v. United States Jaycees - **235**, 236
Rochin v. California - **113**, 114
Roe v. Wade - 117, **118**, 119, 120, 121, 122, 123, 124, 125, 127, 140
Rogers v. Lodge - **330**
Romer v. Evans - 140, **316**, 318
Roper v. Simmons - **146**, 147
Rosenberger v. Rector and Visitors of University of Virginia - 216
Rosenbloom v. Metromedia, Inc. - 162

Ross v. Moffit - 341
Rostker v. Goldberg - **311**
Roth v. United States - **168**, 170, 171
Rumsfeld v. Padilla - 47
Rust v. Sullivan - **214**
Rutan v. Republican Party of Illinois - 238

Sable Communications v. FCC - 226
Sabri v. United States - 31
Saenz v. Roe - **338**
Salyer Land Co. v. Tulare Lake Basin Water
    Storage District - 323
San Antonio Independent School District v.
    Rodriguez - **343**, 345
Santa Fe Independent School District v. Doe -
    260
Scales v. United States - 158
Schechter Poultry Corp. v. United States - 21
Schenck v. Pro-Choice Network of Western
    New York - 212, 213
Schenck v. United States - **153**
Schlesinger v. Ballard - 312
Schmerber v. California - 114
Schneider v. Irvington - 208
SCRAP, United States v. - 369
Screws v. United States - 358
Seaboard Air Line Railroad Co. v. Blackwell
    - 76
Seeger, United States v. - 267
Shapiro v. Thompson - **336**, 338, 339
Shaw v. Reno - **331**, 333
Shea v. Louisiana - 115
Shelley v. Kraemer - **351**, 352
Sheppard v. Maxwell - 203
Sherbert v. Verner - 263, 264, 265, 273, 362
Sierra Club v. Morton - 369
Simon v. Eastern Kentucky Welfare Rights
    Organization - 369
Skinner v. Oklahoma - 116
Slaughter-House Cases, The - **90**, 340
Smith v. Allwright - 348
Solid Waste Agency of Northern Cook County
    v. United States Army Corps of Engineers -
    27
Sosna v. Iowa - 374
South Carolina v. Katzenbach - **359**

South Carolina Highway Department v.
    Barnwell Brothers - 77
South-Central Timber Development, Inc. v.
    Wunnicke - **80**
South Dakota v. Dole - **30**, 31
Southeastern Promotions, Ltd. v. Conrad - 220
Southern Pacific Co. v. Arizona - **76**
Spector Motor Service v. O'Connor - 84, 85
Spence v. Washington - 181
Stanford v. Kentucky - 147
Stanley v. Georgia - 138, 169, 176
Stenberg v. Carhart - **127**
Steward Machine Co. v. Davis - **30**
Stone v. Graham - 254
Strauder v. West Virginia - 279
Sugarman v. Dougall - 318
Sullivan, United States v. - 23
Swann v. Charlotte-Mecklenburg Board of
    Education - **289**

Tahoe-Sierra Preservation Council, Inc. v.
    Tahoe Regional Planning Agency - 106
Tancil v. Woolls - 284
Tennessee v. Lane - 364
Terminiello v. Chicago - 172
Terry v. Adams - 348
Texas v. Johnson - **180**, 181
Texas Monthly, Inc. v. Bullock - 272
Thomas v. Review Board - 263
Thornburgh v. American College of Ob-
    stetricians & Gynecologists - 123
Thornton v. Caldor, Inc. - 273
Time, Inc. v. Firestone - 164
Time, Inc. v. Hill - **164**
Times Film Corp. v. Chicago - **199**
Tinker v. Des Moines School District - **217**,
    218
Torcaso v. Watkins - 267
Town of Castle Rock v. Gonzales - 149
Trafficante v. Metropolitan Life Insurance Co.
    - 369
Troxel v. Granville - 132
Turner Broadcasting System, Inc. v. FCC
    (Turner I) - 224
Turner Broadcasting System, Inc. v. FCC
    (Turner II) - 225

U.S. Term Limits, Inc. v. Thornton - 15
United Building & Construction Trades Council v. Mayor of Camden - **82**
United Public Workers v. Mitchell - **376**
United States v. ___ (see opposing party)
United States Railroad Retirement Board v. Fritz - **277**
United States Trust Co. v. New Jersey - **109**, 111

Vacco v. Quill - **136**
Valley Forge Christian College v. Americans United for Separation of Church and State, Inc. - **371**
Van Orden v. Perry - 257
Vieth v. Jubelirer - **327**
Village of Belle Terre v. Boraas - 130
Virginia v. Black - **194**
Virginia State Board of Pharmacy v. Virginia Citizens Consumer Council - **187**
Virginia, United States v. - **308**
Vitek v. Jones - 149

Wabash, St. Louis & Pacific Railway Co. v. Illinois - 76
Wade, United States v. - 115
Wallace v. Jaffree - **251**
Walton v. Arizona - 145
Walz v. Tax Commission - **246**, 247
Ward v. Rock Against Racism - 212, 213
Washington v. Davis - **285**
Washington v. Glucksberg - **134**, 137
Washington v. Seattle School District - 293
Watchtower Bible and Tract Society of New York v. Village of Stratton - **197**
Weaver v. Palmer Brothers Co. - 94
Weber v. Aetna Casualty & Surety Co. - 316
Webster v. Reproductive Health Services - **122**
Weinberger v. Wiesenfeld - 312, 313
West Coast Hotel Co. v. Parrish - 95
West Lynn Creamery, Inc. v. Healy - **67**
White v. Regester - 329
White Primary Cases - 348
Whitney v. California - **156**
Wickard v. Filburn - 22, 26
Wilkerson v. Rahrer - 62

Williams, United States v. - 358
Williamson v. Lee Optical of Oklahoma - 96
Wisconsin v. Yoder - 265
Wolston v. Reader's Digest Association - 164
Woodson v. North Carolina - 144, 145
Wooley v. Maynard - 232
Wygant v. Jackson Board of Education - 300, 302, 303
Wynehamer v. People - 90

Yakus v. United States - 48
Yates v. United States - 158
Yick Wo v. Hopkins - **284**
Young v. American Mini Theatres, Inc. - **183**, 184
Youngstown Sheet & Tube Co. v. Sawyer (The Steel Seizure Case) - **40**, 42

Zablocki v. Redhail - **131**
Zacchini v. Scripps-Howard Broadcasting Co. - 165
Zelman v. Simmons-Harris - **249**
Zemel v. Rusk - 141
Zobel v. Williams - **337**
Zorach v. Clauson - **253**
Zurcher v. Stanford Daily - **206**

NOTES

NOTES

NOTES

NOTES

NOTES

NOTES

NOTES

NOTES

NOTES

NOTES

NOTES

NOTES

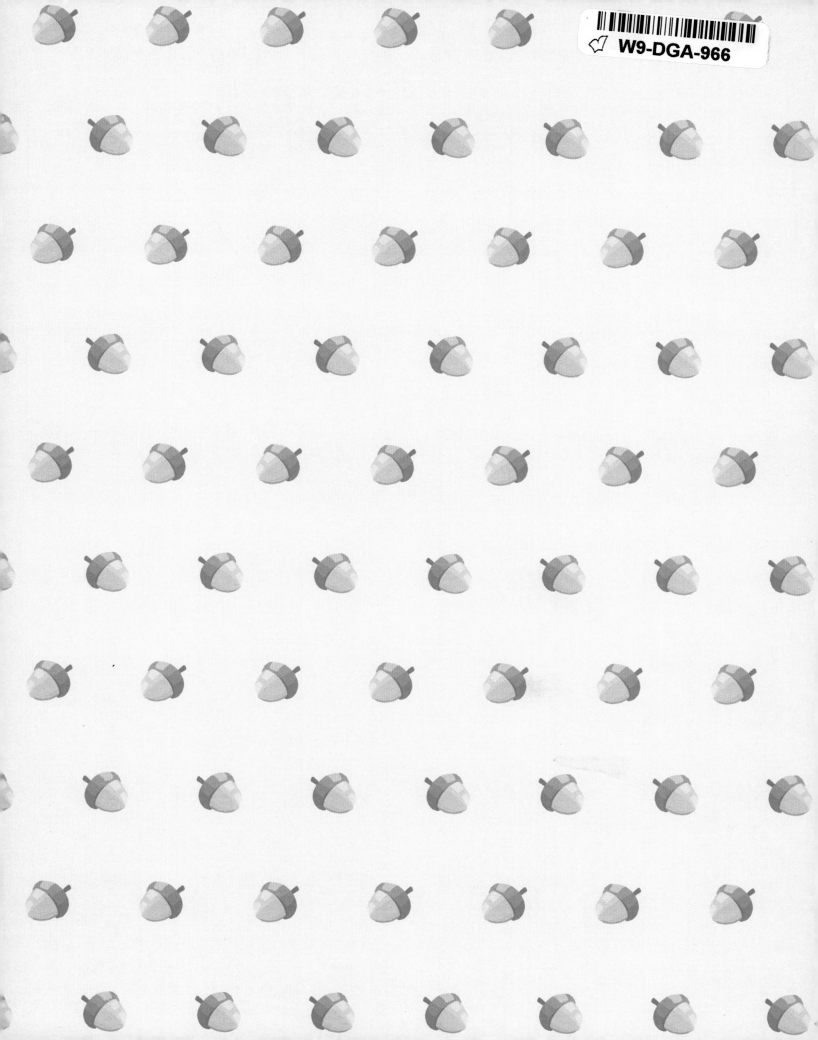

MAGGIE

AND THE

Sprinkle Tree

Written by:
John Bray

Illustrated by:
Christian Jackson

Maggie and the Sprinkle Tree

Text © 2013 John R. Bray
Illustrations © 2013 Christian Jackson
All rights reserved

Published in the U.S. by
Tumbling Acorn Publishing
www.tumblingacorn.com

Designed by John Bray and Christian Jackson

Summary: A fun story about imagination, adventure, and sprinkles.

Printed in the United States

ISBN 978-0-9913962-0-7

For:

Heather and Lennon

Kathryn, Sati, and Raphaelle

With the generous support of:

Tim & Marla Ursiny

John Hammond

With special thanks to:

John W. Bray

Jacob, Maria, Daphne, Violet, and Quinn

Bobby and Lisa Hammond

The Soetaert Family

Katherynn Ramirez

That's Maggie

right there

not that

She's 7 3/4 years old. She's also nearly three inches "taller than average," which is pretty exciting, in her opinion.

At the very farthest end of the street. And behind that house, just past the chimney, is Maggie's favorite tree. It's okay if you can't see it.

When she's not busy exploring, you can usually find Maggie

using her jump rope as a lass

counting the sp🐞ts on a bug

or picking those awful green things off her pizza.

Of course, she's only doing those things if she's not mixing.
And she's almost always mixing. You see Maggie is a mixer.
In fact, there's usually something that's a bit mixed up even
if she's not mixing anything at all.

Maybe it's her paints

or her socks
(if she HAS to wear socks)

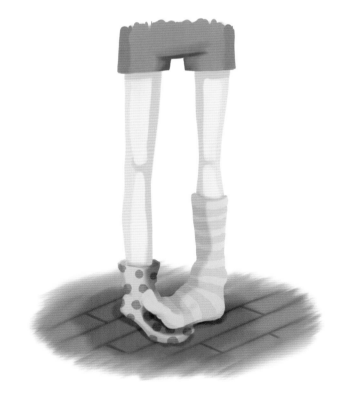

or even her potatoes
and her peas.

But one day she mixed something special.
Something that was just a bit

Something...

and

Something exciting.
Something with...

1 cup of water

5 spoons of sugar

3 blues

5 reds

1 yellow

2 greens

4 mini marshmallows

1 handful of glitter

1 BIG splash of pink lemonade

1 pinch of cinnamon

Then she stirred
and stirred...

and stirred...

and stirrrrrrred some more,

until she spun a tornado
of sparkling colors.

Finally, she went running, as fast as she could without spilling, to dump this

Different

COLORFUL sticky Messy

mixture into her favorite red bucket. A bucket she kept ready for special mixes just like...

But she tripped! Right there, on a rather large, rather shiny acorn. Of course, Maggie didn't have time to figure out why just ONE large, shiny acorn was under a willow tree, of all places. She was too busy watching her mixture - every last different, sticky, colorful, messy drop of it - fly out of the cup and slosh everywhere.

Everywhere EXCEPT the red bucket, that is.

She was more than a little bit sad. That was, after all, her very last handful of glitter. And those were four very fresh and extra squishy marshmallows.

And her mixture was gone.

Sort of...

That night, long after Maggie fell asleep, she woke to a...

TLE CLICK RATTLE! ZZZ

right outside her window.

Then a...

LIE CLICK CLICK

RATTLE CLICK

Or maybe that last sound was a CLACK. She wasn't quite sure.

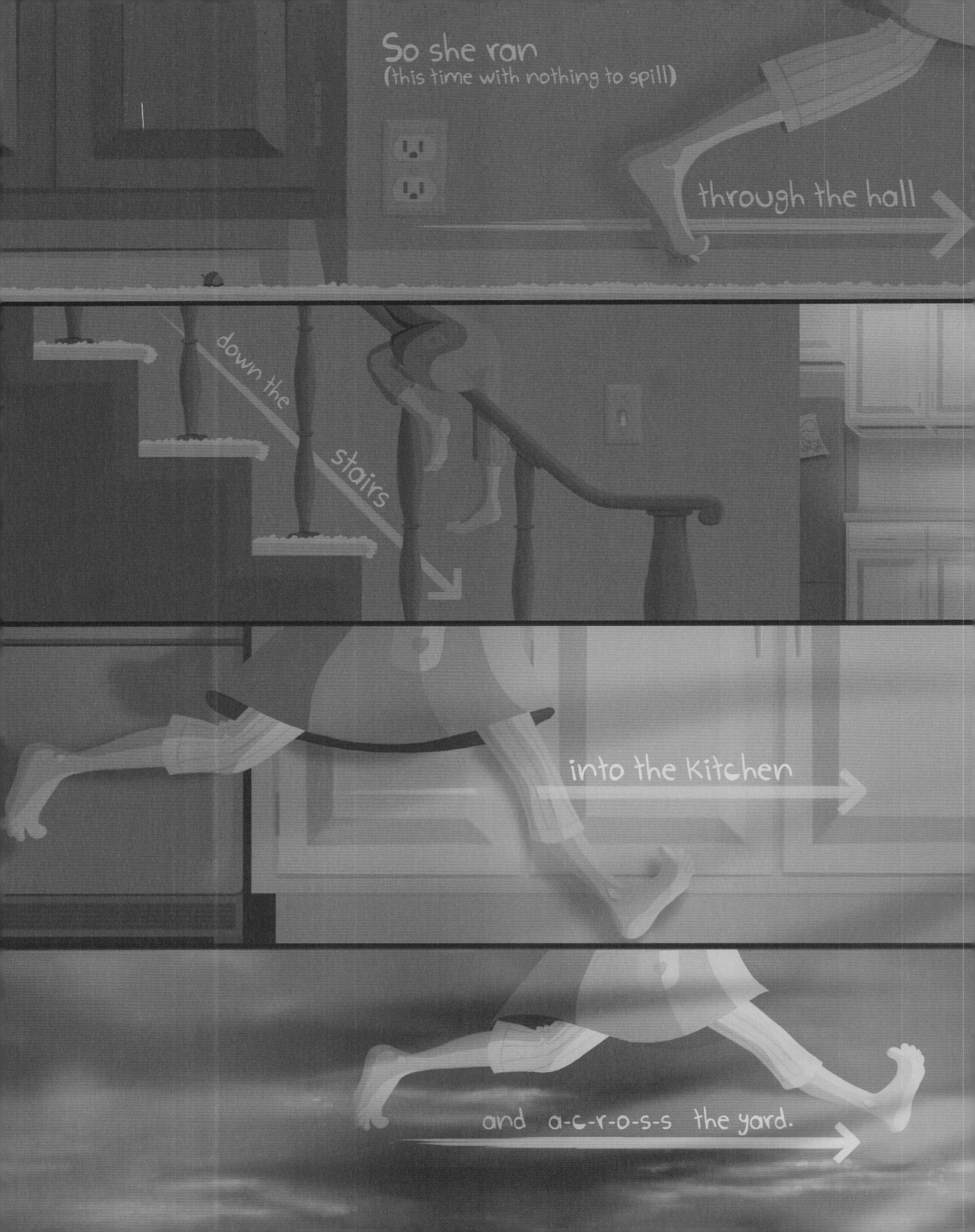
So she ran
(this time with nothing to spill)
through the hall
down the stairs
into the kitchen
and a-c-r-o-s-s the yard.

To the sound. The tree.
Her favorite tree. Now covered
in sprinkles and colorfully CLICK CLACKING
in the breeze.

And she did the only thing you can do when you first see a tree covered in sprinkles:

She POKED it!

First with one finger

Then with two at the same time

Then she grabbed one branch and held her breath

And with two excited fingers, she plucked one little blue sprinkle and tossed it into her mouth before she had time to think.

But after that first sprinkle? After that small, blue sprinkle fresh off the tree? Well, Maggie had only one thing on her mind: SPRINKLES.

From this branch

And that one

And those three

There were more sprinkles than she could carry, even with her pockets. Then, just then with PJs full of sprinkles, she had another thought.

Buckets!

Lots of buckets
and cups
and jars
and bowls
and spoons
and pans
and two delicious

CUPCAKES!

She grabbed as much
as she could carry.
And you'd be surprised
how much you can carry
when you have sprinkles
on the mind.

Then she sprinkled!

Actually, she sprinkled, plucked,
grabbed, chewed, and even SWUNG,
just a little bit higher than normal.

Before long, she had pockets full of sprinkles. The buckets and cups and jars and bowls and spoons and pans were overflowing. There were sprinkles on sprinkles on sprinkles.

There were sprinkles of every color everywhere. And when there's a whole tree of sprinkles, a sprinkle tree of sprinkles, everywhere means **everywhere.**

Even a couple
stuck right there

to the very bottom of her foot. And her toes. And her other foot. And, well, everywhere in sight.

So she picked herself up, held her belly, dropped her cupcake, and dragged her sprinkle-stained feet

across the yard

into the kitchen

up the stairs

and through the hall.

Then she flopped, without a worry or a care, right onto her bed. And with a belly full of sprinkles and a head full of ideas for the morning, she slept with a faint

RATTLE

drifting through her window.

CLICK CLICK RATTLE

But when Maggie woke the next morning, the

RATTLES
WERE GONE!

Her room was quiet. There weren't any sprinkles on her hands.
Or the bottom of her feet. Or even between her toes.

The grass was green, the leaves were back, and the sprinkles were gone. There wasn't a bowl, a spoon, or a half-eaten cupcake to be found.

A little bit sad and a little bit confused, Maggie went back inside for a sprinkle-free breakfast. And the tree? The plain old tree? Well, the tree stayed in the yard.

But a small squirrel with a fuzzy tail, and an even
fuzzier personality, hiding right there by the trunk, kept
it company... with a grin.

The
End?

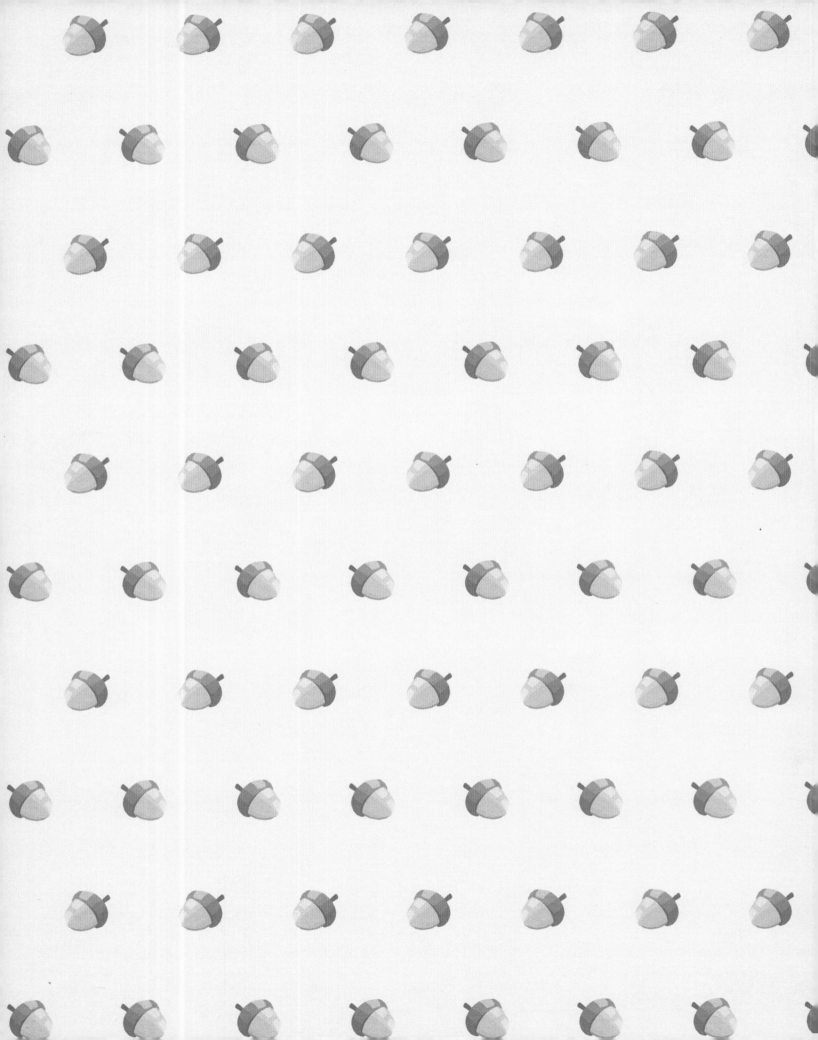